AF529108

REFORMS AND ECONOMIC DEVELOPMENT OF INDIA

REFORMS AND ECONOMIC DEVELOPMENT OF INDIA

Edited by
Talwar Sabanna

SERIALS PUBLICATIONS
NEW DELHI

First Published - 2008

ISBN: 978-81-8387-148-8

Published by

SERIALS PUBLICATIONS
4830/24, Prahlad Street, Ansari Road
Darya Ganj, New Delhi-110002 (India)
Phone : 23245225 Fax : 91-11-23272135
E-mail: serials@satyam.net.in

CONTENTS

PREFACE

Until 1991, India did not witness any major change in its development policy. But, in the meantime, the public-sector-led strategy of industrialization gradually began to yield diminishing returns after 1965. We could not protect the public sector enterprises from extraneous political and bureaucratic influences. Recurrent cost and time over-runs became endemic and the efficiency and profitability of the public sector were further eroded by lack of autonomy and accountability and global competitiveness. They could not generate sufficient resources to finance their future expansion and to pay the general exchequer a decent dividend on investment. The fiscal deficits gradually reached unsustainable levels, frequent increases in tax rates were effected, increasing recourse was taken to borrowing to meet even the minimum essential public expenditure. This, in turn, affected the resources meant for basic services, like education and health. Deficiencies in human resources development and infrastructural bottlenecks emerged as major constraints on the elementary education, neglect of the education of the girls child, and persistent high rates of infant mortality prevented the growth of an environment conducive to a sharp debt crisis as their background. Although the policies of privatization and globalisation-the hallmarks of 'reform' were introduced by Shri Rajiv Gandhi in 1985, these were accelerated by the Union Government only in 1991. Moreover, the 1990's has been the decade of globalisation and privatization.

It is a universal truth that ultimate objective of the economic development is to promote the well-being of all people of the society. In the words of Mahatma Gandhi, 'it is an effort to wipe out tears from the eyes of everyone'. In other words, any policy or reform aiming at economic development should have a 'human face' which makes all people happy both materially and socially. As we now entered into the new millennium, it is opportune time to have a critical look at 'reforms' introduced in 1991 with the particular emphasis on the fact of what extend they have been in tune with 'human face of development' or what can be termed as 'social liberalisation'. In this book an attempt is made to look at the achievements of Economic Reforms and Development of India.

OUR CONTRIBUTORS

R.Meenakshi, Reader, Department of Economics, Sri Sarada College, Salem.

K.S.Eswari, Reader in Commerce, Vellalar College for Women, Erode-638009.

Anupama, Department of Economics, Punjabi University Regional Centre, Bathinda (Punjab).

K.K.Bagchi, Professor, Department of Economics, North Bengal University, Raja Rammohunpur, Darjeeling, West Bengal.

S.B.Akaksh, Faculty, Department of Commerce, Karnatak University PG Centre, Karwar, Karnataka.

H.Y.Kamble, Professor and Head, Department of Studies in Commerce, Karnatak University, Dharwad-3, Karnataka.

A.Xarier Susai Raj, Lecturer (Senior Scale), Sacred Heart College (Autonomous), Tirupattur.V.DT.-635601, Tamil Nadu.

Rudra Prakash Pradhan, Economics and Finance Group, Faculty Division-I, Birla Institute of Technology and Science(BITS), Pilani-333031, Rajasthan.

W.N.Salve, Shri Venkatesh College, Ichalkaranji, Kolhapur District, Maharashtra.

Shashi Arora, Head, Department of Economics, G.D.H.G.College, Moradabad.

Soniya Gupta, Research Scholar, Department of Economics, G.D.H.G. Moradabad.

Ashwini Kant Jha, Professor and Head, P.G. Department of Economics, BNM University(W.C.), P.G.Centre, Saharsa, Bihar.

Bhavna Jha, Lecturer in IRPM, MAM College, Naugachia T.M.Bhagalpur University, Bhagalpur, Bihar.

Rati Kant Jha, M.L.S.M. College, Darbhanga, Bihar.

Sanjay Kr. Jha, Lecturer, Department of Economics, TNB College, Bhagalpur, Bihar.

J.P.Sharma, Department of Commerce, TNB College, Bhagalpur, Bihar.

D.R.Albal, Reader in Sociology, Karnatak University Kittuer Rani Chennamma P.G.Centre, Belgaum, Karnataka.

Z.A.Pathan, Research Scholar in Sociology, Karnatak University Kittuer Rani Chennamma P.G.Centre, Belgaum, Karnataka.Prakash S.Kamble, Venutai Chavan College, Karad, Satara District, Maharashtra.

D.K.Kamble, Research Scholar, Department of Geography, Karnatak University Kittuer Rani Chennamma P.G.Centre, Belgaum, Karnataka.

S.M.Hurkadli, Reader, Department of Geography, Karnatak University Kittuer Rani Chennamma P.G.Centre, Belgaum, Karnataka.

S.B.Javali, Lecturer in Bio-statistics, Department of Public Health Dentistry, SDM College of Dental Sciences and Hospital, Sattur, Dharwad-580009, Karnataka.

Parameshwar V. Pandit, Senior Grade Lecturer, Department of Statistics, Karnataka Arts College, Dharwad-580003, Karnataka.

Mahadevi Kotyal, Lecturer, Department of Geography, JSS College, Dharwad, Karnataka.

S.I.Biradar, Reader, Department of Geography, Karnatak University, Dharwad-3, Karnataka.

G.Saravanan, Research Scholar, Department of Rural Industries and Management, Gandhigram Rural Institute, Gandigrm,Dindigul-624302, Tamil Nadu.

Samvel Kakuko Lopoyetum, Senior Post Doctoral Research Fellow, Department of Rural Social Sciences, Gandhigram Rural Institute, Gandigrm,Dindigul-624302, Tamil Nadu.

P.Selvamani, Department of Political Science and Development Administration, Faculty of Rural Social Sciences, Gandhigram Rural Institute, Gandigrm,Dindigul-624302, Tamil Nadu.

Benjamin K.Muttai, Faculty, Department of Agricultural Economics and Agri-business Management, Egerton University, Post box no. NJORO, Kenya, South Africa.

Shivani Raswan Pathania, 187, Defence Colony, Jalandhar.

J.Cyril Kanmony, P.G. and Research Centre, Department of Economics, Scott Christian College, Nagercoil-629003.

Fr.J.G. Valan Arasu, Vice Principal, St.Aloysius College, Jabalpur.

V.Aditya Srinivas, Lecturer, 606, Sri Appartment Makipool, Nanpura, Surat-395001.

G.N.Joshi, Professor, Department of Economics, Veer Narmad South, Gujarat University, Surat.

S.M.Javed Akthar, Senior Lecturer, Department of Economics, Aligarh Muslim University, Aligarh-202002, U.P.

1

SECOND GENERATION REFORMS IN AGRICULTURE IN INDIA

*R. Meenakshi**

INTRODUCTION

Agriculture is believed to have started in India around 4500 years back and today about one third of Earth's surface (Approximately 11 billion acres) is used for agriculture providing livelihood and food security for a large majority of Indian population. India is a fortunate country ranking 5th in world in terms of total farm area. It is blessed with most suitable conditions by earth and nature providing all types of soils and climatic conditions which entire world has. The total cultivated area in India is 143 million hectares with nearly 40% of cultivated area under irrigation. The average land holding size is 1.6 hectares per household. India is one among the top producers of rice, groundnut, tobacco, sugar and milk. Thanks to green revolution programme and the efforts of Indian farmers. India is an agricultural country and the agriculture and allied activities sector is the second largest sectoral contributor to India's Gross Domestic Product.

Agriculture is the backbone of Indian economy, because of three reasons. The first being, agriculture constitutes largest share of country's national income though the share has declined from 55 percent in early 1950s to about 25 percent by the turn of the Century. Secondly, more than half of India's

* Reader, Department of Economics, Sri Sarada College, Salem

workforce is employed in its agriculture sector. Thirdly, growth of other sectors and overall economy depends on performance of agriculture to a considerable extent.

NATURE OF AGRICULTURAL DEVELOPMENT

The post-independence period made a turning point in the history of Indian Agriculture. It is inferred from the fact that compared with a rate of growth of less than 0.5 per cent per annum during 1904-5 to 1944-45 the agricultural sector recorded an annual growth rate of more than 2.3 per cent during the current period.

AGRICULTURAL POLICY IN INDIA DURING THE PLANNING ERA

Prior to the liberalization of the Indian economy of June 1991, agricultural policy was governed by a planning framework. The entire gamut of macroeconomic policies, notably trade, fiscal and monetary policies, was designed to serve planning objectives. The plans for the agricultural sector, including its financing and production targets, were all decided through a series of governmental processes at the state and central levels. The nature and role of planning for the Indian agricultural sector was primarily determined by the sector's specific characteristic of being under the operation of millions of independent producers. Hence, agricultural planning in India consisted in creating a rural infrastructure combined with providing modern inputs and a framework of incentives for farmers that would enable them to increase output through the adoption of modern technology.

Because food availability emerged as a major concern and constraint to the development process, accelerating agricultural and food grains growth with a view to providing food security became the central objective of India's agricultural policy. There were several agricultural components in the first and subsequent five-year plans. The first and most important was the implementation of land reforms during the mid-1950s with the objective of eliminating intermediaries and bringing about a greater degree of equality in land distribution.

The second agricultural component was the undertaking of substantial investment in rural infrastructure. A very high priority was accorded to public investment in irrigation and power (large-, medium- and small-scale) in both the central and the state plans. Simultaneously, policies were introduced to provide cheap institutional credit and other subsidies to the farmers to encourage private investment in irrigation. Large subsidies were also given for charges to users of both irrigation and power and fees were kept significantly below the costs of operation. The main thrust of this effort was to create a macroeconomic environment to encourage private investment by farmers and, thus, stimulate production. Promotional policies, including the Special Food Production Programme and agro climatic regional planning, land and water development programmes, were aimed at accelerating agricultural development. Large investments were also undertaken for the development of a research system under the aegis of the Indian Council of Agricultural Research and the State Agricultural Universities. Simultaneously, a well-designed extension network was instituted for disseminating new technologies to cultivators. The result was a rapid extension of the land area under high-yielding varieties (HYV).

From 1950 until 1967, the Community Development Programme and a network of extension services were the main instruments in transforming traditional agriculture. These were supplemented by programmes to intensify production in a few well-endowed districts during the early 1960s. The advent of the green revolution in the mid-1960s marked a turning point in the technological "upgrading" of Indian agriculture. The agricultural research and extension system received special attention during this period since Mexican wheat and International Rice Research Institute (IRRI) rice varieties had to be adapted to Indian conditions and made acceptable to farmers through extension and training.

Initially, new technology was confined to wheat production in the northwestern states of India. In the early 1970s, however, new varieties of rice were successfully introduced and the rice revolution spread not only in Punjab and Haryana but also to many other parts of India including the southern coastal areas. The focus of agricultural policy became the modernization of agriculture through extending seed-fertilizer technology to different parts of the country. Measures were also taken to involve small and marginal farmers in the production process by providing them with new inputs, including seeds, fertilizers and credit at subsidized rates.

Administered prices were the third component of policy during the planning era. In the context of pervading food shortages up until the mid-1950s, agricultural price policy had aimed at serving the main planning objective of keeping foodgrain prices low in the interest of food security. With the founding of the Agricultural Price Commission in 1965, price policy also provided incentives to farmers to increase production by establishing remunerative prices and assuring minimum support prices. The objective of the price policy was to reconcile two opposing interests - that of the farmers for fair remuneration and that of the consumers for reasonable prices.

The fourth important component of policy was the establishment of a comprehensive management system for the procurement, storage and public distribution of foodgrains to provide food to consumers at reasonable prices. During periods of scarcity, minimum support and procurement price operations were combined with compulsory procurement, levies on millers, zonal restrictions and other measures to enable the distribution of foodgrains (at subsidized rates) through the public distribution system (PDS). Sufficient food stocks were kept for running the PDS and also to help to stabilize prices through open market operations.

The fifth component was tightly controlled trade and exchange rate policies. In the case of agriculture, except for a few traditional commercial crops, the sector was insulated from world markets through the almost total control of exports and imports. The estimated surplus over domestic consumption requirements determined the quantities to be exported and vice versa for imports. Food grains, sugar and edible oils were imported in times of scarcity to prevent domestic prices of essential commodities from rising and to impart a measure of stability to domestic prices in the interest of both producers and consumers. Foreign trade in most agricultural goods was subject to quota or other restrictions such as minimum price requirements.

Finally, financial policy attempted to mobilize resources for public sector expenditure and for public investment. A system was created to extend cooperative and institutional credit to the rural sector, thus facilitating private investment in infrastructure and encouraging the adoption of new technology.

THE PLANNING STRATEGY AND AGRICULTURE

This overall policy package achieved many of the government's objectives. The land reforms were modest but succeeded in making owner-operators the dominant mode of cultivation. However, the legislation regarding land ceilings failed to a large degree. Policies also succeeded in accelerating the growth of agriculture and foodgrains production. As compared to a paltry growth rate of less than 0.25 percent per annum from 1904 to 1944, agricultural output grew by 2.7 percent and foodgrains production by 2.9 percent per annum. The introduction of HYVs during the mid-1960s resulted in a phenomenal increase in the growth rates of wheat and later rice production.

In addition, new technologies which were confined to wheat in the irrigated areas of Punjab, Haryana and western Uttar Pradesh began spreading to other areas. With a breakthrough in rice, the new technology gradually spread to the irrigated coastal regions of Andhra Pradesh, Tamil Nadu, Karnataka and eastern states of Bihar, Orissa, West Bengal and Assam, resulting in a significant increase in rice production.

Finally, and most important, accelerated growth in foodgrains production resulted in a greater degree of food security for a rapidly rising population and in a reduction of dependence on food imports making India marginally self-sufficient in foodgrains. The steady growth in foodgrains production, over time, increased both physical and economic access to them. The availability of cereals (measured in terms of kilocalories per caput per day) increased by more than 20 percent from 1960 to 2000. Access to food for the poorer sectors of the population improved as the rapid growth in productivity lowered the real price of wheat and rice. The gains from productivity increases were shared by both producers and consumers. Hence, even though the intersectoral barter terms of trade became adverse for wheat and rice growers, their income terms of trade remained favourable because of yield and profitability increases.

Finally, access to food for the poor increased because of anti-poverty programmes such as the Integrated Rural Development Programme, the Rural Landless Employment Guarantee Programme, National Rural Employment Programme and, later on, the Jawahar Rozgar Yojana. Effective mechanisms were developed for the relief of food scarcities and for resolving the problems of extremely severe droughts through the initiation of special employment programmes. In fact for the poor the proportion of per capita income required to buy food declined over time.

GLOBALISATION AND AGRICULTURE

Globalisation of agriculture is not an entirely a new concept but it has acquired a new significance in face of the changed scenario of the world economy. It is a process of reaffirmation of faith in the markets, retaining the character of independence of a country. Here the country follows a pragmatic policy with a shift in the decision making from Government to business. WTO agreement on agriculture throws open competition to our agricultural sector, subsidized at far low levels than in developed countries, where agriculture is business rather than livelihood and these countries have higher productivity levels, irrigation, technology, storage, distribution, value additions, marketing facilities and abilities. With vast population below poverty level, India needs to protect its food security as well. Further it is also a reality that most of our agricultural products are noncompetitive in the international market due to excessive regulation, poor processing technology, low productivity level and cheaper imports. The agreement of WTO relating to agriculture is made up of several elements which seek to reform trade in agriculture and provide the basis for market oriented policies and thereby improving export sector.

It is therefore essential to see how far the agreement has on agriculture succeeded in removing the trade distortions and providing level playing field to our rural economy. This write up is a sincere effort in this direction. This attempts to examine the impact of the second phase of globalization on Indian agriculture and suggests measures to make Indian agriculture viable in free trade global environment.

Indian farmers are no different from other entrepreneurs. They adopt new technologies enthusiastically, respond to price signals and grab opportunities to increase their own well–being. The main reform needed is to free farmers from all domestic restrictions on storage, transport and sale of agricultural products. The present policy of low output prices and subsidised (low) input prices puts a net tax on farmers; we should change to a system of internationally competitive prices on both inputs and outputs. To protect poor consumers, it is much better to provide an effective targeted safety net, than to distort food prices which helps the poor so little when compared with the cost. The responsibility of the government is to ensure that adequate public investments are made in irrigation, agricultural research, and infrastructure that ensures well–functioning markets and facilitates exports. For providing food security, government should follow a mixed strategy of modest buffer stocks supplemented by occasional trade on the world market.

SUBSIDIES TO FARM SECTOR

The initial commitments to WTO indicate that the developed countries were to reduce the domestic support of agriculture to the level of 5% and developing countries were to bring down it to the level of 10% of GDP in agriculture. Further the developed countries had initially committed to reduce the tariff rates by 36% in a period of six years and developing countries like India were to reduce them by 24% in a period of 10 years from 1995. The above commitment by developed countries also applies export subsidies given to farm sector.

In the context of initial commitments, it seems that though the developed countries have followed their initial commitments, the levels of domestic support to agriculture are still very high. The levels of domestic support in 1997-99 was 61% in Japan, 65% in Korea, 66% in Norway, 70% in Switzerland and only 9% of GDP in India [excluding a negative product specific support of (−38.5%) GDP in agriculture]. The developed countries also give several other subsidies to farm sector under the provisions of green box, blue box, special and differential treatment box which are exempted from the initial commitments. In addition to this they also transfer income directly to the farmers for plant protection, as compensation in the event of crop failure, for environmental protection etc., In India the product specific subsidies are negative and non product specific subsidies were 9 % of GDP in agriculture. With this background it is certain that the developing countries like India could not capture the markets of developed countries. The commodity wise data on subsidies clearly indicate that the domestic support in developed countries is still very high. For instance in 1998, the domestic support provided to wheat was Rs.2.82 per Kg. in U.S.A., Rs.2.29 per Kg in Canada and Rs.4.62 per Kg in countries belonging to European Union but it was negative in India. It should be noted that farmers in developed countries are at present getting 4.3 % higher prices than the international prices. Therefore India is under no obligation to reduce domestic support currently extended to the agricultural sector.

Again developed countries provide huge subsidies on exports of agricultural commodities to maintain prices of farm products in the domestic markets. For example the countries belonging to European Union can give Rs.3.5 per Kg export of sugar, Rs.2.8 per Kg on wheat and Rs.38 per Kg on export of butter in 1998. These figures will reveal that the export subsidies are still very high in developed countries and WTO has not succeeded in bringing down the levels of farm subsidies in these countries. Hence reduction commitment in export subsidies does not apply to India and to protect the income level in farm sector, the exports of our agricultural goods are to be promoted by giving subsidies. India has raised this issue in the recent conference of 2001 and pointed out that the agricultural markets of developed countries are not yet opened for products of the developing countries like India.

TARIFFS ON THE AGRICULTURAL SECTOR

Regarding tariffs on imports of agricultural goods, India has achieved some success through negotiations. India is now allowed to impose a customs duty up to 100 % on imports of agricultural raw materials, up to 150 % on imports of processed farm products and up to 300 % on imports of oil seeds. India should take care in this regard because the tariff rates in developed countries are still very high. India will have to rely on adoption of cost reducing production technology in agriculture to become competitive in international market.

INTERNATIONAL TRADE, THE ENVIRONMENT AND SUSTAINABLE AGRICULTURAL DEVELOPMENT

Historically, India's agricultural policies sought to ensure self-sufficiency in two staple grains, wheat and rice. That focus continues today, even though current grain production is more than enough to satisfy consumer demand. The most significant policy changes in the sector have been in market access, including the WTO-required liberalization of import policies completed in 2001. Longstanding restrictions on farm exports that taxed local producers and precluded competitive export industries began to lessen in the mid-1990s. These reforms helped stimulate trade, including the rise in edible oil imports and increased exports of rice and wheat.

In recent years, the collision of environmental and trade interests has emerged as one of the most complex and divisive issues in world trade policy. While the debate is multifaceted, involving legal, economic and environmental perspectives, all sides are generally interested in promoting national and social welfare. Many supporters of liberal world trade believe that reducing trade barriers is environment-friendly as a way of allowing the world to use its resources more efficiently and, as long as impacts on the environment and on natural resources are appropriately priced, more sustainable.

Moreover, by raising incomes, the reduction of trade barriers enables countries to spend more on preserving the environment. Trade supporters also point to numerous studies that show how protectionism often exacerbates environmental problems. For example, a variety of studies document how export bans, import restrictions and consumer boycotts of tropical hardwood products actually discourage conservation and encourage unsustainable rates of cutting.

Agricultural production gave less response to globalization policy. The growth of agriculture has fallen in spite of increase in terms trade and private investment in agriculture. The growth rate of food grains has fallen in spite of successive good monsoons. The compound growth rate is 1.52 % for rice, 3.76 % for wheat, 1.13 % for pulses and 1.74 % for food grains. These annual growth rates worked out for the period from 1990-91 to 1999-2000 indicates that agricultural production grew at a slower rate and economic prosperity in agricultural sector also grew at a small rate. In India the food grains account for about 63 % of country's agricultural output and hence even a marginal decline in food grains production has a ripple effect on the rest of the economy.

QUANTITATIVE RESTRICTIONS ON AGRICULTURAL IMPORTS

To promote competition, the Government of India has lifted numerous Quantitative Restrictions (QR) on import of several items. After many years of imposing QRs or quotas on agricultural product imports, India has finally begun lifting this non-tariff barrier. This would benefit the consumers, improve social welfare particularly the rural and urban poor. In 1997, import restrictions applied to about 1000 agricultural products. Since then nearly 859 agricultural products have been freed for import, including 228 feed in 2000. The remaining 150 agricultural products were freed in 2001 based on the phasing out policy of India on all products including agricultural and consumer goods.

THE TRIPS REVIEW

Finally serious concerns were expressed about provisions made under TRIPs. It was argued that the patent of WTO would bring slavery to Indian farmers. This is not true because the member countries are free to follow either the patent of the WTO or their own patent act prepared as per their guidelines. The Indian Patent Bill provides for patent of "invention" as well as "discovery" patent for a period of 15 years for the reuse of patented seeds by researchers. This clearly indicates that the Indian Government has taken sufficient care of the interests of Indian farmers. However the statistics on India's agricultural exports to GDP in agriculture has declined from 19.2 % (during 1996-97 to 1999-2000). This enables us to conclude that India's exports of agricultural goods could not increase but on the contrary, the share of the developed countries in world agricultural trade has increased during the globalisation period.

PROBLEMS FACED BY INDIAN AGRICULTURE AND THE NEED FOR PRIVATE PARTICIPATION

Agriculture sector in India suffers from poor productivity due to falling ground water levels, expensive credit, a distorted market, the intermediaries (who increase more cost than adding values), controlled prices, inadequate infrastructure, and poor quality of agriculture produce compared to the international standard. Agriculture has also suffered because of farmers wholly depending on the monsoon, poor irrigation facilities, use of traditional practices, farmers' poor economical status, fragmented landholdings, poor yields, lack of post-harvest infrastructure and lack of farm extension. There is an urgent need to invest in infrastructure like irrigation facilities, processing, storage and marketing activities. In this background, it is essential for private agencies to come forward to make the Indian agriculture conditions better and the government to come forward to encourage the public-private participation. Agriculture research institutes have ample of information on how to improve the productivity of the crops but are handicapped in disseminating the researched information because of the lack of sufficient finance and infrastructure. However, the situation has been changing in recent times. The need is not only to increase the crop production over the periods but also to sustain agriculture which can be done by providing the right information at right time about the agriculture inputs application, and the marketing of agricultural produce at a reasonable price.

While the government has social liabilities to uplift the agriculture sector, there are many NGOs, which are actively involved in this sector. The private sector, while having the revenue generating mindset, also takes care of the socio issues. The share of private sector in capital formation in Indian agriculture is approximately three times more than the public sector. This shows the active involvement of the private agencies in the Indian agriculture sector. The existing private participation in the agriculture sector will help in building the image of this sector in the map of the world. By doing so, the agriculture sector will also increase the contribution to the GDP which is decreasing the GDP share every year. Both private and public sector are contributing to the agriculture in a big way. However, there are many things that have to be implemented, especially concerning the financing aspects. The need is how to make the agricultural sector more attractive for private sector to invest.

CHALLENGES FACED BY INDIAN AGRICULTURE

Indian agriculture faces several challenges. These are both internal and external. Internal challenges have been with us for some time; they are well recognised and need to be addressed urgently. External challenges have emerged in recent years and are threatening to weaken the already emaciated agricultural sector. Because external challenges have come to stay and cannot be wished away, addressing internal issues assumes special urgency. Ignoring the challenges will be perilous because the livelihood of two-thirds of the population is dependent on agriculture and allied activities. Internal challenges include those in farm production, processing industry and marketing. Dependence on monsoons, fragmented land-holding, low level of input usage, poor pre- and post-harvest practices and inadequate marketing infrastructure are some of the well-known weaknesses that lead to low yields and high cost of the farm produce.

Providing food security continues to be the central objective of India's agricultural policy. With a large and growing population of 1000 million and an expected acceleration in per capita income over the next decade, the demand for foodgrains is likely to grow at a rapid rate. Policy-makers recognize that accelerating growth in foodgrains production is an essential prerequisite for meeting the rising food demand.

Higher agricultural growth requires both public and private investment in irrigation and other rural infrastructure. However, the rate of investment in agriculture has declined since the early 1980s. An important reason has been that in most states a large proportion of the government budget is required for huge subsidies on power, transport and water and on the inefficient functioning of both power and irrigation systems.

In addition, policy-makers are considering decentralizing and privatizing irrigation projects (with explicit subsidies to be provided for socially important schemes), leasing distribution systems to panchayats and forming irrigation cooperatives to establish and collect water charges and to manage and maintain distribution channels. Private investment in agriculture is likely to increase if public investment grows to allow farmers to adopt yield-raising technology and if farmers have the incentives of remunerative prices.

Faster income growth, together with lower import barriers, helped to more than double India's farm imports during the 1990s to $1.9 billion in 2000-01. Complying with World Trade Organization (WTO) rules, India removed all quantitative barriers to agricultural imports by 2001 and voluntarily reduced tariffs below required levels for a number of commodities, including edible oils, pulses, and cotton. As a result of trade liberalization, India is now the world's largest market for edible oils and pulses.

IMPACT OF ECONOMIC REFORMS ON AGRICULTURE

Agricultural sector is the mainstay of the rural Indian economy around which socio-economic privileges and deprivations revolve, and any change in its structure is likely to have a corresponding impact on the existing pattern of social equality. No strategy of economic reform can succeed without sustained and broad based agricultural development. New import and export policies aim at enhancing export capabilities of the agricultural sector by increasing productivity and promoting modernization and competitiveness. The measures to facilitate export growth include allowing the import of capital for the agricultural sector, reducing the list of agricultural products that cannot be exported, and removing the minimum export price from a number of products.

India's new economic policy was launched in June 1991. The government began to liberalize the economy by reforming trade, financial, tax and investment policies. Public enterprises were restructured and the budget controlled more closely. Specific policy reforms included floating the rupee, abolishing most industrial licensing, removing import licensing, reducing tariffs and relaxing foreign investment regulations. In this context it is important to look at some of the short- and medium-term consequences of these reforms for the agricultural sector.

The short-term stabilization measures included sharp cuts in public spending and fiscal austerity. Consequently, there was a large cut not only in current expenditures but also in public investment. The vagaries of monsoons make it very difficult to establish a link between economic reforms and the growth rate in agriculture over a short period of time. The fiscal adjustments that had the most significant effect on agriculture were the reductions of public investment in irrigation, power and other rural infrastructure, including agricultural research, roads and communications.

All this has resulted in decelerating growth but the economy reviewed subsequently and it is expected to accelerating in future.

Moreover the serious foreign-exchange crisis in 1990 led to a number of well-publicized economic reforms in the early

1990s dealing with trade, industrial licensing, and privatization. The reforms had an impact on the agricultural sector through the central government's effort to withdraw the fertilizer subsidy and place greater emphasis on agricultural exports. The cut in the fertilizer subsidy was a result of the government's commitment to reduce fiscal deficit by removing grants and subsidies from the budget. The government action led to a reduction in the use of chemical fertilizers and protests by farmers and opposition political parties. The government was forced to continue the subsidies but at a somewhat lower level.

THE REFORMS AND AGRICULTURAL EXPORTS

There is a general agreement among economists and policy-makers that India has export potential in some agricultural products. In addition to traditional commodities, such as tea and coffee, exports of many new commodities, including fish products, rice, fruits and processed food, have shown a rapid increase. Some studies argue that there is major scope for increasing exports of foodgrains such as rice and wheat. In the short term, however, the competitiveness of several agricultural commodities is gradually being eroded because of high inflation attributed to the new economic policy.

The extent to which India should free its trade in foodgrains, oils and sugar, as a consequence of becoming a signatory to WTO, is an issue that has generated a great deal of debate. The main argument in favour suggests that India would stand to gain immensely from complete trade liberalization and that even the interest of food security would be served in a much more efficient and less costly way if, instead of relying on huge food stocks, imports and exports of foodgrains were used as a way of countering domestic supply fluctuations.

The opposite point of view argues that India should not free its trade immediately and that its demand for foodgrains should be met through domestic production instead. This view suggests that, because food production is the predominant means of living for a large percentage of the country's workforce whose fortunes depend on the growth rate of output and productivity in the foodgrains sector, India should be insulated from international price changes. This group argues that free trade is likely to accentuate the variability in domestic market prices in the short term as a result of large fluctuations in the international prices of agricultural commodities. This would expose market prices to great risk and uncertainty. These fluctuations would adversely affect food security for the poor.

The practical approach to trade liberalization suggests that the new liberal climate should make it possible to dispense with many coercive instruments such as compulsory procurement, zonal restrictions and limits on stocks, and to make more effective use of markets at both the national and international levels. Important measures include: reducing the costs of procurement and storage through the better functioning of the Food Corporation of India and the association of private trade with procurement operations; correcting many of the existing deficiencies in the PDS through gradually directing assistance only to the poor in both rural and urban areas, removing its urban bias and extending it to most of the rural areas and strengthening the coverage in poor states such as Bihar and Orissa; introducing a more cost-effective strategy for the management of food stocks, which should take into account likely food demands, the extent of fluctuations in domestic output and prices; allowing the Food Corporation of India to enter the international future markets with a view to reducing buffer stocks and cutting down on costs and subsidies; and developing regional cooperation.

SHAPPING INDIAN AGRICULTURE

The policies imposed by the World Bank-IMF have a component directly affecting the agrarian economy. These policies have the following components:

- The gradual abolition of input subsidies on fertilizers, irrigation, electricity, credit etc
- The removal of trade restrictions on agricultural commodities so that the domestic prices are not out of tune with world prices.

- A unification of prices so that the current system of dual markets in food grains and other agricultural commodities disappears.
- A drastic curtailment of food subsidy confining the Public Distribution System (PDS) only to the deserving poor.
- The removal of all restrictions on the choice of what to produce, where to sell etc.
- Freedom of operations for agri-business corporations.
- Abolition of land ceiling laws.

ANTICIPATED BENEFITS DUE TO REFORMS

- Elimination of trade distortions of tariff, domestic support and export subsidy by developed countries to lead to increase in commodity prices
- Increase in commodity prices to attract Indian farmers towards commercialization of agriculture
- WTO regime, if harnessed properly, could become the catalysis for crop diversification (eg., burgeoning floriculture industry in India)
- Adoption of organic farming to cater to growing demand for organic based fruits/vegetables, which could lead to recouping of soil fertility
- In long run, India could adopt cultivation of those crops in which it enjoys competitive edge (and high water consuming crops could be imported)

CONCLUDING REMARKS

India faces major challenges in transforming itself from a sustenance based agrarian country to a vibrant modern Nation State. Immediate need is to use agriculture reforms as an important tool in rural development and poverty alleviation. Creation of world-class infrastructure and proper information systems necessary for accelerating agricultural growth Impact of globalisation of agriculture need to be studied carefully and policies formulated suitably to minimise their negative impacts With less than 1% contribution to global trade, macro level benefits from agricultural exports may not be substantial in the medium term. As large population is dependent on agriculture, policy formulations in other sectors will also continue to be impacted by this sector

In the wake of the macroeconomic reforms, it is possible for the agricultural sector to derive large benefits not only-by catering to increasing domestic demand, but also by making use of the export possibilities brought by increased access to foreign markets. Globalization of Indian agriculture offers both opportunities and challenges to policy makers. Opportunities exist for deriving large benefits through substantial increase in agricultural exports, especially exports of high-value labour-intensive agricultural products. This can become possible, however, only if the agricultural sector is able to generate larger surpluses through increased public and private investment in rural infrastructure, in research and development, new technology and in marketing. The challenges lie not only in modernizing small-scale agriculture and in making it efficient and competitive, but also in involving the mass of rural people including small and marginal farmers and landless agricultural labourers, in all parts of India, in the development process. India is primarily an agrarian economy. It is a well known fact that agriculture across states is facing various challenges and it is extremely important that appropriate reform measures are taken by the respective States so that the agriculture sector, which is so vital, for an economy like India continues to play a pivotal role in the Indian economy.

Therefore the second phase is going to be more important because the country should shift gears of the economy from a crisis driven to a development driven economic reforms. Second generation reforms should take measures to encourage investment in agriculture and rural infrastructure. This will stimulate rural purchasing power and inject further dynamism for the acceleration of rural development in India.

REFERENCES

Prof. G.S. Bhalla, "The Nature of Agricultural Development in India", Jawaharlal Nehru University.

G. Chandrashekhar, "Can India attain global competitiveness in agriculture", Seminar on "WTO v/s Indian Agriculture", Soyabean Processors' Association of India, Indore.

Maurice R. Landes, (2004), "The Elephant is Jogging- New Pressures for Agricultural Reform in India", Economic Research Service/ USDA, Volume 2, Issue 1.

"Sustainable Agriculture and the Global Food Economy View from India" , Virtual Conference, March , 2004.

Deepak Kumar, "Private Sector Participation in Indian Agriculture", A CII Publication of Business Review, July 2005.

Report of the working group on Agricultural Development in the Eastern and North Eastern India for the formulation of the Tenth Five Year Plan, Planning Commission, Government of India, August, 2001.

Agricultural Reforms in Southern States – Issues and Concerns, A CII Publication, Policy Primer No: 4, August 2004.

Tamil Nadu Agricultural Development, Final Report of Government of Tamil Nadu, November 2004.

Information gathered from dailies.

2

GLOBALISATION AND EMERGING CHALLENGES FOR INDIA

*K. S. Eswari**

INTRODUCTION

Globalisation has been understood in very diverse ways, by different entities dealing with this subject. The Commission on Global Governance, conceived of a world economy in the framework of Global neighbourhood, and conceptualized the imperatives of strengthening the institutional mechanisms for governance of the world economic phenomenon. The global neighbourhood dispenses with the diversities with regard to economic, social, and cultural characteristics of different countries of world community. Growing internalionalisation of production and increasing importance of production and trade, consistent increase in the knowledge-intensity of production, increasing share of knowledge-intensive and technology-intensive products in the export and import-baskets of trade flows, and growing integration of capital market across the Globe characterise the process of Globalisation. According to Ricardo Petrella, the principal characteristics of Globalisation consists of the following:

- Globalisation of financial markets
- The internationalisation of corporate strategies, in particular, their commitment to competition as a source of wealth creation

* Reader in Commerce, Vellalar College for Women, Erode-638009.

- Diffusion of technology and related R & D and knowledge world wide
- The transformation of consumption pattern into cultural products with world wide consumer markets.
- The internationalisation of the regulatory capabilities of national societies into a global political economic system.
- The diminished role of national governments in designing the rules for global governance.

Globalisation, in a nutshell, is lowering, if not, elimination, of the artificial barriers created by the host countries to protect the domestic firms and industries from the competition from the businesses of foreign countries. The barriers may be a complete barrier by way of ban on entry of foreign firms to operate in a country or partial barrier in the form of high tariff or quota on goods and services entering the country or in the form of contracts on equity stake holdings in a joint venture between a foreign firm and a local firm or in the form of control over repatriation of funds in the case of strategic alliance.

DRIVERS OF GLOBALISATION

There are many factors which tend to promote globalisation of world economy*

- International trade (lower trade barriers and more competition)
- Financial flows (foreign direct investment, technology transfer/licensing, portfolio investment, and debt)
- Communication (traditional media and internet)
- Technological advances in transportation, electronics, bioengineering and related field
- Population mobility, especially of labour

Each of these drivers of change has accelerated in recent years and each reinforces the other.

BENEFITS OF GLOBALISATION

The basic principle of globalisation is the global welfare and not merely individual benefits. If globalisation is accepted widely, then, it will surely bring forth many benefits:

- The concept of comparative advantage will come in light and the country will produce only those goods in which it possesses more comparative advantage or less comparative disadvantage. This will lead to maximisation of output and increasing the real income of the world economy.
- Globalisation will lead to optimisation of consumption.
- An open economy spurs innovation with fresh ideas from abroad.
- Globalisation prevents the establishment of monopolies and concentration of economic power and wealth, in few hands.
- Rapid integration of financial markets and emergence of several instruments of financial flows across many sectors leading to deregulation of money market.

DRAWBACKS OF GLOBALISATION

While Globalisation has several benefits, it has number of drawbacks also:

- In a competitive environment, a firm can survive only if it is efficient. To achieve cost efficiency many firms try to cut down the size of human resources. Unless these firms get rid of the surplus labour, they can hardly be competitive thus, many fear losing of their jobs.
- Replacement of traditional and indigenous products by modern products, result in the ruin of traditional crafts and industries and the livelihood of people in these sectors.
- The adverse terms of trade lead to economic loss for the developing countries in general.
- It may increase inequality, as inequality increases because of the worsening of the living conditions of poor.

CHALLENGES FOR ECONOMIC DEVELOPMENT

Globalisation, certainly constitutes the main core element of economic development in the newly emerging global economic system. For the successful globalisation of business, the domestic economy and the firm have to satisfy some essential conditions. There are a number of favourable factors for globalisation of Indian business. These include human resources, growing entrepreneurship, growing domestic market and foreign market, niche market, large number of non- resident resourceful Indians, skilled and cheap labour etc. Still, there are several impediments in the successful implementation of Globalisation process. Many in India have pessimistic attitude forwards globalisation. It poses challenges for people at individual level and through Government and economic organisations.

The following section deals with the challenges of globalisation for India:

CHALLENGES FOR INDIANS GOVERNMENT

The first and foremost challenge for India is that the superpower is getting diluted at decision making level. The Government has to adjust and adapt to the most other countries. It can't now decide the degree of freedom, it was used to earlier, to attain its socio economic objectives. It can do so now subject to limits, it has committed to in order to be a part of current globalisation. The agreement between India and U.S. regarding nuclear deal is the best example. Further the people of India, the vast majority of whom are illiterate, are to be educated about the concept of borderless world, which is a difficult task for the Government

FOREIGN DIRECT INVESTMENT

When there is a gap between the savings rate within a country and the rate of investment required for achieving the targeted growth rate, then the gap is usually met by Foreign Direct Investment. Indian savings rate has not touched the required level and hence globalisation has paved way for the global players in the form of capital, technology etc. But the foreign players prefer to invest large amount of capital mainly in the large infrastructure projects. There are only a handful of domestic business firms that are capable of undertaking or willing to make that kind of investment needed for long gestation uncertain projects. Hence the advantages foreign capital can't be fully reaped.

GLOBAL COMPETITIVENESS

Globalisation necessarily implies creation of a competitive environment which would in turn, induce efficiency in production and optimality of resource allocation. The problem is to define, what should be the limit to competition, from the development point of view. The competition is a double edged weapon, which should be dealt with carefully. To reap the benefits of competition, it should be conceived and practised within the framework of normative values that takes into account the differences in the stages of development and the capacities to compete in particular ethos of developing world. The basic rule in any competition is that if we want to compete with some chances of winning, we have to be more or less equal, otherwise we will be cracked down.

India being a socialistic country which adopted protective policy to safeguard the industries before the era of globalisation, can't afford to throw it open to competition, all of a sudden. The major challenge for the Government is to take into confidence various interests and pressure groups including political parties to devise policies that would provide more favourable environment to reap competitive advantage.

POOR STATE OF INFRASTRUCTURE

Our productive prowess and ability to serve global markets are increasingly handicapped by the insufficient and inefficient infrastructure and public goods such as water, electricity, sanitation, transportation, law and order and Governance. These goods can't be provided by any private entity or through market based competitive system. While foreign and domestic capital can flow into infrastructure, the actual provision of public service is necessarily in the public domain. A survey by the World Bank reveals that manufacturers in India face nearly seven significant power outages per month on an average, as against only one in Malaysia and four in china .9% of total output is lost due to power breakdown in India, compared to

2.6% in Malaysia and 2% in China*. Power is an example of poor infrastructure. Yet another example is poor transport management system.

Infrastructure in India is starved of investment. In the words of Economic forum's latest global competitive report. "inadequate supply of infrastructure" was ranked as the highest impediment to doing business in India. Hence efforts should be taken by the Government to attract foreign investment into infrastructure development which has the double benefit of inducing growth as well as kick starting a virtuous cycle of investment in all other sectors.

DEMOGRAPHIC DIVIDEND

India's demographic dividend is a well known fact wherein the labour force is growing much more rapidly than the overall population. There is a diversity in the race, religion, culture, language, education, etc with respect to different states which act as a stumbling block in the path of development. The interest of different groups conflict with each other. The challenge for the government lies in increasing the capabilities of people by providing literacy and means for skill development, so that they become employable or self employed. Only when the productive capacity and skill increase, the benefits of globalisation can be attained in full.

AGRICULTURE

India is primarily an agricultural country with most of her masses living in rural India. The growth of agriculture is very essential for the growth of other sectors as it has multiplier effect. The globalisation will open the door to many multinational corporations to step in the agricultural sector with changes and innovations in agricultural biotechnology. Agricultural inputs like seeds, fertilizers, agro chemicals, etc become high technology products and the use of these inputs requires good formal education and training. Low literacy rate, small and fragmented holding, low infrastructure facilities, farm indebtedness and low capacity to invest are the characteristics of Indian farmers. Hence use of high technology methods of farming or agricultural inputs is a dream rather than a reality for the poor farmers.

WTO TRIPS

This covers intellectual property rights such as copy right, trade mark, trade secrets, geographical indications, industrial design, integrated circuits and patents. By becoming a member of WTO, India has allowed huge inflow of products and their manufacturing which has been restrained till date. The two important areas of controversy are pharmaceutical industry and agriculture. The developed world is adopting hard patent regime which would affect Indian drug industry. India has good scope for generic drugs, the patents for which have expired. But India has been identified as one of the countries with innovative capabilities in the pharmaceutical industry. Factors like availability of cheap and skilled labour, technological infrastructure, educated and skilled manpower, vast market potential and liberalisation policy favourable to investors would all serve as a focus area to develop their business in India for the foreign giants. This will ruin Indian pharmaceutical industry. Further India will be forced to buy life-saving drugs at a very high price.

The IPR on agriculture is yet another gateway for MNCs to enter into agricultural sector. Genetically engineered patented seeds of food and cash crops owned by MNCs will be sold in India and such seeds will have royalty which have so far been absent. Since the seeds are protected by patent the farmers may not be allowed to save them for their own harvest. In that case India will not be able to benefit out of globalisation, by increasing the yield rate of high quality seeds to make the product highly competitive in the world market. The worst sufferers will be small and marginal farmers.

True, globalisation can benefit developing countries. It is also apprehended that unregulated globalisation will cause serious challenges for developing countries. The dominance of industries by MNCs would be on the increase. A number of countries allow high foreign stake even in industries where that is not really required. There will be a number of cases of takeover of national firms by foreign firms. The technology that the MNCs bring may not be suitable to host countries. In the international trading system, the adverse terms of trade may bring loss to developing countries, since only developed countries will be benefited.

CONCLUSION

Despite the challenges and problems, there are chances for developing countries including India from benefiting out of globalisation. If we concentrate on goods, whose production is simple and labour intensive, raising demand for unskilled labour and raising the income of poor relative to those of non-poor. In many cases the better technology brought in by the MNCs would induce many Indian firms to absorb similar technology leading to enhanced competitiveness and market expansion.

In spite of Global challenges, as our Prime Minister has stated in his Independence Day address, "Our country is witnessing an unprecedented economic growth at this point of time. If this growth rate is maintained for 5 to 10 years, it would be possible for us to eradicate poverty, ignorance, hunger and disease from our country". For all these, we need to remove barriers that impede innovation most especially red tape and bureaucracy. There is an urgent need to streamline the government process to mitigate the harmful effects and reap benefits of globalisation.

REFERENCES

Francis Cherunilam,"Business Environment", Himalaya Publishing House, Mumbai, 2003.

Kumar A and Joshi K.M., "Economic Development, some Policy Issues", Anmol Publications, New Delhi, 1998.

Kumar Ratnesh, "WTO, Structure, Functions, Tasks and Challenges", Deep& Deep Publications, New Delhi, 2002.

Mukesh Chaturvedi & Aseem Kumar "Managing Global Business a Strategic Perspective", Parcel Books, New Delhi, 2005.

Business Today "Challenges for India" 14th Anniversary issue, January 15, 2006.

Business India, from BPO to KPO, Aug 29 to Sept 11, 2005.

3

ANALYSIS OF CAPITAL INVESTED BY MULTINATIONAL CORPORATIONS IN INDIA

Anupama*

INTRODUCTION

The main development priorities of developing countries include achieving sustained income growth, for their economies by raising investment rates, strengthening technological capabilities and increasing their competitiveness in export markets. Here, investment is a key factor in economic growth, as it is often seen that the countries that devote a high proportion of output to investment may sustain more rapid growth than countries that invest less(*World Investment Report (1999)*). In a closed economy, the investment is solely financed by domestic savings. Since developing countries generally have a large saving investment gap, they depend largely on foreign sources to fill this gap. Initially, the developing countries depended on foreign aid, then on foreign loans and now it is considered that of all these sources, the source of capital through direct foreign investment is the best one (Moran, 1974) and more over it puts lesser burden than debt financing (Chossudovsky, 1988). Foreign Direct Investment (FDI) is usually preferred because profits are repatriated only when there is return on capital employed, whereas loans involved necessarily a fixed schedule of amortisation and interest payments irrespective of the repaying capacity of the project (Sharan, 1995). Regarding

* Department of Economics, Punjabi University Regional Centre, Bathinda.

foreign aid, it is generally felt that the capitalist countries who are the aid givers have dangerously mixed up aid with politics (Ghosh, 1977). This has led to world's division between exploiters and exploited which is possible explanation of economic development and under development. On the other hand FDI offers certain advantages over other sources of foreign finances to developing host countries. It has proved to be more stable than other type of financials flows. Direct investors show a longer term commitment to host economies than lenders and speculative portfolio investors(*World Investment Report, 2000*). FDI is also easier to service than loans, since profits tend to be linked to the performance and business cycle of the host economy. This is the main feature of FDI which is very important for the countries at the bottom of the development ladder and who have little access to other investible resources.

That is why, the FDI by MNCs has been growing rapidly in the recent past, faster indeed than the international trade and thus sharpening the pace of globalisation (*World Investment Report, 1996 and 2005*). Recently FDI flows by MNCs in developing countries has set new records. Year 2004 registered an increase of 40 per cent for FDI inflows to the developing economies while the world at $648 billion FDI inflows is hardly 2 per cent higher than the same in 2003. during this period the developed countries have actually experienced a 14 per cent decline in their FDI inflows as a result the share of the developing countries in total FDI inflows increased to 36 per cent. However, the developed countries as a group remained significant exporters through FDI (*World Investment Report, 2005*).

Thus, it is observed that in recent years, internationalisation of production has been significantly increasing and becoming the distinct feature of emerging world economic system and MNCs are becoming the main agents for this revolutionary transformation of the world economic order (Panchmukhi, 1997). These trends show certain striking features viz, FDI has emerged as the most dominant source, among other sources of foreign resources i.e. aid, loans and trade, etc. Secondly, out of total private capital flows consisting of both FDI and portfolio investment the relative share FDI is increasing and assuming more importance. Thirdly, most of the FDI originates from and is concentrated in developed countries and developing countries are vying with each other to get a larger share of the cake. That is why the developing countries are gradually opening up their economies to ensure a favourable economic environment for the MNCs. Actually, it is now a widely held belief, that the country who has a larger amount of FDI, has a larger growth rate (Mohanty and Sau, 2000) as the MNEs provide an easy access to various resources viz, capital, technology, skills, market access, among many others, which are necessarily desirable to expedite their growth rates (Kumar, 2000a).

In this race, however, the countries inviting MNCs, overlook the detrimental effects of these MNCs. The problems of MNCs to host economies, arise mainly because the goals of MNCs are different from that of the host developing economies (Dunning, 1981). They are not the philanthropic institutions who have come to serve the poor developing economies, they are strikingly business oriented with main objective of maximisation of global profits (Goyal, 1990). Though these MNCs are invited to increase competition among local firms, yet their mere presence, may frustrate any effective alternative to them and they may even make an oligopoly by takeovers, mergers and acquisitions. In case of India, too, it was observed by various studies that the hopes of the government were belied e.g. Chaudhari (1979) has found that in the case of 50 largest MNC affiliates in India, they had hardly contributed to the growth of the economy and rather it had hindered it through outflow of capital to their respective parent companies through various forms. Similarly Kumar and Chenoy (1982) say that MNCs hardly bring any fresh capital. They showed on the basis of a study of 8 leading MNCs that only 13.5 per cent of total equity share capital was actually brought in to India, the rest was raised through bonus issues or was subscribed to by public security and financial institutions or by the Indian public. Thus, it is blamed that instead of supplementing the domestic savings, the MNCs actually substitute them. This is shown by an econometric model by Ruffin and Rassekh (1986) that FDI and other private flows could be perfect substitutes and an increase in one type of flow may be offset by an equivalent decrease in other type. This is further proved by an econometric study by Agarwal (1987) that the aggregate domestic savings in the developing countries are largely inversely related to FDI. He also emphasised that MNCs can not be relied as a powerful mean to supplement domestic savings in order to achieve faster economic growth as they generally carry their operations from local resources rather than bringing new capital in the host economy. Even Barnet and Muller (1974) in their study of Latin America, have shown that about 83 per cent of total capital invested by MNCs is generated from local resources. Thus, instead of bringing new capital, already existing capital merely changes hands. This tendency erodes the economic base upon which the local firms rest as it leads to a marked decrease in the availability of local funds for locally owned industries (Shariff, 1982). In this way the MNCs, not only thwart the local competition, but overtake it entirely (Lewis, 1978). The MNCs may even crowd out i.e. induce the exit of domestic investment by adopting various anti-competitive strategies. That is why these TNCs are blamed for using new strategies of colonialism and penetrate into the economies of poor developing countries (Rao, 1975).

Despite all these unfavourable effects, developing economies are competing among themselves for MNCs' involvement in their economic growth. This is mainly due to some reasons viz, in the unipolar world of today, the commercial loans and foreign aid to the developing countries are declining. This fact has raised the relative importance of MNCs as a source of investment funds (Subrahmanian et. al. 1996). Further, it is also a fact that the developing economies have disillusioned from their strategies of prolonged protection and excessive state control, which has given to increasing creditability of market guided and out ward oriented strategies.

India, too has followed the same path. Though the inflow of FDI is not new to India, yet it has assumed a special importance in post-liberalisation period. The reforms in India have not only raised the level of foreign equity, amount of foreign investment, but it has also put more sectors open to foreign firms. This is clear from the data for number of approvals.

On the basis of these varying approaches of Indian government the approvals of foreign collaborations in India can be categorised in four phases. This is shown in Table 1. The Table shows that the annual average number of approvals ranged between 244 and 239 in first and second phases, i.e., mid fifties to mid sixties (i.e. 1956-65) and that from mid sixties to late seventies (i.e. 1966-79), respectively. These were, actually the phases of cautious and restrictive attitude towards MNCs.

Table 1
Foreign Collaboration approvals in Different Policy Phases

Phases	*Time Period*	*Annual Average no. of approvals*
I	1956-65	244
II	1966-79	239
III	1980-90	724
IV	1991-2004	1985

Source: *RBI Occasional paper;* August 30, 1996 and various issues of *SIA Newsletter*

The eighties which were characterised by the initiation of the reform process, liberalised various regulations regarding foreign capital and as a result invited more of foreign capital. That is why the annual average number of approvals immediately jumped to 724, showing an increase of about 302 per cent over the previous phase. Then the nineties in Inida, observed revolutionary changes in the economic policy, followed by the adoption of Structural Adjustment Programme (SAP) and signing of MIGA (Multilateral Investment Guarantee Agency) which attracted many MNCs towards India. So, the average number of approvals increased sharply to 1985. This phase is characterised by removal of FERA, various bureaucratic controls, opening up of various sectors to FDI, which were hitherto prohibited. The equity level which was not generally allowed more than 40 per cent was increased initially to 51 per cent in case of 34 priority industries.

However, later, in several sectors, this limit was raised to 74 and then to 100 per cent, thanks to the liberalisation and globalisation wave in India. In the post-liberalisation period, the foreign investment in India entered through two main routes. One is through Reserve Bank of India (RBI) which allowed automatic approval up to 51 per cent in priority industries listed in Annex-III of New Industrial Policy Statement 1991. The other routes are through Foreign Investment Promotion Board (FIPB) and through SIA (Secretariat of Industrial Approvals), which was specially established in 1991 to simplify the procedures related to FDI. Table 2 brings out that the share of RBI in total approvals was about 19.79 per cent in 1991 which increased to 48.42 per cent in 1992 and then gradually declined in later years, finally shrinking to only 22.10 per cent of total approvals in 2000. Similarly the share of SIA, too has declined from 38.49 per cent in 1992 to only 9.40 per cent in 2000. In contrast to this the share of FIPB was hardly 0.21 per cent in 1991 which rose sharply to 68.50 per cent. In case of amount approved, it is shown that the average share of RBI from 1991 to 2000 had remained only 6.42 per cent of total amount invested. It was as high as 13.49 per cent in 1993 and declined to 4.51 per cent in 1999, then increased to 8.80 per cent in 2000, thus giving a average share of 6.42 per cent. In contrast to it the average share of SIA & FIPB combined had remained as high as 48.93 per cent, though this share has declined from 70.80 per cent in 1992 to only 32.80 per cent in 2000, yet it is considerably higher than the 8.80 per cent of RBI route in 2000. This tendency of declining share of RBI route may be indicating two trends that either the MNCs were more interested to enter in the non-annex-III industries or the limit of 51 per cent might be inadequate from their point of view or because of both of these reasons. In other words, the market signals are for investment in non-priority areas.

Before analysing, the sector-wise break-up of the investment by MNCs in India, we first have a glance on overall picture of amount approved and actually invested by MNCs from 1986 to 2004 as given in Table 3. The number of

Table 2
FDI Approvals in Number from Various Routes & Actual Amount Invested (in Rs. Million)

Route / Year	1991	1992	1993	1994	1995	1996	1997	1998	1999	2000**	Total Values	Trend
I. Approvals SIA	760	585	307	382	593	410	167	193	221	137	3755	–
	(80.0)	(38.49)	(20.80)	(20.60)	(25.40)	(17.80)	(7.20)	(10.80)	(9.90)	(9.40)	(20.59)	
RBI	188	736	676	702	799	719	801	432	571	324	5948	–
	(19.79)	(48.42)	(45.80)	(37.90)	(34.20)	(31.20)	(34.40)	(24.20)	(25.70)	(22.10)	(32.61)	
FIPB	2	199	493	770	945	1174	1357	1161	1432	1004	8537	–
	(0.21)	(13.09)	(33.40)	(41.50)	(40.40)	(51.0)	(58.40)	(65.0)	(64.4)	(68.50)	(46.80)	
Total	950	1520	1476	1854	2337	2303	2325	1786	2224	1465	18240	1.05
II. Actual Investment SIA & FIPB	1911.80	4779.50	9851.60	15007.60	38694.40	57589.10	101284	82397.30	61894.30	63425.30	436834.90	–
	(54.40)	(70.80)	(55.14)	(45.63)	(56.74)	(55.43)	(61.70)	(61.80)	(36.70)	(32.80)	(4893)	
RBI	Nil	475.4	2411	3625.80	5301.60	6196.20	8672.20	6106.50	7608.10	16918.00	57314.80	–
	(0)	(7.04)	(13.49)	(11.02)	(7.77)	(5.96)	(5.28)	(4.58)	(4.51)	(8.80)	(6.42)	
Total*	3514.30	6751.80	17867.10	32892.80	68200.30	103892.00	164253.30	133390.40	168677.90	193417.40	892857.30	1.57

Figures in parentheses show per cent of the total.

* Total Includes Investment by GDR and NRI Proposals.

** The data for 2000 shows approvals upto October 2000 only.

SIA - Secretariat for Industrial Approvals.

FIPB- Foreign Investment Promotion Board.

RBI - Reserve Bank of India.

Source: *SIA Newsletter* ; January 2001.

Note: The data after 2000 is not included here due to change in the scope of FDI definition, so, a comparison may lead to wrong results.

Table 3
Number of Foreign Collaboration Approvals; Amount Approved and Actual Investment

Year	No. of approvals	Amount approved (in Rs. Cr.)	Actual inflow (in Rs. Cr.)	Actuals as % of Approvals
1985	1024	126.1	N.A.	–
1986	957	106.9	N.A.	–
1987	853	107.7	N.A.	–
1988	926	239.8	N.A.	–
1989	605	316.7	N.A.	–
1990	666	128.8	N.A.	–
1991	950	534.1	351.43	67.8
1992	1520	3879.1	675.18	17.41
1993	1476	8861.8	1786.71	20.16
1994	1854	14190.0	3289.28	23.18
1995	2337	32070.0	6820.03	21.27
1996	2303	36150.0	10389.2	28.74
1997	2325	54890.0	16425.33	29.92
1998	1786	30810.0	13339.84	43.3
1999	2224	28370.0	16867.79	59.46
2000	2124	37040.0	19341.74	59.28
2001	2270	26870.0	19265	71.70
2002	2273	11140.0	21286	191.08
2003	1874	6040	14302	236.79
2004#	467	1600	5077	317.31
Trend$ values	1.08*	1.71*	1.57	–

* The 't' values are not significant at 5% level of significance.
$ for data upto 2000 only
# upto March only
Source: Compiled from *SIA Newsletter*, January 2001.

approvals, were 1024 in 1985 gradually declined to 660 in 1990, but again rose to 950 in 1991 (the year of SAP), after which the number of approvals increased almost continuously with some variations. These were 2124 in 2000 and 1874 in 2003. this decline in 2003 is actually in consonance with the world trends. However, World Investment Report, 2005 has shown that these declining trends have now caught the path of recovery.

The Table shows that the amount approved has increased from Rs. 126.10 crore in 1985 to about Rs. 128.30 crore in 1990, registering a marginal increase. However, it increased sharply to Rs. 534.10 crore in 1991, when liberalisation wave initiated and after that there had been a continuous increase in the amount approved which increased to Rs. 54890 crore in 1997. In 1998, the amount approved declined to Rs. 30810 crore, it further declined to Rs. 28370 crore in 1999, and then increased to Rs. 32630 crore in 2000. Although during 1998 and 1999, the amount approved had declined, yet the actual inflow of foreign capital had increased. The actual investment inflows in India were of Rs. 351.43 crore in 1991 which increased to Rs. 19341.74 crore in 2000. However, the trend growth rates for the number of approvals were 5 per cent per annum for the period 1991-2000. Another striking feature, in Table 3 is that though in the post-liberalisation period, the approvals had increased rapidly, but actual investment inflow was much lower initially. This is clear from the Table. In the year 1991, though the amount approved was Rs. 534.1 crore, but the actual inflow was only of Rs. 351.43 crore. This amount was about 67.8 per cent of the amount approved. In later year, the situation on this front even worsened, as this percentage fell to about 17.41 in 1992, 20.16 per cent in 1993, 23.18 per cent in 1994, 21.27 per cent in 1995, and then took a positive turn as it increased to 28.74 per cent in 1996, finally reaching at 59.20 per cent in 2000. However, the trends after 2002 seemed to be compensating the original skepticism of the MNCs in Indian market. The trend growth rates upto 2000 have also reflected the gap between the approvals and the actual amount. Whereas the trend growth rate was about 71 per cent per annum for the approvals, it is only 57 per cent per annum for the actual amount invested by the MNCs in India in the post liberalisation period. This gap between approvals and actuals showed a hesitant nature of foreign investors initially to invest in India, even after the economy was liberalised. Although Indian economy is liberalising itself at a larger pace, yet the foreign investors still find the procedures for automatic approvals quite cumbersome as compared to other countries. Despite the reforms in India, U.S. investors could still set business in Mexico in three months compared to a year or more that takes in India. They complain that the repeated changes in the import policies, as has been done in recent past do not permit the investors to effect long term planning. If there is stability in government policies, only then the foreign investors would be encouraged to make suitable investments in India (Katti, 1993). In this case, the literature suggests that even the availability of low-cost labour has not become a point of attraction for FDI (Chaudhari, 1995). Regarding availability of low cost labour, the general perception of foreign investors about India is that the wage rate is low and so is the productivity of labour, along with several traditional inefficient practices. Moreover, the infrastructure is already inadequate, so, they do not find Indian business climate as hospitable as other locations. These seem to be the main reasons of their 'wait and watch' policy which results in a gap between approved amount and the actual inflow of foreign capital.

Table 4 deals with the country-wise break-up of FDI approvals. The data is divided into eight major country groups. Out of these countries, it is seen that U.S.A. took the lead. From 1985 to 2000 the average share of U.S.A. had been about 20.77 per cent of total approvals. The year-wise data shows that U.S.A. had always been taking the lead, with only one exception of the year 1989, when, Germany had the largest share, followed by U.S.A. However, U.K. registered the highest growth rate. The FDI from U.K. increased by 76 per cent per annum, which is the highest growth rate, followed by France, showing growth rate of 65.40 per cent per annum. While in case of U.S.A. the growth rate is 62.40 per cent per annum. Japan, Italy, Switzerland and Germany had recorded growth rate of 61.60, 57.10, 54.40 and 49.00 per cent per annum, respectively. Thus U.S.A had always remained the largest investor in India, despite the fact that her share declined significantly in the post-liberalisation period. During this period, the share of U.S.A. declined from 34.81 per cent of total approvals in 1991 to only 12.26 per cent in 2000. If we analyse the pre and post liberalisation period separately, it is clear that the average share of every country had declined and that of others (which are not separately mentioned in this table) had increased. Since, all of those countries are developed countries, so we can say that though a major share of FDI in India is contributed by the developed countries, yet this share is declining, giving way to FDI from other developing economies. The average share of all

Table 4

Foreign Direct Investment Approved: Country-Wise (In Rs. Million)

Year / Country	1985	1986	1987	1988	1989	1990	1991	1992	1993	1994	1995	1996	1997	1998	1999	2000*	Total	Share in Pre-liberalisation Period
USA	400	294	295	971	623	345	1859	12315	34619	34881	70544	100559	135698	35620	35752	39996	504771	28.72
	(33.14)	(27.48)	(27.57)	(40.5)	(19.67)	(26.89)	(34.81)	(31.68)	(39.1)	(24.59)	(22.0)	(27.82)	(24.72)	(11.56)	(12.6)	(12.26)	(20.74)	
UK	37	77	85	139	335	91	321	1177	6227	12992	17259	15246	44907	32608	29631	3805	163337	
	(3.07)	(7.2)	(7.94)	(5.8)	(1058)	(7.09)	(6.0)	(3.03)	(7.03)	(9.16)	(5.38)	(4.22)	(8.18)	(10.39)	(10.45)	(0.86)	(6.71)	
Germany	118	202	99	310	1203	195	418	863	1759	5694	13395	15379	21558	8538	11430	4441	85602	20.86
	(9.8)	(18.9)	(9.25)	(12.93)	(38.0)	(15.2)	(7.83)	(2.22)	(1.99)	(4.01)	(4.18)	(4.26)	(3.93)	(2.77)	(4.03)	(1.36)	(3.52)	
France	23	20	54	118	85	89	193	296	1291	897	4204	16717	7134	5136	14486	1934	52677	3.82
	(1.91)	(1.9)	(5.05)	(4.92)	(2.68)	(6.94)	(3.61)	(0.76)	(1.46)	(0.63)	(1.31)	(4.63)	(1.3)	(1.67)	(5.11)	(0.59)	(2.16)	
Italy	70	23	30	279	69	68	178	894	1174	3909	4603	1389	11950	2784	17595	1026	46041	5.29
	(5.8)	(2.15)	(2.8)	(11.63)	(2.18)	(5.3)	(3.33)	(2.3)	(1.33)	(2.76)	(1.44)	(0.38)	(2.18)	(0.9)	(6.20)	(0.31)	(1.89)	
Japan	157	56	69	310	88	50	527	6102	2574	4009	15143	14883	19064	12828	15947	8223	100030	7.16
	(13.0)	(5.23)	(6.45)	(12.93)	(2.78)	(3.9)	(9.87)	(15.7)	(2.91)	(2.83)	(4.72)	(4.12)	(3.47)	(4.16)	(5.62)	(2.52)	(4.11)	
Switzerland	8	33	89	27	55	135	355	6898	4268	483	3095	1598	4937	2851	2912	659	28403	3.4
	(0.7)	(3.08)	(8.32)	(1.13)	(1.74)	(10.52)	(6.65)	(17.74)	(4.82)	(0.34)	(0.97)	(0.44)	(0.9)	(0.93)	(1.03)	(0.2)	(1.17)	
Sweden	–	–	–	–	–	–	70	484	6	116	5023	5330	1090	2154	2739	966	17978	–
							(1.31)	(1.25)	(0.007)	(0.08)	(1.57)	(1.48)	(0.2)	(0.7)	(0.97)	(0.3)	(0.74)	
Total @ (Including others)	1207	1070	1070	2398	3167	1283	5341	38875	88593	141872	320717	361468	548914	308135	283665	326314	2423894	–

Figures in parentheses show percentage in total

* Data for 2000 is upto October 2000.

** Significant at 5 per cent level of significance.

@ This includes GDRs & NRI proposals.

\# Trend values are calculated upto year 1999 because year 2000, shows data upto October 2000.

Source : Complied from *SIA Newsletter*, Janauary 2001.

these countries taken together was 76.75 per cent in the pre-liberalisation period, while in the post-liberalisation period this declined to only 40.95 per cent.

The Table shows that the average share of every country discussed above had declined in the post-liberalisation period. However, the decline was found to be the highest in case of Germany with an average share of 20.86 per cent in pre-liberalisation period which declined sharply to 3.44 per cent in the post-liberalisation period. Similarly, the share of U.S.A declined from 28.72 per cent in the pre-liberalisation period to 20.71 per cent in post-liberalisation period. The average share of U.K. declined marginally from 7.50 per cent to 6.71 per cent, respectively in pre and post-liberalisation period. The share of France declined from 3.82 per cent to 2.16 per cent, that of Italy from 5.29 per cent to 1.88 per cent, that of Japan from 7.16 to 4.10 per cent and that of Switzerland declined from 3.4 per cent in pre-liberalisation period to 1.16 per cent in the post-liberalisation period.

Table 5 deals with the sector-wise break-up of pre and post liberalisation period. In the Table, the entries upto serial number 15 are included in the Engineering sector. The Table shows that this sector has the largest share both in the pre and post-liberalisation period, though this share declined in the post-liberalisation period. The share of the Engineering sector came out to be 64.77 per cent of total approvals in the pre-liberalisation period, which declined to 49.21 per cent in the post-liberalisation period. In the post-liberalisation period, the share of the Engineering sector in total amount approved was 44.12 per cent. While the share of Engineering Sector in total approvals had declined, the share of Chemicals (Fertilizers, Drugs & Pharmaceuticals take together) had improved from 10.22 per cent in the pre-liberalisation period to about 11.16 per cent in the post-liberalisation period. Similarly, the share of Textiles improved from 0.74 per cent to 3.70 per cent, that of Rubber and Rubber products improved from 0.97 to 1.11 per cent. This tendency may be justifying the critics that the FDI in India is moving towards non-priority sectors, in the absence of controls. Another striking feature of the sector-wise break-up of number of approvals shows that although the sub-sector of telecommunications had a share of only 3.63 per cent in the pre-liberalisation period and 3.72 per cent in the post-liberalisation period, yet in terms of amount approved, this sector had the largest share. The amount approved in this sector was about 18.74 per cent of total amount approved in the post liberalisation period. This was followed by electrical equipments, which constituted 9.17 per cent of total amount approved and further followed by the sub-sector of transport machinery, which accounted for 7.50 per cent of total amount approved in the post-liberalisation period.

Table 5

FDI Approvals : Industry-wise : Pre & Post Liberalization Period

Sr. No.	*Industry*	*No. of Approvals Approved in*		*Amount Industry 1991-2000*	*% of every out of total amount approved (1991-2000)*
		1981-1990	*1991-2000*		
1.	Metallurgical Industries	316 (4.25)	635 (3.47)	143299.62	5.91
2.	Boilers and Steam Generating plants	36 (0.48)	75 (0.41)	1466.61	0.06
3.	Prime movers (other than electricals)	212 (2.85)	61 (0.3)	917.24	0.04
4.	Electrical Equipments	1220 (16.41)	3505 (19.17)	222120.41	9.17
5.	Tele-communications	270 (3.63)	680 (3.72)	453967.46	18.74
6.	Transport Industry	380 (5.11)	1244 (6.8)	183231.00	7.56
7.	Industrial Machinery	1158 (15.57)	1322 (7.23)	22351.07	·0.92
8.	Machine tools	238 (3.2)	196 (1.07)	3820.96	0.16
9.	Agricultural machinery	16 (0.22)	46 (0.25)	4534.85	0.19
10.	Earth moving machinery	37 (0.5)	66 (0.36)	1058.46	0.04
11.	Miscellaneous mechanical & engineering products	401 (5.39)	790 (4.32)	15061.2	0.63
12.	Commercial, office and domestic appliances	72 (0.97)	85 (0.47)	11600.28	0.48
13.	Medical appliances	51 (0.69)	82 (0.45)	3301.82	0.14
14.	Industrial Instruments	379 (5.1)	174 (0.95)	1235.35	0.05

Contd.....

Sr. No.	Industry	No. of Approvals Approved in		Amount Industry 1991-2000	% of every out of total amount approved (1991-2000)
		1981-1990	1991-2000		
15.	Scientific Instruments	30 (0.4)	43 (0.24)	657.36	0.03
16.	Consultancy	156 (2.1)	575 (3.14)	20582.51	0.85
17.	Chemicals (excluding fertilizers)	708 (9.52)	1574 (8.61)	122775.59	5.07
18.	Fertilizers	N.A.	64 (0.35)	2468.85	0.10
19.	Drugs and Pharmaceuticals	52 (0.7)	403 (2.2)	16161.37	0.67
20.	Textiles	55 (0.74)	676 (3.7)	33598.02	1.39
21.	Cement & Gypsum	58 (0.78)	95 (0.52)	16839.38	0.69
22.	Ceramics	184 (2.48)	217 (1.19)	8764.06	0.36
23.	Paper & Pulp	39 (0.53)	173 (0.95)	31580.55	1.30
24.	Rubber products	72 (0.97)	202 (1.11)	11825.45	0.49
25.	Leather & leather products	50 (0.67)	187 (1.02)	3252.12	0.13
26.	Trading	—	466 (2.55)	20146.42	0.83
27.	Tea & Coffee	—	5 (0.03)	3172.5	0.13
28.	Total (including others)	7436 (100)	18287 (100)	2422945.21	100.00

-Figures in parentheses show percentage of total,

Source: Compiled from *Kothari's 'Directory of Indian Industries*, New Delhi, 1994 And various issues of *SIA Newsletter.*

Further, Table 6 shows the state-wise distribution of FDI in India during August,1991 to March, 2004. The table shows that Maharashtra had invited the largest amount of FDI. It was Rs. 51115 cr for the period 1991 to 2004. Which constituted about 17.48 per cent of total amount approved while in case of number of approvals, its total 4816 approvals accounted for a share of 18.91 per cent in total approvals. Delhi occupied the second rank as it had 12.06 per cent of total amount approved. The table shows that the states of Rajasthan, Punjab, Kerala, Pondicherry, Bihar, Himachal Pradesh etc. got a very marginal share in total FDI approved. This tendency shows that FDI had a bias towards the developed state, which has a good infrastructure, more number of industrial and skilled workers and a huge market.

Table 6
State-Wise FDI in India, (August 91 to March 2004)

State	*(in Rs. Cr.) Amount approved*	*% of Total FDI Approved*	*Number of Approvals*
Maharashtra	51115	17.48	4816 (18.90)
Delhi	35251	12.06	2638 (10.35)
Tamil Nadu	25072	8.58	2607 (10.23)
Karnatka	24138	8.26	2467 (9.68)
Gujarat	18837	6.44	1204 (4.72)
Andhra Pradesh	13745	4.70	1226 (4.81)
M.P.	9271	3.17	242 (0.95)
West Bengal	9317	3.19	670 (2.63)
Orissa	8229	2.81	140 (0.55)
U.P.	4917	1.68	798 (3.13)
Haryana	3870	1.32	858 (3.37)
Rajasthan	3033	1.04	341 (1.34)
Punjab	2434	0.83	199 (0.78)
Kerala	1552	0.53	325 (1.28)
Pondicherry	1286	0.44	129 (0.51)
Goa	990	0.34	245 (0.96)
Bihar	740	0.25	49 (0.19)
Chhattisgarh	633	0.22	47 (0.18)
Himachal Pradesh	1174	0.40	98 (0.38)
Chandigarh	196	0.07	77 (0.30)
Jammu & Kashmir	8	0.00	5 (0.02)
Jharkhand	145	0.05	80 (0.31)
Other States	76327	26.11	6188 (24.28)
Total Investment	292358	Total Approvals	25482 (100)

Source: Compiled from Various issues of *SIA Newsletter*.

Thus we have observed that FDI in India has been increasing both in terms of approvals and actual inflows, from which it is generally inferred that the rate of capital formation is increasing due to additional flows of foreign capital. But as discussed earlier, it is blamed that the MNCs, instead of bringing fresh capital just substitute the domestic savings. To check this tendency, we analyse the sample surveys of selected FDI companies by Reserve Bank of India. The data is given in the form of combined balance sheet data of various companies. It is generally held that the MNCs mainly increase their equity from the profits generated within India over a period of time instead of through net transfer into the country. It is found that these MNCs have high profitability ratios than their local counterparts and rely heavily on retained earnings for increasing their investment (*RBI Bulletin, 1993*). A study by Chander Shekhar (1992) of 144 companies reveals that the share of bonus issues as percentage of equity had been very high, ranging between 65 per cent to about 98 per cent. Though initially ploughing back of profits minimises the burden of profit repatriation, but in the long run, it helps in aggravating the problem, as the ploughing back of profits means larger claim of the foreign investors in the long run (Vyuptakesh, 1978). The extent to which reinvestments take place, the immediate cost to the economy is diminished. But in the long run, the retained profits inflate the total volume of foreign investments implying that, reinvestments are an increasing burden on the economy (Kurian, 1966). These reinvestments, had another serious implication that instead of bringing foreign exchange in the economy, these increase the foreign exchange liability of economy, as more and more dividends will have to be paid in future.

The high profitability of MNCs may be due to their large size, international operations, superior technological capability or even due to their establishment in highly profitable sectors (Lall, 1978). Whatever may be the reason, the host economy will suffer in both the cases, whether, these MNCs plough back their profits or remit these abroad (Streeten, 1971). In both cases, the host economy's balance of payments are adversely affected. In the former case, the balance of payments are adversely affected in the long run, without any net contribution of foreign exchange in the present time-period while in the latter case, the balance of payments are adversely affected in the initial time period itself and higher profitability means larger drain of foreign exchange on account of dividends.

Thus, it would be interesting to observe the paid up capital of the these MNCs. The MNCs in India, accumulate large reserves due to high profitability. Against these reserves they are able to issue liberal bonus shares (Goyal, 1980). To analyse this tendency the share of bonus issues in total paid-up capital (P.U.C) is calculated. These calculations would show the extent of investment on the basis of ploughing back of profits, in various policy phases. The Table 7 gives the country-wise break-up, while the Table 8 gives the sector-wise break-up.

Table 7 shows that, there is a sharp contrast in share of bonus issues during the pre liberalisation period as compared to the post 1995 period when the quantitative restrictions on repatriation of profits were removed after India became the signatory of WTO. For example in case of U.K, 59.04 per cent of total P.U.C was raised by bonus issues in pre-liberalisation period, which declined to 44.33 per cent in the post-1995 period. Similarly, in case of U.S.A the share of bonus issues in pre-liberalisation period was 55.69, which declined to 27.69 in the post-1995 period. However, the case of Germany and Switzerland are very striking. Both of these countries had bonus issues 66.40 and 70.73 per cent of their P.U.C, respectively for the pre-liberalisation period. It declined sharply to 17.89 and 30.58 per cent, respectively, of their P.U.C in the post-1995 period. This implies that these countries are more interested to invest their profits abroad, rather than ploughing back, if the regulations on remission of profits are minimised (Sauvant, 2000).

The Table 8 shows an industry-wise picture. It brings out that all industries taken together, had the 55.51 per cent share of bonus issues in total P.U.C in pre-liberalisation period which declined to only 22.46 per cent in the post-1995 period. The Engineering sector had a lower percentage of P.U.C raised through bonus-issues as compared to the All Industry average. It was 51.06 per cent in the pre-liberalisation period and declined to hardly 21.05 per cent after 1995. This decline is quite significant in case of Trading, Chemicals and Rubber products. In Trading, the share of bonus issues in the pre-liberalisation period was 65.14 per cent of total in the paid-up capital which declined to only 15.10 per cent In case of Chemicals this share declined from 67.34 per cent to 29.10 per cent, in case of Rubber and Rubber Products this share declined from 55.73 per cent to 28.21 per cent and in case Tea this declined marginally from 59.83 per cent to 57.86 per cent in the respective periods. Thus, this table shows that in the post-liberalisation period, there is found a tendency of remitting profits abroad and this tendency is strengthened in wake of removal of quantitative restrictions.

Table 7
Share of Bonus-Issues Out of Paid-up Capital of Selected FDI Companies in India Country-wise (In Percentage)

Country	*1985-91*	*1991-95*	*1995-2003*
U.K.	59.04	46.73	44.33
USA	55.69	64.95	27.69
Germany	66.40	51.55	17.89
Switzerland	70.73	34.37	30.58
Japan	8.05	9.40	6.92
Sweden	61.33	—	—

Source: Compiled from Various Surveys of Finances of FDI Companies, *RBI Bulletins.*

Table 8
Share of Bonus-Issues Out of Paid-up Capital of Selected FDI Companies in India Industry-wise (In Percentage)

Industry	*1985-91*	*1991-95*	*1995-2003*
Engineering	51.06	38.09	21.05
Chemicals	67.34	65.48	29.10
Tea	59.83	61.11	57.86
Trading	65.14	14.13	15.10
All Textiles	44.32	—	—
Rubber & Rubber Products	55.73	43.31	28.21
All Industries	55.51	48.77	22.46

Source: Compiled from Various Surveys of Finances of FDI Companies, *RBI Bulletins.*

Further, it is also blamed that MNCs rely largely on borrowings both from internal and external sources, to generate resources for investment. Thus MNCs' investment is not always associated with a significant capital flows as it may have been generated through reinvestment of earnings or from local borrowings (Hanumantharao, 1985). This tendency not only debars the Indian economy from additional inflow of capital, but also becomes a cause of shrinkage of concessional resources which our financial institutions provide to our domestic industries, in case these are utilized by a foreign company (Goyal, 1982). The heavy dependence of MNCs on local borrowings is shown in Tables 9 and 10 which show debt-equity ratio of the MNCs, country-wise and industry-wise, respectively.

Table: 9

Debt- Equity Ratio of Selected FDI Companies : Country-Wise

Year *Country*	*Average ratio1985-99*	*1999-2000*	*2000-01*	*2001-02*	*2002-03*	*Average ratio 1985-2003*
U.K	43.16	24.2	20.3	25.0	19.2	38.22
U.S.A.	39.49	26.1	23.4	9.3	5.0	33.95
Germany	44.19	54.3	51.2	13.1	10.9	41.41
Switzerland	33.35	32.9	35.8	32.5	33.9	33.45
Japan	82.84	36.4	35.4	57.0	45.4	73.59

Here Debt Comprises: (a) All borrowings from Government & Semi Government financial institutions, other than banks and foreign institutional agencies. (b) Borrowings from banks against mortgages and other long term ecurities.(c) Borrowings from companies against mortgages and other long term securities.(d) Debentures, deferred payment liabilities and public deposits.

And Equity includes: (a) Paid-up-capital (b) Fortified shares (c) All reserves & surplus

Source: Compiled from various Surveys of Finances of FDI, Companies, *RBI Bulletins*, August 91, August 94, November, 94, March 99, June 99, July 2000, February 2001& April 2004.

Table 9 illustrates country-wise debt-equity ratio. Japan had the highest debt-equity ratio at 73.59 and Switzerland had the lowest at 33.45 per cent. U.K, U.S.A, Germany had a debt-equity ratio of 38.22, 33.95, 41.41, respectively and all these three countries were having debt-equity ratios which were less than the All country/All industry average ratio of 47.44 per cent. However, the above table has shown that although the debt equity ratio of the MNCs is still very high, yet it has declined after 2000. That is why the average debt equity ratio for the period 1985-2003 declined from the average during 1985-1999 (with the exception of Switzerland).

Table 10

Debt- Equity Ratio of Selected FDI Companies: Country-Wise

Year *Country*	*Average ratio1985-99*	*1999-2000*	*2000-01*	*2001-02*	*2002-03*	*Average ratio 1985-2003*
Engineering	53.87	33.27	30.1	38.9	29.87	48.97
Chemicals	38.57	24.4	22.2	15.7	11.3	33.82
Tea	20.38	20.8	19.6	11.6	21.1	19.89
Trading	47.12	0.6	0.1	2.4	1.1	36.28
Rubber & Rubber	50.98	45.8	58.2	134.7	110.8	59.54
All Industries	49.27	35.7	31.8	52.9	45.6	47.44
Products						

Source: Compiled from various Surveys of Finances of FDI, Companies, *RBI Bulletins*, August 91, August 94, November, 94, March 99, June 99, July 2000, February 2001& April 2004.

Table 10 shows the sector wise data on debt-equity ratio. In the engineering sector it declined from about 53.87 in 1985-99, to about 48.97 per cent in 1985-2003. the sector of Rubber and Rubber products had the highest average debt equity ratio. The average debt-equity ratio of other sectors was 33.82 for chemicals, 19.89 for Tea and 36.28 for Trading. Now, with such a high rate of debt, it would be appropriate to analyse the data on borrowings and that how much of these borrowings are raised from the foreign sources. Tables 11 and 12 deal with the share of foreign sources in total borrowings country wise and industry wise, respectively.

Table 11

The Share of Foreign Borrowings out of Total Borrowings of Selected FDI Companies : Country-Wise (In Rs. Lakh)

Year *Country*	*Average ratio 1985-99*	*1999-2000*	*2000-01*	*2001-02*	*2002-03*	*Average ratio 1985-2003*
U.K	8.36	6.86	0.43	0.29	1.99	5.85
U.S.A.	9.01	0.78	1.93	0	0	6.45
Germany	0.19	1.80	1.71	0.15	6.20	0.91
Switzerland	0.00	0.00	0.00	0.86	0.84	0.00
Japan	0.40	3.92	2.39	3.28	1.43	1.64

Source: Compiled from Various Surveys of Finances of FDI Companies, *RBI Bulletins.*

The Table 11 shows the country wise break up of the borrowings of selected MNCs for different time periods. It is clear that these MNCs, mainly depend on the Indian sources for their borrowings and hardly bring any additional capital from abroad. In terms of share of foreign sources in total borrowings, it can be observed that upto 1999, this share was only 8.36 per cent in case of U.K, 9.01 for U.S.A, 0.19 per cent for Germany and 0.40 for Japan, which further declined after 1999. due to it the overall average (1985-2003) share of foreign borrowings further declined. It is discouraging to observe that the MNCs from Switzerland had no contribution from the foreign sources, that is all of their borrowings were financed by local sources only.

Table 12

The Share of Foreign Borrowings out of Total Borrowings of Selected FDI Companies : Country-Wise (In Rs. Lakh)

Year Country	*Average ratio 1985-99*	*1999-2000*	*2000-01*	*2001-02*	*2002-03*	*Average ratio 1985-2003*
Engineering	1.56	1.31	0.35	0.62	1.56	1.39
Chemicals	0.14	1.57	1.93	5.80	0.82	0.98
Tea	0.00	0.00	0.00	0.00	0.00	0.00
Trading	4.85	0.00	0.00	0.00	0.00	4.20
Rubber & Rubber Products	0.53	5.74	3.86	0.00	0.00	1.26
All Industries	1.12	2.23	1.63	1.32	1.20	1.37

Source: Compiled from Various Surveys of Finances of FDI Companies, *RBI Bulletins.*

Table 12 shows the sector wise break up. The Table shows that the average share of foreign sources of all companies in total borrowings was hardly 1.12 per cent upto 1999. Although it marginally improved to 1.37 per cent, yet it is still very low. Most of the MNCs in different sectors largely depend upon the local resources, which is clear from the fact that none of the industries mentioned in above table (with tradind sector as an exception) had shown a above 2 per cent share of their total borrowings raised from a foreign source (during both the time periods i.e. before 1999 and after 1999). So, it is clear that though the MNCs have a very high debt-equity ratio, but much of the borrowings had been raised from Indian sources itself. Thus, these MNCs had been using the local sources only, without adding any new capital to the domestic capital formation. Thus, these MNCs belie the hopes of Indian Government that they will fill the saving-investment gap in our economy. Rather, it is obvious that they use only those resources, which would otherwise (in absence of these MNCs) have been used by our local industries. In this way, instead of brining additional capital in the Indian economy, these MNCs, shrink the availability of capital for the domestic entrepreneurs and it is blamed that they even enjoy the facility of concessional loans, which are otherwise, meant for the small and infant indigenous companies.

The host countries, on the one hand invite MNCs, to attract capital, management skills, technology and global market access that these MNCs can provide. On the other hand, they are sensitive to the potential dangers of the transfer of important assets from domestic hands to foreign control (Sauvant, 2000). This danger is impending when the cross border M & As are rapidly increasing. The World Investment Report 2000 says that over the past decade most of the growth in international production has been via cross border M & As rather than greenfield investment. The value of cross border M & As rose from $ 74.5 billion in 1987 to $ 720.1 billion in 1999. With such a high rate of growth, genuine fears are raised about growing international oligopolies and market powers.

The MNCs are specially interested in the entry through M & As rather than through a greenfield entry, mainly due to two reasons viz speed and easy access to proprietary assets. The M & As, make the entry and establishment of any MNC faster into a host economy. They just get the benefits of already established distribution and marketing network of the acquired firm, instead of developing their own. Thus through M & As, the MNCs, try to minimise (reduce) the risks and maximise their efficiency through appropriate synergies (Bhoi, 2000). The World Investment Reports, 2000 and 2005 have shown that cross border M & As were mainly carried out in the developed countries. Table 13 shows that about 90 per cent of cross border M & As are carried out in developed countries. The data is divided into the cross border M & As region-wise i.e. by developed countries and the developing countries and is further sub divided by sale and purchase of M & As. It is clear that the M & As in terms of purchase were always greater than the sales after 1988 in the developed world. While in case of developing countries, the sales had always been greater than the purchases after 1988. Although the developing countries, showed a very small share both in purchases and sale of M & As, yet, it is important to note that the value of cross border M & As sales has gone up from $ 1.7 billion in year 1987 to $ 64.5 billion in 1999 and declined to $54.7 billion in 2004. Cross border purchases among developing countries had also increased from $ 2.6 billion in 1987 to $ 41.2 billion in 1999 and then to $39.09 billion. The M & As on the sales side has been growing at rate of 15 per cent per annum in case of developed countries while this growth rate is 34 per cent per annum for developing countries during this period.

It is further observed that India registered a very small share both by purchases and sales of cross border M & As during this period. This is clear from the Table 14. The Table shows that among developing countries, the majority of sales & purchases were on account of the Asian countries. However, India always had a marginal share, which actually took place from 1992. The purchases of M & As were 0.1 per cent of total M & A purchases by developing countries in 1992, increased to 2.1 per cent in 1993, jumped to 4.0 per cent in 1997 and again fell to 0.1 per cent in 1998 and 1999 and further improved to 4.39 per cent in 2003. Similarly, in case of sales of M & As in India, these were 0.4 per cent in 1992 of total sales of M & As by all developing countries taken together, increased to 0.8 per cent in 1993, 2.6 per cent in 1994, then after fluctuating in the intervening period it finally reached to 3.22 per cent in 2004. Thus, In case of India, the M & As wave had only recently shown increasing trends.

Although, these M & As are mainly dealt by MNCs for their own economic reasons, yet these deals do not have the same effect on the host economy. It is always emphasised by the host

Table 13

Cross-Border Mergers and Acquisitions By Region : Developed and Developing (Figures in US $ Million)

Year	*Developed Countries*				*Developing Countries*				*World*
	Purchase	*% of Total*	*Sale*	*% of Total*	*Purchase*	*% of Total*	*Sale*	*% of Total*	*Total*
1987	71874	96.50	72804	97.70	2614	3.50	1704	2.30	74509
1988	113413	98.10	112749	97.50	2180	1.90	2875	2.50	115623
1989	135786	96.70	135305	96.40	3990	2.80	5057	3.60	140389
1990	143216	95.10	134239	89.20	7035	4.70	16052	10.70	150576
1991	77635	96.20	74057	91.80	3057	3.80	5838	7.20	80713
1992	74431	93.90	68560	86.50	4827	6.10	8119	10.20	79280
1993	72498	87.30	69127	83.20	10439	12.60	12782	15.40	83064
1994	116597	91.70	110819	87.20	10164	8.00	14928	11.70	127110
1995	173732	93.10	164589	88.20	12779	6.80	15966	8.60	186593
1996	198257	87.30	188722	83.10	28127	12.40	34700	15.30	227023
1997	272042	89.20	234748	77.00	32544	10.70	64573	21.20	304848
1998	511430	96.20	445128	83.70	19204	3.60	80755	15.20	531648
1999	677296	94.10	644590	89.50	41245	5.70	64550	9.00	720109
2002	341548	92.36	322502	87.21	27549	7.45	44410	12.01	369789
2003	256935	86.51	244426	82.30	31060	10.46	40166	13.52	296988
2004	339799	89.28	315851	82.99	39089	10.27	54700	14.37	380598
Trend Values	1.16	-	1.15	-	1.27	-	1.34	-	1.17

Source: World Investment Report, 2000, 2005.

developing economies that greenfield entry is always better than the entry through cross border M & As, as the latter raises the danger of increasing market concentration, formation of oligopolies (Singh, 1999) and thus hitting badly the competitive process in the economies, which is so necessarily required for efficient production system.

The cross border M & As, it is blamed, do not add to the capital formation of a host economy and even take up efficient firms which adversely affects the host economy (Panchmukhi, 1997). Thus, the general notion that the MNCs increase the stock of productive capital, may not always be true as when an MNC acquires a firm in the host economy, paying the current owner of the firm in cash, it would not lead to additional stock of productive capital, but only the addition to foreign exchange reserves (that too only when the resources to finance M & As are not raised locally). In the liberalised policy environment Indian entrepreneur seems to have lost his bargaining power and well known Indian brands (like Hindustan Motors, Premier Automobiles, Mahindra and Mahindra, TOMCO and HLL) have been taken over by TNCs providing them a ready market with lesser competition from local industry. The process is continuing. Takeovers have the additional implication that they do not add to new production capacities or employment opportunities. On the contrary these can add to the growing outflow of foreign exchange. Although, the advocates of these M & As give arguments of economies of scale, proper utilisation of idle funds, diversification and renovation of an ailing unit or better and optimal utilisation of capacity, yet the host countries need to be cautious of the adverse affects. So, there is a need of an appropriate regulatory framework. In India, the institutional arrangement which had bearing on the evolution of regulatory framework for M & As were (Bhoi op. cit.) :

(i) Various provisions of MRTP Act, 1969.
(ii) Clause 40 of Listing Agreement
(iii) Amendments to clause 40 in 1990.
(iv) Creation of SEBI in 1992 and adoption of Takeover Code in 1994.
(v) Bhagwati committee on takeovers and adoption of a new Code in 1997 and amendment to the Code in 1998.

Table 14
Total Cross-Border Mergers & Acquisition by Developing Countries

Year	*Asia*	*% of Total*	*India*	*% of Total*	*Total of Developing Countries*
1987	P: 2372S: 256	90.715.0	—	—	26141704
1988	P: 2080S: 1569	95.454.6	22–	1.0–	21802875
1989	P: 2998S: 2089	75.141.3	11–	0.3–	39905057
1990	P: 5438S: 4073	77.325.4	–5.0	–0.0	703516052
1991	P: 2441S: 2182	79.837.4	1–	0.0–	30575838
1992	P: 2624S: 3414	54.444.5	335	0.10.4	48278119
1993	P: 7843S: 7347	75.157.5	21996	2.10.8	1043912782
1994	P: 6486S: 4701	63.831.5	109385	1.12.6	1016414928
1995	P: 8755S: 6950	68.543.5	29276	0.21.7	1277915966
1996	P: 19136S: 13368	68.038.5	80206	0.30.6	2812734700
1997	P: 21690S: 21293	66.633.0	12871520	4.02.4	3255464573
1998	P: 6399S: 16097	33.319.9	11361	0.10.4	1920480755
1999	P: 15875S: 25262	38.539.1	21776	0.11.2	4124564550
2002	P:13816S:17265	50.1538.88	2701698	0.983.82	2754944410
2003	P:18533S:21572	59.6753.71	1362949	4.392.36	3106040166
2004	P:20598S:24768	52.7045.28	8631760	2.213.22	3980954700

Source: *World Investment Report*, 2000, 2005.
P=Purchase, S=Sale

However, since India has gradually liberalised her investment regime, screening mechanisms have gradually given way to automatic approvals. On the other hand, in developed countries, there are several anti-trust laws which examine the possible impact of overseas M & As, even if none of the participants in the deal belongs to the country and these laws provide remedial measures, to deal with their ill-effects (Kumar,2000b). But in India, in the absence of any anti-trust law, a competition policy is suggested (SEBI, 1997) to promote efficiency and maximise welfare by enhancing competition in national market. Bhagwati Committee Report has recommended a pre-notification for a threshold limit for the value of assets of the merged entity at Rs. 500 crore or more and of the group to which the merged entity belongs at Rs. 2000 crore or more. The potential efficiency losses from the merger need to be weighed against the potential gains in adjudicating a merger. If within a specified period of 90 days, the adjudicating authority does not, through a reasoned order, prohibit the merger, it should be deemed to have approved.

To conclude, we can say that the FDI by MNCs in India is rapidly increasing, especially in the post-liberalisation period However, an initial gap was found between the approvals of FDI and the actual flows, the reasons may be administrative delays or the 'wait and watch' policy of the foreign investor or both of these. The most serious feature of growing FDI in India is found that they hardly add to the gross capital formation of the country, as much of the capital invested in India is raised locally either through issue of bonus shares or from borrowings from local financial institutions. This leads to a shortage of already scarce capital for the indigenous industry. Thus, the economic base of the local industry is eroding out and changing hands from local ownership to the foreign ownership. The situation becomes worse for the local competitors, when the MNCs indulge in M & As in name of more efficiency and economies of scale. Due to this activity of MNCs, instead of increasing competition, they just increase market concentration and change the market structure from a competitive to an oligopolistic one. So, there is a need to check this tendency. For this, it is suggested that either a greenfield entry should be preferred or there should be a close monitoring of the merger deals by weighing their potential gains and losses. A competition policy for India under changed domestic and international circumstances, will be necessarily required to promote a healthy and fair competition, which is very important for achievement of economic efficiency.

REFERENCES

Agarwal, M.R. (1987), 'TNCs, Economic Development and Income Distribution in LDCs', *The Indian Economic Journal*, Vol.34, No.3, January-March.

Barnet, Richard J and Mueller, Ronald (1974), *Global Reach: The Power of Multinational Corporation*, Simon and Schuster, New York, p-153.

Bhoi, B.K. (2000), 'Mergers and Acquisitions : An Indian Experience', *Reserve Bank of India Occasional Papers*, Vol.21, No.1, Summer, p-134.

Chaudhari, Sudip (1995), 'Government and TNCs : New Economic Policies Since 1991', *Economic & Political Weekly*, May 6-13, Vol.XXX, No.18-19, 43.

Chossudovsky, Michael (1988), 'Writing off Third World Debt', *Economic and Political Weekly*, Vol.23, No.52, p-2739.

Choudhari, Sudip (1979), 'Financing of Growth of Transnational Corporations in India', *Economic & Political Weekly*, 18th August, , p-1431-35.

Dunning, J.H. (1981), *International Production and the MNEs*, George Allen & Unwin Ltd, London, U.K., Chapter-II, p-307.

Ghosh, B.N (1977) 'Foreign Aid or Neo-imperialism', *Indian Journal of Economics*, No.2, p-89.

Goyal, S.K. (1980), 'Some Aspects of the Operations of MNCs in India', *Social Action*, Vol.30, No.4, October-December.

Goyal, S.K. (1982), 'The New International Economic Order and TNCs', Working Paper No.5, IIPA, New Delhi, December 16-20, p-85.

Goyal, S.K (1990), 'Foreign Capital, Technology and Self-Reliance'-A paper presented in the seminar in 'Debt-Militarisation and Development', held during August 18-19, , IIPA New Delhi, p-2.

Hanumantharao, C.H. (1985), *Structure and Policy in Less Developed Countries*, Heritage Publishers, New Delhi, p-117.

ISID (1999), 'FDI in India Since Liberalisation : An Overview' ISID-ESI-IDPAD workshop on 'Global Capital Flows and Indian Stock Market', April 5-6, New Delhi.

Katti, Vijaya (1993), 'India's Economic Reforms : An Assessment of the Impact on Industry and FDI', *Foreign Trade Review*, Vol. XXXIII, No.1, April-June.

Kumar, Nagesh and Kamal Mitra Chenoy (1982), ' MNCs and Self-reliance : A Case Study of Drug and Pharmaceutical Industry', *Social Scientist*, No.107, April, p-13-34.

Kumar, Nagesh (2000a), 'WTO Regime, Host Country Policies and Global Patterns of MNEs Activity : Implications of Recent Quantitative Studies for India', *RIS Occasional Paper*, RIS, New Delhi, May, p-1.

Kumar, Nagesh (2000b), 'Multinational Enterprises and M & As in India: Patterns and Implications', *R.I.S. Occasional Paper*, June, p-7.

Kurian, K. Mathew (1966), *Impact of Foreign Capital on Indian Economy*, People's Publishing House, New Delhi, Chapter-VI, p-216.

Lall, Sanjaya (1978), 'Transnationals, Domestic Enterprises and Industrial Structures in Host LDCs : A Survey', *Oxford Economic Papers (New Series)*, Vol.30, No.1, March, p-232.

Lewis, D. Solomon (1978), *MNCs and the Emerging World Order*, Kennikat Press, New York, p-40.

Mohanty, A.K. and P.K Sau (2000), 'FDI : Global and Indian Perspectives' *Facts for You*, July.

Moran, Theodre H. (1974), *Investing in Development : New Role for Private Capital* ? Transaction Books, New Brunswick (U.S.A.) & Oxford (U.K.), p-17.

Panchmukhi, V.R. (1997), 'MAI- What Should be the Response of the Developing Countries?', *RIS Digest*, September, p-9.

Rao, G.V. (1975), 'Transnational Monopolies', *Social Scientist*, May, Vol.3, No.10.

RBI (1993) 'Finances of Foreign Controlled Rupee Companies', *RBI Bulletin*, February, p-110.

Ruffin, R.J. and F. Rassekh (1986), 'The role of FDI in U.S. Capital Flows' *American Economic Review*, December, p-1126-30.

Sauvant, Karl P. (2000), 'Cross Border M & As', *Economic Times*, 4th October.

SEBI, 'Justice Bhagwati Committee Report on Takeovers', Stock Exchange Board of India, Mumbai, 1997.

Sharan, Lokesh (1995), 'Economic Reforms and FDI in India', *Facts For You*, September.

Shariff, Ismail (1982), 'MNCs - A Stumbling Block to the Developing Countries', *Indian Economic Journal*, October-December, Vol.30, No.2.

Shekhar,Chander (1992), *Political Economy of India*, Vikas Publishing House, New Delhi, p-45.

Singh, Balbir (1999), 'Foreign Direct Investment and Globalising India', Punjabi University Patiala, p-6.

Streeten, Paul (1971), 'Cost & Benefits of MNEs in LDCs', in Dunning J.H. (ed), *'The Multinational Enterprises'*, George Allen and Unwin Ltd, London, Chapter-9, p-251.

Subrahmanian, K.K. and et. al. (1996) 'Foreign Collaborations Under Liberalisation Policy', *Occasional Paper*, RBI, Mumbai, August 30, p-3.

Vyuptakesh, Sharan (1978), 'MNCs and the Balance of Payments Problems in Developing Host Countries : An Indian Experience' *The Indian Economic Journal*, Vol.20, No.2, October-December.

'World Investment Report (1996) : International Trade and International Policy Arrangements' *Foreign Trade Review*, October-December 1996, Vol. XXXL, No.3.

World Investment Report (1999), U.N. Publications, U.N., New York, Chapter-IV, p-159

World Investment Report (2000) : 'External Financial Resources and Investment', Chapter VI, 'FDI & Development : Does Mode of Entry Matter?' Chapter VI, p-165.

4

RURAL DEVELOPMENT AND SOCIO-ECONOMIC CHANGE AMONG AGRICULTURAL LABOURERS IN INDIA

K. K. Bagchi[*]

I

INTRODUCTION

Rural development has been a priority area in our national economic planning since long. It is sought for an all-round development of rural areas. It is to bring about a change of the rural environs including its people for the better. However, the need for this change is not, perhaps, equally felt for all socio-economic groups. There are more vulnerable and less vulnerable groups. Agricultural labourers, especially the landless agricultural labourers are obviously one of the most vulnerable groups in the rural society. On an average about one third of rural households belong to agricultural labourers in India. Lots of changes have taken place in different spheres of socio-economic and cultural life of people in India. The question is how far the socio-economic condition of agricultural labourers has changed over the last fifty years since the beginning of the rural and community development programmes and especially after the adoption of the

* Professor, Department of Economics, North Bengal University, Raja Rammohunpur, Darjeeling, West Bengal, e-mail: kkbagchi@hotmail.com, kanakbagchi@yahoo.co.in

programmes of economic reforms in 1991? Has this group of people become better off in terms of employment, earnings and literacy in the post-reform period compared to the pre-reform period? Available statistical evidences reveal a mixed picture. However, it appears that on the whole their condition in the above respects has improved slightly in the post-reform period. At present the existence of bonded and attached labour is nil or negligible. Agricultural labourers now, perhaps, enjoy a little more freedom and bargaining power than the earlier decades due to various economic, social and political forces at work. But the extent of improvement of the conditions of their life including levels of living is not satisfactory judged by any standard. India has experienced a reasonable rate of economic 'growth' in the past as well as in recent years but that has not percolated to the grass root level adequately and thus for the poor this 'growth' has not turned into 'development'. This lopsided development has led to a discontent among the deprived people, which is getting manifested in different forms. This indicates that there is the need for implementing the existing schemes under rural development programme sincerely by an honest and efficient rural development administration as well as executing the existing welfare measures for the agricultural labourers earnestly.

The present study is based on secondary data and literature. Data have been gathered from reports conducted and published by the Labour Bureau, Ministry of Labour. Data have also been collected from Economic Survey published by the Government of India and from various journal articles and internet sources.

The remaining part of the paper is organized as follows. Section II makes a review of important and relevant literature. Section III analyzes the changes that have taken place in the socio-economic condition of agricultural labourers in terms of changes in employment, income and literacy in the pre and post-reform periods. Finally, section IV summarizes the discussion, draws conclusions and makes suggestions for the betterment of living condition of agricultural labourers as a social group in particular and rural poor in general.

II

REVIEW OF LITERATURE

Bandopadhyaya (1977) in his paper has examined the cases of sharp increase in the number of agricultural labourers in North Bengal between 1961 and 1971. Through field investigation he has attempted to find out an answer to the question: How far did this rise originate from changes in mode of production and social existence forms?

Mencher (1980) holds that Kerala is regarded by a number of economists and others as an exceptional instance where, without either a radical revolution or a major increase in industrialization or production, things really seem to be getting better in terms of quality of life of common people. Under this backdrop, he has examined in some detail to what extent optimistic statements about the 'miracle of Kerala' will hold up under closer scrutiny. He has done it through an examination of the condition of life of agricultural labourers. Specifically he has examined the following aspects: health and fertility; fertility and employment, land reform; nutrition, education and literacy; and other public facilities.

Gulati (1990) in her paper has examined the principal factors of the pension scheme for the agricultural workers in Kerala, which is said to be the first Indian state to experiment with such a scheme. She has done the study against the background of the demographic trend in Kerala and its impact on the age structure of the state's population. The author has discussed, among other things, the impact of the scheme on an agricultural worker household and the future of the scheme in the light of the likely changes in the population's age structure.

Banerjee (1993) in his paper focuses on the segmented nature of the agricultural labour market. He also examined the basic components of recent economic policy changes with special reference to the farm policy and highlights the implication of such changes for agricultural labour. The study concludes that the condition of agricultural labour is likely to worsen in truncated reform which eludes land reform and the basic structure of production relation in the agrarian sector and which emphasises on agro-industries and infrastructure development by private investment depending on profitability and market condition. According to Banerjee, the condition of agricultural labour will improve if their asset holding and entitlement can be increased through land reform and availability of inputs.

Bhalla (1993) in her paper focuses on selected analytical issues related to wage determination in the long run. She has also dealt with the determination of labour absorption in Indian agriculture in the paper. She holds that there is plenty of scope for the expansion of employment within agriculture in certain regions and in the production of particular crops. The analysis made in the paper also points to the importance of investing in the creation of more productive non-farm jobs.

The paper by Chadha (1994) looks at the changing level of landlessness in different parts of rural India, both conceptually and empirically. It has analyzed the changing incidence of landlessness in terms of (i) the number of rural households owning arable land, (ii) the number of households operating no land and (iii) the number of agricultural labour households. The study concludes that between the years 1964-65 and 1982-83 the incidence of landlessness has increased in each state looked at from each of the three angles above and since expansion in agricultural wage employment is becoming increasingly difficult, therefore wage employment shall have to play a decisive role in years to come.

Pandya (1996) has analysed the problems related to labour absorption in Indian agriculture with special reference to Gujarat. He has done the study using farm level cost of cultivation data. He points out that the farm size has negative impact on labour use and fragmentation of land holding has positive impact on labour use.

Jha (1997) in his study has mainly focused on the socio-economic condition of agricultural labourers in contemporary Bihar. In his study he has utilized secondary and primary sources of data. It is a study at the macro, regional and micro levels. The study analyses the condition of male and female agricultural labourers; money wages and real wages; time rate and piece rate, daily, weekly, off-season, busy season scenario; income level and consumption and so on. It tries to relate the findings of all in one direction, i.e., changes in the labour process in the changing socio-economic scenario in the process of agricultural development.

Bagchi (2002), in his paper has made an assessment of the condition of agricultural labourers in India under the New Economic Policy in terms of the trends in landlessness, employment and wages of agricultural labourers and trends in rural poverty in the post-reform years.

Chadha and Sahu (2004) in their study has looked at the pace and pattern of growth of agricultural employment during the 1990s (post-reform decade) in contrast to the 1980s (pre-reform decade), without making any attempt to ascertain which element of change has been caused by which specific policy change.

Haque and Sharma in their paper entitled" Trends in Crop Output and Employment in India' has made an attempt to primarily at examining the employment potentials of agriculture in different regions of the country and suggesting measures for improvement in employment growth.

Deshpande and Prachitha (2004) in their paper has made an attempt to understand the development performance of the agricultural sector from the vantage view of the nexus between growth and employment.

Kijima and Lanjouw (2005) in their study have analysed NSS data for 1987-88, 1993-94 and 1999-00 to explore the relationship between rural diversification and poverty.

Himanshu's (2005) paper surveys all available sources and estimates agricultural wages in India over the period 1980-81 to 1999-00. he has made an attempt to look at the methodology as well as concepts and definitions used to arrive at the wage figure. He has also looked at the issue of comparability of various wage estimates and offered some possible reasons for the same.

Srivastava and Singh (2005) have focussed on agricultural wages and explored the rate of growth of real wages in different periods, corresponding to the pre and post-economic reform.

Then they have used state level data over the entire time period to see whether the determinants of wages have changed over time.

Sharma (2005) in his paper shows that average daily real wage earnings of adult male and female labourers increased in all the major states both during the pre and post-reform periods. But the rate of increase was lower in most states in the post-reform period as compared to the pre-reform period. The proportion of agricultural labour households under debt also declined continuously in most of the states, though average debt per indebted household increased during both the periods.

III

CHANGES IN THE SOCIO-ECONOMIC CONDITION OF AGRICULTURAL LABOURERS

Changes in the Proportion of Agricultural Labour Households

Table 1 below shows the changes in the proportion of agricultural labour households across the states during the period from 1983 to 1999-00. A comparison between these two years demonstrates that the proportion of agricultural labour households increased in as much as 10 states out of 17 states. In two states (West Bengal and Punjab) it remained more or less constant between these two years, while in 5 states it decreased during this period. The increase was more distinct in Bihar, Karnataka, Orissa, Gujarat and Madhya Pradesh while it was less pronounced in the states of Andhra Pradesh and Uttar Pradesh. On the other hand the decrease was sharp in the case of Kerala and Rajasthan. On all India level a definite increase in the proportion of agricultural labour household can be seen.

Release and Rehabilitation of Bonded Labourers

The system of bonded labour is a scar on Indian society. In 1978 Ministry of Labour formulated a Centrally Sponsored Scheme (CSS) for rehabilitation of bonded labour. Table 2 shows the state-wise details of bonded labourers identified and rehabilitated upto 31st March 2000. It can be seen that the progress in this regard has been more or less satisfactory except in Haryana and Arunachal Pradesh. However, on the whole there are nearly 30,000 released and not rehabilitated bonded labourers, which is a cause of concern.

Table 1
Agricultural Labour Households-Major States: 1983 to 1999-00

State	*Number (000)*			*% of rural households*		
	1983	*1993-94*	*1999-00*	*1983*	*1993-94*	*1999-00*
Andhra Pradesh	3929	4583	5408	41.55	41.56	42.52
Assam	463	816	632	19.45	22.98	17.26
Bihar	4028	4844	4884	37.11	39.22	42.52
Gujarat	1267	1959	2063	30.69	37.83	34.82
Haryana	512	364	464	20.24	15.87	18.71
Himachal Pradesh	17	26	42	2.19	2.85	4.00
Jammu & Kashmir	52	11	59	6.35	3.33	5.30
Karnataka	1762	2180	2943	36.59	37.33	41.70
Kerala	1148	1102	969	31.70	28.22	21.83
Madhya Pradesh	2302	3332	2699	30.15	34.85	34.29
Maharashtra	3031	3937	4851	38.55	41.17	41.73
Orissa	1725	1516	2719	36.41	25.46	43.32
Punjab	561	706	680	25.26	27.69	24.59
Rajasthan	545	576	502	11.10	9.97	7.89
Tamil Nadu	3117	3761	4231	42.24	42.08	45.15
Uttar Pradesh	3040	3061	4189	18.01	15.31	19.68
West Bengal	3139	3252	4305	38.50	32.57	38.23
All India	30867	36262	44184	30.70	30.34	32.23

Sources: (i) *Rural Labour Enquiry: Report on Wages and Earnings of Rural Labour Households, 1983*, Labour Bureau, Shimla; (ii) *Rural Labour Enquiry: Report on Wages and Earnings of Rural Labour Households, 1993-94*, Labour Bureau, Shimla; (iii) *Rural Labour Enquiry: Report on General Characteristics of Rural Labour Households, 1999-00*, Labour Bureau, Shimla.

Changes in Average Daily Real Wage Earnings

The most important determinant of economic condition of agricultural labourers is their real wage earnings. Table 3 below presents average daily real wage earnings of agricultural labour for the period 1983 to 1999-2000 for 17 major states in India.

Table 2

State-Wise Details of Bonded Labourers Identified and Rehabilitated Upto 31-3-2000 Since Inception of the Scheme in 1978-79

Name of the State	*Number of bonded labourers Identified and released*	*Rehabilitated (%)*	*Central assistance (Rs. in lakhs)*
Andhra Pradesh	36,289	29,552 (81.44)	680.10
Bihar	13,092	12,368 (94.47)	314.48
Karnataka	62,727	55,231 (88.05)	1383.84
Madhya Pradesh	12,822	11,897 (92.39)	146.35
Orissa	49,971	46,843 (93.74)	898.13
Rajasthan	7478	6297 (84.21)	69.02
Tamil Nadu	63894	58073 (90.84)	911.93
Maharashtra	1384	1300 (93.93)	8.25
Uttar Pradesh	27797	27797 (100.00)	533.22
Kerala	823	710 (86.27)	15.56
Haryana	544	21 (3.86)	0.42
Gujarat	64	64 (100.00)	1.01
Arunachal Pradesh	3526	1416 (40.16)	70.84
Total	2,80,411	2,51,569 (89.71)	5032.45

Source: Ministry of Labour (http://indiabudget.nic.in/es2000-01/Chap 1002.pdf)

Note: Figures in the parameters indicate percentage of total.

Table 3

Average Daily Real Wage Earnings of Agricultural Labour in Agricultural Occupations at 1986-87 Prices – Major States: 1983 to 1999-00 (Rs.)

State/Year	*Male*			*Growth rate*		*Female*			*Growth rate*	
	1983	*1993-94*	*1999-2000*	*1993-1983 & 1993-94*	*1983 94 & 1999-00*	*1993 94*	*1993-94*	*1999-2000 1993-94*	*1983 &*	*1993-94 & 1999-00*
Andhra Pradesh	5.31	9.69	12.50	6.20	4.42	4.14	6.95	8.34	5.32	3.14
Assam	9.87	13.06	14.00	2.84	1.19	9.75	10.97	12.09	1.18	1.67
Bihar	5.16	8.31	11.68	4.88	5.96	4.39	7.26	10.33	5.16	6.18
Gujarat	6.82	10.17	12.57	4.08	3.67	5.38	9.86	10.74	10.83	1.46
Haryana	7.66	13.35	19.41	5.71	6.57	6.14	11.39	17.97	6.37	8.06
Himachal Pradesh	8.57	14.87	21.82	5.66	6.73	3.43	12.16	19.32	13.49	8.19
Jammu & Kashmir	8.31	18.78	26.76	8.49	6.20	7.84	13.45	-	5.55	-

Contd....

State/Year	*Male* 1983	1993-94	1999-2000	*Growth rate* 1993-1983 & 1993-94	1983 94 & 1999-00	*Female* 1993 94	1993-94	1999-2000	*Growth rate* 1993-94	1983 & 1993-94 & 1999-00
Karnataka	4.49	9.6	12.58	7.89	4.70	3.76	7.14	8.47	6.62	2.95
Kerala	14.17	21.83	30.56	4.42	5.88	11.55	15.16	19.94	2.76	4.77
Madhya Pradesh	4.18	8.45	9.52	7.29	2.05	3.58	7.07	8.81	7.04	3.81
Maharashtra	5.23	10.55	12.33	7.27	2.69	3.59	6.57	7.97	6.23	3.34
Orissa	3.85	8.76	9.06	8.57	0.57	3.44	6.46	7.00	6.50	1.37
Punjab	11.39	19.33	20.20	5.43	0.75	5.61	16.46	25.06	11.36	7.41
Rajasthan	6.35	12.95	16.27	7.39	3.96	3.71	10.83	12.75	11.31	2.81
Tamil Nadu				6.17		13.56	17.15		8.19	4.07
3.98				8.19		10.08	7.48		3.59	
Uttar Pradesh				4.83		9.70	12.33		7.22	4.16
3.56				7.41		9.47	7.61		4.26	
West Bengal				9.91		12.99	14.30		8.19	1.65
5.51				11.26		12.28	7.41		1.48	
All India				5.69		10.78	12.99		6.60	3.22
4.29				7.67		9.18	5.98		3.10	

Source: As in Table 1

It can be seen from the table that there has a varying positive rates of growth in average daily real earnings of both the male and female agricultural labourers throughout the period 1983 to 1999-2000. But except Bihar, Haryana, Himachal Pradesh and Kerala in all other states the rate of growth of wages of male agricultural labourers has been much lower in the post-reform period compared to the pre-reform period. For female labourers the post-reform growth in wages has been higher compared to pre-reform period only in the case of Assam, Bihar, Haryana and Kerala. On all India level also rates of growth in real wages of both male and female labourers have been much lower in the post-reform period compared to the pre-reform period. This indicates that the improvement in economic condition of agricultural labourers has not been satisfactory in the post-reform period unless their incomes were supplemented by accrual from other sources. One common phenomenon that can be observed is that over the entire period across the states absolute average daily real wage of female labourers remained lower compared to their male counterparts.

Growth in Employment

As far as the growth in employment is concerned, table 4 shows that employment of agricultural labourers has expanded over the period across the three most recent NSS surveys. In 1987 nearly 20 per cent of all males aged 15 and above were employed in the occupation of agricultural labour. This increased to 22.5 per cent in 1993 and further improved to 23.2 per cent by 1999. Given the fact that women population as a whole is economically less active, the figures for female agricultural labour indicate an obvious importance of these occupation to women. Figures show that the percentage of women employed in agricultural labour has increased overtime from 11.2 per cent in 1987 to 14.5 per cent by 1999. Since the absolute number of population was growing during this time period,

Table 4
Distribution of Occupation in Rural India
(individuals aged 15 and above)

	Male			*Female*		
	1987	*1993*	*1999*	*1987*	*1993*	*1999*
Agricultural labour	19.9	22.5	23.2	11.2	14.0	14.5
Cultivator	36.4	38.1	34.4	15.0	14.1	13.7
Non-farm regular	6.5	6.5	6.3	1.0	1.0	1.0
Non-farm casual	7.2	6.3	7.7	2.9	1.5	1.6
Non-farm self-employed	13.5	11.8	12.2	5.5	2.7	3.2
Farm regular	1.7	0.7	1.0	0.4	0.1	0.3
Not working	14.8	14.2	15.2	64.1	66.6	65.9

Note: "Not working includes attending school, being unemployed, engaged in domestic duties, recipients of rent, pension, and remittance, and beggars and prostitutes.

Source: Kijima and Lanjouw (2005) this percentage increase overtime has led to a sizeable increase in the absolute number of agricultural labourers in rural areas in the late 1980 and 1990.

As far as the employment share among economically active population is concerned figures in Table 5 shows that there is a wide variation in agricultural wage employment across states in India. States with relatively high percentage of the economically active population in agricultural labour in all the three years in agricultural labour include Andhra Pradesh, Bihar, Karnataka, Maharashtra, Orissa and Tamil Nadu. Agricultural employment increased uniformly in six out of 16 major states between 1987-88, 1993-94 and 1999-2000 and in another seven states, the trend was not uniform but employment shares in 1999-2000 were higher than they were in 1987-88 on all India level by more than five percentage points.

Table 5
Employment Share Among Economically Active Adult Population: 1987-88 to 1999-00

State	*Agricultural labour*	*Cultivator*	*Casual non-farm labour*	*Regular non-farm*	*Non-farm self-Farm*	*regular employed agricultural sector*	*Total non-farm sector*	*Total*
				1987				
All India	29.8	39.5	6.5	8.1	14.2	1.9	71.2	28.8
Andhra Pradesh	39.4	28.6	4.9	8.0	17.7	1.3	69.3	30.6
Assam	13.8	44.7	16.9	12.8	10.4	1.4	59.9	40.1
Bihar	35.1	40.0	4.4	4.7	11.2	4.6	79.7	20.3
Gujarat	30.7	30.9	7.5	17.8	10.0	2.9	64.5	35.3
Haryana	17.9	47.3	8.8	5.8	18.2	2.0	67.2	32.8
HP	4.7	69.7	6.5	9.1	10.0	0.0	74.4	25.6
Karnataka	40.1	33.1	5.5	8.6	11.3	1.4	74.6	25.4
Kerala	24.8	6.5	14.5	29.4	24.8	0.0	31.3	68.7
Madhya Pradesh	27.2	54.5	3.7	3.4	8.4	2.7	84.4	15.5
Maharashtra	36.3	37.7	7.3	6.7	10.0	2.1	76.1	24.0
Orissa	34.6	32.8	5.6	6.7	18.8	1.5	68.9	31.1
Punjab	20.8	34.6	12.6	5.8	20.1	6.1	61.5	38.5
Rajasthan	12.5	47.0	3.9	15.1	20.7	0.8	60.3	39.7
Tamil Nadu	40.3	22.3	10.9	9.1	16.7	0.7	63.3	36.7
Uttar Pradesh	19.7	57.6	4.4	4.1	13.1	1.2	78.5	21.6
West Bengal	33.3	30.4	9.2	7.6	18.6	0.8	64.5	35.4

Contd....

State	*Agricultural labour*	*Cultivator*	*Casual non-farm labour*	*Regular non-farm*	*Non-farm self-Farm*	*regular employed agricultural sector*	*Total non-farm sector*	*Total*
				1993				
Andhra Pradesh	46.1	28.7	4.5	5.2	14.6	0.8	75.6	24.3
Assam	15.6	41.3	15.7	15.3	11.5	0.7	57.6	42.5
Bihar	42.3	39.2	4.1	2.8	11.2	0.4	81.9	18.1
Gujarat	41.3	33.4	7.7	8.9	8.7	0.1	74.8	25.3
Haryana	18.9	41.0	13.0	10.9	15.4	0.7	60.6	39.3
HP	7.8	65.2	9.5	9.0	8.3	0.2	73.2	26.8
Karnataka	39.6	37.3	5.6	5.4	11.9	0.1	77.0	22.9
Kerala	27.3	5.1	13.8	35.1	18.6	0.0	32.4	67.5
Madhya Pradesh	33.2	53.7	3.7	3.4	5.0	1.0	87.9	12.1
Maharashtra	43.4	35.5	7.2	4.7	8.0	1.2	80.0	19.9
Orissa	39.5	36.8	4.7	4.4	14.1	0.4	76.7	23.2
Punjab	29.1	34.9	11.9	7.4	14.7	1.9	65.9	34.0
Rajasthan	16.1	57.4	5.0	11.9	9.0	0.6	74.1	25.9
Tamil Nadu	45.4	21.4	10.0	9.4	13.6	0.2	67.0	33.0
Uttar Pradesh	21.0	55.6	5.1	5.0	13.0	0.3	76.9	23.1
West Bengal	30.8	27.9	9.9	9.4	20.8	1.1	59.8	40.1
				1999				
All India	35.2	36.7	6.6	8.3	12.1	1.1	73.0	27.0
Andhra Pradesh	47.4	27.5	5.5	5.5	13.3	0.8	75.7	24.3
Assam	9.0	37.0	9.0	18.9	14.2	11.9	57.9	42.1
Bihar	41.2	36.5	3.6	5.3	13.1	0.3	78.0	22.0
Gujarat	40.0	34.4	7.2	9.1	9.0	0.3	74.7	25.3
Haryana	17.7	40.3	15.5	10.5	15.0	1.1	59.1	40.9
HP	10.0	52.9	13.5	13.2	9.8	0.6	63.5	36.5
Karnataka	40.8	35.2	5.0	8.5	9.9	0.6	76.6	23.4
Kerala	21.7	3.8	13.8	38.4	19.4	2.8	28.3	71.6
Madhya Pradesh	37.4	47.1	3.6	4.8	6.5	0.5	85.0	14.9
Maharashtra	44.4	33.8	7.5	5.9	7.4	1.0	79.2	20.8
Orissa	45.3	29.9	4.9	6.0	13.5	0.5	75.7	24.4
Punjab	22.7	33.1	12.8	11.2	15.1	5.1	60.9	39.1
Rajasthan	15.7	56.0	5.7	11.1	11.2	0.4	72.1	28.0
Tamil Nadu	45.8	17.5	11.8	10.1	14.0	0.9	64.2	35.9
Uttar Pradesh	20.7	50.7	6.2	6.6	15.3	0.6	72.0	28.1
West Bengal	34.7	24.8	5.9	9.2	23.6	1.8	61.3	38.7

Note: Economically active adult population is defined as those who are between 15 and 60 years of age and engaged in wcrk such as all the market activities for pay or profits (except prostitution, begging, smuggling etc.) and non-market activities relating to the agricultural sector for own consumption and construction of private or community facilities free of charge. Non-farm employment is defined as workers in sectors other than agriculture by using industry code. Employment status is defined in NSS as following. Regular salaried employee is a person who gets in return salary or wage on a regular basis but not on daily basis, casual wage labour is a person who earn wage according to the terms of the daily or periodic work contract and self-employed are persons who operate their own farm or non-farm enterprise.

Source: Kijima & Lanjouw (2005).

Only in three states i.e., in Assam, Haryana and Kerala there is a decline in the importance of agricultural wage employment overtime. As far as employment share among economically active adult population in total non-farm sector is concerned, it can be seen that on all India level there has been a decline by 1.8 percentage point over the entire period.

Growth of Agricultural and Rural Employment and NSDP

Table 6 presents state-wise growth in agricultural employment, rural employment and NSDP from agriculture. The broad trends that can be discerned from the figures of this table are:

Table 6

State-Wise Growth Rates of Employment and NSDP from Agriculture

State	*Growth Rate of*					
	Agricultural Employment		*Rural Employment*		*NSDP from Agriculture*	
	1983-84/ 1993-94	*1993-94/ 1999-00*	*1983-84/ 1993-94*	*1993-94/ 1999-00*	*1983-84/ 1993-94*	*1993-94/ 1999-00*
(1)	*(2)*	*(3)*	*(4)*	*(5)*	*(6)*	*(7)*
Andhra Pradesh	2.26	–0.18	2.27	0.24	3.03	1.47
Assam	1.86	–0.77	1.96	1.68	2.12	1.69
Bihar	1.28	1.17	1.29	1.90	–0.66	–0.80
Gujarat	0.65	2.50	1.65	2.07	0.66	3.08
Haryana	1.79	–0.01	2.54	0.70	5.06	1.67
Himachal Pradesh	1.90	–1.45	2.72	–0.13	3.10	1.91

Contd....

State	Agricultural Employment		Growth Rate of Rural Employment		NSDP from Agriculture	
	1983-84/ 1993-94	1993-94/ 1999-00	1983-84/ 1993-94	1993-94/ 1999-00	1983-84/ 1993-94	1993-94/ 1999-00
(1)	(2)	(3)	(4)	(5)	(6)	(7)
Jammu & Kashmir	2.45	1.59	3.05	1.98	0.27	3.65
Karnataka	1.79	-0.05	2.12	0.17	3.56	2.87
Kerala	-0.43	-2.47	0.17	1.28	4.55	0.16
Madhya Pradesh	1.91	0.25	1.89	0.68	2.81	1.74
Maharashtra	1.24	0.16	1.63	0.37	5.52	1.50
Orissa	1.99	0.10	1.74	0.66	-0.69	1.18
Punjab	-0.88	1.62	0.10	2.00	4.90	1.90
Rajasthan	1.23	-0.02	2.18	0.52	4.08	5.17
Tamil Nadu	0.51	-1.85	1.06	-1.41	4.56	1.24
Uttar Pradesh	1.41	-0.29	1.53	0.69	2.80	2.72
West Bengal	0.81	0.08	2.13	0.45	4.45	5.14
India *	1.39	0.05	1.75	0.66	2.75	3.04

*All India estimates are based on figures for the listed states only.
Source: Chadha and Sahu (2004).

(i) In the post-reform period both rural employment (except in two states) and NSDP from agriculture (except in one state) have grown, but the growth in employment is lower in the case of as many as 14 out of 17 states than that in the growth of NSDP. (ii) Growth of agricultural employment has been negative in the case of 9 states in the post-reform period while this negative growth was experienced by only one state (i.e. Kerala) in the pre-reform period. The former trend implies that technological change in agriculture and change in cropping pattern has been labour saving on the whole and elasticity of employment in agriculture with respect to output is either positive but low or negative. Haque and Sharma's (2004) estimates reveal that out of 13 major states elasticity of employment in agriculture with reference to out put was negative in the case of 5 states during 1981-82 to1990-91 and it became negative for 8 states during the period 1991-92 to 2001-02 (Haque and Sharma, 2004)

Table 7 exhibits that two other important dimension of well being, viz., education levels and caste status are strongly and inversely correlated with agricultural labour employment. Thus there is little to suggest that over time the association between agricultural wage-labour employment and low welfare in terms of these indications has weakened (Kijima & Lanjouw, 2005). We can see that relationship between non-agricultural employment on the one hand, and educational and social status on the other, is strong and positive—especially in the case of regular employment in the non-farm sector. The positive development that can be visualised from the data exhibited in Table 7 is that over the period 1987-1999 there has been a continuous increase in the literacy level of the agricultural labourers as a group. However, at the same time it can be noticed that the proportion of illiterate agricultural labourers has also increased which implies that to an increasing number of rural labour force agricultural labour as an occupation has become the 'last resort'.

Table 7

Distribution Of Occupations By Education And Social Groups

(Adult male individuals aged 15 and above)

	Agricultural labour	*Cultivator*	*Non-farm regular*	*Non-farm casual*	*Non-farm self-employed*	*Farm regular*	*Not working*
			1987				
Not literate	31.3	36.9	2.4	9.0	11.4	3.1	6.0
Primary completed	14.1	38.9	5.9	7.6	17.0	1.1	15.4
Secondary completed	4.0	28.8	18.0	2.3	12.8	0.3	33.8
University completed	2.2	23.2	34.3	0.7	13.5	0.1	26.1
Non SC/ ST	15.4	39.8	7.1	6.0	14.7	3.4	12.1
SC/ ST	32.1	27.3	4.7	10.2	10.2	3.4	12.1
Non Muslim	19.9	37.1	6.6	6.9	12.8	1.8	14.9
Muslim	20.3	30.2	5.6	9.2	19.8	0.8	14.2
			1993				
Not literate	36.5	39.4	2.2	6.9	9.4	1.2	4.4
Primary completed	18.2	41.7	5.2	8.5	14.3	0.3	11.7
Secondary completed	6.1	32.4	14.1	3.0	11.2	0.2	33.2
University completed	2.4	26.8	34.5	0.5	12.6	0.2	23.0
Non SC/ ST	16.0	42.5	7.1	5.4	13.2	0.5	15.3

Contd....

	Agricultural labour	Cultivator	Non-farm regular	Non-farm casual	Non-farm self-employed	Farm regular	Not working
SC/ ST	37.9	27.5	5.0	8.5	8.4	1.0	11.6
Non Muslim	22.8	38.9	6.6	6.1	10.8	0.7	14.3
Muslim	20.0	30.4	5.7	8.2	21.7	0.4	13.8
		1999					
Not literate	39.1	34.1	1.8	8.4	10.1	1.4	5.3
Primary completed	20.1	36.7	4.7	10.0	13.6	1.1	13.9
Secondary completed	7.4	33.0	12.5	4.4	13.0	0.6	29.2
University completed	3.5	29.1	31.3	1.5	14.1	0.5	19.9
Non SC/ ST	17.5	38.5	6.9	6.5	13.8	0.9	16.0
SC/ ST	36.5	24.9	5.1	10.4	8.6	1.2	13.3
Non Muslim	23.4	35.6	6.4	7.4	11.0	1.0	15.1
Muslim	21.7	23.3	5.5	10.3	23.0	0.6	15.7

Note: The figures are summed up to 100 in each educational of social category.

Source: Kijima & Lanjouw (2005).

Changes in Landlessness

Possession of land in rural society indicates economic security of rural households while the lack of it implies vulnerability. Therefore let us look at the profile of agricultural labour households from the point of view of possession of land. Table 8 below shows agricultural labour households with land and without land and average size of land (in ha.) in major states of India. It is revealed that the proportion of household with land has increased in the post-reform period in as much as 8 out of 17 states while in 2 states (Madhya Pradesh and Andhra Pradesh) it has remained more or less unchanged between the years 1983 to 1999-2000. What is additionally worrying is the fact that the average size of land possessed by agricultural labour households across the states has declined steadily. The reason may be increasing demographic pressure on land (Myrdal, 1968), indebtedness among petty land owning households to non-institutional agencies ultimately leading to land alienation (Parthasarathy, 1994), eviction of tenants to evade the provision of tenancy acts (Bagchi, 2002), lack of non-farm employment opportunities (Sharma, 2005) etc. The growing incidence of landlessness and declining size of land holding implies increasing vulnerability of agricultural labour households.

Table 8
Agricultural Labour Households With And Without Land-Major States: 1983 to 1999-00 (per cent)

State	*Households with land*			*Households without land*			*Average size of land (ha)*		
	1983	*1993-94*	*1999-00*	*1983*	*1993-94*	*1999-00*	*1983*	*1993-94*	*1999-00*
Andhra Pradesh	39.43	41.91	39.37	60.57	58.09	60.63	0.62	0.22	0.22
Assam	43.23	50.95	38.43	56.77	49.05	61.57	0.82	0.13	0.09
Bihar	47.93	37.81	28.25	52.07	62.19	71.75	0.26	0.12	0.04
Gujarat	26.45	39.13	43.64	73.55	60.87	56.36	0.60	0.26	0.18
Haryana	4.55	14.97	17.16	95.45	85.03	82084	0.75	0.21	0.06
Himachal Pradesh	77.83	72.27	82.92	22.17	27.73	17.08	0.25	0.22	0.45
Jammu & Kashmir	66.00	57.96	82.17	34.00	42.04	17.83	-	0.22	0.19
Karnataka	45.76	47.63	42.98	54.24	52.37	57.02	0.87	0.36	0.30
Kerala	82.12	24.30	55.89	17.88	75.70	44.11	0.19	0.04	0.08
Madhya Pradesh	49.17	56.68	49.25	50.83	43.32	50.75	0.90	0.45	0.33
Maharashtra	41.90	42.16	44.84	58.10	57.84	55.16	1.19	0.44	0.35
Orissa	55.83	58.00	57.39	44.17	42.00	42.61	0.48	0.26	0.21
Punjab	4.76	5.41	9.03	95.24	94.59	19.97	0.40	0.03	0.03
Rajasthan	53.60	51.85	50.60	46.40	48.15	49.40	1.86	0.60	0.32
Tamil Nadu	28.39	24.89	23.90	71.61	75.11	76.10	0.43	0.09	0.08
Uttar Pradesh	83.62	62.14	61.86	46.38	37.86	38.14	0.36	0.20	0.14
West Bengal	47.00	49.28	36.23	53.00	50.72	63.77	0.89	0.11	0.07
All India	44.05	43.03	42.67	55.95	56.97	57.33	0.70	0.23	0.18

Source: As in Table 1.

Changes in Indebtedness

One of the indicators of economic well being of agricultural labour households is the extent of their indebtedness. Generally low levels of earnings compel them to borrow to meet their subsistence needs. Unproductive expenses such as for consumption of liquor; social ceremonies etc. are also some of the important causes of their indebtedness. Indebtedness of agricultural labour households and average debt per indebted household in major states for the period 1983 to 1999-00 has been shown in table 9 below.

Table 9
Indebted Agricultural Labour Households and Average Debt Per Indebted Household in Major States: 1983 to 1999-00

States	*Indebted Households (%)*			*Average debt per indebted household (Rs.)*			*Growth rate in average debt per household*	
	1983	*1993-1994*	*1999-2000*	*1983*	*1993-1994*	*1999-2000*	*1993-1983 & 1993-94*	*1994 & 1999-2000*
Andhra Pradesh	66.03	51.60	37.60	1206	3636	6478	11.67	10.32
Assam	22.85	46.50	44.90	477	652	609	3.17	–0.68
Bihar	55.46	27.50	17.10	779	1413	2613	3.13	11.02
Gujarat	32.32	35.90	37.50	1313	2477	4933	6.55	12.42
Haryana	44.85	57.80	44.80	26530	5496	10136	–14.56	10.96
Himachal Pradesh	26.02	12.40	12.10	1698	7802	8475	16.47	1.42
Jammu & Kashmir	33.68	21.90	41.60	3337	1479	2845	–7.81	11.76
Karnataka	49.29	36.20	19.50	1236	2844	5797	8.69	12.87
Kerala	52.39	29.30	42.10	1655	7171	10520	15.79	6.73
Madhya Pradesh	37.38	23.20	16.20	1844	3593	7300	6.90	12.81
Maharashtra	48.07	33.40	23.20	1006	3260	6523	12.48	12.51
Orissa	14.75	26.30	17.10	838	2148	3382	9.86	8.02
Punjab	53.06	28.40	37.20	1822	3904	6054	17.92	7.74
Rajasthan	51.13	26.20	24.20	2041	3482	6286	5.49	10.56
Tamil Nadu	60.31	33.50	19.50	1036	3097	7116	11.57	15.19
Uttar Pradesh	47.76	40.20	17.50	1481	3223	6042	8.09	11.27
West Bengal	49.01	43.20	36.40	589	1410	1527	9.12	1.36
All India	51.05	35.50	25.10	1516	2901	5230	6.70	10.54

Source: As in Table 1.

It is apparent from this table that compared to 1983, the proportion of indebted household has decreased in 14 states out of 17 states in 1999-00. This is a desirable change that implies an improvement in the economic condition of agricultural labour households. However, the last column of the table 9 shows that in all the states except Assam the rate of growth of average debt has been positive and in the case of 10 states the rate of growth in post-reform period has been greater than that of the pre-reform period. These positive rates of growth may not be of a serious concern in view of the fact that the absolute increase between the two periods is in money terms and when converted to real term the rate of growth will be of a lower magnitude. But the matter, which is not undesirable, is that except four states (Andhra Pradesh, Bihar, Kerala and Uttar Pradesh) in all other 10 states the percentages of households taking loan for consumption purpose has increased and that for production purposes has decreased.

Trends in Poverty

It may not be out of place here if we look at the estimates of rural, urban and total poverty ratios based on quinquennial survey for the pre and post-reform periods and thereby making an attempt to comprehend the relative level of poverty among agricultural labourers. The estimates based on the expert group method and approved by Planning Commission are presented in Table 10. The data reveal that the 1980s recorded faster decline in rural poverty and the decline slowed down considerably after the introduction of reforms. It is also revealed that urban poverty declined much faster than rural poverty.

Table 10
Estimates of Poverty

Year	*Per cent below poverty line*			*Reduction from previous survey (Percentage point)*		
	All India	*Rural*	*Urban*	*All India*	*Rural*	*Urban*
1973-74	54.9	56.4	49.0	–	–	–
1977-78	51.3	53.1	45.2	3.6	3.3	3.8
1983	44.5	45.7	40.8	6.8	7.4	4.4
1987-88	38.9	39.1	38.2	5.6	6.6	2.6
1993-94	36.0	37.3	32.4	2.9	1.8	5.8
1999-2000						
30 days recall	26.1	27.1	23.6	9.9	10.2	8.8
7 days recall	23.3	24.0	21.6	12.7	13.3	10.8

Source: Data from 1973 to 1994 was sourced from *Economic Survey*, Govt. of India. Data for 1999 to 2000 (30 days & 7 days recall) was sourced from *www.indiastat.com*

However, it can be seen that there has been an accelerated fall in both rural and urban poverty in 1999-00 and in fact there was a faster decline of rural poverty compared to the urban poverty. It can thus be inferred that since there has been a sharp decline in rural poverty in the late 1990s and since agricultural labourers forms the majority of the rural poor, therefore, economic condition of agricultural labourers might have improved to some extent in the late 1990s compared to the pre-reform period.

IV

SUMMARY, CONCLUSIONS AND SUGGESTIONS

The analysis made above reveal that the percentage of agricultural labour households in rural households has increased in 10 states and decreased in 7 states of which in the case of latter, in two states the decline has been marginal in the post-reform period compared to pre-reform period. However, the absolute decline in number has taken place in the case of three states, viz., Haryana, Kerala and Rajasthan during the same period. The proportion of landless agricultural labour households has also increased in most of the states. The average daily real wage earnings of both adult male and female workers have increased in all major states during pre as well as post reform period. But in most of the states the daily real wage earnings of both male and female labourers was lower in the post-reform period than in the pre-reform period. The percentage of indebted agricultural labour households has declined gradually in majority of the states. The average debt per indebted household has increased both during the pre and post-reform periods practically in all the states. However, this is perhaps not a serious thing as the increase is in nominal terms. In real terms the rise in indebtedness is likely to be much less. The matter of concern is, however, the percentage of debt incurred for consumption purposes that have increased in the post-reform period compared to the post-reform period. Estimates of poverty reveal that rural poverty is continuously declining and in the late 1990s the decline has been faster than that of early 1990s as well as than the decline in urban poverty.

Two major conclusions may be drawn from the above analysis of secondary data related to wage, employment, literacy, indebtedness and poverty of agricultural labourers. First, probably in the late 1990s socio-economic condition of agricultural labourers both male and female have improved very marginally as evidenced by a decline in rural poverty, decline in the percentage of indebted rural households, slight increase in rural non-farm employment in some states and increase in real wage earnings by the agricultural labour households and favorable impact of various rural development programmes. The second conclusion is that since the improvement in the socio-economic condition of agricultural labourers has not been to the desired extent, therefore, several measures are to be undertaken to raise their levels of living.

We may therefore make the following suggestions for the improvement of the socio-economic condition and reduce the vulnerability of the agricultural labour households.

First, since employment elasticity of agriculture is very low, therefore, the most effective way to reduce the incidence of poverty among agricultural labour households would be to promote the rural non-farm employment opportunities that do not impose barriers to entry. Agricultural labourers who gain access to such jobs will be directly benefited. It will also indirectly benefit those who remain as agricultural labourers through the improved wage level as access to non-farm jobs tighten the rural labour market.

Secondly, redistribution of ceiling surplus lands, wherever available, among the landless is the first guarantee to build up the asset structure to improve the entitlement and capability of poor agricultural labourers. Thereafter necessary inputs should be provided in order to make the marginal and landless peasants viable against natural odds and exploitation by large farmers.

Thirdly, the ongoing rural employment (self-employment and wage-employment) programmes and the traditional welfare programmes for agricultural labourers such as pension scheme, Targeted Public Distribution system and nutrition programmes and other programmes providing safety net should continue. The newly enacted National Rural Employment Guarantee Bill, 2004 is a step in right direction. If implemented sincerely it will go a long way in mitigating rural poverty in a big way.

Finally, there is the need for an honest and efficient rural development administration for implementing the existing schemes under rural development programmes as well as for earnestly executing the existing welfare measures and if possible to adopt more welfare measures for those in need. There is the need for reform of the governance to deliver goods to the rural common people by making it more pro-poor and outcome oriented.

REFERENCES

Acharya, Sarathi (1989), Agricultural Wages in India: A Disaggregated Analysis, *Indian Journal of Agricultural Economics*, 44(2), 121-139.

Ahluwalia, Montek S. (1990), Policies for Poverty Alleviation, *Asian Development Review:Studies of Assian and Pacific Economic issues;* 8(1).

Bagchi, K.K. and T.K. Roy (2002), Impact of New Economic Policy on Agricultural Labourers oin India, *Economic Affairs*, 47(1), 7-17.

Bandyopadhyaya, Nripendra (1977), causes of Sharp Increase in agricultural Labourers, 1961-71: A Case study of Social –Existence Forms of Labour in North Bengal, *Economic and Political Weekly*, 12 (53), A-111-A-126.

Banerjee, Amalesh (1993), The Impact of New Economic Policy on Agricultural Labour, *Indian Journal of Agricultural Economics*, 48(30), 470-76.

Bhalla, Sheila (1993), The Dynamics of Wage Determination and Employment Generation in Indian Agriculture, *Indian Journal of Agricultural Economics*, 48(3), 448-70.

Chadha, G.K. and P.P. Sahu (2002), Post-reform Setbacks in Rural Employment: Issues that Need Further Scrutiny, *Economic and Political Weekly*, 37(21), 1998-2026.

Chadha, G.K. and P.P. Sahu (2004), Recent Changes in Agricultural Employment in Rural India; A State-Level Analysis, *Agricultural Situation in India*, 41(5), 249-272.

Chakrabarti, H.K., K.K. Bagchi and A. Bhuimali (2002), Impact of New Agricultural Technology on economic Conditions of agricultural Labourers: a Case Study of Two Villaves of west Bengal, *Labour and Development*, 8 (1&2), 62-89.

Deshpande, R.S. and J. Prachitha (2004), Entangled at the Cross-Roads: Growth and Employment in Indian Agriculture, *Agricultural Situation in India*, 41(5), 281-294.

Dhanasekaran K. (2005), agricultural Growth, Employment and Rural Poverty in the Era of Economic Liberalisation in India, *Asian Economic Review*, 47(1), 81-88.

Gulati, Leela (1978), Unemployment Among female Agricultural Labourers, *Economic and Political weekly*, 11(13), A-31.

Haque, T, and Shailaja Sharma (2004), Trends in Crop Output and Employment in India, *Agricultural Situation in India*, 41(5), 273-280.

Himanshu (2005), Wages in Rural India: sources, Trends and Comparability, *Indian Journal of Labour Economics*, 48(2), 375-406.

Kijima, Yoko and Peter Lanjouw (2005), Economic Diversification and Poverty in Rural India, *Indian Journal of Labour Economics*, 48(2), 349-374

Mencher, Joan P (1980), The Lessons and Non-Lessons of Kerala: Agricultural Labourers and Poverty, *Economic and Political Weekly*, Special Number, October, 1781-1802.

Myrdal, Gunner (1968), *Asian Drama: An Enquiry into the Poverty of Nations, Vol.II*, Pantheon, New York.

Pandya, K. (1996), *Agrarian Structure, New Technology and Labour absorption in Indian Agriculture*, Himalaya Publishing house, Bombay.

Parthasarathy, G. (1994), Rural Credit for the Asetless and Poor: Some Policy Changes in G.K. Chadha (ed.), *Sectoral Issues in the Indian Economy: Policy and Perspectives, HarAnand* Publications, New Delhi.

Parthasarathy, G. (1996), Recent Trends in Wages and Employment in Agricultural Labour, *Indian Journal of Agricultural Economics*, 51 (1&20, 145-67).

Patnaik, K. Uma Shankar et al (2003), Determinants of Agricultural Labour Absorption – A Study of East Godavari District of Andhra Pradesh, *Asian Economic Review*, 45(1), 1-12.

Reddy, B. Sambi (2004), Assessment and Identification of Rural Poor in India: A Study Based on NSS Household Data, *National Bank News Review*, April-September, 20-36.

Selvaraj K. (2002), Agricultural Development in India and its Impact on Poverty Reduction, *Indian journal of Social Development*,2(1), 53-77.

Sharma, H.R. (2005), Economic Conditions of Agricultural Labour Househlds in 1990s: A State Level Analysis of Wage Earnings and Indebtedness, *Indian Journal of Labour Economics*, 48(2), 425-436.

Srivastava, Ravi and Richa Singh (2005), Economic Reform and Agricultural wages in India, *Indian Journal of Labour Economics*, 48(2), 407-424.

Sundaram K. and Tendulkar, Suresh D. (2003), Poverty In India in the 1990s: An Analysis of Changes in 15 Major States, *Economic and Political Weekly*, 38(50), 5263-5275.

Sundaram K. and Tendulkar, Suresh D. (2004), Poverty among social and Economic Groups in India in 1990s, *Economic and Political Weekly*, 39(14), 1385-1394.

Sundaram, K. (2001), Employment and Poverty in 1990s: Further results from NSS 55th Round Employment-Unemployment Survey, 1999-2000, *Economic and Political Weekly*, 36(22), 3039-3051.

Unni, Jeemol (1988), agricultural Labourers in Rural Households, 1956-57 to 1977-78: Changes in Employment, Wages and Income, *Economic and Political Weekly*, 23(26), A59 - A68.

Vaidyanathan, A. (1994), Employment Situation: Some Emerging Trends, *Economic and Political Weekly*, 29(50), 3147-3156.

5

PLIGHT OF INDIA'S FOREIGN TRADE UNDER GLOBALIZE REGIME

*S. B. Akash**
*H. Y. Kamble***

INTRODUCTION

Globalization played, significant role in international trade, because, globalization facilitates breaking the political, economic, social, cultural, ecological, geographical and integrating the whole world into global village. Moreover, its have different roles viz., free flow of capital, free flow of technology, increases in industrialization, spread of production facilities throughout the global, balance development of the world economies, national sovereignty at stake, commodities at lower price with high quality, cultural exchange and demand for a variety of products, increases employment opportunities and income, increases standard of livings, welfare and prosperity. In view of this at present there are over 200 countries in the world each trading with the other in a large number of goods and services.

The potential role of trade in economic performance had been recognized by Adam smith as early 1776 and stated that division of labour and specialization moving force behind economic growth, are limited by the extent of the market. Trade

* Faculty, Department of Commerce, Karnatak University PG Centre, Karwar, Karnataka.

** Prof. and Head Department of Studies of in Commerce, Karnatak University, Dharwad.

could expand the market and services and thus facilitates specialized and higher productivity[1] Drucker and Mitches argue that globalization for better or worse has changed the world business, globalization has positive and negative impacts on national economy[2]. However, due to globalization, national economy characterized not only by free trade, by free movement of labour, capital, skill and entrepreneurship.

CONCEPT OF GLOBALIZATION

Globalization played vital role in developing and developed countries. And it had notable impact on big and small enterprises. On one hand they have access to a far grater market and better technology and resources, while on the other hand resulted in an environment of highly competitive local market with imports from other countries flooding local market and threat the very existence of local big and small- scale industry by offering quality product at cheaper price. The concept of globalization defines by different scholars on their own views. IMF argued that globalization as the growing economic interdependence of countries world wide through increasing volume and variety of cross border transaction in goods and services and of international capital flow and also through the more rapid and wide spread diffusion of technology[3].

Charless U L Hill defined globalization as the shift towards a more integrated and interdependent world economy. The globalization has two main components i.e. the globalization of markets and the globalization of production[4]. The term globalization refers convergence of national market into international market and putting international trade on the forefront of strategic importance in the development process[5].

Thus it is clear that globalization means to a constellation of forces, economic, technological, ecological and cultural structure that are emerging on a global scale and it facilitates to increasing the independency and integration of the individual countries in the world. In view of this India has embarked on a major reform of its economy with a complete overhaul of its industrial and trade policies with view to introduce grater transparency and liberalization.

FEATURES OF GLOBALIZATION

The term globalization not only today used widely but also widely interpreted. The globalizations refers a very broad and all most all encompassing concept incorporating moment of persons, concept, images, ideal, values, capital. Trade and services across national boundaries. The globalization include the accelerating of global financial speculation, growth world trade the integration of the world economy with a neo-liberal free-trade oriented framework. The following are the important feature of globalization.

- It is a process of breaking the political, economic, social, cultural, ecological, geographical and educational barriers and integrating the whole world into a global village.
- It facilitates to operating and planning to expand business throughout the world.
- It is erasing the difference between domestic market and international market.
- It facilitates to open business and selling goods and services all over the world.
- Buying and selling goods and services from any country in the world.
- Sources of factor of production and inputs like raw material, machinery, finance, technology, human resources, and managerial skill, from the entire globe.

GLOBALIZATION AND ITS IMPACT

Globalization had notable impact on developed and developing countries and it is in India generally taken to mean integrating the economy of the country with the world economy. Thus it turn opening up of the economy to foreign direct investment by providing facilities to foreign companies to invest in different field of economic action in India; removing constraints and obstacles to the entry of MNC in India and allowing Indian companies to enter into foreign collaboration in India and also encouraging them to set up joint venture abroad; carrying out massive import liberalization programmes by switching over from quantitative restrictions to tariffs in the first place and then bringing down the level of import duties considerably and instead of a plethora of export incentives opting for exchange rate adjournments for promoting export. However, globalization seems to be helping the developed country and big gaps between the developed and underdeveloped countries, there by increasing regional disparities. According to the World Bank[6] latest report nearly 70% of the gain from free trade would go to the developed countries. The USA subsidies on cotton crop will depress world price. The recent report by Oxfam Warned imports of cheap subsidized US cotton warned imports of cheap subsidized US cotton to china would result in loss of $ 208 million income and 720000 jobs[7]. Hitting in particular Gansu and Xinjiang two of China's poorest reasons. Further more than three fourth of rural house hold in China are expected to suffer a cut in real incomes between 2001-07. The International of Conference free Trade Union (ICFTU), study pointed out, the membership of china in WTO has been helping mainly the capitalists the losers have been formers, blue-collar workers, whose income has remained stagnant for the last ten years. The recent ILO's report substantiates above facts, which states that globalization could neither create new jobs nor better jobs. The process of globalization had unequal competitors between giant MNCs and dwarf Indian enterprise even the large Indian industry are just pygmies compared to the multinationals and while some of them have already been gobbled up by latter, some others are awaiting their with bated breath[8]. The globalization has emerged in the post 1991 reform phase, Indian business communication are thus facing unequal competition from MNCs. According to Baldev Raj Nayar[9] the unequal competition steams from many reasons such as cost of capital of Indian companies much higher than MNCs, immense financial strength of MNCs, they are not only in a position to bear losses in any line of business for a considerably more time than Indian enterprise, they have enough muscle power to force out the Indian partners from joint ventures and grab control of their companies, Indian firm continue to suffer from handicaps developed under the earlier regime of control etc.

WTO AND ITS ROLE IN FOREIGN TRADE

WTO came into existence on 1-1-1995 by replace the General Agreement On Tariffs and Trade for strengthening the world economy by encouraging trade, investment, employment and income growth. The main function of WTO are administering and implementing multilateral agreements, seeking to resolve trade disputes, and co-operation with other international involved in global economic policymaking and it played significant role in international trade because, it deals with the rules of the trade between nations. Provides transparency of policies rules and procedures and for multilateral conformism and it is not for insular and protected economic, trade investment regime, facilitates grater and grater market access, not impose import restriction or import substitution, it does not believe in more focus on export orientation, but is consistently and passionately seeking outward orientation in economic policies of member countries, it is not far unrestrained or imprudent use of capital resources in the development strategy, but for developing capital on the basis of comparative and competitive advantage of nations, it is not for subsidies, for wider and effective use of pricing Mechanism for allocation of resources domestically and globally. The WTO framework implies that every country economic policies are framed in conformity with international framework. It strives towards strengthening interrelationships between trade and economic policies affecting growth and development. In substance, it seeks promotion of multilateral trading system based on agreed, effective and enforceable multilateral disciplines.

The WTO agreement deals with agriculture, textiles and clothing, banking, government purchases, industrial standards and product safety, telecommunications, food sanitation regulations, intellectual property etc. However, in case of agriculture sector the commitment by the members was to reduce tariff by 36% by developed countries over a period of 6 years and by developing countries by 24% over a period of 10 years. Domestic support had to be reduced by developed countries over a period of 6 years by 20% and by developing countries by 13.33% over a period of 10 years. De- minimize level of domestic support of 10% in respect of developing countries and 5% in respect of developed countries were also agreed upon the process of tariffication members had to convert non- tariff barriers in place into tariffs and under taken reduction commitments a tariffs thus arrived at. It is now well know that this tariffication process was mis-utilized by developed countries to indicate very high levels of tariffs and this tariffication exercise.

The Uruguay Round commitments the developed countries had reduces tariff by 40% and under developed countries by 30% in five equated instruments ending 1 January 2000. Due to this agreement the weighted average level of tariffs applicable to industrial products was expected to full from 6.3% to 3.8% in the case of forwarded countries, from 15.3% to 12% in developing country. In case of non agriculture sector, Under the Uruguay Round commitments the developed countries had reduce tariff by 40% and under developed countries by 30% in five equated instruments ending 1 January 2000. Due to this agreement the weighted average level of tariffs applicable to industrial products was expected to full from 6.3% to 3.8% in the case of forwarded countries, from 15.3% to 12% in developing country.

Under the General Agreement on Trade in Service (GATIS), India under took commitments in 7 sectors, which spread over 33-sub sector. The service sector classified into 12 broad service sectors and 161 sub sectors. In case of financial services, India's commitments are restricted to banking services. Under insurance service India's agreement are restricted to non- life insurance of freight, reinsurance and insurance intermediation. In case of telecommunication services, India has under taken commitments like voice telephone services, circuit, switched date transmission services, fax services, private leased services, data and message transmission services and cellular mobile services. However, in case of data and message transmission services foreign equity up to 51% is committed. In case of cellular mobile services, foreign equity up to 25% and under other services sector, viz. tourism, health and construction and related engineering services. Foreign equity ceiling restricted up to 51%. These are the bound specific commitment by India's under the Uruguay round.

WTO AND RECENT MINISTER MEET IN HONG KONG

World Trade Organization on December 2005 came out with the draft ministerial text that pro-poses to end farm export subsidies either by 2010or 2013 and the other be-ing five years after the implem-entation of the agreement, which starts in 2008. 'This cla-use will give developed countr-ies time till 2013 to eliminate export subsidies. On the other contentious issue of phasing out trade dist-orting domestic support, the text proposes three bands for developed countries for re-duction, while exempting developing countries from any commitment. India's concerns on special products and special safe-guard mechanisms have been somewhat reflected in the draft but there was not much specificity. The text provided some re-lief to developing countries, as it has prevented developed countries from shifting subsid-ies from one box to another to continue them in a different form.

The draft text also suggests eliminating cotton subsidies by next year, a key demand of poor West African countries. On non-agriculture market access, the draft makes it clear that tariff cuts for industrial goods will be based on Swiss formula though it did not mention a specific formula or the coefficient that would be used for reductions. Reductions in industrial tariffs has been a key demand of rich countries like the Unit-ed States and the European Union, while poor and de-veloping countries like India have been opposing steep re-ductions to protect their domestic industries. The text, released on the penultimate day of the WTO ministerial also shows progress in arriving at an agreement for granting duty free market access to least developed countries. On services negotiations, the text points out that little headway has been made so far and makes it clear that plurilateral negotiation can not be launched in service. Meanwhile, civil society groups have denounced the draft text, saying it was "full of peanuts and full of time tables". Leading international Nongovernmental Organization Green peace said the text was a long way from equity and sustainability. Thus it is clear that from the above discussion negotiations are on wrong track, in view of this it is not much benefited developing countries.

RECENT TREND IN INDIA'S FOREIGN TRADE

Foreign trade played a key role in developing and developed countries in order to increases the high rate of profits. And it act as a multidimensional processes involving structural changes in the economy of the country. Table 1-reveal the item wise export performance. During the year 2004-05 the country export about $ 79247.05 million, against $ 63842.97 million in the year 2003-04. Agriculture and allied exports constitute 7.61%

Table 1

Item wise Export Performance in Recent Year ($ in million)

Items	*2003-04*	*2004-05*
Plantation	592.64	621
Pulses	71.51	123.26
Cereal	1513.92	1973.31
Castor Oil	142.77	228.85
Nuts and seeds	653.62	795.22
Spices	336.05	399.30
Sugar and molasses	268.97	33.19
Marine product	1328.72	1267.53
Poultry and dairy product	90.35	149.42
Spirit and beverage	26.53	30.18
Leather and Mfrs	2163.04	2289.23
Plastic and Linoleum	1752.74	2947.42
Machinery	4872.96	6484.71
Ferro alloys	84.61	182.31
Iron and Steel	2477.78	3631.20
Electronic goods	1804.92	1804.06
Project goods	84.13	49.17
Readymade Garments	6231.47	6026,39
Cotton raw including waste	205.08	81.12
Petroleum products	3568.44	6792.14
Unclassified exports	1881.44	2089.60

Source: DGCI& S Kolkata Provisional data compiled by Economic Division, Commerce Department

in total exports posted a reasonably high growth of 11.60% during the year 2004-05 at $ 6033.94 million against $ 5406.70

million in the year 2003-04. Engineering goods exports constituting 18.41% acquitted themselves well by posting a growth of 38.71%at 14587.37 million, against $10,516.45 million in 2003-04. The exports of gems and jewelry amounting 7.29% notched up growth of 29.62% at $13,705.44 million during 2004-05, against, $10,573.38 million, exports of chemicals and related products registered a growth of 27. 28%, at $12,677.21 million against $9,96012 in the year 2003-2004.

The textile exports share of 15.16 per cent in overall exports put up a tep-id show by notching up a nega-tive growth of 1.53 per cent at $12,017.46 million, against $12,2204.77 million in the pre-vious year. The dip in exports assumes significance in the light of the fact that the quota regime in global trade in tex-tiles and clothing ended in the final quarter of the last fiscal but this did not get reflected in any market rise in export receipts. Destination-wise, India's ex-ports continued its growth sto-ry with -Asia and Oceania as this region absorbed 47.41 per cent of as total exports and recorded a rate of growth of 27 per cent at $37,573.37 mil-lion in 2009-05, against $29,621.10 million in the previ-ous year.

The exports to West Eu-rope amounting 23.30 per cent grew by 1972 .per cent at $18,859.10 million in 2004-05, against $15,752.10 million in the previ-ous year, while exports to the Americas constituting 20.42 per cent logged a growth of 20.50 per cent at it, $101618.76 million in the year 200-3-05, against13.428.35 million during 2003-04. Among the top 15 countries for export; Singapore record-ed the highest growth of 79 per cent at $3,795.51 million during 2004-05, against $2,124,89 million

2003-04, followed by China of 55 percent at $4,536.25 million and the. United Arab Emirates of 38 per cent art $7,098.1 million. Table 2 gives information about item wise export in recent year. The import growth during the year 2004-05 amounting 37 per saw the import bill touching $1,07,066.11 mil-lion, against $75,149.62 million during 2003-04. Petroleum, crude and lubricants, which account for 27.57 per cent of total import, grew by a whopping 45.09 percent during cent at $24,844.10 million in the year 2004-05, against $20,569.60 million in the previous year, partly fuelled by a flare-up in world crude prices which cruised to a level of $50 per barrel. Machinery imports with a weight of 10 per cent in total imports grew by a moderate 15.11 per cent at $10,709.87 million during 2004-05, against $9,303.40 million during 2003-04. Bulk imports with a weight of 39.09 in ag-gregate imports grew by a hefty 43.03 per cent during 2004 05 at $91,351.00 million, against $29,2:9.96 million in 003-04. Equally with a share of 10.11 per cent in aggregate imports, import of gold and silver registered a rate of 57.87 per cent at $ 10824.38 million during 2004-05, against, $6,856.42 million in the previ-ous year, marking a recrudescence of interest in bullion as a safe haven for investment by the public.

Table 2
Item wise Import Performance in Recent Year ($ in million)

Items	*2003-04*	*2004-05*
Edible oil	2542.53	2393.79
Bulk import	29259.46	41851.00
Fertilizers	720.79	1231.08
Sugar	13.65	212.38
Fruits and nuts	174.59	235.31
Cashew nuts	298.53	391.08
Crude rubber	280.77	394.93
Iron and steel	1506.16	2597.20
Metalliferrous ores and metal scrap	1295.92	2370.39
Pearls, precious and semi-precious stone	20569.60	29844.10
Machinery other than electronic	4743.59	6550.64
Project goods	395.99	581.70
Computer software physical form	383.19	649.56
Tea	14.06	34.00
Essential oils and Cos.prep	91.26	118.72
Electric goods	7506.18	9739.04
Chemical products	631.60	788.09
Silk yarn and fabrics	115.32	162.75
Cotton yarn and fabric	142.10	187.89
Coal, Coke and briquettes	1410.79	2801.45
Other commodities	2599.24	4353.75

Sources: DGCI& S Kolkata Provisional data compiled by Economic Division, Commerce Department

India importers from Asia and Ocean-ia, which accounts for a share of 35.40 per cent in total im-ports, grew by close to

40% at $ 37899.26 million against $ 27151.41 million in the previous year. Import' from West Europe amounting (22.60 per cent) was up by 29.45 percent at 524,194.92 million, against$ 18690.45 million in 2003-04. Imports From the Americas (8.36%) per cent; grew by a ro-bust 29.18 per cent a'. $8,947.03 million, against $6,926.20 million in 2003-04

CONCLUSION

Due to globalization business communities are more connected each other than ever before allover the world and information and money flow more quickly than ever. Goods and services produced in one part of the world are available in all parts of the world. However, the globalization not free from problems its have many problems like it kill domestic business, exploitation of human resources, leads to unemployment and under employment, decline in demand for domestic product widening gap between rich and poor, transfer of national resources and commercialization and political colonialism etc. Moreover managing the process of economic integration that is driven by several forces, and the recent WTO negotiations are on wrong track, in view of this developing countries face challenges from a world order and that is particularly burdensome on country like India, hence it is necessary to formulate sound policies by the developing countries to manage the process with a view to maximizing the benefits to its citizens.

REFERENCES

MPEDA Newsletter, October 2004, p.5.

P Subba Rao, International Business, Himalay Publication, 2004 p.117.

University News 43(36) September, 2005 p.8.

Dr. Murthy S, International Trade and Rupee Exchange Rate RBSA Publisher, Jaipur 1995 p.7.

Vijay Time, Jan. 25, 2006.

Vijay Times, op.cit, p.

Business Line, December, 15.

P Subba Rao, Op.cit p.123.

Francis Cherunilam, International Trade and Export Management, Himalay Publication House, 2005.

New Times of India: Dec. 16, 2005.

6

NATIONAL HEALTH POLICY IN INDIA-2002; AN OVERVIEW

*A. Xavier Susai Raj**

INTRODUCTION

Human resources are a very important component for effective implementation of health sector programmes and therefore are an important component of sector reform agenda of any state, the availability of adequate funds, equipments and people to manage the programmes alone may not necessarily lead to successful implementation of programmes and reforms. The state government have been successful in creating impressive net works of health facilities. Dr. Abdul Kalam emphasized more investment in social sector is required so that we can achiev universal health for all at 2010. What type of health system should India have in the 21st century? This was the basic question asked by the government of India when it requested the world bank to work with on an analysis of its health system.

In this paper an attempt has been made to study the general health conditions in India and in the second section health policy of 2002 were critically analyzed. In the final section is about suggestion for the improvement of the health policy in the country were studied.

---

* Lecturer (Senior Scale), Sacred Heart College (Autonomous), Tirupattur.V.DT.-635601, Tamil Nadu.

It is increasingly recognized that good health is an important contributor to productivity and economic growth. But it is first and fore most an end it self. A recent analysis of the world Bank says that the hospitalized Indian spends more than half of his total annual expenditure on buying health care more than 40 per cent of hospitalized people borrows money or sell assets to cover expense and 75 per cent fall below poverty line. The state has to provide universal health care through the public health system. In India the public spending on health is less than 1 per cent of GDP. Most of the low income countries spend more than India. After 58 years of independence the health facilities were not provided to the rural masses. India has the lowest budget allocation for health in the world. Compared to the other less developed countries in the world. Health is an important contributing factor in the utilization of manpower. Table -1 shows the expenditure on health of the government of India in different years.

Table 1
Expenditure of Central and State Governments on Health

Year	*Percentage of GDP at current market prices*
1993-94	1.25
1994-95	1.11
1995-96	1.02
1996-97	0.95
1997-98	1.00
1998-99	1.22
1999-00	0.9
2000-01	0.98
2001-02	0.98
2002-03	0.99

Sources: CMIE; public finance p.12

The World Health Organization 2001, recommended that the public health expenditure should be at least 5 per cent of the GDP or otherwise it will affect our public health system. According to Amartya sen (2003) concluded government could deliver the different kinds of health care to the people it will mainly benefit the deprived groups of population. He has suggested that heath equity and decentralization of public services required in India. Bhore (2001), committee have identified the major weakness in the health care system in India they are lack of availability of trained health personnel in rural areas and inadequate quality of health care. Mia-Defever (1995), the health care policy reform in competition, privatization and inequality. Hilar, Standin (2002), says that health delivery systems could be improved only though the government. Dr. Bhathachariya (2004) emphasized more budget allocation and investment in health sector this will improve development in humanity.

THE CURRENT HEALTH SCENARIO IN INDIA

As outlined by the constitution, the provision of health care by the public sector is a responsibility and shared by the state, central and local governments, although it is effectively a state responsibility in terms of delivery to the people. The trends of public deliver and infrastructure in India in the year 2003. The total number of SC, PHC, CHC, was 163196, dispensaries and hospitals 38031, beds 914543, nursing personnel 836000, doctors 625131. Although the amount of infrastructure in India is low when compare to china. The present challenges focus only on the health sector reforms rather than control of communicable diseases .In India nearly 2.5 million childrens below age of five affected by malaria, T.B and HIV/AIDS in the year 2004.

T.B: This is the second major disease in India nearly 4.17 lak, persons affected and death took place every year because of T.B.

HIV/AIDS: It is another emerging challenges in our country the mounting of HIV positive cases continues to be very high. In the year 2003 the number of persons affected by HIV/AIDS was 5.1 million. The first human clinical trial in the country of a vaccine to prevent HIV/AIDS began in feb 2005 at National AIDS Research Institute in pune. If the present situation continues this will affect the health system in our country for that we need an effective health policy which is required in order to control this diseases.

WHAT DO WE MEAN BY HEALTH POLICY?

Health policy is a comprehensive and it covers all those procedures principles, policies rules and regulations which control the disease and to provide welfare to the people.

India accounted for 16 per cent of the global population the population projection at 1114 million at the end of 2006. (WHO), The population growth rate was 2% per annum in the same year. Since independence there have been a significant changes in health policy and the composition of the health sector. While major transformations have not improve the health system in the country, so for a number of committees where constituted to improve the health care system in the country. The first committee was setup in 1947. The second committee was Mudaliar Committee 1961 under the charmanship of Dr. Mudaliar.

Jain committee 1996 and Kartar sing committee 1974. Srivastava committee each committee has its own objectives and targets. The final committee is known as National Health policy 2002.

NATIONAL HEALTH POLICY-2002.

The government of India in 2002 has revised the national health policy NHP of 1983. Keeping in view the national commitment to attain the goal of health for all by the year 2003. The main objectives of this policy is to achieve an acceptable standard of good.

HEALTH AMONG ALL THE GENERAL POPULATION OF THE COUNTRY

The precise approach of the stated policy is to increase the access to decentralized public health system, ensure equitable access, increase the public health investment through contribution of central govt, to enhance the contribution of NGO and private sector in health, to regulate the services of private and public sector. The policy has set time bound goals for identified national problems like malaria, tuberculosis, blindness, gastroenteritis, cholera, water vector born diseases, leprosy, HIV/AIDS etc. The national health policy also identifies the other public health problem's of accidents, micro and macro nutrient deficiencies, life style diseases and problems of aged to be tackled through concerted efforts to translate the above objectives in to reality. The health policy has laid down specific targets at the end of 2005, they are given in table-2, and steps are already under way to implement the policy.

Table 2
National health policy 2002-2015

Goals to be achieved	
Eradicate polio and years	2005
Eliminate leprosy	2005
Eliminate kala Azars and leprosy	2010
Achieve zero level growth of HIV/AIDS	

Reduce IMR to 30/1000 and MMR to 100 lakh

Improve nutrition and reduce proportion of LBW babies from 30% to 10% 2010.

Increase utilization of public health facilities from current level <20 % to >70% 2010

Reduce mortality 50% on account of TB malaria and other water born diseases 2010

Reduce prevalence of blindness to 0.5% 2010

The followings are the main advantages of the health policy 2002.

The process of formulation of health policy 2002 had the advantages of having access to the experience of implementation of the previous policies, and all the reports were comes out only in that period, economic reforms initiated in 1991 and 73rd and 74th constitutional amendment acts promoting decentralization, local governance and women's participation.

THE COMPONENTS OF NHP ARE CRITICALLY ANALYZED AND ARE BEING DISCUSSED HERE UNDER.

Decentralized planning and implementation of services.

Access to decentralized public health system will be incrcased by establishing new infrastructure in deficient areas and by upgrading the infrastructure in the existing institutions. Health care delivery system in states tends to be centralized at the departmental level but NHP 2002 strongly advocated decentralized management. The health care functionaries at panchayat level now operate under state level. There is an imperative need to bring in convergence in their work and bring them under one administrative umbrella so that effective convergence and delivery of health care at the primary level. NHP 2002 has to ensure that these barriers are broken sooner that later by devolution of powers at the PHC level. The intervention of the state health department may be limited to over all level so that PHCs can function individually.

Financial resources

The public investment in the country over the years has been cooperatively low. The proportion of central budget allocation for health out of the total budget remains stagnant at 1.3%. For the state expenditure declined from 7% to 5% respectively. More than two third of households 69% normally use the private medical sector only 29% use public sector medical services. NHP 2002 emphasis to increase health expenditure to 6% of GDP but so far 0.99% spend for public health, so government expenditure in public health services will always be limited because of constraints in resources allocation.

Urban health services

In India 30% of the population lives in urban areas. Nearly 50% of the population lives in urban slums, under precarious and sub human conditions. The NHP 2002 does not talk of urban slums and its approach is at variance with that of NP 2002. It appears that NHP 2002 beats a different track on the issues of urban slums and indicates disintegrated services for national health programmes. The dichotomy of views and approaches are serious issues for resolution.

Control of communicable disease

The absence of an efficient disease surveillance network is a major handicap. NHP envisages full operationalization of integrated disease control network from lowest rung of public health administration to the central government by 2005 by using high tech information technology and by covering private health care institutions and private practitioners NHP disease surveillance strategy omits PRI and people from the surveillance system. It is quite surprising that surveillance system omits and deprives people as equal partners, whose lives it profoundly affects. Thus the policy document failed to enhance the local capacity to deal with burden of disease and disease surveillance programmes. The NHP policies have synergies and convergence rather than divergence and diverging approaches.

Policy concludes by saying that improved standard of governance is a prerequisite for the successful implementation of any policy. There has been an element of over governance and too title has been done to decentralize and decentralization and devolution should result into peoples health in peoples hand. People have the right to information health accounts on morbidity, mortality malnutrition and disability as also spectrum of services and supplies at various levels should become accessible to people through improved information technology to have their regular reactions and feed backs to improved the efficiency of system.

SUGGESTIONS

1. The following are the suggestions for the improvement of the health services in the country.
2. Expand public health and infrastructure by increasing numbers of subcenters, primary health centers.
3. More involvement of the panchayatiraj institutions and community groups for implementing the NHP.
4. To increase the investment in the health sector in order to achieve the targets set down in the health policy.
5. Regulations in the drug policy and health research should be strengthened higher investment in knowledge based activities.
6. Importance to Indian system of medicine like ayurveda, siddha, unani yoga naturopathy and homeopathy.

REFERENCES

Alan william, 2003, Comment on Amartya Sen Why Health Equity, 2003, *Health Economics.* pp.61.

Ministry of Health and Family Welfare (Govt. of India), *National Health Policy,* 2002 New Delhi.

Economic Survey 2004-2005, (Govt. of India), *Ministry of Finance Economic Division.* pp-13.

World Health Report, 2000, Health Systems Improving Performance. Geneva; *World Health Organization;* 2002.

The World Bank; Financing Health Service in Developing Countries; an Agenda for Reform the World Bank Washington. D. C, 1999.

Rajiv Misra and Rao, 2001, Changing the Indian Health System current issues, future directions Indian Council For Research On International Economic Relations, New Delhi, pp.48-69.

Sundar Lal, 2002, Implementation of Health Policy 2002, Indian Journal of Community Medicine. xxvii (2), pp. 51-57.

Duggal, 2000, The Private Health Sector In India-Nature Trends and a Critique. Independent Commission On Health In India, Voluntary Health Association of India, New Delhi.

Bloom David, E. 2000, The Health and Poverty of Nations; from Theory to Practice Third meeting of the Commission on Macroeconomic and Health, Paris.

Balasubramanian K. 2001, Improvement of Maternal Survival in India; Issues and Strategies for Intervention, SRC, Osmania University, Hyderadad.

W.H.O 2004, Pesketiues Health. The Plan American Health Org. Vol. 9. (12) pp. 31.

7

INDIA'S RURAL POVERTY IN THE GLOBALIZATION ERA: THE STATUS AND ELIMINATION

*Rudra Prakash Pradhan**

INTRODUCTION

During the start of 1990s, India was in twin major crisis such as high deficit balance of payments and socially intolerable inflation rate. This was the most midst of an extraordinary economic and political crisis in the Indian history. It was typically due to excessive public spending, subsidies and a large inefficient public sector during 1980s, resulting in large fiscal deficit year after year, which were financed by internal as well as external borrowing and de-accumulation of foreign exchange reserves. As a result, the access to international credit was completely denied and economy was stagnant and foreign exchange reserves declined to US$1 billions. However with the change of power at the centre, new government came with twin tasks, viz., putting economy into a higher growth path and improving the credibility of the country. This was done with the help of reforms measure, specifically through globalization. It simply represents an integration of economies across the world so that there is free movement of goods and services, technology, capital and even labour across the national boundaries (Datt, 2003). This involved varieties of steps ranging

* Economics and Finance Group, Faculty Division-I, Birla Institute of Technology and Science (BITS), Pilani-333031, Rajasthan.

from fiscal, monetary, price reform, opening of economy for foreign investors, liberalization of trade, de licensing, privatization of agricultural policy, etc. The enthusiasts on globalization considered that this was the only path for accelerating economic growth and reducing poverty.

India has already been covered one and half decades of globalization and during these periods, it received high economic growth and reduction of poverty. But the reduction of rural poverty was not as per with urban poverty and economic growth. Accordingly, the basic objective of this paper is to examine the status of rural poverty in the globalization era and its elimination thereof. The rest of the paper is planned as follows. Section II outlines the salient features of Indian economy during the globalization era. Section III describes the concept of rural poverty and its status in the Indian economy during the pre- and post-globalization era. Section IV examines the causes and determinants of rural poverty in the Indian economy. Section V describes how globalization could affect the status of rural poverty. In the final section, paper highlights some areas to alleviate rural poverty in the Indian economy through globalization.

THE PERFORMANCE OF INDIAN ECONOMY UNDER GLOBALIZATION ERA

The performance of Indian economy during the globalization era can be analyzed in the form of achievements and failures.

Noteworthy Achievements

To begin with its success, India first overcame its worst economic crisis of 1990-91 within the short span of two years. India's balance of payments position was undergone a sea change since 1991. There was favourable impact on macro economic stabilization policies including devaluation of rupee and other structural reforms. The improvements in current account balance, inflows of external finance and accretion of foreign exchange reserves have been seen most remarkable. The foreign exchange reserves raise from a low of US$2.34 billions in 1990-91 to US$141 billions in 2003-04. The current account balance, as percentage of GDP, has been declined from a high of 3.5% in 1990-91 to 0.81% in 2002-03. The rate of inflation comes down to 2.5% in 2000-01 in contrast to a high of 13.6% in 1991-92 (Rakshit, 2003). The share of India's trade, as proportion of GDP, increases from 14.15% in 1990-91 to 23.54% in 2003-04. Both exports and imports have been increasing from a low of $17.98 billions and $23.64 billions in 1990-91 to a high of $57.10 billions and $71.20 billions in 2000-01. India also successfully moves into higher growth path and displayed strong dynamism in selected sectors based on international competitive advantage. Its economic growth increases from a low of 1.3% in 1991-92 to a high of 8.1% in 2003-04. This achievement of economic growth is mostly due to industrial growth and service sector growth, as agricultural growth was very fluctuating in nature in the entire globalization era. The flows of Foreign Direct Investment (FDI) have increased from a low of $0.097 billions in 1990-91 to $4.3 billions in 2003-04. It covers number of sectors including auto components, telecommunications, software, pharmaceuticals, biotechnology, R & D, engineers, technologists and the like. The spillover effects of India's increasing international competitiveness in most of these sectors have helped the Indian economy into a higher economic growth path and thus, directly benefited the Indian poor through better quality and lower prices.

Noteworthy Failures

On the failure sides, the most notable is her fiscal consolidation. It consists of both revenue deficit (varies between 3.6-5.1%, as a percentage of GDP) as well as fiscal deficit (varies between 5.9-10.4%, as a percentage of GDP). Another worrisome picture is the declining trends of tax revenue. It not only declines but also stagnant between 14-15% (as a percentage of GDP). The performance of social sector development is relatively poor, as per country's requirement and by relative standards of many developing countries in the world including some of the least developed countries in the Sub-Saharan Africa. Human development is also very abysmally in comparison to East and Southeast countries and generally due to low social sector expenditure and again mostly by low public expenditure on education and health. The level of infrastructure is comparatively low along with large-scale regional variation across its states. On the employment aspects, it is characterized as 'jobless growth' together with existence of poverty and unemployment. This is because organized manufacturing sector failed to generate additional labourforce in the economy and also accompanied by rigid labour laws of our country. This situation is again aggravated due to growing population. All in all, globalization accelerated economic growth in the Indian economy; but the question remains, whether economic growth reaching the rural poor.

RURAL POVERTY: THE CONCEPT AND DIMENSIONS IN THE INDIAN ECONOMY

Poverty is a perpetual human tragedy. The poor often becomes vulnerable and insecure, which leads to loss of human dignity, optimism and human waste. It is found in all contemporary societies in various forms and in different entities, although it is more visible and manifest in some societies than others. Long ago, it was used to be tackled by communities and was a local concern. With the improvements in communications, distance barriers were broken and poverty became a national issue. The flows of knowledge have played a significant role in bringing about international focus on poverty. It is of interest to both social theory as well as social policy and has received attention from social scientists in Britain, USA, India and other countries for more than a hundred years (Beteille, 2003).

In human terms, poverty means lack of food, cloth and shelter. However, in economic terms, it represents the inability to attain a minimal standard of living. It is natural to view that poverty is a failure to meet basic requirements and to attain a minimum standard of living. Of course, it varies from society to society, person to person and place to place. While biological requirements and nutritional norms provide the most elementary concept of a minimal standard of living, the modern understanding of poverty requires other factors to be taken into consideration like public expenditure on social sector and other indicators of social achievement of the poor like pre-school enrolment, child mortality, immunization, malnutrition, life expectancy at birth and total fertility rate. As per the report of HDR (1997), human poverty focuses the denial of opportunities and choices most basic to human development- to lead a long, healthy, creative life and to enjoy a decent standard of living, freedom, dignity, self-esteem and the respect of others.

Poverty, as commonly understood, is concerned with absolute standard of living of a part of society- 'the poor'. It is the inability to attain a minimum standard of living, which is identified by a country specific poverty line, which distinguishes the 'poor' from the 'non-poor'. Measurement of poverty involves two distinct and interrelated exercises. First, by identification, which is the method of identifying a group of people as poor. Second, by aggregation, which is the method of aggregating the characteristics of the poor people into an over-all index of poverty [Sen (1976, 1981)]. If Z denotes the poverty line (PL), which is derived on some basis, and the income profile is $y_1 \leq y_2 \cdots \leq y_q < Z \leq y_{q+1} \leq \cdots \leq y_n$ then the individuals with income less than Z are identified as poor. The identification issue involves various criteria of defining the poor and arriving at a level of income, which defines the poverty line. However in the context of developing countries, nutrition based approach has been generally followed, so that the consumer at the poverty line has to meet a pre-specified nutritional norm (Panda and Rath, 2004).

Since India is a rural economy, its development depends upon the status of rural economy. But unfortunately, the dimension of poverty is much higher in rural India. Rural poverty, in India, has gone so mysterious into the marrow of our bones that the nation has dutifully acquired the knack of living with it. In present, it is a more challenging tasks to all responsible persons- administrators, ecologists, politicians, planners, social workers and alike.

Rural Poverty during Pre-Globalization Era

As per National Sample Survey Organization (NSSO) data on consumption expenditure, rural poverty in India declined from

56.5% in 1973-74 to 53.1% in 1977-78, 45.7% in 1983 and 39.1% in 1987-88. In absolute term, it was reduced from 261.3 millions in 1973-74 to 231.9 millions in 1987-88 (See Table 1). The rate of decline was, however, faster during 1980s in contrast to 1970s. A faster decline in rural poverty during the 1980s could be attributed to higher growth in agricultural production, slower growth in foodgrains prices and presence of safety nets. In fact, safety nets are in the form of drought and flood relief programmes (especially during the years of natural calamities) are comparatively high in 1980s in contrast to 1970s. Furthermore, the decline of rural poverty in the 1980s was also due to large volume of PDS, achieved by depletion of government stock rather than increase in procurement. This process of increasing PDS prevented the flows of grain from the rural areas to the urban areas. This is the single largest factor in the decline in rural poverty in 1987-88 (Tendulkar and Jain, 1995; Ahluwalia, 1978). In the state-wise, rural poverty is higher in the states like Bihar, Assam, Madhya Pradesh, Maharashtra, Orissa, Tamil Nadu, Uttar Pradesh and West Bengal. On the contrary, it is relatively low in the states like Haryana, Himachal Pradesh, Punjab and Andhra Pradesh (See Figure 1).

Rural Poverty during Post- Globalization Era

It is true that the reform process, started since 1991, covered wide range of steps including price, tax, fiscal, monetary and trade reforms. These reforms had impact on prices and income and thus, indirectly affect rural poverty. Liberalization of agricultural trade and removal of agricultural trade embargo for private traders shifted cropping pattern and increased prices of foodgrains at least in the short-run. At all India level, there is evidence that rural poverty increased significantly during the initial phase of reforms period. Incidence of rural poverty has been increased from 36.43% in 1990-91 to 43.37% in 1992 (Chandrasekhar and Sen, 1996). However, as per NSSO estimates, rural poverty has declined from 39.1% in 1987-88 to 37.1% in 1993-94 and 26.8% in 1999-00. In the absolute term, it has reduced from 231.9 millions in 1987-88 to 193.2 millions

1999-00 (See Table 1). In the state-wise comparison, an existence of rural poverty is relatively high in the states like Assam, Bihar, Madhya Pradesh, Orissa, Tamil Nadu and West Bengal and moderate in Himachal Pradesh, Karnataka, Kerala and Maharashtra and relatively low in Haryana and Punjab (See Figure 1). In brief, the dimension of rural poverty has substantially been increased in the early period of globalization era and than declined in the later phase. However, as per World Bank estimates of head count ratio, poverty gap ratio and squared poverty gap ratio, the picture of poverty is somewhat worsening in the Indian economy since 1990-91.

Table 1
Rural Poverty and Its Trend in Indian Economy

Year	Poverty Ratio (in %)			No of Affected People (in Million)		
	Rural	Urban	Total	Rural	Urban	Total
1973-74	56.4	49.0	54.9	261.3	60.3	321.3
1977-78	53.1	45.2	51.3	264.3	64.6	328.9
1983	45.7	40.8	44.5	252.0	70.9	322.9
1987-88	39.1	38.2	38.9	231.9	75.2	307.1
1993-94	37.3	32.4	36.0	244.0	76.3	320.3
1999-00	27.09	23.62	26.1	193.2	67.0	268.0

Source: Planning Commission, Government of India, New Delhi

Table 2
The Characteristics of Rural Poverty during 1987-88 to 1993-94

Low and Increasing	*High and Increasing*
Haryana and Himachal Pradesh	Assam, Bihar and Uttar Pradesh
Low and Decreasing	*High and Decreasing*
Andhra Pradesh, Gujarat, Karnataka, Kerala, Punjab and Rajasthan	Madhya Pradesh, Maharashtra, Orissa, Tamil Nadu and West Bengal

Characteristics of Rural Poverty during Pre- and Post-Globalization Era

The characteristics and nature of rural poverty has been changed a lot in the Indian economy between pre- and post-globalization era. In order to understand the same, we have classified the change into four different heads such as low and increasing, high and increasing, low and decreasing, and high and decreasing (See Tables 2 & 3). During 1987-88 to 1993-94, Haryana and Himachal Pradesh are in low and increasing trend group; Assam, Bihar and Uttar Pradesh are in the groups of high and increasing; Andhra Pradesh, Gujarat, Karnataka, Kerala, Punjab and Rajasthan are in the groups of low and decreasing; and Madhya Pradesh, Maharashtra, Orissa, Tamil Nadu and West Bengal are in the groups of high and decreasing (See Table 2). During 1993-94 to 1999-2000, no state is in the groups of low and increasing and high and increasing. The states like Andhra Pradesh, Gujarat, Haryana, Himachal Pradesh, Karnataka, Kerala, Punjab, Rajasthan and Tamil Nadu are in the groups of low and decreasing. On the contrary, Assam, Bihar, Madhya Pradesh, Maharashtra, Orissa, Uttar Pradesh and West Bengal are in the groups of high and decreasing (See Table 3). Overall, there is little bit diversification on the alleviation of rural poverty across the Indian states in the post-globalization era.

Figure 1
State-wise Trends of Rural Poverty in the Indian economy in the Pre- and Post-Globalization Era

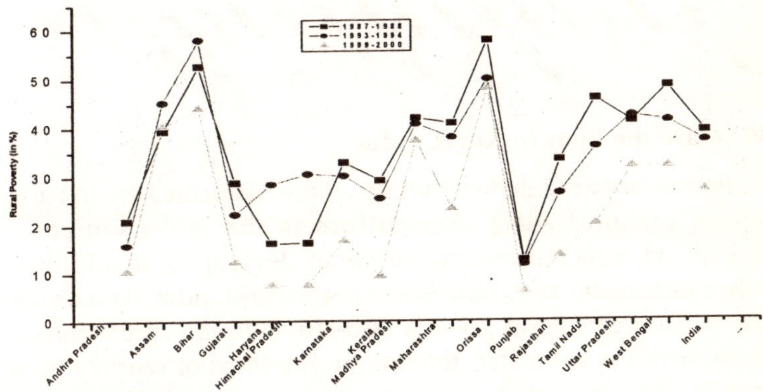

Table 3
The Characteristics of Rural Poverty during 1993-94 to 1999-00

Low and Increasing No States	High and Increasing No States
Low and Decreasing Andhra Pradesh, Gujarat, Haryana, Karnataka, Kerala, Punjab, Rajasthan and Tamil Nadu	High and Decreasing Assam, Bihar, Madhya Pradesh, Maharashtra, Orissa, Uttar Pradesh and West Bengal

Figure 2
Rural Poverty by Occupation for 1993-94

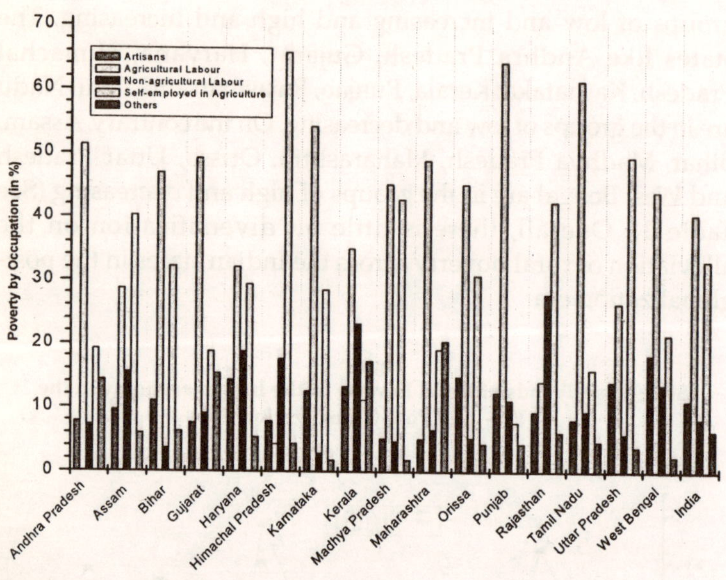

Who are the Poor in Rural India

India is a unparalleled economy, where majorities are in rural sector (around 74%). Agriculture is the main source of livelihood, which is somewhat under developed. In addition, other sectors are also undersized in the rural India. As a result, the existence of rural poverty is relatively high in the Indian economy. It is estimated that about one-third of world's poor live in India and there are more poor people in India alone than in the whole of Sub-Saharan Africa. In other words, Indian poverty is predominantly rural based, where landless labourers and casual workers are the worst-off economic group. Among them, scheduled castes and scheduled tribes, women and female-headed families, old people, and female children face more deprivation than others. The rural poor are the primarily those with limited ownership of assets-including land. They are in various forms like self-employed in agriculture and allied activities (about 38.50%), agricultural labourers (23.32%), non-agricultural labourers (15.80%), self-employed in non-agriculture (15.01%), salaried earners (5.66%) and others (1.71%). This is coexists with large-scale inter state variations in the distribution of rural poor across different groups. In Andhra Pradesh, Gujarat, Kerala, Maharashtra and Tamil Nadu, agricultural labourers have major share of poor. In Bihar, poor are more or less evenly distributed across all the groups. In Haryana, poor's are more or less evenly distributed across self-employed in agriculture, agricultural labourers and non-agricultural labourers. Punjab and Kerala have maximum proportion of poor from non-agricultural labourers. In Andhra Pradesh, Bihar and Assam, the proportions of poor are self-employed in non-agriculture group. Over and above, except Andhra Pradesh and Kerala, the relative incidence of Indian rural poverty is highest among agricultural labourers followed by non-agricultural labourers, self-employed in non-agriculture, self-employed in agriculture and allied activities, and salaried persons (See Figures 2 & 3).

THE DETERMINANTS OF RURAL POVERTY

In general, rural poverty is determined by multi number of factors. It includes both economic and social factors. These are employment, income, economic growth in general, agricultural growth in particular, government intervention on poverty alleviation, price fluctuations, education, health, sanitary facilities, etc. Out of several factors, economic growth in general and agricultural growth in particular are the most outstanding factors that determines the level of rural poverty in the economy. According to Ahluwalia (1978), the fluctuations of rural poverty mostly depends upon the fluctuations of agricultural performance. It is observed that the year, where agricultural growth is high, the rate of decline of rural poverty is relatively low and vice versa. This is probably due to the evidence of trickle down associated with agricultural growth. According to Datt and Ravallion (1998), besides agricultural growth, the availability of infrastructure and human resources also contributing significant poverty reduction in the rural areas. However, in the present context, we have considered some selected variables that can substantially determine the level of rural poverty in the Indian economy in the globalization era of 1990s. Here, we have used a multi-variate regression model to examine the same, which is as follows:

Figure 3
Rural Poverty by Occupation for 1993-94

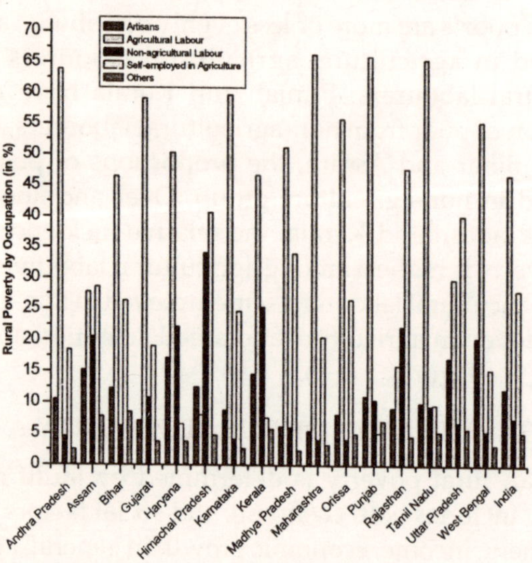

Source: Radhakrishna, R. and Ray, S. (2004-05)

$$RPOV = \beta_0 + \beta_1 CPIAL + \beta_2 RAW + \beta_3 RNFLF + \beta_4 PCNSDP + \beta_5 AgGDP + U$$

Where, RPOV = Rural poverty (in percentage); CPIAL = Consumer price index on agricultural labour; RAW = Real agricultural wage; RNFLF = Rural non-farm labour force; PCNSDP = Per capita net state domestic product; AgGDP = Percentage share of agriculture to Gross Domestic Product; U = error term; and all others are parameters.

The estimation has been done here for two cross sectional years in the post-globalization era (i. e. 1993-94 and 1999-2000). The estimated results reflect that per capita net state domestic product is the most significant factors that affecting rural poverty in the Indian economy in the 1990s. The estimated coefficients ensured negative sign, which indicates that an increase of per capita income leads to decline of rural poverty in the economy. In addition, growth of real agricultural wage also negatively influenced rural poverty (see Table 4) and can be concluded that increase of agricultural wage leads to decline of rural poverty. The other variables also affect the dimension of rural poverty at a positive and negative level, but they not statistically significant.

HOW GLOBALIZATION COULD AFFECT THE RURAL POVERTY

Globalization often works on poverty through higher economic growth and other macro economic indicators (Ahmad, 2005; Jha, 2002). But despite higher economic growth and other socio-economic development in the Indian economy during the globalization era of 1990s, the rate of rural poverty is substantially low in contrast to 1980s. There are lots of reason involve for the same. Some of are as follows:

- Though economic growth has been increasing but not so high, as per our country's requirement. In fact, the growth of per capita income is somewhat insignificant. Besides, some of other factors like rising income inequality and high unemployment rates accompany the poor performance on economic growth.
- The existence of high fiscal deficits of public sector have not allowed much space for undertaking redistributive policies and poverty oriented programme in the economy.
- The ratio of development expenditure has consistently declined. If we consider the leakages, there is waste and inefficiency of public expenditures. This leads to

Table 4
Estimated Regression Results

Year	*Dependent Variables*	*Independent Variables*	*Estimated Coefficients*	*Standard Error*	*t-Statistics*	*Significance Level*
		Constant	53.143	7.220	7.362	0.000
1993-94	RPOV	PCNSDP	-0.008	0.003	-2.812	0.013
		R^2	0.345			
		F	7.908			0.013
		Constant	63.971	7.396	8.469	0.000
		PCNSDP	-0.003	0.001	-4.198	0.013
1999-00	RPOV	RAW	-0.65	0.257	-2.532	0.024
		R^2	0.714			
		F	17.51			0.000

Note 1: RPOV = Rural poverty; CPIAL = Consumer price index on agricultural labour; RAW = Real agricultural wage; RNFLF = Rural non-farm labour force; PCNSDP = Per capita net state domestic product; R^2: Coefficient of Determination; F: F-statistics.

Note 2: The estimated results are obtained through step-wise regression.

severe imbalances in the demand and supply of public goods, which affects the benefit of ıural poor.

- The poor governance of public sector institutions and controlling of public goods by the well-to-do segments of the society in a general environment of congestion and shortages have led to reduce access of poor.
- The worrisome aspect of this poor governance is that opportunities for human capital formation for those below the poverty line have diminished considerably both for the current cohorts and the future additions to the labour force.
- In the era of globalization, financial integration and technological revolution of the 1990s has not benefited much in India. While world exports has been growing at 5% annually during the last five years, India's exports have remained stagnant. In the agricultural sector, it is more worrisome. This is because its share to total export has been declining, and thus, affects the rural poor.
- Foreign direct investment flows to India have remained modest in relation to the size of its economy and very less effective in the rural areas and not at all helpful for rural poor.
- The existence of high external debt burden again affects the servicing capacity of the nation and thus, the rural poor.

Over and above, globalization has been in favour and against rural poverty in some aspects and in some areas. But hopefully, it can bring positive effects in the long run, if it is properly implemented.

HOW GLOBALIZATION CAN HELPFUL TO ALLEVIATE RURAL POVERTY

Globalization helps in alleviating rural poverty through rapid economic growth; both directly and indirectly. Accordingly, we have to first observe here how globalization can bring economic growth in the economy. The following possibilities are as follows:

- **Increasing Trade Openness:** Increasing trade openness will always have direct impact on production and employment and thus, helpful for poverty alleviation. Here, steps must be taken to increase the volume of agricultural exports. This requires removing trade barriers (tariffs and licensing), establishing creation of special export oriented units and export processing zones. Trade openness can also helps the poor in getting the products at a cheaper rate, at least in the medium and long run.
- **Flows of Foreign Capital:** Foreign capital especially Foreign Direct Investment (FDI) has a positive impact on economic growth and employment and thus, helpful for reducing rural poverty. It will be more effective, if it is designated towards labour intensive sectors.
- **Labour flows:** Globalization helps the international migration of labour both in the short run and long run. This process certainly enhances the employment generation capacity in the economy and thus, helpful for rural poor.
- **Technological Change:** There is need of assimilation and adoption of technology, which improves efficiency in resource use and thus, gains in employment and reduces rural poverty. Though new products and new processes broaden the choice of consumers (particularly the rural poor), the solutions are found form gains in productivity only.
- **Public Expenditure:** In the globalization era, there is falling growth public expenditure especially on primary health, education and other skill up-gradation and training programmes. If it could be protected, there will be reduction of rural poverty. Besides, direct poverty alleviation program should be given priority in the public sector development.
- **Establishing Rural-urban linkage**: This helps free flows of labourforce from rural to urban areas and thus, reduces rural poverty. This requires developing socio-

economic infrastructure in the economy and its integration with non-farm activities. The above transformation patterns can improve the quality and pattern of growth and hence, rural poverty too.

v **Poverty Targeted Interventions**: An investment in human development and social safety nets are additional and complementary steps to reinforce the movement towards poverty alleviation. This requires that domestic policies, institutions and governance can either accelerate or hinder the process of transmission from economic growth to poverty reduction.

Over and above, globalization can bring down the dimension of rural poverty in the economy through enhancing economic growth. But the generation of economic growth is not sufficient condition to achieve this objective. This requires sectoral policies, direct employment programmes and other institutional arrangements. In other words, there is need of comprehensive rural development approach to alleviate rural poverty in the Indian economy by the net of globalization. The effects of globalization can differ over the long run and short run. But, in true sense, it can provide a better guidance in the long run.

REFERENCES

Ahluwalia, Montek, (1978), "*Rural Poverty and Agricultural Performance in India*", *Journal of Development Studies*, 14 (3): 298-323.

Ahmad, M. I. (2005), "Impact of Globalization on Poverty in India", in (F. K. Sudan, ed.), Globalization and Liberalization: Nature and Consequences, pp. 34-45. Serials Publications: New Delhi.

Beteille, A. (2003), 'Poverty and Inequality', *Economic and Political Weekly*, 38 (42): 4455-4463.

Chandrasekhar, C.P. and A. Sen, (1996), *"Has Poverty Really Come Down Following the Reforms?"*, Macroscam, Business Line, January 15.

Datt, R. (2003), "Globalization, the WTO and Its Impact on India: A Developing Country Perspective", in (K. Kalirajan and U. Sankar, eds.), *Economic Reforms and the Liberalization of the Indian Economy*, pp. 107-123. Massachusetts: Edward Elgar.

Datt, G. and M. Ravallion (1998), 'Why Have Some Indian States Done Better than Others at Reducing Rural Poverty', *Economica*, 65 (1): 17-38.

Jha, R. (2002), "Reducing Poverty and Inequality in India: Has Liberalization Helped", Departmental working Papers 2002-04, Australian National University, Australia.

Panda, M. K. and K. P. Rath (2004), 'Price Changes and Some Underlying Aspects of Measurement of Poverty', *Journal of Quantitative Economics*, 2 (1): 25-43.

Radhakrishna, R. and Ray, S. (2004-05), "Poverty in India: Dimensions and Character", Indian Development Report, pp. 40-61. Oxford University Press: New Delhi.

Rakshit, M. (2003). "External Capital Flows and Foreign Exchange Reserves: Some Macroeconomic Implications and Policy Issues", *Money and Finance*, 2 (13-14): 63-95.

Sen, A. (1976), 'Poverty: An Ordinal Approach to Measurement', *Econometrica*, 46: 437-446.

Sen, A. (1981), Development as Freedom. New Delhi: Oxford University Press.

Tendulkar, Suresh D. and L. R. Jain, (1995), "*Economic Reforms and Poverty*", Economic and Political Weekly, June 10, Vol. 30: 1373-1377.

HDR (1997), Human Development Report, UNDP. New York: Oxford University Press.

8

CROP DIVERSIFICATION AND FOOD SECURITY IN HILLY TRIBAL AREAS OF EASTERN INDIA

W. N. Salve *

INTRODUCTION

Agricultural is the mainstay of the Indian economy. Agricultural and Allied sectors contributes nearly 22% of Gross Domestic Product, while about 65-70 % of the population is dependant on agricultural for their livelihood. The agricultural output, however, depends on monsoon, as nearly 60% of area sown is dependent upon rainfall. The production of food grains during 2004-05 is estimated at 210.44 million tones, India has become self sufficient in agricultural production due to green revolution in India. However, majority of small and marginal farmers cultivate mainly low value, subsistence crops. They are facing the various problems like low productivity, low income and, low investment and capital formation, low prices, high production costs, low purchasing power, infrastructure deficits etc. therefore, agricultural diversification is often suggested as a means of rapid development in India in order to solve various problems in Indian economy. The concept of diversification conveys different meaning to different people at different levels. In terms of agriculture, diversification is considered as shift of resources from one crop to a larger mix crops and live stock. The government identified various crop development schemes, such as technology mission on oilseeds, pulses and maize; maize based cropping

* Shri Venkatesh College, Ichalkaranji, Kolhapur District, Maharashtra.

system for food security in India, integrated cereals development programs in rice base cropping systems areas.

Since the mid- eighties, the government identified horticultural crops as a means of diversification for making agriculture more, profitable through efficient land use, optimum utilization of natural resources and creating skilled employment for rural masses (India, 2000). In this paper, an attempt has been made to study about crop diversification and food security in hilly tribal areas of Eastern India. The specific objectives of the study are

- to know the nature of crop diversification in North-Eastern region.
- to study about food security in tribal and hilly areas of Eastern India.
- to characterize the agricultural growth in the tribal and hilly areas of Eastern India.

The study is based on the available secondary data, which have been collected from different sources.

NORTHEASTERN INDIA

The North-Eastern region comprises eight states of Arunachal Pradesh, Assam, Manipur, Meghalaya, Mizoram, Nagaland, Tripura and Sikkim. It Covers 8% of the total area of the country and has a population of 39.04million i.e. around 3.80% of the countries population. However, North-Eastern india is a land-locked region with 98% percent of its border being international. Density of population varies from 13 Arunachal Pradesh to 42 Mizoram to Assam 384(Madhab, 2005). Eastern India is an economically underdeveloped and ecologically fragile region of the country. The Per capita income in the North-Eastern region on an average is Rs.12918 only as compared with the national average of Rs 17823 at the current prices of 2001-02. The North-Eastern Council (NEC) was established in 1972 for securing the balanced developed of the North-Eastern region and interstate coordination. In addition, a Department Of North-Eastern region (DONER) was created to look after and to coordinate all the programs of the North-East region. The government has declared India's look East policy in order to develop the North-East region. According to Barthakur (2005), the terrain is by and large hilly and mountainous, interspersed with valleys of different length and breadth. Besides, the entire north eastern region, experience heavy to very monsoon rains, generally varying from 2000mm to around 17000 mm per annum. Besides, the soils of this region, by and large, are strongly acidic. Consequently, it is low productivity and poor quality of crops compared to other states of the country. The soils are not suitable for farming, less than a quarter of its land is arable, whereas the national average of land availability for cultivation is about 60%. Worse still, less than 17% of the cropped land in the North-East enjoys the benefit of irrigation versus the all India average of about 39 %. Barely, 21 % of the land under rice cultivation is irrigated in Assam as against almost cent percent in Punjab (Chakraverthy,2005).

PLAN INVESTMENT AND GROWTH

According to India's look East policy in 1998, a non-lapsable central pool of resources (NLCPR) was created by the government of India for supporting infrastructure development projects in the North-East region. All the north Eastern states are considered as special category states .According to George (2005), the total state plan expenditure of the North-Eastern states increased from Rs1752.64 crore in 1992-93, to Rs.2341.6 crore in1994-95, and Rs.4208 crore in 2001-02 and declined to Rs.3938.27 crore in states. However, the North-Eastern states generally spend 80-85% of the approved plan outlay. It has been observed from Table –1 that the real state plan expenditure showed significant positive growth rates only in respect of Nagaland (7.8%), Meghalaya (6.0%), Mizoram (3.0%), and Tripura (2.8%). The growth rates were negative in respect of Assam (0.3%), and Manipur (2.5%), Arunachal Pradesh (0.8%), the growth rate of North-Eastern states was 1.8 percent per annum.

The aggregate plan expenditure of the North-Eastern states shows that the share of Agriculture and allied activities has declined steadily from 15.79% in 1985-86 to 9.03% in 1997-98 and further to 7.95 % in 2002-03. The expenditure under irrigation, flood control and energy declined from 31.26% to 16.73 % and further to13.99% during the above period. The agricultural sector tends to growth at a slower pace than manufacturing and service industries. The share of transport and economic services increased from 14.67 % to 19.84 % and then declined to 15.91%. The share of social services, which includes education, heath and water supply, increased from 26.61% to 38.3% and further to 44.66% in 2002-03. The major contributor to the GSDP is the tertiary sector, which includes transport, trade and restaurants and the services (George, 2005). As compared to the other parts of the country, the quantum of investment in the North-Eastern region is very low. In order to active higher levels of growth it was therefore imperative that investment in the region be increased. Therefore, the Prime Ministers of India during their visit to the North-Eastern region from time to time has announced socio-economic packages for the development of the region. During the period 1996-97, the government tried to set up the Prime Minister's high level commission on the North-East(Shukla Commision).The Shukla Commission identified four basic need deficit an infrastructure deficit, a resources deficit and a two way deficit of understanding with the rest of the country. The multiple effects of plan investments in the North-East region are very weak due to the regions dependence on the outside world for many consumptions and capital goods.

CROPPING PATTERN

Now, we shall try to discuss about cropping pattern and land holding pattern in the states of North East region. Tripura State and its economy is permanently agrarian including traditional shifting Jhum cultivation engaging 51% of the total working force and is the main source of livelihood particularly in the rural areas. The net area, under cultivation is 26.88%. The cropping pattern demonstrates food grains, largely rice, followed by pulses, vegetables, maize, condiments, and spices, oilseeds, rape, mustered, jute and cotton. In terms of land holding pattern of the Tripura state brings out that 68% of the farmers lie in marginal farmers category owning 28% of land,

22% of farmers in the small farmers category owning 34% of the land and 9% to Semi medium farmers category owning a farmer category owning a quarter of land and Top 1% owning about 13% of the land (Sahaya, 2005).

Besides, Mizoram is a land of hills. Agruculture is particularly the only occupation in Mizoram. The cultivation method Jhum is very primitive and destructive. Now terraced farming is being tried .The entire Mizoram is a notified backward area. Nagaland is entirely trible. Agricultute involves 73% of the population. Cultivation is vitiated by what is called Jhumming. Meghalaya is the homeland of the three India's ancient hills communities the Khasis, the Jaintias, and the Garos. The majority of the people depend on the land for their livelihood. But the potential for agriculture expansion is very limited in Meghalaya due to terrain. Besides, Arunachal Pradesh is a thinly populated hilly tract on the eastern part of India. The population of Arunachal Pradesh is predominantly tribal. All the tribal belong to scheduled tribes. Nearly 80% of the population is engaged in agriculture. The traditional method of agricultural is Jhumming, a kind of shifting cultivation.

Assam agriculture sector occupies an important place even among the seven North-Eastern region states of India. Almost all other neighboring hilly North-Eastern states can depends on Assam's food grains and other agricultural products because it is easier to transport food grains from Assam to other neighboring of North-Eastern states. In terms of output, more than 70 to 80 percent of food grains and other output come from Assam. (Goyari,2005).Table-2 shows the position of Assam in North-Eastern Region of India in the production of various crops. Assam is the only state with large plain areas; other North-Eastern states are hilly and mountainous, Practicing mostly sifting cultivation. Assam can be made the food grains basket for the whole North-Eastern Region of India While developing regional food security grid. But it has been facing many difficulties in its march towards high level of agricultural production and productivity. Frequent floods have been responsible for many problems in the state. (Goyari,2005).The North-Eastern Region suffers from a serious food grains deficit of 1.6 million tones per annum. The North-East is a net imparter of oil seeds, sugar, meat, fish, eggs, and other civil supplies from distant parts of the country (Gorge, 2005). It has been observed from that agriculture has very slow growth rate in the region. The declining share of plan expenditure on agriculture, irrigation, flood controls etc. may be one of the reasons for the slow growth rate of agriculture in particular and of the North-East economy in general.

TRIBAL AND HILLY AREAS

The tribal communities live in about 15 percent of the country's area. In varying ecological and geo-climate conditions, plains, forests, hills, and inaccessible areas. The sixth scheduled under article 244 of the constitution relates to those areas in states of Assam, Meghalaya, Tripura and Mizoram which are declared as tribal areas. Table-1 shows the percentage of ST to total population in the state i.e. Tribal population.

Table 1
Selected Socio-economic Indicators– North-eastern States:

States	*Percentage of ST to population*	*Population below poverty line (%)*	*Estimated trend growth rates of state plan expenditure of NE states(1.8%)*
Arunachal Pradesh	64.2	33.47	0.8
Assam	12.4	36.09	–0.3
Manipur	34.2	28.54	–2.5
Meghalaya	85.9	33.87	6.0
Mizoram	94.5	19.47	3.0
Nagaland	89.1	32.67	7.8
Tripura	31.1	34.44	2.8
Sikkim	20.6	36.55	—
All India	8.2	26.1	—

Source: Yojana, December 2005,Vol 49 India, 2006.
ST:: Scheduled tribes. — :: Not Available.

Besides, Table-1 shows the population below the poverty line in the states of North-Eastern Region. It has been observed that about 36.55% of the population is below the poverty line in the Sikkim state, followed by Assam 36.09%, Tripura 34.44%,

Meghalaya 33.87%, Arunachal Pradesh 33.47%, Nagaland 32.67%, Manipur 28.54% and Mizoram 19.47%.

It has been observed from Census Report 2001 that the proportion of scheduled tribes below the poverty line is substantially higher than the national average. A majority of scheduled tribes continue to live below the poverty line, have poor literacy rates, suffer from malnutrition and diseases and are vulnerable to displacement.

DIVERSIFICATION OF THE AGRICULTURAL SECTOR

Now we shall try to discuss the nature of diversification of the agricultural sector in the North-Eastern Region. It has been observed that the level of agricultural production is not high due to low percentages of irrigated areas, hilly, and rugged terrains, sedimentary, rocks, susceptibility to soil erosion, fragmentation of land holding, inadequate agricultural mechanism, prohibitive cost of fertilizers due to high transport costs, unfavorable seasonal conditions, on certain market conditions, abrupt fluctuations in prices and lack of availability of quality planting materials (Sahya, 2005)

Due to rising cost of production and shortage of agricultural labor, returns from agricultural activities are being reduced in the states of North-Eastern region. Therefore, the government has taken decision for diversification of the agricultural sector. As a new initiative, a centrally sponsored scheme; on farm water management for encouraging crop production in eastern India has been launched in March 2002. The objectives of the scheme are to increase the production and productivity of food grains through focus on exploitation of ground /surface water and its efficient utilization. The scheme will help in enhancing the income of the farmers and diversifying agricultural production in eastern India. The scheme is being implemented on a credit linked back-ended subsidy basis through NABARD in coordination with the state governments (India-2006).

For increasing income and improving the standard of living of the people, diversification in agriculture, low yielding and low value crops has replaced by high yielding and high value crops. Horticulture has a great role to play in the economy of the people. It has heartening to role that Arunachal Predesh, Mizoram, Nagaland and other states have made significant progress in pisiculture, floriculture, sericulture, horticulture, medicinal and aromatic plantations, vegetables, livelihoods etc. as a part of diversification of the agricultural economy. Sericulture programs have been set up, in spite of the difficulties, small and medium scale industries have come up. Most of which are forest-based industries such as sawmills, veneer mills and play wood mills.

Table-2
Relative Production Positions Of States.
As a percent to North East India total output

Year	*State*	*Rice*	*Wheat*	*Food grains*	*R&M*	*Tea*	*Jute*	*Sugar cane*
	Assam	70.9	89.6	70.1	88.9	99.0	92.8	89.3
1980	Arunachal	2.9	1.6	4.1	4.9	0.0	0.0	0.0
81	Manipur	7.7	0.0	7.4	1.0	0.0	0.0	2.8
to	Meghalaya	3.7	3.5	4.2	2.4	0.0	4.5	0.0
1984	Mizoram	1.0	0.0	1.0	0.0	0.0	0.0	0.2
85	Nagaland	2.8	0.0	3.0	1.2	0.0	0.1	4.7
	Tripura	11.0	5.3	10.3	1.6	1.0	2.6	3.0
	Assam	71.7	85.3	69.7	79.8	98.7	94.0	83.5
1990	Arunachal	2.9	6.5	4.2	10.0	0.0	0.0	0.0
91	Manipur	6.9	0.0	6.6	0.7	0.0	0.0	3.1
to	Meghalaya	2.6	2.4	3.0	2.0	0.0	4.0	0.0
1994	Mizoram	1.8	0.0	2.1	0.0	0.0	0.0	0.3
95	Nagaland	3.6	0.9	4.3	3.8	0.0	0.2	8.9
	Tripura	10.5	5.0	10.0	3.7	1.3	1.8	4.3

R&M:: rapeseed & mustard.
Source: Economic &Political weekly, June 25, 2005

Traditional farming system in North Eastern India are now being transfered within a developmental frame work that seeks of the green revolution of the 1960's in the context of today's globalising world (Krishna, 2005). Animal Husbandary and Dairy development plays a prominent role in the rural economy in supplementing the income of the households, particularly, the landless and small and marginal farmers. It also provides subsidiary occupation in semi-urban areas and move so for people living in hilly tribal and drought prone areas where crops output may not sustain the family

FOOD SECURITY

Sustainability of agriculture is determined by the sustainable use of natural resources, land, water and agricultural bio-diversities including that of plaints and animals (Goyari, 2005). The government has taken various measures for food security of the people in the North-Eastern region. Major emphasis was given on agricultural research for the benefits of tribal and hilly regions. The horticulture sector has established its credibility in improving productivity of land, generating employment, improving economic conditions of farmers and entrepreneurs, enhancing export potential, and above all, providing nutritional security. Horticulture is being vigorously promoted in the entire region and market linkages with South-East Asia are envisaged.

The union ministries for the development of North-Eastern region and state governments have taken various measures for food security of the people through new agriculture policy and national Agricultural technology projects. However, the states of North-Eastern regions have been facing the problem of poverty and food security. About 35% of the people, who are living below the poverty line in the states of NorthEastern region. According to the Krishna's study (2005), Atlas of the sustainability of food security in India 2004, uses 17 selected indicators and states have classified in five groups ranging from the sustainable. According to this mapping, Nagaland is the most unsustainable, and only such state in the country (mainly because of land degradation). Arunachal Predesh is sustainable because it has more forests and fewer people. The comparison reveals that Arunachal Pradesh, which has high gender disparity, is sustainable in terms of food security, while Mizoram with least gender disparity is moderately sustainable in terms of food. Nagaland, which is the most unsustainable state for food security in the entire country, has a moderately high level of gender disparity. Goyari (2005), shows that development of rice and other food crops, based on endogenous resources is the only way to meet the food and livelihood securities in the

Assam state. The need for controlling flood menace in Assam is very critical for ecological security, livelihood security and food security of the state, its neighboring states and the country as whole. Despite the incentive given under the North-East industrial policy and enormous natural, mineral and bio-diversity potential, the North East has not been able to develop as it should.(Madhab,2005) .

SUGGETIONS

1. In the flood force lands, the state government may introduce HYVP of paddy seeds that matures the crop during September to early October. It will bring about a Quantum jumps in the yield about of paddy and enable cultivation of several rabbi crops.
2. Monetary credit should be provided to farmers. The agriculture, horticulture, water shed development, irrigation and energy sectors should be given adequate focus in the development strategy so that the food deficit will remove in the Eastern India.
3. Increase in agricultural production a wide variety of food processing industries with appropriate technological and finacial tie up should be encouraged.
4. Development of human resources, plantation and horticultural crops, medicinal plans etc. should be given priority and focused alteration.
5. It is necessary to give focus on agricultural, horticulture, food processing, and watershed development, irrigation, rural connectivity, internal markets ,co-operatives, institutions and above all development of human resources. It is also necessary to ensure adequate capital content in the state plans of the North-Eastern states.
6. The state government should give priority for development of agriculture and allied enterprises, tourism, floriculture, sericulture, horticulture, small-scale village industry and cottage industry, handicrafts, medicinal and aromatic plantations which are most important. Cottage industries in the whole of the

North-Eastern region. These have large potentially for generally income and employment for people in the rural sector of the state.

7. For increasing income and improving the standard of living of the people. There must be diversification in agriculture, low yielding and low value crops should be replaced by high yielding and high value crops.
8. The private sector should take initiative in setting up food processing units.

REFERENCES

Barthkur, I.K. (2005), Entwined Imperatives, Yojana Vol.49.

Chakravathy, Nilish (2005) Reframing Look East Policy,Yojana Vol.49.

George, N.D. (2005), Plan Investments And Grown, Yojana Vol.49.

Goyari Phanindra, (2005), Flood Damages And Sustainability Of Agriculture In Assam, Economic & Political Weekly, June 25,Vol.26.

Krishna, Sumi(2005), Gendered price Of Rice In North-Eastern India, Economic & Political Weekly, June 18, Vol.25.

Madhab Jayanta (2005), Enabling The North-East,Yojana,Vol.49.

Sahaya, D.N. (2005), Socio-Economic Challenges Yojana, Vol.49.

India (2006), Government of India, New Delhi.

Manorama Year Book 2003.

9

SMALL SCALE SECTOR IN INDIA: AN ENGINE FOR EMPLOYMENT GENERATION

*Shashi Arora** &
*Soniya Gupta***

INTRODUCTION

The promotion of small scale sector has been widely recommended as one of the most appropriate means of developing industry in developing countries. The doctrine of small scale sector received strong official support in India. There are a number of reasons for this. The most important reason is the legacy of Gandhian teaching. In addition, the very wide distribution of existing 551s in India, the great pressure of population and the shortage of capital have all tended to direct attention towards the small scale sector as a possible means of increasing output and employment in Indian industry for at least the next few decades. The small scale sector is growing fast and is capable of addressing itself to the basic problem of Indian economy i.e. unemployment and regional development.

In the post independence era, The government had to synchronize and harmonize the twin consideration of rapid industrialization and the parameters of r1 welfare state. In the context of the major problems of poverty and unemployment

* Head, Department of Economics, G.D.H.G. College, Moradabad.
** Research Scholar, Department of Economics, G.D.H.G. Moradabad.

faced by the Indian economy, the development of the small scale sector was considered essential because of its being:

- Labour intensive
- Having implications for equity
- Flexibility
- Capability to contribute decentralization
- Promote entrepreneurship
- Optimum use of local resources and talents etc.

The small scale sector is a significant part of the Indian industrial economy of India and offers an important means of addressing the problem of under-employment and unemployment by absorbing increasing numbers of the urban and rural poor. The critical importance of this sector is that in a modern globally oriented economy it is the 551 sector which can absorb low income groups into high growth productive sectors of the economy. In this sense the 551 sector, if supported and nurtured in the right manner through strategic intervention on the part of government, can be seen as one of the main channels of sustainable poverty reduction. Unlike investment in other poverty alleviation programmes, investment in 551 sector infrastructure will offer a long term competitive means of employing low income labour. A part of this challenge, however, will be to ensure that public investment in the sector does lead to sector expansion and a growth in the demand for labour rather than simply an increase in the profit margin of existing entrepreneurs. Small scale industries (SSI) are defined as those with less than Rs. 0.5 million in fixed assets, excluding land and buildings. SSIs account for over 95 percent of total industrial units in the country producing 40 percent of total manufacturing output, 35 percent of exports, employing around 17 million people producing over 7,500 products. The sector covers a wide range of establishments from artisans, cottage industry through to modern production units. As a sector with significant employment potential and low investment it has long enjoyed protection as a priority sector and benefited from special assistance in concessional credit, technology, marketing and infrastructural support.

INSTITUTIONAL SUPPORT

The 551 sector has remained a high priority area for government intervention of the years. The reason for this is due to the sector's importance in employment generation, regional disbursal of industries and a seedbed for entrepreneurship. The Department of Small Scale Industries in the Ministry of Industry was established in 1991 to promote the sector. The department is responsible for a plethora of schemes and programmes covering the sector. A number of agencies then provide specific forms of assistance to the sector including consultancy, training, testing, marketing support through agencies such as the Small Industries Development Corporation (SIDO), Small Industries Service Institutes (SISI), National Small Industries Corporation and other research and testing agencies. Central government policies serve as guidelines but each State has evolved its own initiatives for the sector under the Commissioner/Director Industries who oversee the activities of the District Industries Centres which in turn provide support in:

- Economic studies
- Supply of machinery
- Raw materials
- Credit
- Marketing
- Quality assurance
- Consultancy and extension

At State level a variety of other institutions are involved in SSI promotion including:

- State Financial Corporations providing term loans, direct subscriptions to equity debentures, guarantees, discounting bills of exchange and seed capital
- State Industrial Development/Investment

Corporations which develop land and infrastructure as well as plots and sheds along with water, power, drainage and other amenities as well as loans

- State Small Industries Development Corporations which help to procure raw materials, supply machinery, marketing assistance, estates, capital and management assistance

- Other agencies including State Infrastructural Development Corporations, Co-operative Banks, Regional Rural Banks, Handloom and Handicraft Corporations,

TECHNICAL CONSULTANCY ORGANISATIONS ETC

- Industry Associations including Confederation of Indian Industry,Federation of Indian Chambers of Commerce and Industry, PHD Chamber of Commerce and Industry, Associated Chambers, Federation of Exporters etc

POLICY INITIATIVES

There have been around six policy resolutions from 1948-91 which all give some emphasis to the SSI sector. The key initiatives are:

- Reservation which has been designed to protect SSIs from competition from large scale manufacturers giving them the exclusive rights of production. At present 812 items are reserved for SSI production. However, more recently it has been felt that this policy has not been particularly beneficial and recommendations have been made for deregulation of the sector.
- Upward revision of investment ceilings in plant and machinery in 1991 and 1997 to extend protection from competition.
- Some relaxation of reserved items for large scale production where 50% or more is for export Foreign equity participation up to 24% and higher for items with export obligations.
- Foreign technology agreements and removal of restrictions on use of foreign brand names/trade marks.
- Reduction of customs duty on various items and import of capital goods and liberalisation of export procedures.

EMPLOYMENT PROJECTION

The small scale sector is poised to be the engine of employment generation or growth in the just ten years as is clear from the projections made by the subgroup -I of the working group on SSIs for the tenth five year plan. The growth in employment is dependent on the growth in the number of units, growth rate of the small scale sector and nature of growth Le. capital intensive or labour intensive. Taking all these factors into account, the subgroup has made a projection of growth I the number of units, Production and employment with Year wise breakup as given in the following table.

Table 1
Projection Of SSI Output and Employment in 10th plan

Year	No. of Units (Lakhs)	Production (Rs. Crore)		Employment (Lakhs)
		Current Prices	Constant Prices (93-94)	
2002-03	36.71	824363	527837	200.79
	(4.5)	(12.5)	(8.5)	(4.0)
2003-04	38.36	932354	527837	209.03
	(4.5)	(13.1)	(9.1)	(4.1)
2004-05	40.09	1060087	575871	217.80
	(4.5)	(13.7)	(9.7)	(4.2)
2005-06	41.89	1213800	631730	227.17
	(4.5)	(14.5)	(10.5)	(4.3)
2006-07	43.78	1401939	778339	237.17
	(4.5)	(15.5)	(11.5)	(4.4)
Average Growth (10th Plan)	x	13.9	9.9	4.2
Total growth in 5 years Base year (2001-02)	x	91.3	60.0	22.8
Average	X	18.3	12.0	4.6

Note: Figures in brackets indicate the percentage growth over the previous year. Source: Laghu udyog samachar (various issues)

FACTORS AFFECTING EMPLOYMENT

The special group is targeting ten million opportunities per year in its report. Some of the major Problems and constraints experienced by the small scale sector in India in the form of:

- Lower productivity
- Increased competition due to globalization Removal of QRs
- Cheaper imports from china
- Increased capital intensity
- Power related inadequacies
- Credit related insufficiencies

Of these problems the problem of lower productivity is most serious and needs special attention through measures designed to upgrade technology, improvement in quality of products and skill development of the workers etc.

The employment generation through induced measures can serve a successful supplement to the autonomious measures. Direct employment should not be viewed in the isolation It has both forward and backward linkages and generate large scale employment. In addition the role of fast emerging information and biotechnological sector should not be ignored. In many ways they are catalyst to employment generation.

CLUSTER DEVELOPMENT

In spite of the complex institutional support arrangements at Central and State level combined with various policy initiatives designed to offer protection to small industries there has still been a failure in the sector to generate adequate levels of employment and reduce levels of under employment and poverty in the economy as a whole. At the same time as domestic protectionist policies begin to give way to a more liberal global industrial order new challenges now face the SSI sector calling for a radical change in SSI policy. One such change would be to provide a much greater thrust on the concept of industrial clustering, defined as the sectoral or geographical concentration of around related and complementary production and to maximise {he advantages of such clusters to provide a sound competitive base for SSI production. Research has shown that industrial clusters benefit from forward and backward linkages where business have similar economic and cultural characteristics. Clusters encourage specialisation, inter-firm linkages division of labour and information sharing. Small and

Medium Enterprises (SMEs) . operating in clusters have been seen to be particularly innovative and able to compete globally. India has numerous industrial clusters. It has been estimated that there are over 350 SME clusters and over 2,000 artisan clusters in a wide variety of areas such as leather in Tamil Nadu, UP and West Bengal, automobile components in Haryana and Punjab, hosiery and garments in Delhi, Gujarat and Madhya Pradesh, woollens in the Punjab, footware in Agra, carpets in UP, Powerlooms in Maharashtra etc. However, many of these clusters compete on the basis of labour costs and gain little advantage from inter-firm linkage.

CLUSTER DEVELOPMENT PROGRAMMES

The Government of India has launched a number of initiatives to support cluster development. SIDO has established technical support services through production cum development centres (PPDCs) in different parts of the country which provide research and development, product design and innovation, process improvements, common facility services and manpower training. SIDO has also set up sector specific cluster initiatives such as the Central Footwear Training Centres (CFTCs) which assist with design for export. However, in order to strengthen the existing SSI clusters government needs to assess the requirements of individual clusters more closely and formulate sector specific strategies. The main problems that need to be addressed are as follows:

- Formulation of sector policy for the development and promotion of new SSI clusters and for strengthening existing SSI clusters.
- Common information systems and access to IT.
- Shared R & D and training facilities.
- Procurement (stores and supplies) arrangements.
- Common business support and marketing services.
- Marketing and branding services.

Research on the SSI sector has shown that the main requirements for the expansion of the sector depend on:

- Enlargement of the definition of SSI to include tertiary sector

- Simplification of laws and procedures
- Enhancement of excise duty exemption limit
- Action to address delayed payments from suppliers
- Special schemes for women entrepreneurs
- Rationalisation of taxes
- Comprehensive information base/data bank for SSI
- Common testing facilities

As far as credit is concerned there have been some important changes in recent years. The Central Bank has declared that 40 percent of funds may be extended to all segments of the SSI sector. The RBI has advised banks to adopt simplified procedure for sanctioning credit for working capital to SSIs on the basis of 20 percent of projected annual turnover to all SSI units. Delayed payments Act has been amended to assist SSIs in securing interest on delayed payments. Banks have been advised to open more SSI branches and banks with a good track record of servicing SSIs are being offered lower spreads over PLR.

RECOMMENDATIONS

It is in this context that the recommendations below are made and all investment in the sector should be tied to some element of growth in employment as well as productivity. This may be direct expansion of employment any particular unit or indirect expansion of employment through the growth of subcontracting. The main recommendations in pursuit of this objective are as follows:

PROMOTING CLUSTERING

Worldwide experience shows that there is considerable benefit in promoting the formation of effective clusters. Attention needs to be focused on strengthening and building upon existing clusters by extending support in a range of areas that would encourage effective collaboration and inter-firm linkage.

PUBLIC-PRIVATE PARTNERSHIPS

There is a need to shift away from traditional public sector support services operating on bureaucratic principles to those where business support services are delivered by business development organisations aimed at developing commercial transactional relations with client SMEs.

CREDIT SUPPORT

Although the flow of credit to SSIs has increased there is still a need to focus on the discounting of bills of exchange in less developed regions and creating an environment for mobilising low cost funds through tax free bonds etc. Banks and financial institutions need to have adequate incentives to service this sector

SCIENCE PARKL UNIVERSITY LINKAGE

There needs to be greater encouragement of SMEs to forge links with universities and IITs. Universities may be encouraged to establish business liaison services covering research, training, consultancy, licensing, recruitment of graduates etc.

RESEARCH & DEVELOPMENT (R&D)

There needs to be stronger co-ordination between research centres and encouragement for SSIs to work with Industry Associations and the Technology Bureau of Small Industries to create awareness for R & D.

INFRASTRUCTURE THROUGH PRIVATE FINANCING

Surveys have shown infrastructure for SSIs to be inadequate. Private industrial estates should be encouraged to provide competition in the provision of industrial infrastructure. The growth centre scheme could be remodelled to include private sector participation. Streamlining and Corporatising Support Services At present in India there is considerable overlap in extension services between agencies. Central government should confine itself to policy issues concerning the sector and certain high cost shared services while state governments should be charged with the exclusive implementation of front line services. A number of agencies should be restructured in such a way as to enable joint venture activity and facilitate subcontracting arrangements.

RESTRUCTURING DISTRICT INDUSTRY CENTRES

District Industry Centres (DICs) need to be restructured as a single window agency and should be upgraded through closer associations with the SISIs. DICs could be emodelled along the lines of the BL programme in the UK with professional secondments from the private sector.

Strategic Alliances between SMEs and large enterprises Large firms should be encouraged to draw upon the competitive advantages of certain SMEs to enhance their own profitability. SMEs provide a high degree of flexible specialisation and through subcontracting arrangements can offer significant low fixed cost advantages to large firms.

FINANCIAL INCENTIVES

- Earmarking 70 percent of priority sector credit to the SSI sector for tiny units
- Simplification of procedures for grants and loans for working capital
- Central Bank may consider the viability of setting up a SSI Development Fund for infrastructure provision.
- SIDBI should assist with the setting up of a new credit rating agency for SSI financing . Financial incentives to export units.

REFERENCES

The development Commissioner, Small Scale Industries in India, An engine of growth, Ministry of Small Scale Industries.

Laghu Udyog Samachar (Various Issues).

Sahoo S.K., SSIs in India, Indian Economic Journal, Vol. 51.

10

GLOBALISATION AND AGRICULTURAL CRISIS IN BIHAR: OPPORTUNITIES AND WEAKNESSES

Ashwini Kant Jha[*], *Bhavna Jha*[**] *and Rati Kant Jha*[***]

INTRODUCTION

The crop yield depend on the efficiency in the use of resources viz. land, labour, irrigation, power technology, extension services, fertilizers, pesticides, seed, agricultural machinery and marked infrastructure. The availability of these various resources have a bearing on investments in agriculture, both public and private, and the extent of use these resources depends on the access to credit. This section examines the constraints operating in the accessibility to these various resources and assesses the available potential through which these constraints can be removed.

During the period of first generation reform there has been a steady deceleration in the rate of growth of agricultural output as compared with the same achieved during the decade immediately before the reform. In fact, the growth rate of food and non-food crops have fallen remarkably from 3.54 and 4.84 per cent per annum during the period from 1980-81 to 1989-90 to 1.66 and 2.36 per cent per annum during the eight years period of reform, *i.e.* for 1990-91 to 1997-98. All India yield

* Professor and Head, P.G. Department of Economics, BNM University(W.C.), P.G.Centre, Saharsa, Bihar.

** Lecturer in IRPM, MAM College, Naugachia T.M.Bhagalpur University, Bhagalpur, Bihar.

*** M.L.S.M. College, Darbhanga, Bihar.

indices of major crops rice and wheat recorded annum growth rate of about 2.77 and 3.73 per cent respectively during 1970-71 to 1990-91 whereas their respective growth rates are just 1.27 and 1.85 per cent during 1990-91 to 1995-96. Firstly, the growth rate of agriculture both in terms of gross production and in terms of output has visibly decelerated during the nineties. For some crops and in some regions, the deceleration has been quite steep. This has resulted in immense hardships to farmers, driving some of them to commit suicide. During the Kharif harvesting season of 2000 the refusal of FCI to procure paddy on time has further added to the woes of the Indian farmers. Secondly, in some of the poor rainfed states of India the diversification of the cropping pattern coarse cereals oilseed crops has slowed down considerably during the recent years. Thirdly, after liberalisation and devaluation the initial spurt in agriculture has now almost come to a halt. Lastly, with the new policy paradigm, there appears to be backtracking on institutional issues like land reforms, ceiling on holding and on security of land tenure.

Agriculture in the State performed very well during 70s and 80's by recording rates of growth move than 2 per cent per annum, respectively. But in the 90s the rate of growth declined to 1.32 per cent. This deceleration in the growth of output in the 90s is a serious cause of concern. The main contributing factors for the growth are yield in the 70s, cropping pattern followed by yield in the 80s and yield followed by cropping pattern in the 90s. In fact, area had a negative effect on growth in the 90s. This pattern of growth indicates that agriculture sector in the state as been subjected to some constraints operating in the areas of land use pattern, cropping pattern and yields. Therefore the policy interventions for pulling out the agricultural economy from the constraints operating in land use, choice of crops and raising crop yield is necessary.

Growth for all crops taken together decelerated from 2.65 per cent per annum during the eighties to 1.30 per annum during the nineties. There was a sharp decline in the yield growth rates of wheat, rice and cotton. Growth rate of yield in rice decelerated from 3.21 to 1.27 and in wheat from 3.15 to

2.32 per cent per annum. In the case of cotton yield growth rate has slowed down from 4.15 per cent annuam the eighties to only 0.59 per cent during the nineties.

Table 1
State-wise Growth of Agricultural Output, 1962-65, 1970-73, 1980-83, 1990-93 and 1996-99

State	*1970-73 over 1962-65*	*1980-83 over 1970-73*	*1990-93 over 1980-83*	*1996-99 over 1990-93*
Harayana	4.65	3.02	5.04	1.98
Himachal Pradesh	3.33	0.96	2.74	-0.11
Jammu & Kashmir	5.37	3.47	0.17	0.43
Punjab	6.36	4.74	4.22	0.73
Utter Pradesh	2.54	2.77	3.06	2.47
North-West Region	3.6	3.21	3.55	1.91
Assam	1.85	2.8	2.42	1.31
Bihar	1.12	-0.41	2.12	3.33
Orissa	0.99	2.65	2.92	-5.14
West Region	2.37	0.68	5.97	2.99
Eastern Region	1.57	1.09	3.63	1.25
Gujrat	1.78	3.12	0.86	6.83
Madhya Pradesh	1.97	1.28	4.53	3.86
Maharashtra	3.64	6.57	2.12	3.29
Rajasthan	4.29	1.26	6.06	4.9
Central Region	0.73	3.13	3.33	4.5
Andhra Pradesh	0.93	3.61	3.42	1.52
Karnataka	2.64	2.32	3.68	3.62
Kerala	4.09	-0.19	1.92	3.6
Tamil Nadu	2.76	-0.57	4	3.25
Southern Region	2.4	1.08	3.43	2.19
All States	2.08	2.38	3.44	2.83

Source: GOI Area and Production of Principal Crops in India, Various Issues Ministry of Agriculture

LAND AS A RESOURCE

Bihar is endowed with wide range of agro-climatic conditions and natural resources conducive for the development of agriculture. Regionally, it has well-irrigated and rich land in the south districts, backward and under development areas in North west scants rainfall drought prone areas and the hilly areas along the south eastern borders. The State has also a threat of floods in northern districts and droughts in the rest of the area. The study of changes in the land use pattern shows that the proportion of under utilized land i.e. current fallows, other fallows undated land and cultural waste lands, is much higher in the State compared to all India average. (The fallow lands, both current fallows and other fallows increased at an accelerating rate until 1990 and declined only marginally in the 90s.) It appears that the government initiatives taken in terms of land and irrigation development programmes are not adequate to reduce the size of these land is a constraint for agricultural development in the State. Many studies shows that under utilization of land in the State is largely due to the non-availability of resources, especially water, with the farmers and the nature of investments in relation to expected returns from the land. The Naxalite problem in the state is also observed to be factor behind the increase in under utilization of land (Parthasarathy, 2000).

IRRIGATION

Although there has been a continuous increase in the area under irrigation in the State over the last fifty years rain fed agriculture still remained more than 60 percent. The decline in the surface irrigation i.e. both canal and tank irrigation and the phenomenal increase in the irrigation through ground water source in the 90s is not a desirable trend as it may lead to desertification of lands after some time and cause environmental problems. This phenomenon is the consequence of the decline in public investments that implemented the creation of additional canal irrigation facilities and proper maintenance of existing irrigation structures and increase in the private investments in irrigation. The minor irrigation programmes of the government and NABARD implemented in the State have contributed significantly to the increase in ground water irrigation. The exploitation of ground water at a faster rate is already causing depletion of water table at an alarming rate and the failure of bore wells in many regions.

Estimates show that irrigation facility created in the State, so far, is only 30 per cent of the potential. Therefore there is a possibility for creating additional irrigation facilities through proper intervention. Intervention made for improving efficiency of the large and medium irrigation projects made earlier are not very effective and they are to be made more effective. Establishment of "Water Users Association"' an initiative of the state government, is indeed a right step in this direction.

In the areas where is no possibility for creating surface irrigation structures, interventions are to be made on the lines of promoting micro irrigation techniques such as drip, sprinkler and sub- surface irrigation along with proper maintenance of existing structures, rather than expanding the ground water source of irrigation. There is an urgent need to desilt the minor irrigation tanks and undertaken repairs to the breached tanks and distributaries.

The low and erratic rainfall (fig –1) is a high constraint for the development of rainfed agriculture in the State. The State receives an annual average rainfall ranging between 300mm and 1200mm with significant regional variations. (The average rainfall ranges between 800mm and 1600mm and 1400mm in Telangana and between 500mm and) A major constraint in providing irrigation water in the State is that

In the regions where rainfall is low, surface irrigation is also low and the dependence on ground water source is more. The frequency of occurrence of droughts in the State is also very high. Half of the state

For the development of rainfed agriculture watershed management is the key approach. This involves a package of creation of water harvesting structures, crop diversification in favour of less water intensive crops and horticultural crops and livestock and fisheries production. The Government in many parts of the State implemented watershed development programme. Evaluation studies indicate that this programme showed good results during the project period. After that effectiveness of the project slowly declined due to lack of proper maintenance of the structures created. This calls for government interventions on the lines of proper maintenance of the structures created. This calls for government interventions on the lines of promoting people's participation in watershed management by forming farmers associations for watershed management like the Water Users Associations functioning in the surface irrigated areas.

CROPPING PATTERN

The crop-pattern changes that have been taking place in the State are in favour of water intensive crops and commercialization. These changes have been taking place at the cost of coarse cereals. These changes may pose problems of sustainability and food security. The increase in area under water intensive crops like rice and sugarcane put heavy pressure on the limited water resources and poses a threat to sustainability. The increasing commercialization of agriculture at the cost of coarse cereal crops in resource poor areas may pose severe problems of food security in the event of crop failure, which are very often experienced by the farmers in the State due to the use of substandard inputs. Also, it may be difficult for farmers in the economies where agricultural subsidies are low to compete with farmers in the economies where agriculture is highly subsidize and gain from international trade. This calls for a policy intervention to regular the cropping pattern taking into consideration the available resources and the existing conditions.

AGRICULTURAL YIELD

The growth of agricultural output in the state was contributed mainly by increase in yield in the 70s and increase in yield coupled with crop shifts from low value crops to high crops, in the 80s. In the 90s the growth was contributed by yield and area had a negative effect. But during this period all prominent crops recorded deceleration in the growth of yield. Also, the yield levels of these crops are relatively lower in the State.

The yield gaps point out that there is an untapped yield potential in the State and it can be tapped through proper interventions. In this connection, the knowledge of the constraints operating in the use of various yield-increasing input is highly useful.

SUPPLY OF LABOUR:

The labour supply, as such, is not a constraint for agricultural growth in the state. In fact there is surplus labour in agriculture. When it comes to the quality of labour, the determining factors are education and health and nutrition. Majority of the agricultural labourers in the state are illiterate and their ability to collect the information and understanding it, is very low. The agricultural wages, the determining factor for health and nutrition has been on a continuous rise in the state. The average daily wages of male agricultural workers, at current prices increased from Rs. 2.68 in 1971 to Rs. 24.35 in 1992-93 and in 2000 for male and female agricultural labourers, the wages were Rs. 50.00 and Rs. 40.00 respectively. But the availability of employment throughout the year may be a problem due to seasonality of agricultural work and population pressure. As the agriculture in the state is not very much modernized, the requirement of skilled labour is low and the relatively higher level of illiteracy among agricultural labourers may not stand as a constraint for agricultural growth in the state. However, for efficient management of agriculture, the farmers require skills. These illiteracy levels in the rural areas are low at 60 per cent as in 2001. Many studies also show that farmers' access to skill improvement programmes offered through extension services is limited. The low literacy levels of the farmers and their limited access to skill upgradation programmes through extension services stand as a constraint for agricultural development in the state.

HYV SEEDS

Among the factors contributing to crop yields, seed is the most prominent one. It is also the least expensive one. The rate of adoption of HYV seeds is very high in the State, and it is almost 100 per cent in respect of some crops. As far as the adoption of HYV seed by farmers is concerned, there are no problems. However, some constraints have been operating in the State in ensuring the supply of good quality seed to the farmers due to foul play of the private traders in the seed market. Multinational companies, attract the innocent farmers, through exhibitions of demonstration plots, and thrust on them seed varieties that are unsuitable for their crop conditions. Such deception by traders is observed in many places especially in case of Sunflower & Maize crops. But in the crop development programmes of the state government an important component is the supply of good quality seed. Therefore, it appears that the implementation of these programmes is not very effective.

A large number of seed companies are in operation in the State. The national seed Corporation is also producing large quantities of seeds of crop varieties released by PUSA and distributing in the other states. The Agriculture University has released many high yield crop varieties and they are very popular in the country. The State government has launched a programme know as 'seed village' under which the farmers can produce their own seed at low cost with the Breeder and Foundation seeds supplied by the University. This will ensure quality seed to the farmers, provided the programme is made more popular.

USE OF FERTILIZERS:

There are large variations in the use of fertilizers across the irrigated and dry regions and within region across crop varieties. These varieties are due to excess use (more than the recommended dose) in some areas on some crops and deficient use in some other regions and other crops. There is also an imbalance in the ratio in which N,P and K are used. The excess and imbalanced use of fertilizer in the state increase the cost of production and depress the yield through depletion of secondary and micro nutrients and as a constraint for agricultural development in the State.

UNWANTED PESTICIDES :

Although the pesticides consumption is relatively more Bihar, it has been declining over time with the promotion of Integrated Pest Management (IPM) ad Integrated Disease Management (IDM) methods. But all the farmers are not adopting these methods. So there is an excessive and misuse of pesticides by some farmers on some crop like chilles and tobacco. The cost of pesticides in the total operational costs account for about 20 per cent in Potato and 15 per cent on sugarcane. The excess use of pesticides not only increases the cost of cultivation, but also adversely affects the crop yield and human and animal health. Also high rates of pesticide residues in the product will have adverse effect on our exports. Field survey has shown that pesticide adulteration by private traders is quite common in wheat growing areas, which subjected the farmers to much suffering. Thus the excess and indiscriminate use of pesticides and imperfections in the pesticide markets, stand as constraints for agricultural development in the State.

To overcome these problems, IPM and IDM programmes have been introduced. Bur their implementation is not spread over all farmers in all regions There is a need make these programmes more popular among the farmers.

INADEQUATE FARM MACHINERY AND IMPLEMENTS:

The use of various types of farm machines and implements has been increased at a very rapid rate. But as per the recent data the stock available is quite inadequate. But increasing the mechanization of farm operations replacing rural labour force is neither feasible nor desirable because of the small size of individual holdings and the dependence of large number of people on agriculture. Selective or partial mechanization should be attempted to reduce the labour cost, minimize drudgery for labour, and improve work efficiency, timely conduct of ploughing sowing planting and other farm operations.

POOR CREDIT FACILITIES

There has been a significant improvement over time, in the access to organized sources of credit to the farmers; yet, there exists still a gap between demand and supply. Several studies show that small and marginal farmers yet, there exists still depend on informal and non- institutional sources of credit, particularly from money lenders for 60 to 80 per cent of their credit requirements. Moreover the rates of interest charged by these money lenders are also very high. After the introduction of economic reforms in 90s, there is a virtual breakdown of the extension machinery and decline in the access to institutional sources of credit. As a result, the small and marginal farmers are decline in the access to institution sources of credit. As a result, the small and marginal farmers are becoming increasingly dependant upon private trade for credit and extension services and often become victims of exploitation by unscrupulous traders and moneylenders interested in selling spurious materials, like pesticides.

UNDERDEVELOPED MARKETS:

The state intervention in the markets is more only in the product markets. It appears that the product markets are functioning well, though, the available market infrastructures is not adequate in the sense that each market has to cover a very wide area handling large quantities of commodities with poor road and transport facilities. Also the weighing machines used in the markets are traditional type leaving the farmers complaining of under weighment of the product. But a cause for concern is that the WSP of agricultures commodities in the state is lower than the WSP at all India level during the 80's and 90's.

In the input market, private sector is playing a dominant role. About 90 per cent of the seeds of HYV, fertilizers and plant protection chemicals, farm implements and machinery are being supplied to the farmers through private agencies. Agro-Industries corporation supply seeds of HYV and agro-chemicals to only limited extent. With regard to seed processing most of the units are in the private sector. Further cold chains for storage of fruits and vegetables are also in the hands of private sector. Studies show that there are imperfections in these input markets and farmers are very often subjected to exploitation.

EXPORT POSSIBILITIES OF AGRICULTURE PRODUCTS:

The liberazation and globalization policies that the country has been adopting and its membership in W.T.O. is expected to promote exports and gain from trade. In order to assess, to what extent the state can gain from these policies, and to identify the constraints, if any, the aspects like production in relation to requirement, cost of production and the production and the growth of factor productivity need to be examined.

Towards the end of 90s per capita net production of food grains is about 170 kgs per annum, hardly adequate to meet the nutritional requirements. Per capita net production of pulse is 10 kgs per annum, a meager amount especially for a vegetarian country like India. Per capita net production of oilseeds continues to be low despite recent high rates of growth of oilseeds.

The cost of production of many crops is relatively higher in the state. For instance in the 80s and 90s, the cost of production of in Bihar was higher than that of Punjab and the excess cost varied between 9 to 18 per cent. Under these conditions, unless the factor productivity is stepped up, the possibilities for export of food grains are limited.

In the 70s the total factor productivity grew at a rate of 1.13 per cent annum and contributed one-third to the growth of output. But, in the 90s the growth rate of total factor productivity declined to 1.05 per cent showing a decline in the resources use efficiency (Subrahmanyam, 2003). Therefore the decline in total factor productivity in crop economy is a constraint for taking advantage of the new trade arrangements under W.T.O.

On the other hand, imports of agricultural commodities may increase under W.T.O agreement depressing the domestic prices and causing damage to farming in the state. For instance the imports of large quantities of palm oil since 1996, depressed the groundnut prices. As such, the imports need to be regulated through appropriately bound tariffs.

However the state has an advantage in fishing and aquaculture in north Bihar and horticulture in north eastern and northern regions. The state can gain through the export of these products, through, there do exist certain limitations which will we discussed in the following sections.

RICH HORTICULTURE:

Bihar has an advantage for the development of horticultural crops due to its varied agro-climatic conditions. There has been acceleration in the rate of growth of area under horticulture during the 90s, it grew at rate more than 5 per cent per annum. The area under mangoes, Litchi and Banana also recorded quite high rates of growth. The state rank very high in area and production of fruits in the country.

There is much untapped potential in the yield of horticultural crop, since the yield on farmers' plots are found to be much less than those observed in the experimental stations

(Parthasarathy, 2000) A number of constraints have also been operating in the marketing of fruits and vegetables, such as, lack of coverage under regulated markets, lack of cold storage facilities and inadequate processing facilities. The New economic policies and the W.T.O. agreements open a vast arena for global marketing of agri-goods and agro-processed products. Export potential of these products could be realized only if adequate infrastructure especially, the one related to post harvest treatment of product, is developed. Agro-processing, by and large has not developed to the derived extent. This is a major constraint operating in the horticultural sector in the state.

Promoting horticulture, for export, through crop shifts has an adverse effect on the poor people. As the horticulture crops are less labour intensive, it may cause decline in employment and erosion of wages of the landless agricultural labourers. A shift to horticultural crops may also cause decline in food grain production and increase in further marked dependence and food grain production and increase in further marked dependence and food insecurity. In order to protect the poor from these effects, there is a need for better targeting of pubic distribution system.

ALLIED ECONOMY:

The need of the hour is to increase the incomes of the farmers. Given the small size of holding, it cannot be achieved merely through increase in crop yield and production. What is required is gainful employment in the activities allied to agriculture such as dairying, popultry, piggery sheep farming, fish culture, bee culture, sericulture, mushroom culture, etc., Bihar has an advantage in the sector of animal husbandry and dairying, fisheries and forestry. Development.

ANIMAL HUSBANDRY AND DAIRYING:

As observed in the earlier chapters, in the total livestock, the major component is bovines and they play a very important role in the resource poor agricultural economies. Their size and composition is conditional by the changes in the crop economy. In Bihar, there has been a continuous decline in the work animals and increase in the milch animals while the total stock of bovines remained more or less the same. Therefore the problem of increase in the bovines and the consequent increase in the pressure on grazing lands and environmental degradation due to soil erosion is not serious one in the state.

The decline in the work animals indicates the substitution of mechanical power for animal power in agriculture. It is taking place at a fast rate in the agriculturally progressive region i.e., south and middle Bihar and it is indeed a desirable trend. But in northern Bihar regions the dependence on animal power in agriculture is more even in the present times. Studies show that there is an under utilization of anima power in these regions due to the indivisibility of bullock unit and low work efficiency of the animals. For carrying out agricultural operations a unit of two animals is required and even marginal and small farmers maintain a unit, through they do not have sufficient work to engage the animals through out the work season. This may be due to lack of proper hire markets. The studies also show that the low work efficiency of the animals is due to under feeding and poor management.

The increasing on the number of milch animals and a shift in favour of buffaloes indicate the increase in dairying activities on the State. After 1970, the milk production in the state increased at a rate of about 10 per cent per annum, which is a remarkable achievement. But still, the average yields are relatively low in the state. Studies indicate that this is due to limitations in technology adoption, under feeding and poor management. Through there are shifts from local cow to local buffalo and from local buffalo to graded buffalo; shifts are rarely taking place from local cow and crossbred cow. In fact a shift from local cow to crossbred cow has a greater impact on milk production than any other shift i.e., from local cow to local buffalo or graded buffalo and from local buffalo. Although many programmes were implemented in the state to improve the quality of the animals through cross breeding programmes were implemented in the state to improve the quality of the animals through cross breeding programme, the success rate was observed to be very low. Thus the main constraints operating in the bovine economy in the state are improper adoption of technology, under feeding and poor management.

A large part of the milk produced in the state is processed through co-operative and consumed locally in the fluid form. Milk is also converted in to products like khova, curd, ghee, buttermilk, paneer, etc. and sold in the domestic market. There is a potential in the state to tap the global markets and gain from WTO, through quality improvement and product diversification. This requires adoption of an improved technology like the one product diversification. This requires adoption of an improved technology like the one adopted by AMUL, for converting milk into various products, through SUDHA is doing commendable job.

The small ruminants (sheep and goat), constritute the second largest component in the live stock. Their number grew at a faster rate in the state in 90s. Their meat and wool as main products and skin as by-product have good demand in both the domestic and international market. But the productive efficiency of these ruminates is very low in the state and efforts made in R & D for upgradation of this stock are very limited. The declining size of grazing lands stand as a constraint for their development. Since mostly the weaker sections rear these ruminates, sheep rearing and goat rearing are important schemes in the rural development programmes.

UNORGANIZED FISHERIES:

But constraint operating in the development of fisheries sector is the marketing. In fish marketing middleman's role is very high and price spread is larger than that of any other crop products or live infrastructure is very poor.

In addition to the marketing problems there are some constraint that the development of fisheries is experiencing. These are: 1) The inappropriate use of technology and the consequent problem of the occurrence of disease to fish and prawn and 2) Ground water pollution. Inland fish culture also has an adverse effect on small and marginal farmers and agricultural labourers as fish and prawn culture are less labour intensive that very few small marginal farmers can afford.

LOST FORESTRY:

Forests role in the economy in terms of maintaining ecological balance provision of timber, firewood, fodder and minor forest product need not be emphasized. In the state with Jharkhand the forest area constitute only about 22 per cent of the geographical area, which is very much less than what is suggested by the ecologists (33%) for maintaining ecological stability. But NRSA estimates basing on satellite imageries show that only about 18 per cent of the geographical area has forest cover. The rate of increase in the forest area over the last 50 years is very marginal. Studies indicate that it is

Uncontrolled grazing and construction of river valley project and roads. It appears that forest development programmes implemented in the state is not very effective especially in the social forestry programme. Forests are the major source of livelihood for many tribals. Dwindling of the forests reduce the production of NTFP's and affect adversely, the livelihood of the tribals, apart from causing ecological imbalances. Forests in the state need to be protected and development in the interest of the poor who are dependent on them and in the larger interest of maintaining ecological stability and protecting environment.

SWOT ANALYSIS:

The SWOT analysis pointed out that the strengths, weakness, opportunities and threats for agricultural development in the state are following.

STRENGTHS

- Endowed with good stockes of unexploited natural resources, abundant sunshine, varied agro-climatic conditions and different type of soil conducive for growing a variety of crops.
- Have very knowledge and enterprising farmers.

- Has comparative advantage in the export of horticultural, animal and fish products.
- Have ideal conditions for large-scale commercial production, storage and marketing of quality seeds and plant material.
- Has the second largest coastline in the country location centrally with easy access to all parts within and outside the country.

WEAKNESS

- Has long Himalayan terrain very often subjected to food and drainage problems.
- Only less than 40 per cent of the gross cropped area is covered by assured irrigation and the rest is rain fed.
- Large number of small holdings.
- Literacy levels of the farming community are low.
- Inadequate infrastructure facilities.
- Majorities of the farmer are resource poor.
- Precarious power supply.

OPPORTUNITIES

- Location of several National Institutes, International Institute Agriculture University and several public and private.
- Location of one of the Farm Machinery Training and Testing Institutes.

THREATS

- Erratic distribution of rainfall.
- Frequent occurrence of droughts and floods.

REFERENCE

V.S.Vyas (2000-01), "Agriculture: The Second Round of Economic References, *The Indian Economic Journal,* Vol. 48, Jan-March, No.-3.

Economic Survey (2003-04), GOI, New Delhi.

Hand Book of Statistics, Bihar (from 1960-2001).

Bihar Ankro Mein, Bihar Ek Jhalak, Directorate of Statistics & Evaluation, GOB, (1960-1996).

Various issue of Bihar Through Figures: I bid.

Singh, RKP (2004) Agricultural Development of Bihar: Problems and Prospect, Agricultural Situation in India, New Delhi.

AERC(2001), Report of 'Flow of Credit to small and Marginal Farmers in Bihar, Agro-Economic Research Centre, T.M.B. University Bihar.

AERC(2002), Impact of minimum support prices on agricultural Economy in Bihar Agro-Economic Research Centre, T.M.B. University Bihar.

Subrahmanyam S. & Satya Sekhar. P. (2003)' Agricultural Growth: Pattern and Prospects Economic and Political Weekly, March 22-29.

11

THE ECONOMICS OF HEALTH CARE AND HUMAN RIGHTS IN INDIA

*J. Cyril Kanmony**

INTRODUCTION

Development today involves both economic development, which includes national income and per capita income and human development, which covers health indices, infant mortality rate, nutritional standards, life expectancy and literacy. The health of a nation is the sum total of the health of its citizens. The survival of any human society is inextricably related with the health of its population. Since ancient times human beings and societies have tried to formulate rules and protocols that would enhance chances of sustained good health (Yadavendu, 2003). Health is considered as a fundamental human right indispensable for the exercise of other human rights (Mohd. Yousuf Bhat, 2005). The right to health is recognised by numerous international and regional institutions. It is recognised by the Universal Declaration of Human Rights, 1948, the International Covenant on Economic Social and Cultural Rights, 1966, the International Convention on the Elimination of All Forms of Discrimination against Women, 1979 and the International Convention on the Rights of the Child, 1989 and other regional human rights instruments like European Social Charter, 1961 and the African Charter of Human Rights and People's Rights, 1985.

* P. G. and Research Centre, Department of Economics, Scott Christian College, Nagercoil-629003.

The Universal Declaration of Human Rights in Article 25(1) says "everyone has the right to a standard of living adequate for the health and well-being of himself and of his family including food, clothing, housing, medical care and necessary social services ......". The ILO Convention, 1969 also adopted article 25 (1) which says "governments shall ensure that adequate health services are made available to the people concerned or shall provide them with resources to allow them to design and deliver such services under their own responsibility and control, so that they may enjoy the highest attainable standard of physical and mental health". India is signatory to almost all the international instruments. India promised Health For All (HFA) in 2000 by signing the Alma Ata Declaration, 1978 in the WHO and UNICEF sponsored international conference on primary health.

Hence, this paper tries to find out what happened to the people especially the rural people of the Indian subcontinent regarding health care services. In this paper, only secondary data are made use of to substantiate every point.

REVIEW OF RELATED STUDIES

It is necessary to review the relevant a few studies to understand the important concepts related to health care system functioning in India.

Abhijit Banerjee et. al (2004) point out that the quality of public health service is extremely poor and it has an adverse influence on the people's health. But, the private health providers, who account for the bulk of health care provisions in rural Rajasthan are unqualified.

Gargai Parsai (2004) is of the view that in India especially in States like Madhya Pradesh and Jharkand in most of PHCs and CHCs, there is lack of doctors and in Sub-centres there is lack of buildings.

Aarti Dhar (2005) says that the main problem faced by rural people is the lack of doctors and medical providers in health centres. So the Accredited Social Health Activists must create awareness on health and mobilise the community towards health planning.

R.C. Mishra (2003) points out that in less developed countries less investment is made on health care service and research and only a small percentage (10%) of investment is allotted to research on diseases which affected majority people (90%).

Santhosh Rajagopal (2004) complains that public health sector is completely neglected. The buildings meant for health centres are not properly planned to house a health care institution. Personnel were well trained and experienced but less motivated and corruption is endemic. The primary health centres focus only on family planning and immunization and other urgent issues like epidemic control.

Jean Dreze (2004) tells that as a ratio of GDP public expenditure on health in India is the lowest among countries and this neglecting tendency gets intensified in the period of liberalisaton. This view is upheld by Sharma, 2004, R.C. Mishra, 2003, Abusalam Shariff et.al, 2004 and P.R. Panchmuki, 2004.

Jacob John (2004) brings to light that unless much importance is given to public health by central and state governments, the people of India will face a series of health problems. To ensure better health, the involvement of people through Panchayat Raj Institutions should be ensured.

K.R. Nayar (2004) asserts that the primary health care is utterly neglected and it leads to a worsening epidemiological profile in the country. We require a cost effective intervention, and such rational distribution of medical and financial resources.

Mohamed Imranullah (2005) explains that staff shortage at government hospitals comes severe hardship to patients who throng them from far off places.

Rupa Chinai and Rahul Goswami (2005) tell that there has been a misplaced emphasis on maintenance and strengthening of private health care services at the expense of broadening and deepening of a public health care system.

S. Irudaya Rajan and K.S. James (2004) explain that the proportion of underweight children under three years of age is very high. More than one third of the women in urban areas who maintain high standard of living are either over weight or obese, while the same proportion of women in low income households is underweight in rural areas.

Sharda Jain observes (2005) that India has the highest number of cases of anaemia in the world. In developed countries hardly there is adolescent anaemia, while in India as per the district level health survey by the Ministry of Health and Family Welfare and Department of Women and Child Development 95 per cent of adolescent girls and 92 per cent of children less than three years are anaemic.

Deepa Sankar and Vinish Kathuria (2005) point out that not all states with better health indicators have efficient health systems and investment in the health sector alone will not result in better health indicators. Hence, the need of the hour is efficient management of the investment.

Ajit Madhu (2004) illustrates that the use of IT has a significant role in the development and diffusion of advanced treatment and in the reduction of cost and inefficiency improvement. But there is still a need for more research on how IT affects costs of diagnosis and treatment with regard to specific diseases.

Arunkumar Bhatt (2005) narrates that more than 50 per cent of injections administered are unsafe especially in the developing countries. He points out the WHO Report in support of his view. The WHO estimates that of the 1,200 to 1,600 crore injections administered in the world every year at least 50 per cent are unsafe. In India it is nearly 63 per cent.

It is very clear that the health care system especially public-health care in India requires a complete overhaul and a serious consideration from the governments to enjoy better health indicators.

EMPIRICAL EVIDENCE

In India, it is a generally accepted fact that, today, though science and technology contributed much to the field of medicine, health care services did not reach rural areas which are mainly covered by primary health care systems. A health system has two components, namely public health care and private health care. In the public health care system the responsibility is on the government to protect the public from both communicable and non-communicable diseases. Public health is the art and science of preventing disease, promoting health and prolonging quality life (Jacob John, 2004). Public health is one of the most important areas of human development but sadly it is one of the most neglected in modern India (Santhosh Rajagopal, 2004). The health services in rural areas are very meagre and even the meagre health services, which are available do not percolate to remote corners of the rural areas. And so, the utilisation of public health facilities by the people of India was only 20 per cent in 2002 (Sanjay Sangole, 2003). Though, 73 per cent of the population lived in villages only 25 percent of medical services reached them. For instance, nearly 72 per cent of the patients with eye ailments were being treated by private hospitals (Anbumani, 2004).

It is also observed that the health care facilities available in rural areas are not enough to meet the growing demand of the people (Murugaia, 2004). Although most states have managed to provide one Primary Health Centre (PHC) for 30,000 persons and a sub-centre for 5,000, the poor are forced to resort to private health care because these facilities are not fully functional. According to the CEHAT (Centre For Health and Allied Themes), only 38 per cent of all PHCs have all the critical staff and eight out of 10 PHCs have no essential obstetric care drug kit, only 34 per cent have facilities for delivery and postnatal care, 3 per cent have safe abortion facilities, eight out of 10 have no paediatrician and seven out of 10 have no obstetrician. The ratio of hospital beds to population is 15 times lower in rural areas than in urban areas. The ratio of doctors to population is 6 times lower in rural areas than urban areas. The government spending on health in rural areas is seven times lower than in urban areas (Kalpana Sharma, 2004). Jean Dreze (2004) pointed out that only 69 per cent of PHCs had only one bed, 20 per cent had a telephone and 12 per cent had been maintained regularly.

Lack of facilities in primary health centres are due to the neglect of health care services by the government. The compound growth of per capita health expenditure for the period from 1985-86 to 1998-99 turned to be – 1.63 per cent.

The total expenditure on health was 4.9 per cent of GDP (including private expenditures) against 13 per cent in the USA in 2000. The per capita expenditure on health was $3 in India (K.N. Prasad, 2003) against 4499 in the USA (The World Bank Health Report, 2002). The government expenditure on public health infrastructure has declined especially after globalisation. As a percentage of GDP, the public health investment has declined from 1.3 per cent in 1990 to 0.9 per cent in 1998 (Jean Dreze, 2004). It is lower than the average of 2.8 per cent of GDP spent by some less developed countries. (Rupachand and Rahul Goswani, 2005). Even in Sri Lanka, it is 3 per cent of its GDP. The absolute expenditure on medical, public health and family welfare shows an increase from year to year. But the relative share does not show much improvement. Table-1 shows the central government's share of expenditure on medical, public health and family welfare to total expenditure and the absolute expenditure at constant price from 1991-92 to 1999-2000.

Table 1
Total Expenditure (Centre & State) and Central Government's Share of Expenditure on Medical, Public Health and Family Welfare to Total Expenditure from 1991-92 to 1999-2000

Year	*Total expenditure at constant prices (in Rs. Million)*		*Centre's Share*	
	Medical, Public Health & Family Welfare	*Medical & Public Health*	*Medical, Public Health & Family Welfare*	*Medical & Public Health*
1991-92	20.7	-	6560	-
1992-93	23.0	-	6884	-
1993-94	23.5	-	7263	-
1994-95	23.9	-	7470	-
1995-96	21.9	12.4	8007	5655
1996-97	21.5	15.1	8505	6487
1997-98	22.6	17.1	8648	6775
1998-99	23.0	18.2	9390	7601
1999-00	23.8	19.4	11842	9672

Source: Abusalam Shariff et. al, 2004, pp. 768 & 771.

Though the share of central government's expenditure does not show much improvement there is no heavy fall in the share. But the share of state governments has declined from 16.3 per cent in 1991-92 to 14.9 in 1999-2000. The details are given in the following Table:

Table 2
State Government's Expenditure on Medical, Public Health and Family Welfare Cumulative Expenditure during 1991-92 – 1999-2000

Year	*Percentage Share*	*Cumulative Expenditure (Revenue +Capital)at constant prices(in Rs.million)*
1991-92	16.3	6,346
1992-93	16.1	6,574
1993-94	17.0	6,950
1994-95	16.4	7,048
1995-96	15.7	7,434
1996-97	15.5	8,082
1997-98	15.7	8,229
1998-99	15.4	8,897
1999-2000	14.9	10,382

Source: Abusalam Shariff, 2003, pp. 771 & 774

It is clear from the above Table that the state's expenditure has increased from Rs.6, 346 million in 1991-92 to Rs.10, 382 million in 1999-2000. But in relative term it has declined from 16.3 per cent in 1991-92 to 14.9 in 1999-2000. The relative plan expenditure, shows a decline, is illustrated in the Table-3.

Table 3
Growth of Plan Investment outlay on Health in Different Plan Periods (Centre, State & Union Territories)

Plan	*Health Expenditure (in Rs. Million)*
I	652 (3.3)
II	1409 (3.0)
III	2259 (2.6)
Annual	1402 (2.1)
IV	3355 (2.1)
V	7608 (1.9)
1979-80	2231 (1.8)
VI	20252 (1.8)
VII	36941 (1.7)
1990-92	19656 (1.6)
VIII	75759 (1.7)

Source: Govt. of India Records (Planning Commission & Central Bureau of Health and Intelligence in P.R. Panchamuki; 2004 P841.

It is obvious from Table 3 that the Plan Expenditure has declined from 3.3 per cent in the First five-year plan to 1.7 per cent in the Eighth five year plan.

The next negative factor in health care is the high absenteeism of health providers in primary health cer.tres. The rate of absence among health workers range between 35 and 58 percent in different Indian states (Jean Dreze, 2004 and Abhijit Banarjee et al, 2004).

The next most important factor working in the opposite direction is inefficiency in the working of health care system in different states. Given below are the relative efficiency scores of different states.

Table 4
Relative Efficiency Scores and Ranks Across States

State	*IMR/1000 Population*	*Potential IMR (FE)*	*Efficiency Ranks (FE)*
Andra Pradesh	76	58	7
Assam	86	67	5
Bihar	81	66	4
Gujarat	80	60	13
Haryana	76	54	14
Himachal Pradesh	73	56	8
Karnataka	79	56	12
Kerala	19	19	1
Maharashtra	64	53	3
Madhya Pradesh	112	81	15
Orissa	115	79	16
Punjab	59	45	9
Rajasthan	93	72	6
Tamil Nadu	68	51	10
Uttar Pradesh	104	78	11
West Bengal	67	55	2

Source: Deepa Sankar and Vinish Kathuria, 2004 P/431

The IMR Column Table 4 indicates the average IMR for the years 1986-97. The potential IMR column shows the Infant Mortality Rates the states could have achieved if they had performed efficiently. The efficiency rank indicates the ranks scored by different states in terms of the efficiency scores. The relative efficiency is a measure of actual to the potential. Kerala stands first in efficiency but Orissa scores the last among the 16 states for which efficiency ranks are calculated. Though Kerala stands at the top, it is not comparable with developed countries and even some of developing countries.

While the public health is in such a bad shape, in cities the growth of five star health care centres with facilities that match some of the best in the world is very high. Importance is given to maintenance and strengthening of private health care service at the expense of the public health care system. So private health care is expanding rapidly and nearly 82 per cent of all health spending in India is private (Rupa chinai & Rahul Goswami 2005), against 50 per cent in Latin America ,25 per cent in Europe and only 15 per cent in Britain. (Sanjay Sangole, 2003). While public health facilities are highly in efficient, private services are virtually un-regularised, leaving patients at the mercy of unscrupulous practitioners. Fraud, over medication, unnecessary surgery and enormous fees are the bread and butter of the private health sector (Jean Dreze, 2004). Many private practitioners are prescribing irrationally and giving patients a long list of totally unnecessary and expensive medicines for fairly routine problems. In India 300 to 600 crore injections are administered every year. Of these 63 per cent are unsafe and about 1/3 carry the risk of transmitting blood-borne viruses including HIV. The unsafe rate is 68.7 per cent in government health centres against only 59.9 per cent in private clinics and hospitals. Area wise analysis indicates that it is 65.9 per cent in rural areas while the rate is 59.9 per cent in urban areas. It is also observed that a large numbers of injections are unnecessary, administered for common ailments such as fever, cough and diarrhoea (Arunkumar Bhatt, 2005). Many drugs, out of 70,000 branded drugs are sold at 200 to 500 per cent profit margin (Kalpana Sharma, 2004). In Mumbai, about 65 per cent of deliveries performed in the private sector end up with a caesarean, compared with only 9 per cent in the public sector. (Jean Dreze, 2004). The prescribing habits of some doctors are highly influenced by drug companies (R. Prasad, 2005). Hence due to these reasons patients are either forced to borrow money to pay the medical expenses in the private hospitals or kept away from treatment. It is reported that really 21 per cent of Indians no longer seek medical treatment of any kind for their diseases against only 11 per cent a decade age (Sainath, 2005) though India is having over 17,000 hospitals, 24,000 primary health centres and 1,40,000 sub-centres as well as over five and a half lakh registered allopathic doctors, (Kalpana Sharma 2004).

Because of all these, India is not in a position to fulfill the Health For All (HFA) promise given in the Alma Ata conference even in 2005 and is considered the worst in health care in the world as shown by health indicators. The targets of India for the year 2000 are given in the following table.

Table 5
Health Targets for 2000

Indicators	Targets
Infant Mortality Rate (rude Death Rate)Mortality Rate (1-5) Life ExpectancyCrude Birth RateAnnual Growth Rate of populatiorTotal Fertility Rate	Below 60 person live births. 9 per thousand.10 per thousand 64 years 21 per cent 1.2 per cent 2.3 Children per woman.

Source: Directorate of Health Services, New Delhi in Suresh Malhotra et. al 2005.

India did not achieve almost all the targets in the stipulated period. Only the life expectancy has increased from 60.43 years in 1991-92 to 65 in 2001-02 and the rural urban gap in life expectancy has also declined from 10.9 years to 6.9 years between these two periods. But, the life expectancy is as high as 86.91 in Kerala against only 53.4 years in Madhya Pradesh and 54.3 in Orissa (NHDR, 2001). Further, eighteen lakh children die every year before they reach five years. Only 42 per cent Indian children are fully immunised (Kalpana Sharma,2005). According to the second National Health Survey nearly 47 per cent of children under 3 years of age are under weight in India. In Maharastra alone 2,675 children died of malnutrition within four months, from April to July 2005. According to data from the National Nutritional Monitaring Bureau 5.4 per cent children or 8 lakhs in Maharastra suffer from acute malnutrition whole another 21.2 per cent or 32 lakhs suffer from moderate malnutrition (Kalpana Sharma, 2005).

The maternal mortality ratio has increased from 424 deaths per 1,00,000 live births in 1991-92 to 540 in 1997-98 (Kalpana, 2004). Another survey reported that 30 per cent of all the children under the age of 3 had fever, another 20 per cent had diarrhoea and another 20 had symptoms of acute respiratory infection (Jean Dreze, 2004). The IMR rate is very high in almost all states especially in rural areas. The IMR in rural areas was 87 per thousand against only 53 in urban areas. It is also observed that the IMR is low only in highly literate states like Kerala (Pratima Trivedi, 2000). As reported by the HDR, 2005, in India the annual rate of decline in child mortality fell from 2.9 per cent in the 1980s to 2.3 per cent since 1990. But, in Bangladesh, child and infant mortality has been falling at more than 5 per cent. (Kalpana Sharma, 2005). In India 1,30,000 women die each year during childbirth and pregnancy related complications. Further, India is the second largest country, with the maximum number of AIDS patients (5.1 million) next to South Africa (5.3 million). The average annual number of deaths due to AIDS is 3 million. Communicable diseases continue to spread at a frightening rate (Ajay Mahal, 2004). India has the largest number tuberculosis cases in the world with one to two million new cases being reported every year. India has also the highest number of anaemia cases in the world and the resultant economic loss is more than $ 2 billion due to loss of man hours and productivity. Anaemia is responsible for 40 per cent of the total maternal deaths a year in India. Malaria continues to strike over 2.6 million people each year with over 20,000 people dying from it (Kalpana Sharma, 2004). India is the capital of diabetics, with an estimated 33 million diabetic patients (Vijay Vishwanathan, 2005). Due to vitamin-A deficiency, in India 45 million people suffer from problems of sight out of the total of 180 million in the world.

Pollution now-a-days is a menace as it is the cause for many diseases which affect not only children and the old but also the young and the energetic and all animals and plants. A recent WHO report points out that over 20,00,000 children worldwide suffer from environmental hazards.

Air Pollution occurs when Suspended Particulate Matter (SPM) and noxious gases occur in the air. Air pollution may be either outdoor or indoor. Impact of indoor pollution, which is caused by burning of dung, firewood and crop residues for cooking especially in rural areas is more serious than outdoor pollution. Nearly 50 per cent of the world population continues to cook food with solid fuels. This includes more than 75 per cent of people in India, China and nearby countries. The indoor use of solid fuel causes 35.7 per cent of lower respiratory infections, 22 per cent of chronic obstructive pulmonary diseases and 1.5 per cent of trachea, bronchitis and lung cancer. It is also associated with tuberculosis, cataracts and asthma (The World Health Report – 2002). A UN report says that of the 3 million people who die every year because of illness caused by air pollution, the majority are women and children who contract respiratory illness (D. Aravahi 2003). The Tata Energy Institute estimates that of the 3 million premature deaths due to air pollution, 2.8 million are due to indoor pollution (The Hindu 21.6.2003). But, the World Bank report says that an estimated 5,00,000 women and children die due to indoor pollution in India each year (Aruna Chandaraju, 2004).

Outdoor air pollution is generally an urban and industrial phenomenon. In urban areas the main source of air pollution is vehicular pollution or emission from automobiles. This contributes to nearly 60 per cent of the total air pollution (R.N. Bhatacharya 2001). The Centre for Science and Environment has found that between 1975 and 1995 the country's GDP grew about 2.5 times against the total amount of pollutants emitted by vehicles which grew by 8 times (Anil Agarwal-2000). In the industrial sector thermal power plants top the list of industries contributing to air pollution due to very high emission of discharge of smoke and ash. A thermal power plant designed to generate 500 mw of electricity per day typically discharges about 2000 tonnes of fly ash per day. There are 66 thermal power stations in India and together they generate one-lakh tones of fly ash per day apart from the smoke coming from them. The WHO estimates that the maximum quantum of SPM in the air that does not affect human health is 90 micrograms per cubic meter. As per the World Bank Study, 1998, ambient air pollution levels exceeding WHO standards in 26 major cities account for 40,350 premature deaths, 19,85,00,000 hospital admissions or sickness requiring medical treatment and 1210 million cases of minor sickness annually (Mohd. Yousuf Bhat, 2005).

In Kolkatta the SPM in the air is at least 410 micrograms per cubic meter, which is the highest in the country. It is also estimated that a non-smoker in Kolkatta suffers the same consequences as those of smoking 20 cigarettes a day simply by breathing the air (R.N. Bhattacharya, 2001).

In India the Central Pollution Control Board estimated the air quality for 70 cities in1997. of the 70 cities, Shillong is the only town where the air quality in terms of SPM is clean round the year. Of the remaining 69 cities 29 cities (42 per cent) are critically polluted (more than 1.5 times the standard) 22 cities (32 per cent) have high pollution levels (between 1-15 times) and 18 cities, including Chennai (26 per cent) have moderate pollution levels (between 0.5 and 1 times) (Anil Agarwal, 2000).Air pollution causes bronchitis and lung cancer, in about 5 per cent of the total population and cardio respiratory mortality due to its hazards is 3 per cent globally. In absolute terms it causes 0.8 million deaths and 7.9 million (DALYS Disability Adjusted Life Years) (The Health Report-2002).

In most Indian cities the average noise level in residential, commercial and even sensitive areas exceed the standard prescribed by the Central Pollution Control Board during the day as well as night. CPCB prescribes 75 decibels in daytime and 60 decibels at night in the industrial area, 65 decibels in day time 55 decibels at night in the commercial areas, 55 decibels in day time and 45 decibels at night in residential and silent areas (The Hindu, 7.8.2003).

The health hazards of noise are not uniform. The most immediate and acute one is deafness. Nearly 16 per cent of hearing loss is attributable to occupational noise exposure. Noise has its ill effects on other bodily functions such as the cardiovascular system. A recent report indicates that blood is also thickened by excessive noise. Changes in breathing amplitude have also been reported due to impulsive noise. Eosinophilia, hyperglycaemia, hypokalaemia, hypoglycaemia are also caused by change in blood and other body fluids due to noise. It also affects the nervous system and psychomotor performance. Pupillary Dilation impairment of night vision and decrease in the rate of colour perception are some of the effects. Noise also causes irritation and affects sleep and work performance. Moreover, as noise causes headaches and irritability, work, which needs a high degree of skill considerably affected (N. Manivasakam 1999).

Water is not fit for consumption if it has biological organisms like guinea worms, tape worms and cholera and typhoid creating bacteria and excess chemicals such as fluoride, iron, arsenic and nitrate (Joseph J. Seneca & Michael K. Tausig 1984). It is estimated that a global annual discharge of 440 cubic kilometers of sewage and a considerable amount of 510^8 tonnes of diverse agricultural, industrial and other wastes get into the biosphere (John Kurian 1983). The Ministry of Environment and Forests points out that in India alone the municipal sewage accounts for 22900 million litres a day (mld). It is almost twice as much as the 13,000 million litres a day of industrial wastewater. But the treatment capacity available in domestic wastewater is only for 6,000 mld and for industrial wastewater 8,000 mld (N. Gopal Raj, 2003).

W. Carty (1991) points out that 90 to 95 per cent of all domestic sewage and 75 per cent of industrial wastes are discharged into surface water without any treatment. The solid waste generated has increased from 6 million tones in 1947 to 60 million tonnes in 2002 (Aarti Dhar, 2003). The quantum of hazardous wastes generated by 13,011 industrial units spreading over 373 districts of the country was estimated at 4.4 million tones and the three states, namely Maharashtra, Gujarat and Tamil Nadu account for over 63 per cent of the total hazardous wastes generated in the country (N. Gopal Raj, 2003). The National Environmental Engineering and Research Institute reveals that almost 70 per cent of our surface water is polluted (Helen Matzgar and Marcus Moench, 1994).

Excessive application of nitrogenous fertilizers has resulted in nitrate pollution of ground water. In 1991, India's fertilizer use per hectare was 60 per cent higher than in the U.S.A. India uses over 11 million tones of nitrogenous fertilizers annually.

All these affect over 100 million households, which depend on ground water for theii daily needs

(N. Gopal Raj,2003). Some other areas have been affected by the presence of excess chemicals such as nitrate, arsenic, nickel, chromium and chrome based dyes. In India 37,000 villages are facing the problem of excessive fluoride in water and 26,300 villages are having water with excessive salinity (Vasavada, 1996). About a million people are drinking arsenic contaminated water and approximately 2 lakh people have arsenical skin manifestation (Dipankar Chakraborthi 1996).

Polluted water is one of the reasons for many diseases and deaths in the world. The majority of infectious and parasitic diseases in developing countries are related to water. According to an estimate made by James Winpenny (1994) each year nearly 3 million deaths occur among children under the age of five due to diarrhea, about 200 million are affected with diarrhea diseases, nearly 300 million people with round worm infections, about 150 millions with schistosomiasis, and about 300 million with trachoma which makes nearly 1.5 million people blind. In India water-borne diseases alone cause deaths of nearly 1.5 children annually (S.K. Pant, 1996). While K. Balachandra Krup (1994) explains that 100 million children below 5 years of age may have 300 million incidence of diarrhea per annum, of which 30 million may develop into dehydration, 3 million require hospitalisation and many face death. Nearly 2,500 children die every day for want of adequate safe drinking water. Guinea worm disease, which is a debilitating illness, affects 40 to 50 lakhs people each year in African and Asian countries. A.S. Anand, the NHRC Chairman (2004) says that 66 million people in 19 states and 196 districts were affected by flourisis.

From all these, it is very clear that the government is unable to provide enough health care facilities to its citizens especially to the rural people and thereby violating human rights.

POLICY IMPLICATIONS

Death and sickness of persons especially in the productive age certainly reduce economic growth. Hence, suitable steps should be taken to control the occurrence of all types of diseases. The following points are worthwhile to consider for reaching a steady growth in the availability of health care facilities.

(i) The expenditure on primary health must be enhanced and as share of GDP it must be raised at least to 3 per cent.

(ii) The recently started Rural Health Mission must be introduced vigorously in all states in such a manner that in every nook and corner in the rural areas there must be enough health care facilities.

(iii) The efficiency of the working of the Primary Health Centres must be improved and steps should be taken to provide all medical facilities required by the rural people in all PHCs.

(iv) By strictly following the existing rules, absenteeism of health providers should be checked and if necessary new laws may be introduced.

(v) The consumption of iodised salt must be encouraged and it will help in reducing certain type of diseases in India especially in rural India.

(vi) Expenditure on IT, which provides new technology in the world of health care should be encouraged. Research in the IT-based health care systems must be given importance and IT-based health care should also be available to all rural areas.

(vii) An integrated approach to medical care should be considered. Steps should be taken to integrate modern and traditional medicines. Regulation of private hospitals in all channels must be strictly enforced. Otherwise, it is certain that by following those who charge excessively all private practitioners may exploit the poor rural patients. Priority must also be given to child health care. Every student must be made aware of health care by introducing public health a part of the school syllabus.

Hence, by taking all possible steps, governments must try to provide health care facilities required by the rural masses, who actually feed the whole country. Certainly the health of the people will make the country economically healthier.

REFERENCE

Banerjee, Abhijit; Deaton, Anugus; Duflo, Esther, "Health Care Delivery in Rural Rajasthan". Economic and Political Weekly, XXXIX, 9 February, 28,2004.

Bhat, Mohd. Yousuf *Environment and Human Rights,* Reference press, New Delhi, 2005.

Chinai, Rup and Goswami, Rahul " Are we ready for medical tourism? The Hindu Magazine, 17.03.2005.

Dev, Arjun; Indira and Das, Gupta *Human Rights.* A Source Book (Ed) NCERT, New Delhi, 1996.

Dreze, Jean "Health Checkup", The Hindu, 12/03/2004.

John, T. Jacob, Public Health Priorities, The Hindu. 25.05.2004.

Kanmony, J. Cyril "Drinking Water in Kanyakumari" Economic and Political Weekly, XXXVIII, 35 30, August 2003.

Mahmud, Simeen, "Health and Population Making Progress Under Poverty" Economic and Political Weekly, XXXIX, 36 Sept 4, 2004.

Malhotra, Suresh; Upadhayay Pratibha; Gupta, Meena; Srivastava, Ranjana; Pandey Saroj. *Human Rights, Emerging Issues* (Ed) Kilaso Books, New Delhi, 2005.

Mathur, Aject "Designs of Health Care Trade: Role of Information Technology" Economic and Political Weekly, XXXIX,20, May 15,2004.

National Human Development Report – 2001, Planning Commission, Govt. of India, Oxford, New Delhi, 2002.

Nayar, K.R. Rural Health – Absence of Mission or Vision? Economic and Political Weekly, XXXIX, 45, 6/11/2004.

Parsai Gargi, "Health Mission Needs Fine-Tuning, say states, The Hindu, 3-11-2004.

Prasad, R "Health Comes with a dash of iodised salt" The Hindu, 30/6/2005.

Rajagopal, Santhosh "A Vision for the Public Health Sector, The Hindu, 30/03/2004.

Rajan.S, Irudhaya, James, K.S. "Second National Family Health Survey, Emerging Issues" Economic and Political Weekly, XXXIX, 7, 14.02.2004.

Sangole Sanjay Primary Health Care in Disadvantaged Urban Areas, Employment News 5-11, April, 2003.

Sankar, Deep & Kathuria, Vinish "Health System Performance in Rural India". Economic and Political Weekly, XXXIX, 13,27/3/2004.

Sharma, Kalpana, "How Healthy is Our System? The Hindu, 08/6/2004.

The World Health Report, 2002, WHO, AITBS, New Delhi – 2003.

Trivedi, Pratima, Economic Programme and Social Justice (Ed) Deep & Deep, New Delhi, 2000.

Yadavendu, Vijayakumar, "Changing Perspectives in Public Health, From Population to an Individual" Economic and Political Weekly, XXXVIII, 49 December 6, 2003.

Winpenny James, *Managing Water as an Economic Resources*, Routledge, New York, 1994.

Bhattacharya Robindra, N., *Environmental Economics: An Indian Perspective* Oxford, New Delhi, 2001.

Manivasakam, N., *Environmental Pollution* National Book Trust India, New Delhi, 1999.

Helen Mitzgar and Marcus Moench, " Ground Water Availability for Drinking in Gujarat, Quantity, Quality and Health", Economic and Political Weekly, XXIX, 13, January 26,1994.

Gopalraj, N., "How Safe is our Water". *The Hindu* 24.8.2003. P.14

The Hindu 3.5.2004, 23.08.2004, 05.09.2004, 01.10.2004, 05.10.2004, 06.10.2004, 24.10.2004, 19.01.2004, 20.06.2005, 02.07.2005, 07.07.2005, 17.07.2005 & 19.07.05.

12

GLOBILISATION AND PROTECTION OF WORKER INTEREST

*Shivani Raswan Pathania**

INTRODUCTION

When the countries in South Asia became independent, the State had to set up enterprises because investments were not coming in the desired magnitude from Private Sector. Also , the economic planning model being followed by the countries was for state ownership in the core sector. Some of them permitted enterprises in the core sector, and the same were governed by price control. This was the approach followed by India, Pakistan and Sri Lanka, and later, by Bangladesh. Also, when Private Sector enterprises became sick or were financially not viable, the state stepped in and nationalised them. Today, the approach of the state is not to nationalise the loss making units, but ask the entrepreneur to continue running it. The state will have to recognise that a company cannot continue to live in comatose situation.

The process of liberalisation in South Asia occured largely in the late 1980s and early 1990s(although Sri Lanka started the process in late 1970s).The timing may differ and the degree of liberalisation reforms may vary in each country of South Asia. However, some of the common features of liberalisation are:

- Attracting foreign direct investment.

* 187, Defence Colony, Jalandhar.

- Removing/reducing bureaucratic/government interference on Industrial Licensing.
- Reduction of import tariffs (Guidelines of WTO).
- Realistic exchange rate.
- Privatising state enterprises (in some cases by selling the equity and in certain other cases, giving autonomous structure).
- Higher benefits in export processing and free trade zones.
- Restructuring the manning norms by downsizing/rightsizing through Voluntary Retirement Schemes.

While the South Asian countries have undertaken structural adjustment through economic reforms, they have not been able to bring forward any meaningful amendments to the existing labour laws because of the unemployment levels, the vocal power of the unions and the large vote bank of the working class. There are legal provisions regulating employment and job security and also inflexible wages in relation to productivity and market conditions prevalent in each of these countries.

POLITICAL AFFILIATION AND MULTIPLICITY OF TRADE UNIONS

The trade union movement in South Asia is a part of the freedom movement of each country. We have very few guilds/trade based trade unions, but we have trade unions with political party affiliation. Every political party in power, tries to form unions having affiliation to their political party. Quite often, the office of the Commissioner of Labour (ie. Government Labour Department) is pressurised by the ruling party to help the ruling party's trade unions. This has led to multiplicity of trade unions in the South Asian countries. There are pockets where we find guild/trade based unions like in Plantation sector, Jute and Cement Industry, Banking Institutions. Also, the laws in each of the South Asian Countries have permitted outsiders to be office bearers of the Trade Union. This was probably valid when the trade union movement was at its infancy. However, in today's environment, the law has not changed because the external trade union leaders are politically connected and want to continue in the trade union movement. One problem that we find in South Asia is multiplicity of unions and this does create problems in identification of the recognised bargaining agent.

Managements of Private Sector enterprises in South Asia are interested in successful running their business, hence most of them do not have any political affiliation like the trade unions. They are mostly politically neutral and deal with policy matters on Industrial relations (including amendments to labour laws) through their Employer Organisations

The management of Public Sector enterprises in South Asia are controlled by the Government and quite often, the ruling party in power is interested in having a say in the management of these enterprises. In a large number of cases the public sector enterprises presently are loss making units and the Government has a real dilemma of deciding, how to restructure these enterprises. Each country in South Asia is re-looking at the Government's role in running state enterprises and has set up disinvestment corporations. There are also cases of politicians who have set up enterprises or the owners of existing business enter politics. In this case, the managements of these enterprises are either close to the ruling party or close to the opposition party. Margaret Thatcher has said "The business of government is not to run business" and hence she denationalised industries. Also, the Japanese Government privatised the Japanese National Railway(JNR).Malaysia privatised its telecom business.In India, Modern Bakeries (a publilc sector enterprise) was sold very recently to Hindustan Lever Ltd. The approach on privatisation is to improve efficiency of the enterprise. If that is not achieved, then privatisation will not help.

INDUSTRIAL RELATIONS-ENTERPRISE LEVEL

Indsutrial Relations at an enterprise level is dependent upon the following factors:

1. History of Trade Union Management relation in the organisation and their past style in resolving the IR issues Communication methodology: (a)among management personnel (b) among union members

(c) between management and union (d) between management and workers.

2. Political party affiliation of the trade union / unions.
3. Relationship of Management to the Political Party in power.
4. Profile and attitude of the key management personnel in resolving disputes.

The approach on solving the Industrial Relations issues in organisations differs from organisations to organisations and country to country.However, there are three distinct levels at which Industrial Relations Issues are bargained and settled which involves Unions, Managements and Governments.

1. National level
2. Industry/Region level
3. Company/Enterprise level

There is a greater tendency today to have enterprise level settlements. This is because even in a particular industry, the level of technology, manning norm, market share and profitability of individual enterprises differ.

RELATIONS APPROACHES OF TRADE UNIONS AND MANAGEMENTS IN INDUSTRIAL

Experience has indicated that Trade Union leaders in South Asia adopt four distinct types of approach to reach settlements on Industrial Relations issues.

Approach	*Symptoms*
(1) Frontal	(a) Settle only on their termsb) Keep a total control on the work forcec) Claim that they are championing the cause of labour movement in the çountry
(2) Guerrilla	(a) File cases under existing labour law and use it for bargaining/delay tactics.
(3) Flanking	(a) Initially oppose, but later agree
(4) Bypass	(a) Understand the problems and find a solution to problems

Also, there are managements in South Asia that adopt four distinct approach to settle disputes.

Approach	*Symptoms*
(1) Lion	(a) Settle only on their termsb) Decision making is a management prerogative.
(2) Fox	(a) Blow Hot, Blow Coldb) Firm on Issuesc) Tolerant on people
(3) Teddy Bear	(a) Deal conflict (b) Find solution maintaining relationships
(4) Turtle	(a) Avoid conflictb) Honourable surrender

Each country has its own labour laws. However, in South Asia, there has been too much of regulatory type of labour legislation. Excessive labour legislation and third party involvement of the Government builds a litigatory culture in enterprises. Since litigation is high and the courts are not adequately equipped with the requisite number of Judges, there is a delay in the judgements. Once a delay culture builds in, both labour and management really use the ligitation process to buy time, because with passage of time, they try to settle dispute rather than having social dialogue. In a study conducted in 1999 by NIKKEIREN International Corporation Center along with employer Organisations of South Asia, it was found that excess labour legislation has led to shift in employment from the formal sector to the informal sector or contract labour.

PRINCIPLED NEGOTIATIONS

There is a concept of Principled Negotiations which was built up by two Harvard Professors (ie. Roger Fisher and Ury).They have documented this approach in their book Getting to Yes.The concepts in Principled Negotiations are:

- Separate the people from the problem
- Understand the interest and perceptions on either side so as to invent options for mutual gains

- Avoid commencing negotiations by starting from position
- Use objective criteria to understand each others point of view
- In the event a negotiation fails, also be ready in advance with the Best Alternative to Negotiated Agreement (BATNA).

There applied the concept of "Principled Negotiations" on a Two Union Situation in resolving the dispute on modification of the Dearness Allowance Scheme" that was applicable to the workers of Sandoz (India) Ltd. The concept was applied by evolving alternatives in every meeting and finally a mutually acceptable solution was evolved and the Long Term Settlement concluded. Data Compilation, information sharing, evolving alternatives, setting deadlines are some of the other inputs needed to evolve a win-win situation.

It is true that sometimes coercion / pressure tactics / power play are used by either side in industrial relations to achieve their desired objective. The example of power in negotiations are:

- Expert power (scientist ,legal luminary)
- Ritual or symbolic power(religious person , ie. priest)
- Coercive power (threat of prosecution, confiscation, penalty, closure used by bureaucracy / concerned government official
- Positional power (Hierarchy i.e rank of the individual in the Management or the Union).

APPROACHES OF IMPLEMENTING CHANGE IN ENTERPRISES

Enterprises in South Asia have to become competitve and implement change In order to achieve this, there are three distinct approaches adopted by managements and all three approaches have succeeded depending upon the situation, size of the enterprise, type of ownership, attitude of the management and workmen towards change, relationship of the management with the union and workers. Here, the approach is that contract of employment is not negotiable. As per the contract of employment, vocational and locational mobility is for the management to decide. Also, the norms of work and output performance expected by the management are within an 8 hours shift and since employees are time rated, they have to perform and achieve the output for the wages received.Also, behaviour and conduct of employees are governed by their contract of employment and service conditions, any negative behaviour needs correction and hence the management enforces Acts.

Collective Bargaining: Here, the approach is that the enterprise is dealing with employees and they, as an organized group, are represented through their trade union/unions. Historical performance has built up an existing manning and output norm with certain work methods and procedures.Improvement in output will result in gains to the enterprise and employees expect to get a share in that gain.This would, then, result in collective bargaining between management and the trade union .

Faciliation: Here, the approach is that all the employees (bargainable and non-bargainable) work for achieving the Vision/Mission of the organisation and any change/ innovation on performance improvement is a key factor for an organisation. The attitude of all employees is to perform better compared to earlier performance and for this, the enterprise facilitates the employees by empowering them to perform. In order to achieve this, extensive training is provided, good housekeeping is maintained, employees are encouraged to self inspection, team work is the order of the day, efforts on technology and product upgradation are regular and continuous. Employees are rewarded for their performance, apart from their normal monthly remuneration. In today's competitive world, survival of enterprises in South Asia is getting threatened and enterprises are being driven by market machanisms. For survival, enterprises will have to effect changes in their product portfolio, manufacturing/work practices They will also have to build strategic alliances. All these changes can be successfully implemented, if we have a positive industrial relations climate.

CONCLUSIONS

For success in Industrial Relations, it is essential to take decisions which are not only firm and fair, but they must be taken in time. Delays in decision making quite often leads to grievances not being solved in time. The greviance over a period of time becomes a collective dispute and then leads to an industrial relations problem. Line managers in enterprises need to be trained to tackle routine grievances and industrial relations issues. It is only the collective bargaining agreement which should go to the top management for being discussed.

REFERENCES AND NOTES

Bare Act-The Persons with Disabilities (Equal Opportunities, Protection of Rights and Full Participation Act, 1995), Alankar Publications.

Bare Act-The Factories Act, 1948, Kalyani Publications.

Bare Act- The Industrial Disputes Act, 1947, Kalyani Publications.

Bare Act- The Workmen's Compensation Act, 1923,Kalyani Publications.

Bare Act- The Payment Of Wages Act, 1936, Kalyani Publications.

R. M. Pal, Protection of Human Rights - A Critique, Indian Social Institute, 1999.

Parduman Singh, Friedrich Ebert Stiftung, 1996.

R.C Chawla, K.C Sareen, V.K. Sareen, Commercial and labour Laws, Kalyani Publishers, New Delhi,1999.

Social Security Systems in Developing Countries - Asia, Africa and South America, 2000.

Rationalisation of Labour Laws to Meet WTO Challenges at http://www.googles.com.

Worker's Rights at http://www.rediffmail.com.

13

GROWTH OF MICROFINANCE AND BANK LINKAGE– SPECIAL REFERENCE THROUGH CHINNA PAPPA SHGS OF SUBRAMANIYAPURAM PANCHAYAT IN THOOTHUKUDI DISTRICT.

*G. Saravanan**

INTRODUCTION

NABARD, in partnership with various stake holders, is facilitating SHG – Bank linkage programmes to enable the banking system to transcend the confies of supply driven savings and credit delivery mechanisms, which was neither cost effective for the banks, nor user friendly for the poor. The programme provides a savings and credit history for the number of SHG, auguring well at the time of taking loans from the banks. Simultaneously, it helped the banks in reducing their transaction as well risk cost in delivering small loans. On account of these positive features, the SHG – Bank linkage programme caught the imagination of not only the financial institutions, but governmental and non governmental agencies also joined hands with NABARD in its efforts. Today unique initiative in India of more than 3.024 partners has blossomed into the fasted growing and the most cost effective microfinance initiative in the world, enabling 16.7 million poor families to access sustainable financial services from the banking system,

* Dept. of Rural Industries and Management, Gandhigram Rural Institute, Gandhigram, Dindigul– 624 302.

through a network of over one million Self Help Groups. An SHG has an average size of about 15 people from a homogenous class. They come together for addressing their common problems. They are encouraged to make voluntary thrift on a regular basis. They are encouraged to make voluntary thrift on regular basis. They use this pooled resource to make small interest bearing loans to their members. The process helps them imbibes the essentials of financial intermediates including prioritizations of needs, setting terms and conditions and accounts keeping. This gradually builds financial discipline in all of them. They also learn to handle resources of a size that is much beyond individual capacities of any of them. The SHG members begin to appreciate that resources are limited are have a cost. Once the groups show this mature financial behaviour, banks are encouraged to make loans to the SHGs in certain multiples of the accumulated savings of the SHGs. The bank loans are given without any collateral and at market interest rates. The group continues to decide the terms of loans to their own members. Since the group own accumulated savings are part and parcel of the aggregate loans made by the groups to their members, per pressure ensures timely repayments.

OBJECTIVES OF THE STUDY

The specific objectives of study are

1. To study the growth of micro finance and bank-linkage of Chinna pappa SHGs of Subramaniyapuram Panchayat in Thoothukudi District.
2. To discuss on agency wise members of SHGs financed in India and common problems and suggestion to SHGs.

METHODOLOGY – DESIGN OF THE STUDY

The present study is based on primary as well as secondary data. The secondary data was collected from NABARD. Secondary data collected from NABARD Report, Mumbai and Records of SHGs in Subramaniyapuram Panchayat as well as primary data collected through interview of the respondent. SHGs respondents were purposive random sample selected for the interview. The study period pertains to secondary data collected for the years 1999-2000 to 2003-04. The primary data collected from the respondent of SHGs of Subramaniyapuram Panchayat in Thoothukudi District during one month of December 2005.

DATA ANALYSIS

Data Analysis is to be based on secondary data of SHG – Bank linkage cumulative progress during period of years 1999 – 2000 to 2003 – 04 as follow as below Table.

Shgs Bank Linkage Cumulative Progress

Years	*Shgs Financed*	*Bank Loan (Rs. Million)*
1992-1999	32,995	571
1999-2000	114,775	1,930
2000-2001	263,825	4,809
2001-2002	461,478	10,263
2002-2003	717,360	20,487
2003-2004	1,079,091	39,042

Source: Nabard Report

As may be seen from Table 1, the bank loans aggregating Rs.1,930 million were disbursed to 114,775 SHGs and increased from Rs.39,042 to 1,079,091 SHGs in 1999-2000 to 2003-04 years respectively. Various impact evaluation studies revealed that the on time repayment loan is around 95 percent.

MICRO-FINANCE OF CHINNA PAPPA SHGS OF SUBRAMANIYAPURAM PANCHAYAT IN THOOTHUKUDI DISTRICT.

Chinna Pappa SHGs was started in 2001 and their group savings increased per members Rs.50 in 2001, Rs.80 in 2002, and Rs.100 in 2003. They are conducting meeting among the groups every month of first week. This groups mobilized to micro finance through savings upto 2004, Rs.62,900. Primary data was collected on age, occupation, education, savings, meetings, training and awareness of Anti-poverty programmes as given in the below table.

Occupation wise of Respondents

Occupation	*Yes*	*No*	*Total*
Small farmer	7 (4.12)	-	7 (4.12)
Farmer Labour	4 (23.5)	-	4 (23.5)
Daily Wagers	6 (35.3)	-	6 (35.3)
Total	17 (100)	-	17 (100)

Source: Computed from primary data

From table 2, it is identified that 42.2 percent of the respondents are small farmers, 23.5 percent of the respondents are Farmer labours and 35.3 percent of the respondents are Daily wagers. Occupation is the vital role determination of poverty level.

Community of Respondent by Agewise

		Age		*Total*
Community	*15-30 yrs.*	*31-45 yrs.*	*Above 46 yrs.*	
BC	1 (5.9)	7 (41.2)	2 (11.7)	10 (58.8)
SC	2 (11.7)	3 (17.6)	2 (11.7)	7 (41.2)
Others	-	-	-	-
Total	3 (17.6)	10 (58.8)	4 (23.2)	17 (100)

Sources: Computed from primary data

From table 3, it is identified that under the age group of 31-45 years, 41.2% of the respondents belongs to Backward community (BC) and 17.6% of the respondents belongs to Scheduled Caste (SC). In the remaining age group of respondents, 17.6% belongs to Backward community and 23.4% belongs to Scheduled caste.

Education of Respondents by Age wise

		Age		*Total*
Education	*15-30 yrs.*	*31-45 yrs.*	*Above 46 yrs.*	
Illiterate	1 (5.9)	-	5 (29.4)	6 (35.3)
Primary School	2 (11.7)	4 (23.4)	-	6 (35.3)
Middle School	1 (5.9)	2 (11.7)	-	3 (17.6)
High School	-	1 (5.9)	-	1 (5.9)
Higher Secondary	-	1 (5.9)	-	1 (5.9)
Total	4 (23.5)	8 (47.1)	5 (29.4)	17 (100)

Source: computed from primary data

Table 4 reveals that under the age group of 31-45 years, 23.4% of the respondents belongs to Primary School, 11.7% belongs to Middle School, 5.9% belongs to High School and Higher Secondary School respectively and there is no illiterate. Under the age group of 15-30 years, 5.9% are illiterates, 11.7% belongs to Primary School, 5.9% belongs to Middle School, and no respondents from High School and Higher Secondary School. 29.4% of the respondents are illiterates under age group above 46 years.

Marital Status of Respondent by Age wise

Marital Status	*Age* 15-30 yrs.	31-45 yrs.	Above 46 yrs.	*Total*
Married	2 (11.8)	10 (58.8)	3 (17.70)	15 (88.3)
Widow	-	-	2 (11.7)	2 (11.7)
Unmarried	-	-	-	-
Total	2 (11.8)	10 (58.8)	5 (29.4)	17 (100)

Source: computed from primary data

Table 5 gives the details of marital status of respondents. Out of 88.3%, 58.8% are married respondents under the age group of 31-45 years, 17.7% above 46 years and 11.8% between the age group of 15-30 years. Only 11.7% of the respondents are widows who come under the age group above 46.

Micro Finance of Respondent by saving upto December 2005

Years	*Savings (Rs. In 1000)*	*Average*
2001-2002	20860	1227.06
2002-2003	30600	1800
2003-2004	50075	2945.59
2004-2005	62900	3700

Source: computed from primary data

Table 6 shows that savings per member increased from 1227.06 to 3700 in 2001-02 to 2004-05 respectively.

Loan provided by Bank to Respondents

Loan Repayment	*Credit*	*Average*	*Subsidy*	*Average*	
Revolving Fund	25,000	1470.59	10,000	588	100%
Direct loan	1,20,000	6000	-	-	Nil
Economic Activities	-	-	-	-	-

Source: computed from primary data

Table 7 reveals that out of Rs.2,500/-, Rs.1470.59 is provided to each member from the Revolving fund and got subsidy of Rs.588/- per member. Rs.1,20,000 will be provided as direct loan to all respondents after they repaid revolving fund loan. After completing 4 years, the respondents did not get Economic Activities loan.

Meeting and Training of Respondents

Source	*Attended*	*Not Attended*	*Total*
Meeting	4 (23.5)	13 (76.5)	17 (100)
Training	-	17 (100)	17 (100)

Source: computed from primary data

Table 8 identified that 23.5% of the respondents attended meetings, 76.5% did not attend meetings, and 100% of the respondents did not attend training programmes. There are lack of interest for attending meetings and trainings by respondents and lack of support from higher government authorities.

Awareness about Anti-poverty programmes of Respondents

Programmes	*Yes*	*No*	*Total*
RDP	-	17	17
RYSEM	-	17	17
DWCRA	-	17	17
MWS	-	17	17
RPWP	-	17	17
NRY	-	17	17
JRY	-	17	17
SGSY	2 (11.86)	15 (88.2)	17 (100)

Source: computed from primary data

Table 9 shows that 0% of the respondents didn't get awareness about Anti poverty programmes like R.D.P., RYSEM, WCRA, MWS, RPWP, NRY and JRY. 11.86% respondents got awareness about SGSY. Each and every respondent should know about Anti-poverty and implementation programmes.

PROBLEMS

There is lack of support from NGO, DRDA Mahalisthittam Panchayat President, B.D.O. and Bank Manager for skill upgradation of SHGs. Meetings and trainings were not given properly to these SHGs.

After completion of four years, this group hesitates to start business because their village didn't have adequate facilities like Road, Sanitation, Health and Transport. Due to these reasons many people migrated from rural to urban places. There is lack of awareness about Anti-poverty programmes to SHG Respondents. These groups didn't come forward from poverty through group savings. Group savings is useful to SHG respondents for urgent needs. Till now these groups didn't get economic assistance from DRDA.

SUGGESTIONS

Government funds and loans should be reached properly to SHGs through implementation programme.

Politicians and Government Authorities should take necessary steps to improve SHG activities, qualities, meetings and trainings and expenses in proper way.

Trainings should be based on traditional work of SHGs and motivated through innovative technology.

CONCLUSION

Growth of village as its progress nation, said according to Mahatma Gandhi. In this concept, Rural Development is plays important role to improve SHGs status, and mobilized micro finance through various forms and training programmes have to be conducted at village level to skill upgradation of SHGs.

REFERENCES

NABARD Report, Page No.1-5.

P.M.Mathew, Institute of Small Enterprise and Development, 1998, Page No.63-70.

Bhagwati Prasad, "Co-operative Sector Changes Required to Operationally Internalize Concept of Micro-finance". The Co-operator, Vol. 43, No.8, February 2006, Page No. 353-359.

14

TELECOME SECTOR: IT'S PERFORMANCE SUBSEQUENT TO GLOBALISATION IN INDIA

*J. G. Valan Arasu**

INTRODUCTION

Telecommunication is considered as one of the prime support services needed for rapid growth and modernization of various sectors of the economy. Telecommunication is now universally recognized as one of the prime movers of modern day economy because of the enormous growth of Information Technology and its significant impact on the rest of the economy. Telecommunication, Information and Globalization are restructuring every aspect of business and society. Hence its vital importance is experienced even within a developing economy like India. In this transformation, it is acknowledged that the telecom professionals are the key players, who will play a crucial role as leaders in the changing dynamics of global communications, internetworking, the Internet, e-commerce, mobile and wireless communications strategy.

Modern age is the age of convergence and telecommunication is a key to modern economic development. Telecommunication when linked with computer becomes Information Technology. This is the most dominating technology of today as it influences the entire spectrum of the economy. It covers all aspects of business, technology,

* Vice Principal, St.Aloysius College, Jabalpur.

manufacturing and other services. Telecommunication is significant for economic development since 1% increase in telephone density leads to a 3% increase in the GDP.[1] Today the networks and companies will no longer be categorized on the basis of only voice, data or video services that they provide rather they have to become info-communication companies providing a bundle of services. The benchmark for any country's communication infrastructure therefore is not tele-density any more, but it is the fancy term "per capita bandwidth".

HISTORY OF TELE-COMMUNICATION:

Indian telecommunication liberalization in the 1990s is driven by a state which has seen its capacity and consensus fritter away over the last fifty years under the weight of pluralistic pressures and personalistic rule. Indian reform efforts in the 1980s were halting and nepotistic even though demands from businesses, urban residential users and government administrations continued to grow. India was pushed toward further telecommunications liberalization after a severe fiscal and balance of payments crisis in 1991 which weakened the status quo constituencies in the country and empowered many businesses to demand liberalization. India, like many other countries of the world, has adopted a gradual approach to telecom sector reform through selective privatization and managed competition in different segments of the telecom market. To begin with, India introduced private competition in value-added services in 1992 followed by opening up of cellular and basic services for local area to private competition.

The National Telecom Policy (NTP) of 1994 introduced the concept of 'telecommunication for all and telecommunication within the reach of all'. It visualized universal service covering all villages. Under this, out of nearly 6-lakh villages in the country, about 4-lakh villages have been provided with telecom services. The objective of the government is to see that before the end of year 2020 all villages are provided with basic telecom services. The 1994 policy announced ambitious goals for provision of telephones (20 million lines by 2000) and also liberalized the telecommunications sector further. The state owned monopoly, the Department of Telecommunications (DoT), could not be corporatized or privatized due to resistance from its 480,000 workers. But DoT will now compete with a private player in each of the 21 regions (known as Telecom Circles) announced by the state.

Further in 1995 a multimedia center with video conferencing facility was opened followed by providing commercial ISDN services. As a result of liberalization followed by competition in the telecom services, the Government of India set up the Telecom Regulatory Authority of India (TRAI) in 1997. This was restructured in 2000 and an appellate authority Telecom Disputes and Settlement Appellate Tribunal (TDSAT) was set up. The biggest landmark in 2001 was when MTNL invested U.S. $300 million for operations in Bangladesh and Nepal and this year government control over the country's telecommunication sector undergoes a change with the privatization of Videsh Sanchar Nigam Ltd. (VSNL) and competition was also introduced in national long distance (NLD) and international long distance (ILD) telephony at the start of the current decade[2]. The privatization of India's largest telephone service provider is being considered a milestone in telecommunication history of India.

Two state-owned public sector incumbents with a large existing subscriber base dominate the fixed line service. As on December 31, 2004, the two Public Sector Enterprises (PSEs), BSNL and MTNL[3] owned 44878118 Direct Exchange Lines (DELs) against 4301891 privately owned DELs. These two PSEs were allowed belated entry into the cellular segment in the beginning of the present decade. Consequently, their cellular subscriber base is tiny compared to the private operators. Out of 48013971 mobile phones subscribers in the country in December 2004, they had only 9671810 subscribers where as private operators owned 38342161 mobile phone subscribers[4]. The share of private sector in the numbering of telephone sector is of 45.91 % where as the share of public sector is 54%.

ECONOMIC GROWTH AND TELECOMMUNICATION:

It is observed that there is a direct correlation between the availability of, and access to telecom infrastructure and a country's economic growth. According to International Telecom Union (ITU), the number of main telephone lines has nearly doubled from 546 million in 1991 to 1.12 billion by the end of 2002. Mobile subscribers have grown phenomenally from 91 million in 1995 to 1.5 billion in 2002. In 1991 the total telephone penetration was 49% in developed countries, 3.3% in emerging nations and 0.3% in least developed countries. The above fact indicates a strong association between economic development and growth in telecommunication sector.

Over and above this there are plenty of evidences[5] to show that telecom is improving life chances across the strata of the society. A whole range of information based industry and applications have created new sources of employment and earning with welfare enhancement for the wealthy and the poor. "As a meta-technology, ICT has caused rapid innovations to occur in all other areas of material sciences. As a fabric of information society, ICT has improved access in the fields of education, healthcare, governance and all aspects of business services. It has also improved the abilities of the poor to manage risks and mitigate vulnerabilities through provision of timely information."[6] Manas Bhattacharya thus has rightly said, "Telecommunications have emerged as a springboard of ICT applications with economy-wide ramifications."[7]

According to former World Bank economist Surjit Bhalla, every 10 million new phone lines add 0.5 percent to annual economic output. This means increased productivity because these inexpensive phones prove to be a lifeline for business. "Some Indian business owners hope that if allowing private investment improves telecom services, the government will then surely be encouraged to do the same for India's limping power networks, road system, and airports, all of which are languishing under state control."[8]

PERFORMANCE OF TELECOMMUNICATION

At the World Ranking:

The act of opening up of the market unleashed dynamism that was so far latent in the sector. This is evident from a number of performance indicators. First and fore most in terms of overall size of main telephone lines in operation, India ranked 14th in the world in 1995. The rank improved to 7th position in 2001.This is mainly due to opening of market in the telecommunication sector.

Table 1

Number of main telephone lines in operation in terms of the World

Country	*No. of lines in 1995 ('000)*	*Ranks (1995)*	*No. of lines in 2001('000)*	*Ranks (2001)*
USA	159,735.2	1	190,000.0	1
Japan	62,292.0	2	76,000.0	3
Germany	42,000.0	3	52,280.0	4
China	40,705.7	4	179,034.0	2
France	32,400	5	34,032.9	9
UK	29,411.4	6	34,710.0	8
Russia	25,018.9	7	35,700.0	6
Italy	24,845.0	8	27,303.0	10
Korea, Rep.	18,600.0	9	22,724.7	11
Canada	17,567.0	10	20,319.3	12
Brazil	13,263.0	12	37,430.8	5
India	11,978.0	14	34,732.1	7

Source: World Telecommunication Development Report 2002, ITU[9]

Physical Growth of Telecom Network

Greater and impressive growth has been realized in the telecom sector after 1995. In the year 1997 there were only 148.80 lakh of telephone connection. However the total telephone connections as on December 2004 increased to 928.92 lakh which comprises 342.67 lakh fixed lines and 480.14 lakh cellular connections provided by the public and private sectors. The table below shows the significant increase of telephone connection from the 1997 to December 2004. In the year 2003-04, 219.20 lakh telephones were added. This is equal to the total number of phones installed as of 1999. During this period the actual growth has been nearly 6.24 fold when we compare this year with 1997.

Table: 2
Growth of Telecom Network (PSUs & Private)

Year	Private Network	Total Network	PSUs Network
1997	145.40	3.40	148.80
1998	178.00	8.80	186.80
1999	215.90	12.20	228.10
2000	265.10	20.20	285.30
2001	324.40	38.50	362.90
2002	381.58	68.06	449.64
2003	431.71	114.46	546.17
2004(March)	464.83	300.56	765.40
2004(December)	502.48	426.44	928.92

Source: Annual Report 2004-2005[10]

Figure 1

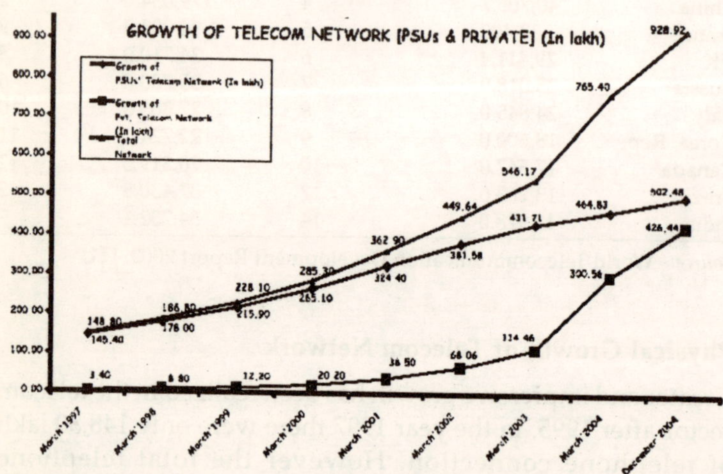

The structure and composition of telecom growth has too undergone a substantial change in terms of mobile versus fixed phones and public versus private participation. In 1999, both mobile phones and private sector separately accounted for 5 per cent of total number of phones. In December 2004 mobile phones accounted for 57 of total phones. The share of mobile has thus surpassed the share of the landlines and this trend is likely to continue. During the same period the private sector accounted for 46 per cent of total phones. Of the 163.52 lakh additional phones provided during 2004-05, major share i.e. 125 lakh (about 77%) was provided by the private sector. So in the years to come the private sector will continue to play a significant role in the growth of telecom sector.

Mobile Telephone

Cellular mobile telephony industry was opened to the private sector in 1992. Initially there were great hopes for profits in this business. Several new entrants have done well, and the industry is quickly moving to maturity, due to the attractive technology, marketing and competitiveness. Stiffer competition, new entrants, and developments in the limited-mobility industry have given opportunities as well as posed challenges, generating appropriate responses. India's cellular phone industry is considered as one of the world's fastest growing markets.

The cellular phone industry market is affected by the hesitation of investors in new technologies and networks. The industry is also affected by the changing telecom and tariff policies on profit prospects and competition. For example: COAI (Cellular Operators Association of India) was recently disappointed at the revision in monthly rentals for WLL (Wireless in local loop) and limited mobility services announced by TRAI. It stated that "by abstaining from prescribing either a ceiling or a floor in the monthly rental, consumer interest has been sidelined, as there is no protection to the consumer from an upward revision in tariffs at any time."[11]

In spite of all this the cellular subscribers are growing at an exponential rate. They are expected to touch 2.15 crore by March 2005. This means mobile phones would account for 20.5% of total telephone connections in India. The mobile telephone services today cover 480.14 lakh subscribers in 900 cities and 60,000 villages. In addition to this, there are 4,67,131 WLL subscribers in urban areas and 9,98,976 subscribers in rural areas. Today the share of mobile phones has surpassed the share of landlines and this trend is likely to continue. The figure below highlights shift towards wireless telephony.

Figure 2

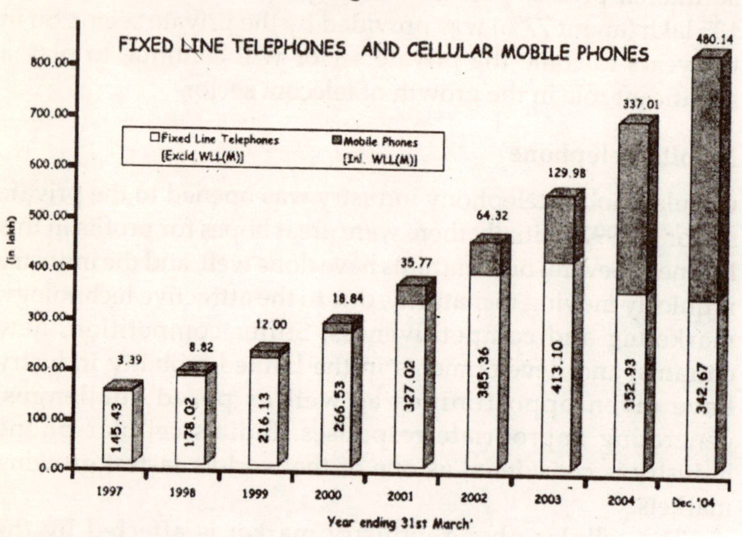

With falling tariff rates for cellular phones, there has been a greater increase in the number of cellular subscribers. From a mere 3.39 lakh cellular subscribers on March 1997, the number increased to 480.14 lakh as on December 2004. The share of the cellular subscribers in the total telephone subscribers has gone up from 10 per cent in March 2001 to 21 per cent at the end of December 2002. It shows that there has been rapid expansion in the telecom sector, accompanied by a significant technological change. As a result there has been continuous shift in the technology of access from fixed line to mobile telephony. In 2003-04 fixed lines grew by less than 3 per cent, while mobile telephones grew by 159.2 per cent.

BSNL and MTNL alone have provided 90.56 lakh GSM and 6.51 lakh WLL mobile phones as on December 31, 2004. This shows that there is a positive shift in the use of mobile telephony. This is confirmed from the rising share of mobile phones. Use of mobiles has increased from 44% as on March 31, 2004 to 52%

as on December 2004. Mobile phones once considered a luxury is no more considered to be a luxurious item at all. In recent years due to low price telephony affluent households and middle income groups are going from one fixed line per family to one mobile phone per person.

Table 3
Growth of Mobile Phones

Mobile including WLL (in Million) *Year*	*PSUs* *% of PSUs*		*Pvt.*	*Total*
2001-02	0.26	6.28	6.54	3.98
2002-03	2.64	10.35	12.99	20.32
2003-04	5.99	27.70	33.69	17.21
2004-05(October)	8.99	35.50	44.49	20.21

Source: Economic Survey 2004-2005[12]

The above table reveals that in the mobile phone segment the private sector is having 79.79 per cent of the market share and the PSUs is having only 20.21 per cent of the market share

Figure 3
Market there of Mobile Subscribers*

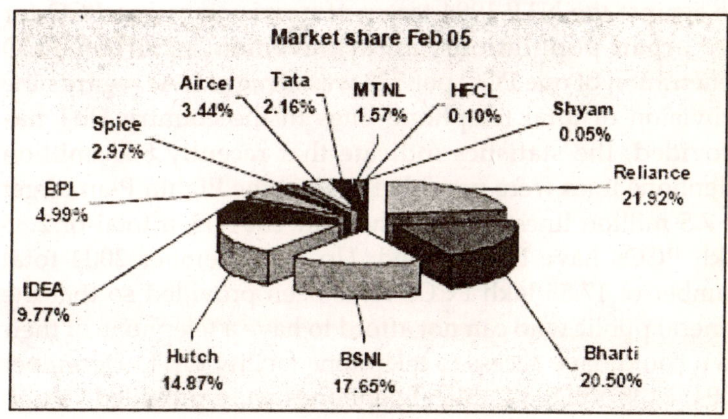

Source: COAI, AUTSPI, Statistics Ex. MTNL (WLL)[13]

in mobile telephony. However it is interesting to note that the PSUs actual gain in the market share in mobile telephony increased from 3.98 per cent in 2001-02 to 20.21 per cent towards the end of October 2004. But as on February 2005 its market share decreased to 19.22 per cent. Among the private sector it is Reliance that has the highest market share with 21.92 per cent and Bharti has the second highest with 20.50 per cent of market share of mobile telephony as on February 2005.

The private sector is also providing other value added telecom services that include paging services, VSAT services for providing data services to closed user groups. Government is issuing licenses for opening up of Global Mobile Personal Communication by Satellite (GMPCS). Recently one of the most notable mergers was that between Birla-Tata-AT&T and BPL Communications to form the country's largest mobile phone company (BPL-Batata) which is now known as "IDEA-Cellular".

PCO's

One of the unique innovations of Indian telecommunications is the public call office spread all over the country for urban population and Village public Telephones (VPTs) for rural population so that people can call any place in India or abroad. As against the NTP 1994 target of provision of one PCO for 500 urban populations, an achievement of urban PCO penetration of one PCO per 522 was achieved. As regards the provision of total telephone lines in the country DoT has provided, the statistics indicate that recently 8.73 million telephone lines were provided against the Eighth Plan target of 7.5 million lines. During the year 2004-05, a total of 2.35 lakh PCOs have been added. Up to November 2004 total number of 17.55 lakh PCOs have been provided so that the general public who can not afford to have a telephone of their own could have access to telephone facility. Up to December 2004, 3138 Village Public Telephones were provided. As on December 31, 2004, the total number of villages having VPT is 512820. The telecom density that was hardly 1 at the time of the introduction of the reforms in 1994 has nearly gone up to 3, which though less is remarkable.

Internet

The explosive growth of the Internet is another important development during this decade. Government recognized the significance of Internet, and in 1998 came up with the Internet Service Providers' Policy that threw open the opportunity of providing the backbone services to other private organizations. Total internet connection as on December 2004 is 2368709, and dial up connections increased from 754220 to 913163. CLI Based Account less Internet Service too increased from 363827 to 750869. Number of cities where CLI made operational too increased from 31 to 100.

Net Telephony

Today Voice over IP networks is leading the communications revolution worldwide. As per the recommendations of TRAI recently internet telephony has been legalized in India. As a result "Net telephony has opened new business opportunities for India's ISPs and cyber cafes. India's telecom consumers now simply enter a cyber cafe and can talk over the Net, paying Rs 5 per minute, depending upon the destination. For example, a call to the United States, that uses to cost about Rs 40 per minute, now costs Rs 5 through the Internet. This offers stiff competition to international long distance service providers but at the same time also helps lower charges for long distance communication both for STD and ISD." [14]

According to forecast estimation, India's IP telephony market is expected to grow at a rate of 119% to reach Rs 13,000 core by 2005. But to maintain its competitiveness globally, India must invest in building its telecom infrastructure and increase PC and Internet penetration. Number of Internet subscribers likely to exceed 7.7 million in the years 2004-05. The first batch of internet telephony products hit the retail market with three Internet service providers namely Caltiger, Net4India and IceNet. More and more cyber cafes are mushrooming across the country that has resulted in net access rates falling to Rs 10 per hour.[15]

Internet and PC

India is perceived to have a special comparative advantage in IT and in IT enabled services. However, sustaining this advantage depends critically on high quality telecommunication. Like the per capita income today number of PCs and internet users are considered as indicators of development. Therefore substantial growth of broadband is necessary to meet the needs and development of IT related sectors. Two important indicators of IT penetration in Indian market are Internet use and availability of Personal Computers (PCs). There has been significant expansion in both during the last decade.

Table 4

Growth in Personal Computers and number of Internet users

Year	*Estimated number of Internet users*	*Availability of Personal Computers*
1992	1,000	410,000
1993	2,000	560,000
1994	10,000	800,000
1995	250,000	1,200,000
1996	450,000	1,500,000
1997	700,000	2,000,000
1998	1,400,000	2,700,000
1999	2,800,000	3,300,000
2000	5,00,0000	4,600,000

Source: Yearbook of statistics, 1991-2000, ITU[16]

Despite impressive growth in the number of Internet users and availability of PCs, number of users of Internet is still a negligible fraction in comparison to India's total population. Per capita availability of PC is also comparatively low in relation to many developed nations. As on December 2001 number of personal computers available per 100 persons in USA are 62.25. At the same period world average on number of personal computer available per 100 persons was 8.42. However in India the situation is not encouraging because only 0.58 personal computers are available per 100 persons.

Table 5
PC and Internet – International Comparison
(As on Dec. 2001)

Country	*Internet Users*	*No. of PCs*
per 100 persons	*per 10,000 persons*	
USA	62.25	4995.10
UK	36.62	3995.01
Australia	51.71	3723.05
Brazil	6.29	465.58
Mexico	6.87	362.23
South Africa	6.85	700.58
Egypt	1.55	92.95
Japan	34.87	4547.10
Malaysia	12.61	2394.96
China	1.93	260.00
Pakistan	0.41	34.49
India	0.58	68.16
Asia	3.31	437.49
World	8.42	823.24

Source: World Telecom Development Report 2002.[17]

Internet booths and cyber-cafes have played an important role in expanding and popularizing IT among the masses and promoting domestic market for personal computers. However, their expansion crucially hinges on the growth of telecommunications infrastructure. In India, a spectrum of technologies has been utilized to connect remote villages, which includes Wireless in Local Loop (WLL), wireless cum wired technology developed by C-DOT[18], radio systems, switching systems of different capacities integrated with underground cables, CorDect and medium capacity satellite systems. It is visualized that with the growth of telecom infrastructure, creation of information at the finger tips of society is not so distant a future.

Call Centers

Call Center business in India is experiencing a very favourable atmosphere presently, because the leased line prices have fallen dramatically due to competition. The local loop has improved significantly. Over and above high bandwidth links are also being built. This new environment has created an opportunity for foreign companies to either outsource their call center operations to India-based companies or set up their own call center/ integrated back-office hub in India. This has allowed foreign companies to capitalize on the availability of cheaper labour and better telecommunications.

India has become a favourite destination for outsourcing of back office operations. This has opened the doors for India's highly skilled and educated resource pool. Today graduates as well as undergraduates from all disciplines are acquiring comprehensive training in soft skills, English language and accent neutralization. It is estimated that nearly 1.1million jobs will be created in the IT-enabled services sector in India by 2008. Analysts in India say that the demands for personnel to man these call centers are explosive. Greater development of call centers, and highly skilled educated resource pool became a reality mainly due to the quality and quantity enhancement that has taken place in the telecom sector.

Cyber-cafes and Internet Use

In the initial stage Cyber cafes and internet usage was considered an urban phenomena in India. According to Steward the cyber-cafes appeared on the Indian scene in the mid-1990s, mainly in metropolitan cites like Mumbai, Delhi, Bangalore and Chennai. However cyber-cafes over the years have mushroomed throughout India and today can even be found in small towns and some of the bigger villages mainly due to home use of the Internet which earlier remained out of reach for substantial proportions of the society in India. Cyber-cafes seem to serve a crucial portion of Indian society as access points for the use of computers and the Internet. In general, the cyber-cafe users are young, the average age being 26 years. More than 70 percent of the users are below 30. The biggest group of users are employees (44.9 percent), followed by students (36.8 percent), housewives (6 percent), and the self-employed (5.5 percent); with others (unemployed, retired etc.) being 6.8 percent.[19]

This does not mean that cyber-cafes and internet usage is limited to educated population only rather illiterate people are also using cyber-cafes and internet for various reasons. The general secretary of the Internet Cafe and DTP Owners Association of Kerala, Mujeeb Poolakal, says "Nowadays, compared to the last two years, also illiterate people are coming for their needs. They come to collect information and mostly they want to send emails to other places or other countries. So now illiterate people are starting to come and they ask do you have this or that facility here, do I get this or that information here and so on."[20] This statement shows that illiterate people are recognizing the utility of cyber-cafes and internet. But we have to accept the fact that the use of caber-cafés and internet by illiterate people at present are only to a minimum extent.

Since there is a lack of regulation for registration, and authoritative measurement, the exact number of cyber-cafes in India can be estimated only roughly. In 2001 the Indian Market Research Bureau (IMRB) estimated around 12,000 cyber-cafes in India. Caslon Analytics estimates the number of cyber-cafes for all of India as approximately 50,000 in 2004.[21] These estimates show that cyber-cafes are slowly becoming as access points to the Internet to a large proportion of the Indian population. That is why Amitabh Kumar, Chairman and Managing Director of Videsh Sanchar Nigam Limited visualizes greater growth of internet usage in India and says, "India has an advantage that the size of the market which can potentially go online is extremely large. Our middle class segment can exceed 200 million and take advantage of discounted airfares, online publications, online education as well as business-to-business transactions."[22]

3.2.4. Audio, Video and Digital Technologies:

Convergence of audio, video and digital technologies is another important development in the global telecom scene today. The NTP 1999 declared, "Access to telecommunication is of utmost importance for achievement of the country's social and economic goals and availability of affordable and effective communication for the citizen is the core of the vision and goal of telecom policy". The policy promised that a balance between the provision of universal service to rural areas and the provision of high level services capable of meeting the needs of the country's economy would be provided, aiming to create a modern and efficient telecommunication infrastructure. Convergence of IT, media, telecom, and consumer electronics is planned to propel India into becoming an IT superpower. Another objective of the policy was to convert PCOs wherever justified into public tele-info centers having multimedia capability of ISDN services, remote database access, government and community information system etc.

Software Exports

India has seen remarkable growth of software exports from the country. This was possible because of the high-speed data connectivity of at least 64 kbps. The Software Technology Parks (STPs), introduced in the 1990s have boosted software exports of India from 100 million dollars in 1990 to more than four billion dollars recently. The heart of STPs is the earth station with connectivity to satellites for speedy communication overseas. Today, nearly 75% of the software exports are taking place from the STPs. The policy initiatives taken by the government has created an environment where Indian telecommunication can take a great leap forward.

The Indian IT Industry recorded a compound annual growth rate of more than 42.4 per cent between 1995 and 2000. Software continues to contribute a major portion of the Indian IT industry's revenues. India's exports of computer software beat global recession in 2001-2002 (April-March) to grow by a healthy 31.4 per cent. In absolute terms, software and services exports went up to $7.8 billion in 2001-02 as against $5.9 billion in 2000-01. This represents 13.3 per cent of India's manufacturing exports.

The steady growth in exports of software is due to effects of software giants setting up bases in India to meet their global software requirements. India's exports of electronics hardware grew by 13.6 per cent in 2001-02 to $1.183 million from $1.041 million in 2000-01. The IT manufacturing industry has over 150 major hardware players supported by over 800 ancillary units and small time vendors engaged in sub-assemblies and equipment manufacturing. The combined export of software and services, and electronics hardware registered a growth of 28.7 per cent in 2001-02. In absolute terms, India's overall IT exports grew to $9.04 billion in 2001-02 from $7.0 billion in 2000-01. In 1999-00, more than 185 of the Fortune 500 companies outsourced their software requirements to Indian software houses.

Nirupam Bajpai therefore strongly feels that the government could do more for this industry by allowing new entry of major international players in telecom. These companies could lay down a tremendous fibre optic network in India and increase the bandwidth available for Indian business and put India even closer to the international scene,[23] so that India's world-class engineers and scientists could keep India in the very forefront of this new technology.

THE TREND IN SUPPLY AND DEMAND OF DELS

The number of DELs in operation (i.e., main line in operation) has been taken as supply whereas demand has been computed by adding the number of subscribers in the waiting list to the number of DELs in operation. However, it is required that we keep in mind that the number in the waiting list, in certain cases, is unlikely to reflect potential demand for telecom services in the economy. The actual demand may be much more than what is revealed through waiting list. In the areas where telecom infrastructure is not adequate, demand may not get registered at all and remain suppressed.

The figure below shows an interesting phenomenon. Total demand tends to exceed supply by a margin, which does not get narrowed down as supply expands. Despite the increase in the number of mainlines for every hundred inhabitants, the waiting list for a connection is higher now than at the beginning of the 1990s. More than 2.92 million people are waiting for about 20 percent of the current number of lines. Expressing its view on the unmet effective demand in telecommunication, the 1994 World Development Report on infrastructure for development said that, "Excess demand for infrastructure, coupled with very low rates of compensation to infrastructure staff, breeds corruption in both service and investment decisions. Where connections are late and service is poor, employees often demand side payments from users to install or repair connections especially in telecommunications...."[25] It shows that market for fixed line is supply constrained and demand tends to increase as supply expands. The table 6 also reveals that there is significant growth in supply of DEL in the 90s, with the eventful decade of sectoral reforms and the growth momentum is sustained in the current decade with a positive supply gap.

Table 6
DEL: Supply and Demand (millions)

Year ending March 31	*Direct Exchange Lines(DELs)*	*Waiting List*	*Demand*
1981	2.15	0.45	2.6
1983	2.47	0.66	3.13
1985	2.90	0.84	3.74
1987	3.49	1.12	4.61
1989	4.17	1.42	5.59
1991	5.07	1.96	7.03
1993	6.80	2.85	9.65
1995	9.80	2.15	11.95
1997	14.54	2.89	17.43
1999	21.59	1.98	23.57
2001	32.44	2.92	35.36

Source: Indian Telecommunication Statistics 2002, Ministry of Communications, Government of India.[24]

TRENDS IN TELECOM TARIFF

The globalization policies of the Government in telecommunication sector have resulted in substantial decline in tariffs for both basic and cellular services. This was done with the objective that rates should move in line with costs in a manner that growth of tele-density and affordability are not affected. During the reform period tariffs for all telecom services have shown a significant downward trend. It is evident from the table given below.

Table 7
Decrease in Tariffs for Local Calls

Distance	*2000*	*2001*	*2002*	*2003*	*2004*
Upto 50 kms.	1.20	1.20	1.20	1.20	1.20
Above 50 kms. and upto 200 kms	6.00	4.80	4.80	2.40	2.40
Above 200 kms and upto 500 kms.	15.60	12.00	4.80	4.80	2.40
Above 500 kms and upto 1000 kms.	21.60	18.00	9.60	4.80	2.40
Above 1000 kms.	30.00	24.00	9.60	4.80	2.40

Source: Annual Report, 2004-2005[26]

Table 8
Trends in Tariffs

(Rs. per minute)

	1998-99	*1999-00*	*2001*	*2002*	*2003*
NLD (Beyond 1000 km.)	30.0	30.0	24.0	9.6	4.8
ISD (United States)	61.2	61.2	49.2	40.8	24.0
Mobile	14.5	6.1	2.4	1.9	1.6

Source: Economic Survey 2003-2004[27]

Consistent with the worldwide trend and keeping in view the market reality, Indian telecom sector has rebalanced the tariff structure. The chief features of the tariff order of TRAI were substantial reductions in long distance and international call charges, increases in rental and local charges, and steep cuts in the cost of leased lines. The first phase of rebalancing was done on May 1, 1999 when long distance STD and ISD tariff were reduced by about 23 per cent. The second tariff rationalization was done on October 1, 2000 and it further reduced long distance STD rates by an average of 13 per cent and ISD rates by 17 per cent. The third rationalization of tariffs came to effect from 14th March, 2002. This has resulted in reduction of STD tariffs by up to 56 percent and of ISD tariffs by up to 47 percent. It is clear from the above table that the STD charges for various distance slabs have declined during this period.

Besides International Long Distance charges have also come down during this period. Globalization period definitely brought greater benefits to the consumers in the form of decrease in tariffs. Though the rationalization of tariffs brought about revenue stress on the operators but it also brought about greater efficiency in the telecom sector and various policy measures incited by the government have resulted in significant reduction in long distance tariffs due to competitive pressures introduced in the telecom sector. Liberalization also caused some operators to promote a more rapid reduction in rates than planned. For example, mobile cellular tariffs were forced to reduce their monthly rental rates to Rs. 160 and maximum call charge to Rs. 1.90 per minute.

GROWTH IN TELE-DENSITY

The telecom network in India is not small in absolute terms. With over 12 million lines, it is the 14th largest in the world. Yet

Figure 4
Tele-Density (Number of Telephones per 100 Population) Since 1995-96

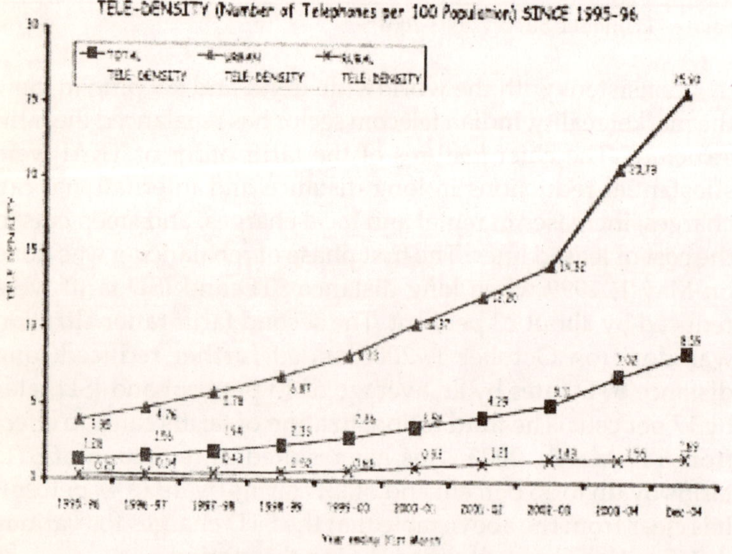

it suffers from an abysmally low penetration of 8.59 per 100 populations as on December 2004 when the world average is over 17.2 as on 2001.[28] Several steps were taken to improve the tele-density in the country during globalization period. For this purpose additional Direct Exchange Lines were added to the existing ones. Over and above intensive efforts were made to cover more villages through Village Public Telephones. Also private sectors were encouraged to provide telecom facilities at a faster pace. As a result the total tele-density[29] in the country has increased from 1.28 as on March 1996 to 8.59 as on December 2004. The urban tele-density was 3.95 as on March 1996, but it increased to 25.90 as on December 2004. The rural tele-density was only 0.29 as on March 1996, but it increased to 1.69 as on December 2004.[30] Within nine years the total tele-density has grown by 6.71 fold and the urban tele-density has grown by 6.55 fold and the rural tele-density has grown by 5.82 fold. This is a positive indication to prove that the globalization and liberalization policies introduced by the government in telecommunication sector has resulted in positive growth.

When we compare India with other developed countries in terms of total tele-density, India's tele-density is very low. Despite greater achievement in terms of network expansion and mobile technology, India's tele-density is low. For this many hold the size of the population responsible. It is also true that countries with smaller network sizes than India are having much higher tele-densities. This is evident from the table given below.

Table 9

Number of main telephone lines per 100 inhabitants

Country	*1995*	*2001*	*2003*
USA	60.73	66.45	116.43
UK	50.18	57.78	143.13
Brazil	8.51	21.69	42.38
China	3.30	13.81	42.32
India	1.29	3.38	6.60
Indonesia	1.70	3.7	9.17
Pakistan	1.70	2.4	4.42
World	12.3	17.2	—

Source: World Telecommunication Development Report 2003, ITU[31]

However, in terms of total tele-density, i.e., the sum of fixed-lines and mobile subscribers per 100 inhabitants, India's comparative ranking in the world improved from 160 in 1990 to 145 in 2000, an improvement by 15 positions[32]. But the table shows that countries like China and Brazil have gone much ahead of India in terms of tele-density. China started out with a higher tele-density than India as of 1995, and obtained a higher growth rate over the following years. However there is a consensus that the country needs a much higher volume of voice telephony, and tele-density needs to go up from existing levels of 8.2 per cent eventually to developed country levels of over 100 percent.

TRENDS IN MANUFACTURE AND EXPORT OF TELECOM EQUIPMENTS AND SERVICES:

India is a major manufacturer and exporter of a wide range of telecom equipments and services. The total production of telecom equipments and cables in terms of value has increased from Rs.3985 crore in 1992-93 to Rs.8300 crore in 1996-97 which further increased to Rs. 10760 crore during 1999-2000. During 2001-02, it further increased to Rs.15437 crore. The growth in telecom equipment production is as follows.

Table 10
Manufacture of Telecom Equipments

Year	*Production (Rs. In Crore)*	*Year*	*Production (Rs. In Crore)*
1992-93	3,985	1998-99	10,000
1993-94	5,500	1999-00	10,760
1994-95	7,000	2000-01	12,271
1995-96	7,750	2001-02	15,437
1996-97	8,300	2002-03	14,400
1997-98	9,960	2003-04	14,000

Source: Annual Report 2000-01 and 2004-05[33]

The above table reveals that manufacture of telecom equipments reached total production of Rs. 15,437 crore dring the year 2001-02. This is the highest production of telecom equipments that the telecom sector has ever achieved. From the year 2002-03 telecommunication manufacturing sector has experienced decline in its total production and its production has reduced to Rs.14,000 crore for the year 2003-04. But India has been recognized as a key supplier of products and technologies for rural Telecom. Significant efforts are undertaken by the government to increase the exports of telecom equipment services. Growth in exports of telecom equipment and services is seen in the following table.

Table 11
Export of Telecom Equipments

Year	*Service (Rs. In Crore)*	*Consultancy (Rs. In Crore)*	*Hardware (Rs. In Crore)*
1993-94	456	118	58
1994-95	598	207	131
1995-96	1,108	235	310
1996-97	1,458	270	240
1997-98	2,232	313	296
1998-99	2,376	383	250
1999-00	3,230	337	180
2000-01	2,882	368	450
2001-02	4,149	378	150
2002-03	3,050	327	402
2003-04	****	388	570

Source: Annual Report- 2004-2005[34]

From the above table it is noted that there was a burst in the exports of services, consultancy and hardware in 1995-96 and the growth has been maintained both in the case of services and consultancy. Export of hardware has displayed a declining trend up to the year 1999-00. But for the year 2000-01 the export of hardware achieved significant growth and for the year 2003-04 the export of hardware obtained Rs. 570 crore.

DEVELOPMENTS IN FOREIGN DIRECT INVESTMENT

Foreign Direct Investment up to 100% has been allowed in the telecom-manufacturing sector and services like e-mail, voice-mail and internet etc. For Infrastructure Providers up to 74% DDI is allowed in case of Radio Paging Service and end-to-end bandwidth providers. Incase of Basic, Cellular, National and International Long Distance Service and Value Added Services, FDI is limited to 49%. FDI up to 49% is also permitted in an investment company, set up for making investment in the telecom companies' license to operate telecom services. During the period August, 1991 to September, 2004, 930 proposals of foreign direct investment of Rs. 41,369.11 crore were approved. The actual inflow of FDI up to August, 2004 was Rs. 10,273.05 crore.

Table 12
Inflow of FDI in Telecom Sector

(Rs. in crore)

Year	FDI Inflow	Year	FDI Inflow
Till 1993	2.06	1999	212.67
1994	14.02	2000	288.58
1995	206.74	2001	3,970.90
1996	764.83	2002	1,081.50
1997	1,245.19	2003	301.40
1998	1,775.64	2004 (August)	409.52
		Total	10,273.05

Source: Annual Report, 2004-2005[35]

Figure 5
FDI Inflow Year-wise (August' 1991 to January' 2004

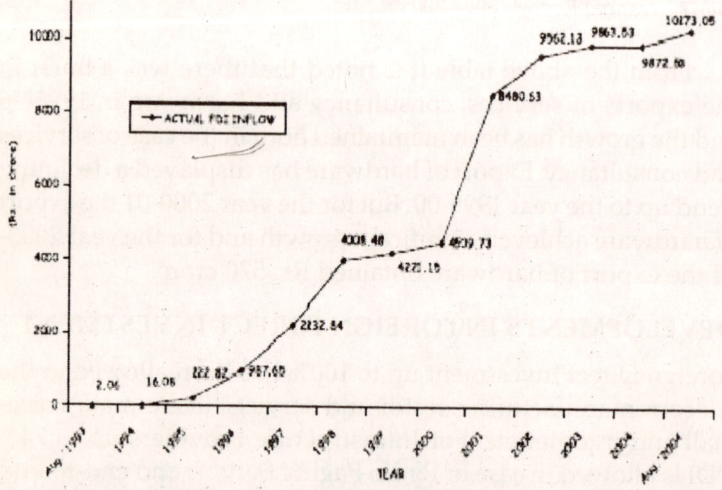

The above table and figure reveal that there has been greater inflow of Foreign Direct investment since the year 1993. Until the year 1993, only Rs.2.06 core has come into India in the form of foreign direct investment. But actual inflow of FDI has increased to Rs. 3,970.90 crore during the year 2001. Out of this Rs.10,273.05 crore was received through foreign direct investment from August 1991 to August 2004, manufacturing and other Vas services received Rs. 6822.55 crore as foreign direct investment and cellular, basic and telephone services received Rs. 3359.50 as foreign direct investment. Thus the globalization process incited in India created greater confidence and security in the minds of investors towards telecom sector which in term attracted greater foreign direct investment in the telecom sector. That is why in terms of foreign direct investment telecom sector stood second.

FINANCIAL PERFORMANCE

Table 12 indicates the financial performance of the department of telecommunication, which indicates a positive growth when we compare post globalization data with the year 1980-81. The net receipts was only Rs. 157 crore in the year 1980-81 but it increased to Rs. 7898 crore during the year 1999-00, which shows a considerable growth of 50.30 fold within 20 years of development. Comparative study between the year 1980-81 to 2002-03 shows that the net receipts has grown by 16.17 fold. Surplus over its expenditure was Rs.125 crore in the year 1980-81, but for the year 2000-01 surplus recorded was Rs. 5265 crore which is a growth of 42.12 fold. The positive growth in its financial performance is due to the spread of wireless access technology. The adoption in this technology has resulted in substantial reduction in the jelly filled cable and other associated wireless infrastructure.

Though the telecom sector is performing well with regard to performance for finance, yet the internal resources generated by the telephone companies are quite inadequate to meet the needs for the sector. The finance ministry has therefore claimed that unless FDI limits are lifted large investments of Rs. 1,60,000 crore cannot be made. The table below shows the current annual surplus and reserves of six telecom companies – BSNL, MTNL, Bharati Televentures, Tata Telecom, Reliance Infocom and VSNL are in the excess of Rs 57,000 crore in the financial year 2003,

Rs 65,834 crore in 2004 and Rs 39,637 crore (Reliance Infocom information not available). It shows that Indian telecom sector is not having sufficient reserves and surplus to carry out the entire expansion work that is necessary in urban and rural areas.

Table: 13
Financial Performance of the Department of Telecommunication
(Rs. Crore)

Year	80-81	90-91	96-97	98-99	99-00	00-01	01-02	02-03
Gross Receipts	632	3405	12266	17744	18257	10175	4274	5911
Net Working Expenses	475	1857	6089	9846	10763	4798	2427	3371
Net Receipts	157	1548	6177	7898	7494	5377	1847	2540
Dividend to General Revenue	32	220	292	252	172	112	—	—
Surplus/Deficit	125	1328	5885	7646	7322	5265	—	—

Source: Department of Telecommunications, Ministry of Communications.[36]

Table 14
Reserve & Surplus of Indian Telephone Companies (Rs in crore)

Company	2003	2004	2005
BSNL	8400	9500	10500
MTNL	8867	9861	10906
Bharati Televentures	1803	2400	3350
VSNL	5265	7004	9860
Tata Teleservices	3701	4013	5021
Reliance Infocom	28978	33056	N.A
Total	57014	65834	39637

Source: Websites of all Companies[37]

WORK EFFICIENCY

Work efficiency of an organization is measured in terms of modernization and total number of staff employed to maintain and operate various capital equipments. Number of staff employed to operate and maintain 1000 DELS shows the ratio between the staff and DELS and the working efficiency of the staff undertaken. The table and the figure below indicate that there is increasing decline in the total staff employed per 1000 DELs.

Table 15
Staff Per 1000 DELs

Year	*Staff per 1000 DELs*	*Year*	*Staff per 1000 DELs*
1990-91	74	1997-98	24
1991-92	64	1998-99	20
1992-93	57	1999-00	15
1993-94	49	2000-01	12
1994-95	43	2001-02	9
1995-96	35	2002-03	8
1996-97	29	2003-04	5

Source: Annual Report 2004-05[38]

Figure 6
Staff Per 1000 DELs

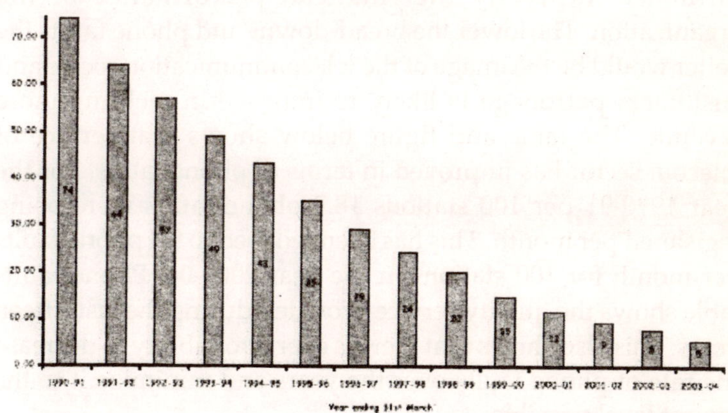

The figure indicates that the manpower of the corporation has been employed in an efficient manner. In the year 1990-91 total number of staff employed per 1000 DELs was 74 and the ratio was 1:13.51 i.e. for 14. DELs 1 person has been employed to look after the working and maintenance of the same. Within 10 years of reforms the work efficiency has improved considerably because during the year 2000-01 only 12 persons were employed for 1000 DELs, which means the ratio between per DELs and the staff employed was 1:83.33 i.e. for 83 DELs 1 staff was employed. For the year 2003-04 the ratio between the Staff employed and per DELs has further declined to 1:200. This indicates that the telecommunication sector has been employing its staff in an efficient manner to bring about greater cost effectiveness in telecom sector. However well-run phone companies worldwide use only 5 to 10 employees per 1000 phones.[39] A reduction from 74 (1990-91) to 5 (2003-04) employees per 1000 phones has taken nearly fifteen years. Taking nearly 15 years objectively cannot be considered as a satisfactory state of cost minimization and work efficiency.

Work efficiency can also be measured in terms of quality service provided by telecommunication sector. Quality service can be interpreted to mean an ideal situation where minimum phone faults, breakdown free services, and punctual in attending to the demands and complaints of the consumers. World over it is recognized today that quality service would influence indirectly the financial performance of the organization. The lower the bread-downs and phone faults the better would be the image of the telecommunication sector and customers patronage is likely to improve in yielding more revenue. The table and figure below shows that service of telecom sector has improved in terms of phone faults. For the year 1990-91 per 100 stations 18.5 phone faults were being registered per month. This has been reduced to 9.4 phone faults per month for 100 stations in the year 2003-04. Phone faults table shows the quality service provided during the last fifteen years. This also shows that there is every possibility to decrease the rate of phone faults over the years and minimize it to the lowest level possible.

Table 16
Phone Faults

Year	*Per 100 Stations per month*	*Year*	*Per 100 Stations per month*
1990-91	18.5	1997-98	17.4
1991-92	19.0	1998-99	16.4
1992-93	18.2	1999-00	15.5
1993-94	18.3	2000-01	13.8
1994-95	17.6	2001-02	12.5
1995-96	15.8	2002-03	10.5
1996-97	17.2	2003-04	09.4

Source: Annual Report 2004-05[40]

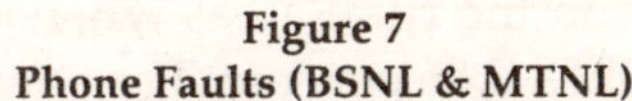

Figure 7
Phone Faults (BSNL & MTNL)

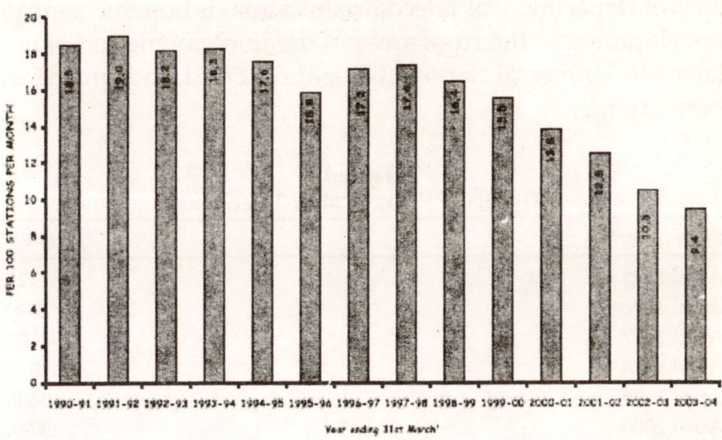

RURAL TELEPHONY

The Rural Sector plays a very important role for the balanced growth of our country and as found out by a survey every single effect in the telecom sector has a six-fold effect on the economy of India. To achieve sustainable development it is essential that people away from the capital city, representing the bulk of society, are given the opportunity to participate in and obtain benefit from the global information revolution, in the most basic ways. As Hudson rightly said, "Information is critical to the social and economic activities that comprise the development process. Telecommunications, as a means of sharing information, is not simply a connection between people, but a link in the chain of the development process itself."

The table above reveals that there is constant growth in providing Village Public Telephones. Out of the 607491 villages in the country, 524606 villages have been provided with VTPs as on December 31, 2004. Of this, 511941 VPTs have been provided by BSNL. The number of rural DELs in the country has increased from 122.72 lakh as on March 31, 2004 to 130.37 lakh as on December 31, 2004. But the share of rural areas DELs to the total DELs is comparatively low to the urban areas share to the total DELs. As on December 2004 only 14 per cent of

DELs are installed in the rural areas wherein the urban areas share in the total DELs is 86 per cent. The annual report of 2004-2005 of Department of Telecommunications is hopeful of greater development in the rural areas in the implementation of non-lapsable Universal Service Obligation Fund and broadband networking.

Table 17
Details of Village Public Telephones

Status as on	*Total VPTs*
April 1995	172511
April 1996	204008
April 1997	260727
April 1998	303582
April 1999	340640
April 2000	374605
April 2001	408922
April 2002	428214
April 2003	513127
April 2004	522263
December 2004	524606

Source: Various Annual Reports of Department of Telecommunication.

Figure 8
Share of Rural and Urban Areas in the total DELs as on December 2004

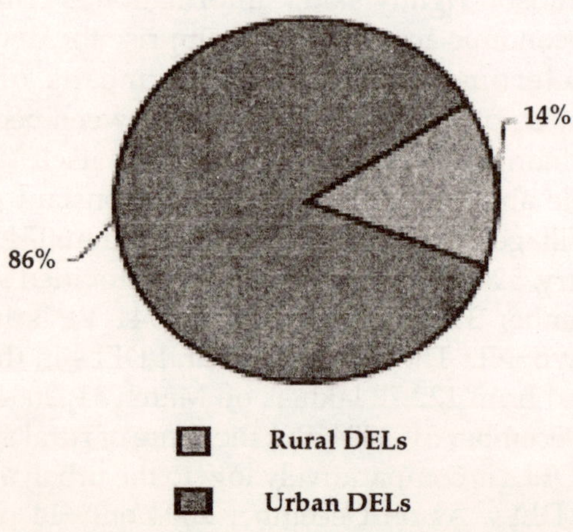

Today in rural areas the economy is much lower than that in urban areas. One of the reason is that the telephone traffic is mainly confined to villages that are close by or to villages within the same telecom center itself. It is obvious therefore that unless and until telephone service is made available in all the villages, it is difficult to expect higher calling rates and better traffic loading. Long distance calls revenues are less and hence phones are far less to justify the provision of rural telephone service and consequently the service has to be subsidized. This is a heavy burden on the exchequer.

CONCLUSION

Economic liberalization has been very fruitful for Indian telecommunications industry. It has brought about significant progress. One of the important features of the liberalization process was that the entire spectrum of telecom services and the operation of market dynamics were open to the private sector. Starting from basic telephone with manual exchange to formation of Mahanagar Telephone Nigam Limited (MTNL) in 1986, India has seen a lot of changes in this effect. Globalization process introduced in telecom sector has brought about following opportunities. Following are the few achievements of globalization process introduced in telecommunication sector.

Indian telecommunications sector has always been like a "Natural Monopoly". But this monopoly could not sustain itself with the technological changes taking place in the telecom sector. Dismantling of monopolies lead to emergence of keen competition and lowering of tariffs, leading to consumer satisfaction, better services, technological up gradation and sound infrastructure.

All telecom services like basic, national long distance, cellular, VSAT etc were opened to the private sector with free competition except those limited by Spectrum (cellular). The Indian telecom sector is the eighth largest network, with annual growth rate of more than 22% for basic services and almost 100% for Internet and cellular services. The lines added to basic services in last 5 years are one-and-a half times more than that added in the last 5 decades.

Before liberalization VSNL had a monopoly over international long distance calls. The end of government monopoly has made a tremendous impact on the telecom sector as far as customers are concerned. While on the one hand VSNL will begin to face the challenge posed by private companies such as Bharti Telesonic, on the other hand consumers have already started enjoying a decline in ISD tariffs and improved services in international telephony. In fact, prominent Internet service providers have announced tariffs slash of upto about Rs. 25 from Rs. 55 per minute.[41] India has a huge ISD market which accounts for transactions of about Rs. 7,500 crore.

India is proud today because various telecom reforms committed under NTP-99 are almost complete, some ahead of schedule. The impact of these reforms has been overwhelming because national long distance charges dropped by more than 60%, cellular air time charges are down by 8 times with even cheaper handsets. There is also an increased availability of bandwidth with efficient usage.

The period of intensified globalization process has contributed many changes in the telecom sector. In certain areas the changes have been more profound. Despite these transformations, the pace of progress continues to be slow in the telecom sector in India. In a number of areas the reform process undertaken is yet to be touched. Apart from this, reform process in telecom sector is faced with several problems which are to be addressed to achieve the ideal type of development. The following are the limitations that are foreseen in the development of telecom sector in India.

- Slow reform process and slow liberalization affect the changes and makes the progress slow.
- Foreign companies wanting to invest in India are put off due to continuously changing rules and Tax policies.
- Since 1994 reform process, telecom density has only gone up to 3 as compared to the global average of 14.
- Though cellular is the most attractive business today, but still the overall number of cellular subscribers is very low and this market really needs to be tapped.

- China's early liberalization and the fast growing economy may prove to be a hindrance for India.
- Price regulations based on pre-set rate of return hinder the growth.
- Young, hardworking and intelligent workforce want to leave the country due to poor economic conditions and exploitation.

Despite the fact that the number of cyber cafes in the urban areas of India has increased significantly, cyber cafes are mostly ignored in scientific research and political programs, which seem to prefer to concentrate on other public access services in libraries, community access centers, village information centers, schools or universities. Little attention has been paid so far to this obviously successful market-driven access model and there is a lack of empirical data, as well as a lack of user surveys measuring the usage patterns of these enterprises. Therefore the users, the usage patterns and the relevance of cyber cafes for particular social groups in India remain almost unknown.

In early 90's the Government recognized that private investment and association of the private sector would be absolutely necessary to bridge the resource gap. Reforms and investments are possible by placing primary responsibility for investment and service provision with the private sector and by placing sector planning and regulation responsibility with the government. As a result the Basic telecom services are to be privatized. The private sector in telecom sector is seen to be concentrating on 200 million middle class population of India, resident in about 300 cities and about 4500 towns. The rural sector consisting of about 0.6 million villages does not seem to be their cup of coffee.

The bid held in 1994 had no companies bid for the telecom circle in Assam, North Eastern States, Andaman and Nicobar, Jammu & Kashmir and Himachal Pradesh. It seems that the naxalites affected areas and terrorism affected area carry no commercial value for these companies. All the sectors whether in difficult terrorist affected areas, rural, or urban should get an equal opportunity for development. So far, the public sector incumbents have spearheaded expansion of rural telephony with very little contribution by the private sector. By the end of December 31, 2001, out of 0.4 million villages, the private operators covered only 718 villages and the rest was by the public sector. Private sector presence is prolific in Public Call Offices (PCOs) and Internet Kiosks in the cities and towns. However, there are certain pilot projects in the rural sector working to evolve cost effective wireless technological solutions in partnership with local service providers.

Affordability is the key to success in India. Till about two years ago, telephone infrastructure in India cost about Rs 30,000 per line. Hence, the yearly revenue had to be 35 per cent of the investment (15 per cent finance charges, 10 per cent depreciation and 10 per cent operation) to break even which was next to impossible as it implied revenues of Rs 11,000 per year per line, or a bill of Rs 1,000 per month for a subscriber. Only 2-3 per cent of India's population can afford this. The scenario, however, is changing. The cost of telephone and Internet connection can easily be brought down to Rs 10,000 per line. When the cost comes down to Rs 10,000 per line, 50 per cent of the Indian population will be able to afford a telephone connection. India is a potential market size of 150-200 million telecom and Internet connections.[42]

Regulation assumes the objective of profit-maximization on the part of those being regulated. It is in this context that incentive regulation makes sense. However, public sector undertakings controlled by government do not necessarily follow a profit maximization objective, nor do profits typically form an important element in performance. Government public sector undertakings are governed and controlled by vote bank norms rather than profit maximization and financial performance. It is in this context that private operators also fear "irrational competition" from the Government-owned incumbent. Globalization process has not made any significant change in the philosophy on the basis of which various decisions are made within the government owned public sectors like BSNL and MTNL.

The traditional strategy in India has consisted of using cross-subsidies, charging urban consumers more and rural consumers less. "The Universal Service Obligation Fund (USOF) in India's telecom sector is a unique institutional innovation which ensures provision of services at minimum cost in rural areas through a system of open bidding. At present, USOF is funded by imposing a levy of 5 per cent of adjusted gross revenue of telecom companies."[43]

It is said that many of the distortions in the Indian telecommunication system have their origin in the universal service objective. There is a basic conflict between achieving universal service objectives through prices and service conditions, and allowing competitive market forces to operate unfettered. At times, the universal service objective has been utilized to serve other interests. The Universal Service Fund was set up in order to resolve this basic conflict and achieve the universal service objective in a competitively neutral manner. The universal service argument must, therefore, be used most sparingly for justifying constraints on competitive market forces through license conditions, tariffs or access charges.

One of the prime concerns of the Government has always been to ensure accessibility and availability of telecommunication services, which may not be viable on pure commercial considerations. Universal Service Obligation thus arises from the requirements imposed as a result of government policy, legislation, or regulation for providing telecommunication services, to certain customers, which can only be met at a loss or under cost conditions.

So for, Rs. 1700 crore have been made available to the operators for rural telephony of which Rs. 1200 has been provided during 2004.05. For the year 2005-06, a provision of Rs. 1200 crore has been made for USOF support. As per the claims of Ministry of Communications and Information Technology 76000 Public Tele-Info Centers and 5000 High Speed PTCs will be set up to provide broadband connectivity in the rural areas. Further, the support is being used for the replacement of 1.84 lakh Multi Access Radio Relay based VPTs. 50 per cent of such VPTs has already been replaced and the remaining shall be replaced by the middle of 2006. In spite of these claims we have not succeeded in providing telecom facilities to entire villages in India. Nearly 15-20 per cent of our villages in India is not yet connected with telecommunication facilities, and has not yet seen telephones in these areas. However, even if it is connected it does not function for many months and no one is there to repair the already established telecom installations in the rural areas.

One of the objectives of National Telecom Policy 1994 was to achieve Universal Service covering all villages as early as possible. The Universal Service Obligation was built into the license of Basic Service providers itself in the form of DELs & VPTs targets that a private basic service provider was obliged to meet. Due to various reasons, the goal set out in NTP 94 for VPTs as well as USO was not achieved.

Each stage of the liberalization process in India has been marked by awarding of contracts and licenses to those with most access to the state's decision-making processes along with many court battles and scandals. Liberalization concept has not emerged strongly at the ground level due to more democratic and pluralistic nature of our society. Many things going on simultaneously in the Indian telecommunications reveal the many influences at work on the Indian state. The most powerful liberalization coalition includes international and domestic businesses supported by foreign governments and international organizations. The opposing group also includes trade unions and politicians. As a result the Indian state's are juggling between these interest groups is producing one of the most complex liberalization programs ever undertaken.

India offers an interesting case of a state facing pluralistic pressures which has liberalized its marketplace, but safeguards and checks against unrestrained authority are few. Political institutions have long succumbed to the party in power, usually driven by special interests, and only recently have opposition parties started playing a significant role.

Telecommunications have played a critical role in shaping India's march towards progress and the importance they hold for the future of India cannot be overstated. "A new framework for infrastructure policy, consisting of competition between multiple players, under a regulatory framework defined by the state has made much headway in the area of telecom. The successful implementation of reforms since 1991 has resulted in unprecedented growth of the sector. It has enabled the adoption of latest available technologies. The perception about telecom services, until recently considered an elitist luxury, has changed to a preferred good of mass consumption with increasing usage of telecom an IT services. The benefits from increased market access for the masses, improved productivity and market efficiency, and unprecedented innovation in business models and organizational structures are now widely recognized."[44]

Therefore we can conclude by saying that "The liberal argument is in favor of making the best possible use of the forces of competition as a means of coordinating human efforts, not an argument for leaving things just as they are. It is based on the conviction that, where effective competition can be created, it is a better way of guiding individual efforts than any other. It does not deny, but even emphasizes, that, in order that competition should work beneficially, a carefully thought-out legal framework is required and neither the existing nor the past legal rules are free from grave defects."

REFERENCES

Abhinay, Taneja: "Rural Telecommunications in India an Analysis", Delhi College of Engineering (University of Delhi), New Delhi.

Anikar, M. Haseloff: "Cybercafes and their Potential as Community Development", Tools in India The Journal of Community Informatics, Vol. 1, No. 3 (2005).

Annual Report, 2000-2001: Department of Telecommunications, Ministry of Communications and Information Technology, Government of India, New Delhi.

Annual Report, 2001-2002: Department of Telecommunications, Ministry of Communications and Information Technology, Government of India, New Delhi.

Annual Report, 2002-2003: Department of Telecommunications, Ministry of Communications and Information Technology, Government of India, New Delhi.

Annual Report, 2003-2004: Department of Telecommunications, Ministry of Communications and Information Technology, Government of India, New Delhi.

Annual Report, 2004-2005: Department of Telecommunications, Ministry of Communications and Information Technology, Government of India, New Delhi.

Bhattacharya, Manas: "Telecom Sector in India : Vision 2020", India Vision 2020, Planning Commission, Government of India, New Delhi, 2004.

Business Line: November 10, 2004.

Businessworld: The Marketing Whitebook 2005. New Delhi, India. (2005).

Chennappa, D.: FDI in Telecom in India: A Study, Southern Economist, Vol. 44, No.10, Setemper, 15, 2005.

Dasgupta, S. Somik Lall and David Wheeler: Policy Reform, Economic Growth and the Digital Divide: An Econometric Analysis, Working Paper No. 2567, World Bank, March, 28, 2001

Economic Survey, 2002-2003: Government of India, Ministry of Finance, Economic Division.

Economic Survey, 2003-2004: Government of India, Ministry of Finance, Economic Division.

Economic Survey, 2004-2005: Government of India, Ministry of Finance, Economic Division.

Indian Infrastructure Report, 2001: 3i Network.

Indian Infrastructure Report, 2002: 3i Network.

Indian Infrastructure Report, 2003: 3i Network.

Indian Infrastructure Report, 2004: 3i Network.

Indian Infrastructure Report, 2005: 3i Network.

IndianInfoline.com: "Telecom Sector Update, India infoline feature, Feb. 2005", March 11, 2005.

India Development Report, 1997: Ajay Shah, "Telecommunication – Monopoly vs Competition".

International Telecommunication union: "Competition policy in Telecommunication: The Case of India," November 2002.

International Telecommunication union, "Competition policy in Telecommunication: The Case of India," November 2002.

Noronha, Frederic: Internet for all: Indian villagers to get access at prices they can afford, www.tenet.res.in.

Nirupam, Bajpai: Ten years of Indian reforms: The unfinished agenda. Infrastructure, February 2003, CMIE, Mumbai.

Pratibha, B. Munot: Study of Telecommunications Structure in India, Oklahoma state university, October 10th 2002.

Sasikumar, K.C. John, "Present Status and Challenges of Rural Telecommunications in India", s. Ganesan (ed.), "Infrastructure Development and Financing", Kanishka Publishers, Distributors, New Delhi, 2001.

Shyamal Ghosh, "Indian Telecom Scenario", Yojana, Vol. 48, January 2004, 19-22.

Singh, J.P. "Evaluating Telecommunication Privatization and Liberalization in India and the Far East" Paper prepared for presentation at the conference on "Has Privatization Worked? The International Experience," Columbia Institute of Tele-Information, Columbia University, New York, June 12, 1998.

Sood, Aditya Dev, 'How to Wire Rural India, Problems and Possibilities of Digital

Development', *Economic and Political Weekly*, October 27, 2001.

Tenth Five Year Plan (2002-2007), Infrastructure, Vol. II.

Uday Lal Pai, "India Tops Internet Reliability in Asia,"

http://asia.internet.com/cyberatlas/0913-india.html

Warrior, Shoba: Telecom sector offers big growth Opportunity, Rediff Report, May 18, 2002.

World Bank and Public-Private Infrastructure Advisory Facility: "India Country Framework Report for Private Participation in Infrastructure", 2000.

World Employment Report: Life at Work in the Information Economy, 2001, ILO, Geneva.

World Telecommunication Development Report, 2002: ITU, Geneva, 2002.

NOTES

1. http://www.indiainfoline.com/nevi/vsmt.html
2. Government divested 25 per cent strategic stake of Videsh Sanchar Nigam Limited (VSNL), a public sector monopoly incumbent in ILD telephony to Tata Group in the private sector out of 52.97 per cent equity held by the government. This was followed by opening up of ILD business to private players from April 1, 2002,

terminating VSNL monopoly two years ahead of schedule, VSNL, 16th Annual Report, 2001-2002, p.5.

5. Till 1986 telecommunication was a public utility owned by the Government of India. Mahanagar Telephone Nigam Limited (MTNL) was created in 1986 as a PSE to take out telecommunication services from the Government entirely in the cities of Delhi and Mumbai. It was in the same year that VSNL was created in the ILD segment. Bharat Sanchar Nigam Limted (BSNL) was formed as a PSE on October 1, 2000 as a telecom service provider in all other places. Both these incumbents inherited the entire pre-existing subscriber base with the Government.

4. Annual Report, 2004-2005, Department of Telecommunications, Ministry of Communications and Information Technology, Government of India, New Delhi, p. 111.

5. See for example, Life at Work in the Information Economy, World Employment Report 2001, ILO, Geneva; Dasgupta, S., Somik Lall and David Wheeler, Policy Reform, Economic Growth and the Digital Divide: An Econometric AnalysisWorking Paper No. 2567, World Bank, March, 28, 2001; Sood, Aditya Dev, How to Wire Rural India, Problems and Possibilities of Digital Development', Economic and Political Weekly, October 27, 2001.

6. Manas Bhattacharya, "Telecom Sector in India: Vision 2020", India Vision 2020, Planning Commission, Government of India, New Delhi, p. 665.

7. Ibid.

8. http://www.indiabandwidth.com/dir1/longdist21.html.

9. As quoted by Manas Bhattacharya, Op.cit., p. 656.

10. Annual Report 2004-2005, Op.cit., p. 97.

11. http://www.india-cellular.com/News-July-2002.html.

12. Economic Survey 2004-05, p.199.

13. IndianInfoline.com, India infoline feature, "Telecom Sector Update, Feb. 2005", March 11, 2005.

14. http://www.indiabandwidth.com/dir1/longdist32.html.

15. Ibid.

16. As quoted by Manas Bhattacharya, Op.cit., p. 656.

17. Tenth Five Year Plan (2002-2007), Infrastructure, Vol. II, p.1052.

18. Noronha Frederic, Internet for all: Indian villagers to get access at prices they can afford, www.tenet.res.in.
19. Businessworld, The Marketing Whitebook 2005, New Delhi, India, 2005, p.72.
20. Anikar M. Haseloff , "Cybercafes and their Potential as Community Development Tools in India" The Journal of Community Informatics Vol. 1, No. 3 (2005), p.14.
21. As referred by Anikar M. Haseloff , "Cybercafes and their Potential as Community Development Tools in India" The Journal of Community Informatics Vol. 1, No. 3 (2005), p. 2.
22. Uday Lal Pai, India Tops Internet Reliability In Asia, http://asia.internet.com/cyberatlas/0913-india.html
23. Nirupam Bajpai, Ten years of Indian reforms: The unfinished agenda.
24. Infrastructure, February 2003, CMIE, Mumbai, p.254.
25. World Development Report, 1994, p. 31.
26. Annual Report 2004-2005, Op.cit., p.vi.
27. Economic Survey 2003-2004, p. 182.
28. Indian Infrastructure Report 2004, 3i Network.
29. The tele-density means telephone per 100 population.
30. Annual Report 2004-2005, Op.cit., p.98.
31. Economic Survey 2003-04, and 2002-03, Government of India, p.180 and p.188, India's tele-density as on December 31, 2004 was 8.59.
32. ITU, World Telecommunication Development Report 2002, Geneva, 2002, p.56.
33. Annual Report 2000-01 and 2004-05, Department of Telecommunication, Ministry of Communications and Information Technology, Government of India, New Delhi, p. 4 and p. 11.
34. Annual Report 2000-01 and 2004-05, Op.cit., p. 11.
35. Annual Report 2004-2005, Op.cit., p. 13.
36. Economic Survey, 2004-05, p. s-48.
37. As given by D. Chennappa, "FDI in Telecom in India: A Study", Southern Economist, Vol. 44, No. 10, September 15, 2005, p.31.

38. Annual Report 2004-05, Op.cit., p. 103.
39. Ajay Shah, "Telecommunication– Monopoly vs Competition", India Development Report 1997, p.243.
40. Annual Report 2004-2005, Op.cit., p. 102.
41. It is between Delhi and New York.
42. Shoba Warrior, Telecom sector offers big growth Opportunity, Rediff Report, May 18, 2002.
43. Economic Survey, 2004-2005.
44. Economic Survey 2003-04, p. 180.

15

FOREIGN EXCHANGE– USE OF CURRENCY DERIVATIVES IN GLOBALISATION

V. Aditya Srinivas & G. N. Joshi***

INTRODUCTION

In the present era of Globalization, where the boundaries of the countries are no longer a barrier to trade and where the cross border trade has become a matter of necessity, the importance of foreign exchange cannot be undermined. Today every country and every company who deals with their counter part located in other country requires foreign exchange to import the goods and avail the required services. The WTO era which has been put in practice from in India from 1st January 2005, has also removed the trade barriers for the business opportunities. Today Indian corporates can raise the foreign exchange from the international markets in the form of External Commercial Borrowing. The 1991 crisis of Indian economy which made it compulsory for our country to make the structural changes in the economy and adopt the liberalization, Privatization and Globalization policy for the survival and growth of the economy is now giving the country a strong platform to compete at the global level. In 1991 our foreign exchange reserve was only about Rs. 2400 crores which was sufficient for only two weeks of import. Today we have come

* Lecturer, 606, Sri Appartment Makipool, Nanpura, Surat-395001.
** Professor, Department of Economics, Veer Narmad South, Gujarat University, Surat.

to a stage where the foreign exchange reserves of the country at a$ 140 billion which makes India among few countries in the world to have such huge reserves which can satisfy the import requirements for seventeen months. The huge foreign exchange reserves have installed faith of the world developed countries in the Indian economy. The Multinational Corporations and the Foreign Institutional Investors are investing in India due to our strong Balance of Payment position. The movement of the foreign exchange has significant impact on the earnings of the country as the earning comes from export. The appreciation and depreciation of the rupee in relation to dollar has significant impact on the earning of the companies in the sectors like the Information Technology, Tourism and other service oriented companies. The RBI is the authority which intervenes in the currency markets to control the movement of the rupee against the dollar. As the people of our country have started investing in the products of the international markets, even they are affected from the movement of the foreign exchange. Hence a comprehensive mechanism is required which can provide the corporates and the individuals to hedge their risk. The RBI now allows that a individual can invest upto $ 25000 anywhere in the world without any prior approval of the RBI. This has also created enough room for the investments to be made the international equities and the bonds and also in the currency trading that takes place in the exchange like the London International Financial Futures and Options Exchange (LIFFE).

WORLD MONETARY SYSTEM

In order to understand the present world monetary system, it is helpful to look at the developments during the last few decades. From the end of the Second World War until February 1973, an adjustable peg exchange rate system, administered by the International Monetary Fund, prevailed. Under this system, the US dollar which was linked to gold ($ 35 per ounce) served as the base currency. Other currency were expressed in the terms of dollar and, through this standard, exchange rates between currencies were established. A special feature of this system was that the close control was exercised over the exchange rates between various currencies and the dollar a fluctuation of only plus or minus one per cent was allowed around the fixed exchange rate. What happened when the central bank of a country found it extremely difficult to maintain the exchange rate within limits? If a country experienced continued difficulty in preventing the fall of its exchange rate below the lower limit could, with the approval of the International Monetary fund, devalue its currency. India for example devalued its currency in 1966 in a bid to cope with its balance of payments problem. JA country enjoying continued favorable balance of payments situation would find it difficult to prevent its exchange rate from rising above the upper limit. Such a country would be allowed, again with the approval of the International Monetary fund to revalue its currency. West German, for example was allowed to revalue its currency in 1969.

PRESENT SYSTEM OF FLOATING EXCHANGE RATES

In 1971 the US dollar was delinked with gold. Put differently, way allowed to "floating". This brought about a dramatic change in the international monetary system. The system of fixed exchange rates, where devaluations and revaluations occurred only very rarely, giveaway to a system of floating exchange rates. In a truly floating exchange rate regime, the relative prices of currencies are decided entirely by the market forces of demand and supply. There is no attempt the authorities to influence exchange ate movements or to target the exchange rate. Such an idealized free float probably does not exist. Governments of almost all countries regard exchange rate as an important macro economic variables and attempt to influence its movements either through direct intervention in the exchange markets or though a mix of fiscal and monetary policies. Such floating is called managed or dirty float. Unlike the Breton Woods, era, there are few if any rules governing exchange rate regimes adopted by various countries. Some countries allow their currencies to float with varying degrees and modes of intervention, some tie their currencies with a major convertible currency while others tie it to a known or unknown basked of currencies. The general prescriptions that a country must not manipulate its exchange rate to the detriment of international trade and payments. The exchange rate of the rupee is managed by the RBI More specifically during the last two years or so the RBI has been intervening heavily in the market to hold the rupee dollar rate within tight bounds while rupee rates with other currencies fluctuate as the US dollar fluctuates against them. These changes in the exchange rate regime have been accompanied by a series of measures relaxing exchange control as well as significant liberalization of foreign trade.

FOREIGN EXCHANGE MARKETS

In the foreign exchange market, currencies are bought and sold against each other. It is the worlds largest market with a daily turnover of around $3.5 trillion a day. Most trading takes place in a few select currencies – US dollar, Deutschmark, Japanese yen, British pound sterling, Swiss franc, Canadian dollar, French Franc, Australian dollar, Dutch guilder, Belgian franc and Italian lira. It takes over two months average trading on New York Stock Exchange to mach one day trading on the forex market. The Indian foreign exchange market is very small compared to the global 24 hours foreign exchange market. The Indian turnover is only around 5-10 billion a day. Amongst this, spot transactions constitute about 50% of the turnover, outright forward 25% and the rest in the swap transactions.

The foreign exchange market is worldwide in scope and the major worlds trading center are in Tokyo, Singapore, New York, Frankfurt, Zurich and San Francisco. Many other centers are also coming up. Banks and professional dealers and brokers obtain exchange rate quotes on desktop computer screens and communicate with each other by telephone, computer, fax and telex. The communication network connecting all the centers is very efficient such that an exchange rate change in one center has an almost immediate impact on forex trading in other centers.

INFORMATION AND COMMUNICATION SYSTEM:-

Communication, pertaining to international financial transactions, is handled mainly by a large network called Society for Worldwide Interbank Financial Telecommunications called as (SWIFT). This is a non profit Belgian cooperative with main and regional centers around the world connected by data transmission lines. Depending on the location, a bank can access a regional processor main center, which then transmits the information to the appropriate location. Even in our country RBI and SEBI have started implementing the this software for the speedy transformation of the currency and securities in the capital market. The proposed system of T + 1 which is likely to be implemented from 1st April will be dependent on the installation of the SWIFT software. This software is used worldwide for the transfer of the currency from one country to other country.

FUNCTIONS OF THE FOREIGN EXCHANGE MARKET

The foreign exchange market is the market in which individuals firms and banks buy and sell foreign currencies or foreign exchange. The principle function of the foreign exchange market is the transfer of funds from one nation and currency to another. Transfer of purchasing power is necessary because international trade and capital transactions usually involve parties living in countries with different national currencies. Each party wants to trade and deal in his own currency but since the trade can be invoiced only in a single currency, the parties mutually agree on a currency beforehand. The currency agreed could also be any convenient third country currency such as the US dollar. For, if an Indian exporter sells machinery to a UK importer, the exporter could invoice in pound, rupees ;or any other convenient currency like the US dollar.

NEED FOR FOREIGN EXCHANGE

Why do individuals, firms and banks want to exchange one national currency for another? The demand for foreign currencies arises when tourists visit another country and need to exchange their national currency for the currency of the country they are visiting, when a domestic firm wants to import from other nation's when an individual wants to invest abroad and so on. On the other hand, nation's supply of foreign currencies arises from foreign tourist expenditures in the nation, from export earnings, from receiving foreign investment and so on. For example, suppose a US firm exporting to UK is paid in pounds sterling. The US exporters will exchange the pounds for dollars at a commercial bank. The commercial bank will then sell these pounds for dollars to a US resident who is going to visit the UK or to United States firm that wants to import from the UK and pay in pounds, or to US investors who want to invest in the UK and needs the pounds to make the investment.

TYPES OF EXCHANGE RATE MECHANISM

There have been various approaches through which the foreign exchange mechanism has gone through in the world. According to the International Monetary Fund there are five types of the exchange rate mechanism that were prevalent in the world during the different times. The major ones among them are as under:

FIXED RATE EXCHANGE SYSTEM

This system was followed after the Bretton Woods Conference where it was decided that the exchange rate would be fixed at one US dollar was equal to 35 ounces of gold. This system was prevalent till 1971 but then there was balance of payment crisis in the United States and ultimately in 1973 the system was changed to floating exchange rate system.

MANAGED FLOAT

Under this system the exchange rate mechanism is controlled by the Central bank of the country. Whenever the country faces any problem regarding the exchange rate mechanism the central bank comes into the picture and takes the control over the movement of the exchange rates. When the rupee depreciates the Reserve Bank of India would come into picture and sell dollars in the markets so that the rupee appreciates and by this way it manages the exchange rates and so it is called as the managed float.

TARGET ZONE ARRANGEMENT

In this type of arrangement the member country of any regime like the European union may decide the upper limit and the lower limit within which the currency rates are allowed to move. In other words a band is created which is acts as a upper control limit and the lower control limit. In the European countries it is also called as the "Snake in the tunnel".

FLEXIBLE RATE SYSTEM

This is the system where the exchange rates are determined by the demand and the supply rules and the market forces determine how the currency rates will move. If the demand of a particular currency moves up then the currency rates would appreciate and corresponding currency rates would depreciate and when the supply of a currency moves up the currency rates would depreciate and the corresponding currency would appreciate.

FOREIGN EXCHANGE MARKETS (BASIC TYPES)

An exchange rate can be defined as the number of units of one currency that must be given to acquire one unit of a currency of another country. It is the price paid in the home currency to purchase a certain quantity of funds in the currency of another country. For example, it takes about Rs. 42.35 to purchase one US dollar and Rs. 6.60 to purchase one French franc. The exchange rate is the link between different national currencies that make international price and cost comparisons possible.

The foreign exchange market includes both the spot and forward exchange rates. The spot rate is the rte paid for delivery within two business days after the day the transactions takes place. If the rate is quoted for delivery of foreign currency at some future date, it is called as the forward rate. In the forward rate, the exchange rate is established at the time of the contract, though payment and delivery are not required until maturity. Forward rates are usually quoted for fixed periods of 30,60 or90 or 180 days from the day of the contract.

SPOT MARKET:

Almost all major newspapers print a daily list of exchanges rates. For major currencies, up to four different quotes are displayed. One is the spot price. The others might include the

30day, 90 day and 180 days forward prices. These quotes are for trades among the dealers in the interbank market. When the interbank trades involved dollars these rates will be expressed in American terms (number of US dollars per unit of foreign currency) or the European terms (number of foreign currency units per US dollar).Banks do not normally charge a commission on their currency transactions but profits from the spread between the buying and selling rates. Quotes are always given impairs because a dealer usually does not know whether a prospective customer is in the market to buy or sell a foreign currency. The first rate is the buy, or bid price and the second is the sell or the ask rate. Suppose the pound sterling is quoted at $1.7019-36. This means that the banks are willing to buy the pounds at $1.7019 and sell them at $1.7036. In practice, the dealers not quote the full rate to each other, instead, they quote only the lat two digits of the decimal. Thus, sterling would be quoted at 19-36. Any dealer who does not understand this will not be able to remain in the business for a long time.

The most common way of stating a foreign exchange quotation is in terms of the number of units of foreign currency needed to buy one unit of home currency. Thus, India quotes its exchange rates in terms of the amount of rupees that can be exchanged for one unit of foreign currency. For example, if the Indian rupees the home currency and the foreign currency is the French Franc then the exchange rate between the rupee and the French franc might be stated as

FF 0.1462/Rs.1 reads "0.1462 French Franc per rupee". This means that one Indian rupee can buy 0.1462 French franc. In this method known as the European terms the rate is quoted in terms of the number of units of the foreign currency for one unit of the domestic currency. This is called as the indirect route.

The other method is called as the direct route called as the American terms, the expresses the home currency price of one unit of the foreign currency. Rs. 6.84/FF read as "Rs.6.84 per French Franc" Both direct and indirect quotes are in use. In the US, it is common to use the direct route for domestic business. For international business, banks generally use European terms.

BID ASK SPREADS:-

Interbank quotations are given a bid and ask price. A bid is the price at which the dealer will buy another currency. An offer or ask is the price at which a dealer will sell the other currency. Dealers generally bid (buy) at one price and offer (sell) at a slightly higher price, making the profits from the spreads, i.e. the differences between the buying and selling prices.

EXAMPLE

All foreign exchange dealers are interested in making a profit out of each transaction. Therefore, a when a dealer in India tries to sell foreign currency he will try to get as high a price as is possible for every unit of foreign currency sold. But when the dealer is buying foreign currency, his aim will be to get the most reasonable price for every unit of the foreign currency he buys.

A dealer in New Delhi may give the following quotations

US $1 = Rs. 43.30000 - 43.7300

L1 = Rs. 69.9200 - 71.3100

This means that the dealer will buy dollars from the exporter at US $1 = Rs. 43.30000 and sell dollars to an importer at US $1 = Rs. 43.7300. Similarly, he will buy pounds at L1 = Rs. 69.9200 but sell pounds at L1 = Rs. 71.3100.

THE FORWARD MARKET

The spot market is for foreign exchange traded within two business days. However, the some transactions may be entered into on one day but not completed until sometime in the future. For example, a French exporter of perfume might sell perfume to a US importer with immediate delivery but not require payment for 30 days. The US importer has an obligation to ay the required francs in 30 days so he or she may enter into a contract with a trader to deliver dollars for francs in 30 days at a forward rate - the rate today for future delivery. The difference between the spot and forward rate is called as the spread in the forward market.

Consider the following example suppose the Japanese Yen of August 6, 1991 sold at $0.006879 while 90 day forward yen was priced at $ 0.006902. Based on these rates, the swap rate for the 90 day forward yen was quoted as a 23 point premium (0.006902-0.006879).

THE NEED FOR FORWARD MARKET

The actual need for the existence of a forward market is not speculation. Today, there is no clear cut line of distinction between hedging and speculating. However, there are a couple of characteristic categories of people who use the forward market in order to cover for time lags. The first group includes exporters and importers. As receipts and payments do not usually coincide time wise, these people buy forward the currency that they will have to pay and sell forward the currency that they will receive. In this way they over come the undesirable market fluctuations and take care of future cash flows. The second group consists of the people who use the forward markets to preserve the value and nature of their assets without speculating against future trends. These operators use both the spot and forward markets through swaps.

MARKET STRUCTURE

Options are purchased and traded either on an organized exchange (such as the PHLX) or in the over the counter (OTC) market. Exchange traded options are standardized in nature with predetermined exercise prices, standard maturities (one, three, six, nine and 12 months) and fixed maturities (March, June, September and December). Options on the Philadelphia stock exchange are available in the ECU and seven currencies like Deutsche mark, pound sterling, French franc, Swiss franc, Japanese yen, Canadian dollar and the Australian dollar are traded in standardized contract.

OTC options are contracts whose specifications are generally negotiated as to the amount, exercise price and rights, underlying instrument, and expiration. Commercial and investment banks in virtually all-financial centers trade OTC currency options. OTC activity is concentrated in London and New York and it centers on the major currencies like the US dollar, Deutsche marks, Swiss franc, Pounds sterling, Japanese yen and Canadian dollars. For example, Australian banks in London writer options on the Australian dollar. OTC options are generally traded in round lots, commonly $5-10 million in New York and $2-3 million in London. The average maturity of the OTC options ranges from two to six months, and very few options are written for more than one year. The OTC market consists of two sectors (1)a retail market composed of non-bank customers who purchase from banks what amounts to a customized insurance against adverse exchange rates movements. (2) a wholesale market among commercial bans, investments banks, and specialized trading firms, this market may include the interbank OTC trading or the trading on the organized market.

THE PARTICIPANTS

The major participants in the foreign exchange markets are the large commercial banks, foreign exchange brokers in the interbank market, commercial customers, primarily multinational corporations, and central banks, which intervene in the market from time to time to smooth exchange rate fluctuations or maintain target exchange rates. Central banks intervention involving buying or selling in the market is often indistinguishable from the foreign exchange dealings of commercial banks or of other private participants.

Only the head offices or regional offices of the major commercial banks are actually market makers that is actively deal in foreign exchange for their own accounts. These banks stand ready to buy or sell any of the major currency on a more or less continuous basis. A large fraction of the interbank transactions in the United states is conducted through foreign exchange brokers. In India the Reserve Bank of India is the prime authority who controls the foreign exchange market in the country. Initially we had the FERA (Foreign Exchange Regulation Act) to deal with the foreign exchange transactions but now it has been repealed by FEMA(Foreign Exchange Management Act). Some of the leading Foreign exchange markets are the International

Monetary Market, The London International Financial Futures Exchange(LIFFE) and Philadelphia Stock exchange trade foreign currency options.

USE OF CURRENCY FUTURES AND CURRENCY OPTIONS FOR HEDGING AND SPECULATION AND ARBITRAGE

Currency Futures

Apart from the spot and forward markets, foreign currencies are traded in the market for currency futures and the market for currency options. These two are known as derivatives because such contracts derive their value of a spot price time series. The market for currency futures and options is known as the market for derivatives because the prices in these markets are driven by the spot market price. These markets for currency futures and options have growth rapidly due to the increase in the transactions in the foreign exchange, which has the risk of exchange rate fluctuation. Both the importers and exporters have to hedge their positions which otherwise would make them incur losses. Moreover the speculators and the arbitrageurs are also the persons who use the currency futures and options to take the advantage of the currency fluctuations. The corporate also use the exchange traded currencies futures and options to take the advantage of the exchange rate movements.

In 1972, the Chicago Mercantile Exchange opened its International Monetary Market (IMM) division. The IMM provides an outlet for currency speculators and for those looking to reduce their currency risks. Trade takes place in currency futures, which are contract for specific quantities of given currencies, the exchange rate is fixed at the time of the contract is entered into, and the delivery date is set by the board of directors of the IMM. Currency futures contracts are currently available for the British pound, Canadian dollar, Deutsche mark, Swiss franc, French franc, Japanese yen, Australian dollar and the European Currency Unit.

Contract specifications for Foreign Currency Futures

	Australian Dollar	*British Pound*	*Canadian Dollar*	*Deutsche Mark*	*French Franc*	*Japanese Yen*	*Swiss Franc*
Contractsize	$100,000	62500	$100,000	125,000	250,000	12,500,000	125,000
Symbol	AD	BP	CD	DM	FR	JY	SF
Margin Required							
Initial	$1200	$2000	$700	$1400	$700	$1700	$1700
Maintenance	900	1500	500	1000	500	1300	1300
Minimum Price change	1 point	2 point	1 point	1 point	5 point	1 point	1 point
Value of One point	$10	$6.25	$10	$12.50	$2.50	$12.50	$12.50

Trading hours are from 7.20 Am to 2.00 pm and the last day of trading is the Third Wednesday of the delivery month.

Forward Contract Versus Futures Contract

The main differences between the forward and the futures contract is that forward contracts are Over the Counter Traded and therefore they are customized while the futures contacts are standardized and they are exchange traded. The terms and conditions of the futures contract are standardized and hence the risk of liquidity and the counter party defaults no longer exists. The other important differences that exists between the Forward and the Futures contracts are as under:

Trading

Forward contracts are traded on the Over the counter markets whereas the futures contract are traded on the recognized stock exchanges.

Regulations

The forward markets are as such not regulated and they have their owns norms and rules that the parties themselves decide whereas the futures contract are regulated by the Commodity Futures Trading Commission.

Frequency of Delivery

More than 90% of the forward contracts are settled by delivery of the underlying asset whereas in case of the futures contract less than 1 % of the contracts are settled by delivery.

Size of Contract

Forward contract are individually tailored and tend to be much larger than the standardized contracts on the futures market whereas the futures contracts have the standardized contracts in terms of currency amount.

Delivery dates

Delivery dates in forward contracts are flexible and they are fixed as per the mutual understanding of the parties that have entered into contract while in futures contract only the specified dates are there on which the transactions can be squared off.

Settlement

Forward contracts are settled between the bank and the customer while in case of futures contracts the trade is settled via the Exchange Clearing House, gains on positions values may be withdrawn and losses are collected daily. This practice is called as mark to market.

Quotes

Forward prices are generally quoted in European terms and in Futures contract they are denoted in the American terms.

Transaction Costs

Costs of forward contracts based on bid-ask spread while futures contract entail brokerage fees for buy and sell orders.

Margins

Margins are not required in the forward markets while in futures markets all the participants are required to pay the margins upfront.

Credit Risk

The credit risk is borne by each party to a forward contract and in futures contract the Exchange Clearing House becomes the opposite side to each futures contract, thereby reducing the credit risk substantially.

FUTURES FORWARD ARBITRAGE

Arbitrageurs find the discrepancy between the forward and futures rates and play a vital role by taking the advantage of the price movement. This can be explained as;

Suppose the interbank forward bid for June 18 on pounds sterling is $1.2927 at the same time that the price of IMM sterling futures for delivery on June 18 is $1.2915. The dealer would simultaneously buy the June sterling futures contract for $80,718.75 (62500 * 1.2915) and sell an equivalent amount of sterling forward, worth $80,793.75(62500 * 1.2927) for June delivery. Upon settlement the dealer would earn profit of $75.

MARK TO MARKET

In the futures market the participants have to settle their accounts on the daily basis which is referred to as the mark to market and the profits and the losses are added to the account of the dealer on every day. This can be explained to as that on say Tuesday morning the investors buys Swiss Franc futures contract with a price of $0.75 and at the end of the day the price goes to $0.755 so the investors receives 125,000(0.755-0.750) = $625. On Wednesday say the price drops to $0.752 then the investor will have to pay 125000(0.755-0.752) = $375.

SPECULATION WITH CURRENCY FUTURES

Speculators make the use of the currency futures to make the profit by speculating the futures prices and then take a position which would results into positive cash flow in the future. This can be explained with the following example:

Suppose the futures rate is US $1.75 per pound and the spot rate on maturity is expected to be $1.76. The speculator will purchase pounds 62000 at the rate of $1.75 and the expectation comes true and so sells that pound at the rate of US $ 1.76 in the spot market, the profit will be US $ (1.76-1.75) * 62500 = US $ 625. In case of the situation where the speculator expects that the prices will fall in the future then he would sell futures say at the rate of $ 1.75and at the maturity the price comes to $1.74 the speculator would make gains of (1.75-1.74) * 62500 = $ 625

HEDGING USING CURRENCY FUTURES

Currency futures are used for the purpose of hedging which protects the firms involved in the foreign exchange transactions to protect themselves from the movement of the foreign exchange. This can be explained with the help of following example:-

Suppose that on July 1 an American company makes a sale for which it will receive DM 125,000 on September 1. The firm will want to convert those DM into dollars, so it is exposed to the risk that the mark will fall below its current spot rate of $0.6922. The firm can protect itself against a declining Deutsche mark by selling its expected DM receipts using futures contract.

	July 1	September 1
Spot	$0.6922	$0.6542
September futures	$0.6956	$0.6558

In the above situation if the firm remain unhedged then it would yield a loss of

125000 * (0.6922-0.6542) = $ 4750 If the firm decides to use the futures contract and sells the futures contract then it would yield (0.6956-0.6558) * 125000 = $ 4975 profit.

CURRENCY OPTIONS

What ever advantages the forward or the futures contract might hold for their purchaser, they have a common disadvantage: While they protect the holder against the risk of adverse movements n exchange rates, they eliminate the possibility of gaining a windfall profit from favorable movements. This was apparently one of thè considerations that led some commercial banks to offer currency options to their customers. Exchange traded currency options were first offered in 1983 by the Philadelphia Stock Exchange (PHILX).

In principle, an options is financial instrument that gives the holder the right but not the obligation to sell (Put) or buy (call) another financial instrument at set price and expiration date. The seller of the put option or call options must fulfill the contract if the buyer so desires it. Because the option not to buy or sell has value, the buyer must pay the seller opt he option some premium of r this privilege. As applied to foreign currencies, call options give the customer the right to purchase, and put options give the right to sell the contracted currencies at the expiration date. An American option can be exercised at any time up to the expiration date a European option can only be exercised at maturity.

An option that would be profitable to exercise at the current exchange rate is said to be in the money. Conversely, an out of the money option is one that would to be profitable to exercise at the current exchange rate. The price at which the option is exercised is a called the exercise price or strike price. An option whose exercise price is the same as the spot exchange rate is termed at the money.

BASIC TERMINOLOGY IN OPTIONS

Option Buyer: A persons or a firm who get the right to buy options is called as option buyer or he is also called as option holder.

Option Seller: A person who sells the options is called as the option seller or he is also called as the option writer.

Call option: Call options gives the buyer of the option the right to buy but not an obligation to do so.

Put option: Put options gives the buyer of the options the right to sell but not an obligation to do so.

Exercise price: it is the price at which the contract is entered into that is it is the rate at which the buyer and the seller decide to enter into the contract.

In the money option: A options that would generate the cash flows immediately on the exercise of the option is said to be an in the money option. In case of the call option the spot price has to be greater than the strike price for the option to be in the money.

Out of the money option: A options that would generate negative cash flow if it was exercised immediately is said to be an out of the money option. In case of call option if the spot price is less than the strike price then it is called as out of the money option.

At the money option: A option that would generate no cash flow it is exercised immediately is said to be at the money options. In this case the spot price and the strike price would be same.

Premium: This is the amount paid for the purpose of buying the option. It is also known as the option value. The premium consists of the time value and the intrinsic value.

Factors Affecting The Option Value: The following factors have a impact on the value of the option and they affect the option price.

Spot Price: This is the fundamental factor that affects the price of the options. In case of call option the rise in the spot price will lead to an increase in the value of the call option while a fall in the spot price will lead to a fall in the value of the call option.

Strike Price: The second factor that affects the value of the options is the strike price. A rise in the strike price will lead to a rise in the value of the put option while a rise in the strike price will lead to a fall in the value of the call option.

Time to maturity: The time available for the option to be exercised also determines the value of the options. If the time available for the option to be exercised is more the value of the option would be more and if the time available for the exercise of the option is less than the value of the options would also be less.

Volatility in Exchange rates: When the volatility is more the chances that a the options would be exercised will also be more and so the value of the option would also be more and if the volatility is less then there are less chances that the options would be exercised will also be less and so the value of the option will also be less.

Hedging With Currency Options: Options are used for the purpose of hedging the exchange rate movement risk and they are used by the importers who have to make the payment and also by the exporters who have to received the payment.

In case of an Indian importer who has imported goods for pounds 62500 and the amount is to be paid after a period of two months. If an appreciation in the pound is expected the importer will buy will the call option of two months coinciding with the maturity of the payment to be made after the period of two months. If the strike price is Rs. 60.00 per pound and the premium is Rs. 0.05 per pound and the say the spot price at the maturity is Rs. 60.20, the importer will exercise his option. He will have to pay Rs. 60.05 * 62500 = 37,53,125. If the importer had not purchased the call option then would he ave to pay 60.20 * 62500 = 37,62,500 Rs. Buying of the cal option reduces the importers obligation by Rs. 37,62,500 - Rs.37,53,125 = Rs. 9375

In case of an Indian Exporter, he will received the payment of pounds after the period of two months. In this case he would buy the put option as he fears a depreciation of pound within two moths when payment are to be received. In order to avoid the risk he will buy put option for selling the pound for a two moth maturity. Suppose the strike rate is Rs. 60.00 and the premium is Rs. 0.05 and the spot rate at maturity is Rs. 59.80 In case of the hedge he will receive Rs. 60.00-0.05*62500 = 37,46,875 Rs. In the absence of the hedge, he would have received only 62500 * 59.80 = Rs.37, 37,500. The buying of the option helps increase the exporters earning by Rs. 37,46,875 - 37,37,500 = 9375 Rs.

Various strategies using call and put options: There are various strategies which can be used by combinations of call and the put options. They can be explained as:

Bull spread: A spread is created by buying one call options and selling one call option. A bull spread is created with the objective of gaining with the rise in the movement of the exchange rate. Suppose a speculator purchases a call on the British pound with a strike price of Rs. 60.00 with a premium of Rs. 0.05 and sells a call with strike price of Rs. 60.90 with the same premium of Rs. 0.05. If the spot rate at the expiry moves up to Rs. 60.20 he will exercise the option and make a profit of Rs. 60.20-60.00-0.05 *62500 = Rs.9375. Since the other call will not be exercised the speculator will receive the premium amounting to Rs. 3125 (62500 * 0.05). His total income would be Rs. 12500 through this kind of bullish spread.

USING CURRENCY OPTIONS

The use of the currency options can be explained with the help of the following example. U.S. importer that has a DM 62,500 payment to make to a German exporter in 60 days. The importer could purchase a European cal option to have the Deutsche marks delivered to it at a specified exchange rate the strike price on the due date. Suppose the option premium is $0.02 per DM, and the exercise price is $0.64. The importer has paid $1,250 for the right to buy DM 62,500 at a price e of $0.64 per mark at the end of the 60 days. If at the time the importer's payment falls due, the value of the Deutsche mark has rise to, say $0.70 the option would be in the money. In case the importer exercises its call option, and purchases Deutsche marks for $0.64. The importer would earn a profit of $3,750 (62,500*0.06), which would more than cover the $1,250 cost of the option. If the rate has declined below the contracted rate to, say $0.60 the option would be out of the money. Consequently, the importer would let the option expire and purchase the Deutsche marks in the spot market despite losing the $1,250 option premium the importer would still be $1,250 better off than if it had locked in a rate of $0.64 with a forward or futures contract.

OPTION PRICING AND VALUATION

The value of an option consists of two things and they are the intrinsic value and the time value. The intrinsic value of the options is the difference between the spot price and the strike price at which the contracts is entered into. The intrinsic value of the call option on the Swiss francs with an exercise price of $0.74 and a spot rate of $0.77 would be $0.03(0.77-0.74). The time value of the options is determined with the time left for the options to be exercised that if more time is left for the options to be exercise then the time value is more and as a result the premium paid for the option would also be more as it provides greater flexibility and on the other hand if the time value of the options is less that is there are only few days for the options to be exercised the premium on such a options would also be less as there is less time availability.

WORLD SCENARIO ABOUT THE USEAGE OF DIFFERENT TYPES OF DERIVATIVES

The International Swaps and Derivatives Association is the global trade association representing participants in the privately negotiated derivatives industry, a business covering swaps and options across all asset classes (interest rate, currency, commodity and energy, credit and equity). ISDA was chartered in 1985, and today numbers over 600 member institutions from 46 countries on six continents. These members include most of the world's major institutions who deal in, as well as leading end-users of, privately negotiated derivatives. The membership includes associated service providers and consultants.

OVER 90% OF THE WORLD'S 500 LARGEST COMPANIES USE DERIVATIVES TO HELP MANAGE THEIR RISKS, ACCORDING TO NEW ISDA SURVEY

At its annual general on 9th April 2003, Japan Tokyo, the International Swaps and Derivatives Association announced the results of a survey of derivatives usage by the world's 500 largest companies.

According to the survey, 92% of these companies use derivative instruments to manage and hedge their risks more effectively. The companies using derivatives are located in 26 countries around the world and represent a broad variety of industries, ranging from aerospace to wholesalers of office and electronic equipment.

Of the companies using derivatives, 92% use them to help manage interest rate risk. This represents 85% of the total sample. 85% of the companies (78% of the total) use derivatives to help manage currency risk, 25% (23.5% of the total) to help manage commodity price risk and 12% (11% of the total) to help manage equity price risk

DERIVATIVES USAGE BY WORLD'S 500 LARGEST COMPANIES

Present Scenario: In the current scenario India's position is very strong in terms of the foreign exchange reserves. The current foreign exchange reserves of the country are above 85

billion dollars. Recently the RBI Governor who has now retired and became a member of the Rajya Sabha said in his recent interview that the rising rupee was a worrying factor and so the companies who had the foreign exchange exposure should

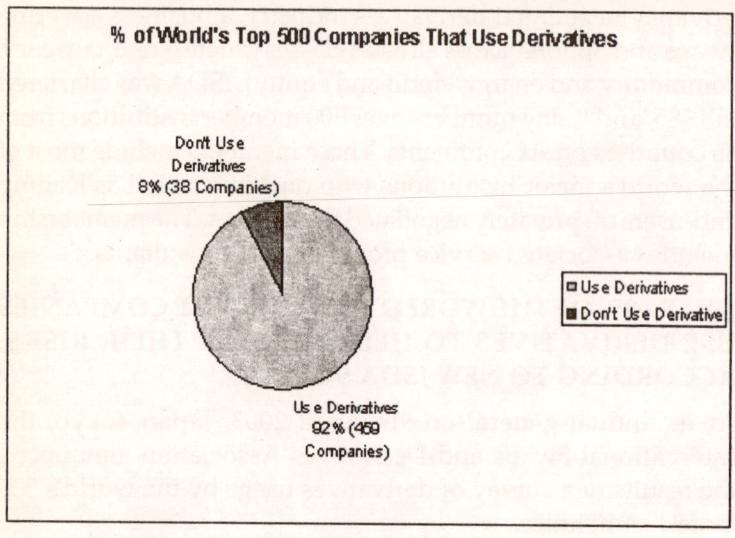

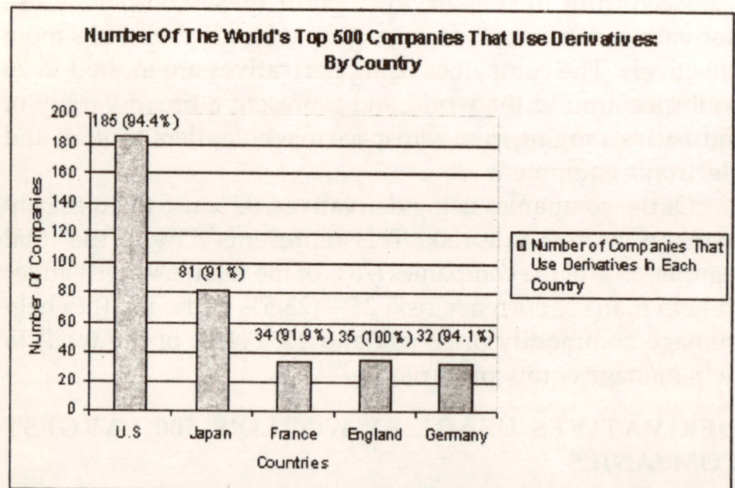

take the hedging positions to protect themselves from the rising rupee which would reduce their profit margins. According to

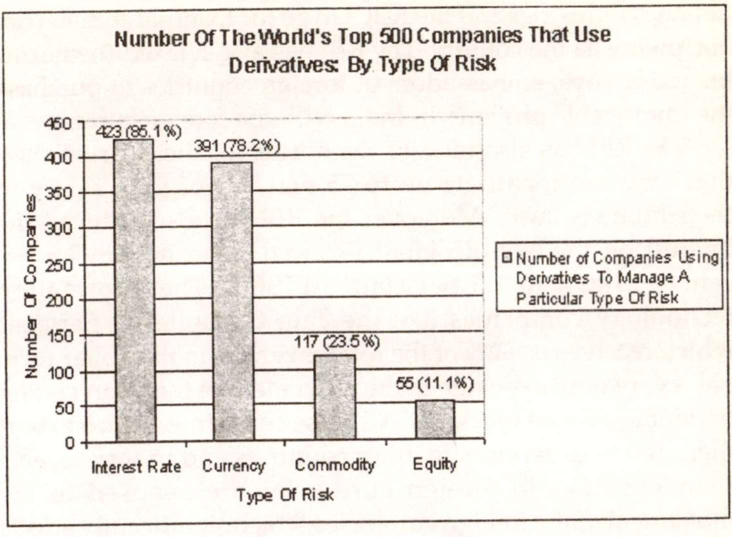

the report published in the Times of India one per cent rise in the rupee values reduces the profits of the companies by about 5 per cent. The continuous rise in the value of the rupee has eroded the profits of the particularly software sector which has majority of its earning from the exports. Players like the Infosys have their exporting earning about 65 per cent and Wipro has earning about 45 per cent form their export earning which are in the form of dollars. Even the players in the industry feel that the exporters should move to the Euro currency as the exchange rate is 50 Rs. While in case of dollars it is about 45 Rs. The euro currency accounts for 20 per cent of the world GDP and 20 per cent of the world trade while euro currency population accounts for about 290 million people. The full account convertibility of the rupee on the capital account is not granted by the Government as such facility was responsible for the South East Asian crisis which was responsible for the collapse of those economies. The Dhabol power project, which has now struck, in the mud is a result of the non-convertibility of the rupee in full sense. GE (General Electrical) and Betchel, which have invested $120 million, are now demanding a compensation of $600 million each in their arbitration procedure, which is carried out in London. The Government has recently not allowed

Reliance industries and the ICICI to go for External commercial borrowing as the country. The RBI has also relaxed the norms for the envoys, ambassadors of foreign countries to purchase the immovable property in India with the foreign currency.

The RBI has also relaxed the norms for the salaried class that they can repatriate up to 75 per cent of their salary to their home country. Moreover the RBI has also reduced the interest on the Non Resident External Deposit from 2.5 per cent + LIBOR to 1.5 per cent + LIBOR. The information technology companies like the Tata Consultancy Services which receives its 62% of the total revenues in the dollar form has a very high exposure to the movement of the appreciation or depreciation of the dollar. All those companies which export their goods or services to other countries and in turn receive their earnings in foreign currencies are exposed to the movement of the foreign currencies which significantly affects their projected earnings.

SUGGESTIONS

1. **Currency Derivatives be allowed:** As we have the equity derivatives market and now the recently launched commodities derivatives market, the Government should allow the currency derivatives market so that the corporates and even the individual investors can hedge their foreign exchange risk with the exchange traded products. This would also create another investment avenue for the individuals and the institutions.
2. **Currency Derivatives exchange be allowed:** The currency derivatives should be traded on the regular exchange like one we have in the equity market and the commodities market. This would reduce the risk of illiquidity in contracts; counter party risk would be removed as the exchange provides the country party guarantee to all the trades carried out on the exchange.
3. **Exchange traded products be launched:** The currency derivatives should be in form of the exchange traded products like the futures and options which would

provide ideal combinations for the strategy formations for the purpose of hedging, speculation and arbitrage. The futures can be used for those who can take high exposure in the currency derivatives as futures involve payment of high margin money while options can be used by those participants who do not want to have very high exposure but want to take the benefit from the movement of the currencies.

4. **Stringent risk management system:** As the currency derivatives world over have high volatility, it is very much necessary that the market should be very strong risk management system. Membership of the exchange should be given only to those participants who have sound financial standing, proper knowledge of the currency market, high integrity. The risk management of the market should also have the stringent margin requirement system so that no excess positions are taken by the market participants.
5. **Foreign Institutional Investors should not be allowed:** In the initial stages of the market, only the retail investors should be allowed to trade in the currency derivatives market. FIIs should be allowed only after the market has gained enough depth and liquidity. This would ensure that the market is not exposed to systemic volatility and that the confidence of the retail investors is not shaken because when the FIIs suddenly moves out of the market, it creates lot of panic and then the investors sell their holding in panic and incur losses.

POLICY IMPLICATION

India has now emerged as one of the fastest growing economy and Indian corporates have now high exposure in the international markets. Presently the Indian corproates use the forward market to hedge their risk due to the movement of the foreign currencies in which they trade but if the exchange traded market of currency derivatives are started then it would be of more utility for the corporates and also for the retail investors as they would get another opportunity for investment. The corporates which raise the money in the form of External Commercial Borrowing and pay interest rather they can use the options to acquire the required amount and if the spot rate is lower then the strike rate, they can let the option expire and purchase the currency from the spot market. The reserves which are at $ 140 billion, lying idle with the RBI can also be used for the purpose of Settlement Guarantee Fund which would install faith in the currency derivatives market. As the Government is encouraging the people to go for the market linked products and the as the assured returns instruments are getting lesser and lesser, the currency derivatives would provide another instruments for investment to the people and which would also generate lot of employment opportunities for the professionals.

CONCLUSION

The currency derivatives are not a luxury product but a need of the hour. The creation of such a market would make the Indian financial market at par with the global level market and attract more foreign capital as the hedging facilities would be more easy and at hand. The investment avenues for the people would increase and they would get more better returns with proper risk management. The employment opportunities would also increase with the new market for the educated class. The corporates can protect their projected earning with the instruments available in the currency derivatives market.

Under this system the exchange rate mechanism is controlled by the Central bank of the country. Whenever the country faces any problem regarding the exchange rate mechanism the central bank comes into the picture and takes the control over the movement of the exchange rates. When the rupee depreciates the Reserve Bank of India would come into picture and sell dollars in the markets so that the rupee appreciates and by this way it manages the exchange rates and so it is called as the managed float.

REFERENCES

Bhalla, V.K. International Financial Management, 2nd edition., New Delhi, Anmol 2001.

Bhalla, V.K. Managing International Investment and Finance, New Delhi, Anmol, 1997.

Shapiro Alan c., Multinational Financial Management, New Delhi, Prentice Hall of India, 1995.

John C. Hull., Options, Futures and other Derivatives, 3rd edition, New Delhi, Prentice Hall of India, 2000.

www.isda.com

16

WTO AND ITS IMPACT ON INDIAN ECONOMY

*S. M. Jawed Akhtar**

INTRODUCTION

The General Agreement on Tariffs and Trade (GATT) was established on 30th October 1947. GATT was established in order to promote international trade. India was one of the founder members of GATT. It was concerned with the promotion of international trade through tariff reduction, doing away with non-discriminatory practices among trading partners, and evolving rules to counter protectionism. The guiding principle of GATT was most favoured nation (MFN) clause. The purpose of this clause was to discourage bilateralism and encourage multilateralism so that the world trade could expand in an orderly manner. GATT provided for reduction in tariffs and trade restrictions in a phased manner over a period of time. It laid down that this task would be accomplished in different 'rounds' of trade negotiations to be held from time to time. In all, eight rounds of Multilateral Trade Negotiations (MTNs) were held under the auspices of GATT. The eighth and last round of negotiations was launched in Punta del Este, Uruguay in 1986, known as 'Uruguay Round'. This Round took more than eight years of complex negotiations as considerable differences existed among the member nations on the various issues such as agricultural subsidies, Multi-Fiber Arrangement,

* Senior Lecturer, Department of Economics, Aligarh Muslim University, Aligarh-202002, U.P.

market access, trade in services, anti-dumping, intellectual property rights etc. Because of the substantial differences among member nations on these issues, the then Director General of GATT, Arthur Dunkel came up with a Draft Final Act, known as Dunkel Draft. It was only after a great amount of persuasion and threats by the developed countries that the governments of developing countries succumbed and on April 15, 1994 the Final Act was ultimately approved and signed at Marrakesh by 104 member nations.

However, it was the signing of the Final Act of the Uruguay Round by the member nations of GATT which paved the way for the setting up of the World Trade Organisation (WTO). The WTO Agreement came into force from January 1, 1995. India is a founder member of the WTO by ratifying the WTO Agreement on December 30, 1994, and at present there are 146 members. The former GATT was merely a legal arrangement, while WTO is a permanent organization and it has a legal status, and enjoys privileges and immunities on the same footing as the IMF and the World Bank. The WTO is the only international organization dealing with the global rules of trade between nations. It has following five functions as set out in Article 111 of WTO (Debroy, Bibek 1996).

(i) The WTO 'shall facilitate the implementation, administration and operation, and further the objectives, of this Agreement and of the Multilateral Trade Agreements, and shall also provide the framework for implementation, administration and operation of the Plurilateral Trade Agreements'

(ii) The WTO 'shall provide the forum for negotiations among its members concerning their multilateral trade relations in matters dealt with under the Agreements in the Annexes to this Agreement'

(iii) The WTO 'shall administer the understanding on rules and procedures governing the settlement of disputes

(iv) The WTO 'shall administer the Trade Policy Review Mechanism'.

(v) 'With a view to achieving greater coherence in global economic policy-making, the World Trade Organisation shall cooperate, as appropriate, with the IMF and with the IBRD and its affiliated agencies'.

In a broader sense, WTO Agreements consist of three main issues - goods, services and intellectual property rights. First, trade in goods of all descriptions (agricultural, industrial or others) is to be governed under GATT reformulations. Second, trade in services of all kinds (business services including professional and computers, communications, construction and engineering, financial services, health services, tourism and travel services etc.) is to be regulated under General Agreement on Trade in Services (GATS). Third, Trade-Related Aspects of Intellectual Property Rights (TRIPs) would set out the terms and conditions for the international flow of intellectual property (Chadha, G.K. 2001). Hence, it should be absolutely clear that there would be no economic activity in the world which will remain unaffected from the influences of the WTO Agreements. At the same time, WTO's mandate can not be bypassed by any member of the world trading community since it is having the support of a sound and comprehensive legal system, and its agreement having been duly signed and ratified by the governing systems of the member countries.

India's decision to continue with the membership of the WTO necessitates a parallel decision to strengthen the country's administrative infrastructure to deal with WTO-related issues. India joined WTO with the objective that it will bring higher growth, accelerated export expansion, and a better earning and living standard to the so-called average citizen of India. So far, India has done well in observing its commitments to WTO. However, as a member of WTO, India has to absorb the shocks that may come under its expanding regime. Hence, it is essential to determine our present status and accordingly decisions are to be taken on various issues.

OBJECTIVE OF THE STUDY

The main emphasis of the WTO is to promote an open, equitable and non-discriminatory multilateral trading system. It is a rule-based organization that seeks to foster a world where persuasion supersedes coercion, where the principle of non-discrimination among members imparts fairness, giving small countries as well as big ones a voice, and where decisions are taken by consensus (Kumar, Arun 2000). The members themselves decide on the rules governing their trade relations, and periodically enter into rounds of negotiations aimed at further opening up of markets and reforming the agreements. Regardless of the size of individual economies, they would all enjoy the same rights and be subject to the same obligations, and so on (Bhattachrya, B. 1995). In particular, when WTO was setup, a great promise was held out to the underdeveloped economies. It appeared that, they would gain as much as the developed countries, and perhaps a little more than that because of the fact that the developed countries would have to remove all trade restrictions making way for a world of free multilateral trade. But in reality, the developed countries seem to be raising new barriers to international trade in the guise of environment and social standards. At the same time, both inside and outside the WTO meetings, much pressure is being put on the developing countries to remove all barriers to trade to make their economies global. The purpose seems clear- developing countries have a market potential and that must be tapped to the advantage of rich countries. The history of clash of interest indicates that the real economic purpose is never revealed, it has to be understood as the fact unfolds itself (Sen, A. 1998).

In the light of the above, this paper attempts to examine the performance of the Indian economy under the WTO regime. For this purpose following parameters have been selected:

(i) GDP growth rate,

(ii) Sectoral contribution to GDP,

(iii) Employment scenario, and

(iv) Structure of trade.

The study is exclusively based on secondary data. These data have been collected from various issues of CMIE Reports and Economic Survey.

PERFORMANCE OF INDIAN ECONOMY:

The WTO Agreement will be completing ten years of its existence on December 31, 2004. It is of national importance to find out the impact of WTO Agreement on Indian economy during these periods being the member countries of the organization. However, a more clear picture will emerge only when all agreements are implemented world-wide. Hence, we can analyse the performance of the Indian economy on the basis of the parameters mentioned in the objective of the study. Table

Table 1
Annual Growth Rates of Real GDP by Industry of Origin
(At Factor Cost, 1993-94 Prices)

(Percent)

Year	*Primary Sector*	*Secondary Sector*	*Tertiary Sector*	*GDP at Factor Cost*
1981-82	5.7	7.4	17.1	6.0
1985-86	1.0	4.7	24.6	4.5
1990-91	4.6	7.4	16.7	5.6
1991-92	-1.1	-1.0	17.1	1.3
1992-93	5.4	4.3	16.1	5.1
1993-94	3.9	5.6	24.0	5.9
1994-95	5.3	10.3	19.2	7.3
1995-96	-0.3	12.3	29.4	7.3
1996-97	8.8	7.7	21.1	7.8
1997-98	-1.5	3.8	31.1	4.8
1998-99	5.9	3.8	25.5	6.5
1999-00	0.6	5.0	31.3	6.1
2000-01	0.1	7.0	16.0	4.4
2001-02	6.1	3.5	18.8	5.6
2002-03 (Q)	-4.0	6.2	21.6	4.0
2003-04 (P)	8.6	6.7	23.2	8.1

Source: Economic Survey -2003-04
P: Provisional Estimates
Q: Quick Estimates

1 gives the annual growth of real GDP by industry of origin. The GDP growth rate has shown a highly uneven growth pattern during the 1990s, in the same way as it did during the 1980s. The annual growth rate of the tertiary sector has been very much impressive particularly in the later half of the 1990s compared with the first half. On the other hand, the performance of primary as well as secondary sectors have not been much satisfactory except for few years. The failure of primary and secondary sectors in generating higher level of

output may be regarded as one of the important factor responsible for low GDP growth rates in some of the years. Table-2 shows the sectoral contribution to the GDP. The secondary and tertiary sectors have steadily improved their share in the GDP, while the share of primary sector has been declining reflecting a consistent restructuring of the economy. More than half of the GDP has been contributed by the tertiary sector showing its rising importance in the GDP. Table 3 estimates employment in organized public and private sectors.

Table 2

Sectoral Contribution to the GDP (At Constant Price)

(Percentage Share in GDP)

Year	*Primary Sector*	*Secondary Sector*	*Tertiary Sector*
1980-81	39.71	23.70	36.59
1985-86	36.30	24.80	38.90
1990-91	32.20	27.22	40.58
1991-92	31.30	26.72	41.98
1992-93	31.50	26.43	42.07
1993-94	30.97	26.26	42.77
1994-95	30.32	26.97	42.71
1995-96	28.00	28.05	43.94
1996-97	28.46	27.86	43.68
1997-98	26.50	27.72	45.78
1998-99	26.42	27.00	46.58
1999-00	24.99	26.68	48.33
2000-01	23.92	27.23	48.85
2001-02	24.08	26.62	49.30
2002-03	21.95	27.25	50.80
2003-04	22.12	26.86	51.02

Source: CMIE Report on National Income Statistics, Oct. 2004.

It shows a marginal increase in the total employment in the organized sector and that too is only upto 1997, then after it started declining. The growth rate of employment has been higher in private sector than in public sector. Private sector reflects continuous increase in total employment except for few years, while employment in the public sector increased continuously only upto 1997, after that there has been continuous decline in the total employment of the public sector. Table 4 gives structure and composition of India's trade. The

1990s have clearly witnessed a much faster pace of globalization, compared with the 1980s. Exports and imports as percentage of GDP have witnessed a steady expansion, especially during the most recent years. Also the structure of India's trade has been steadily tilting in favour of manufactured

Table 3

Estimates of Employment in Organised Public and Private Sectors

(Lakh persons as on March 31)

Year	*Public Sector*	*Private Sector*	*Total*
1990	187.72	75.82	263.54
1991	190.57	76.76	267.33
1992	192.10	78.46	270.56
1993	193.26	78.51	271.77
1994	194.45	79.30	273.75
1995	194.66	80.59	275.25
1996	194.29	85.12	279.41
1997	195.59	86.86	282.45
1998	194.18	87.48	281.66
1999	194.15	86.98	281.13
2000	193.14	86.46	279.60
2001	191.38	86.52	277.90
2002	187.73	84.32	272.06

Note: (i) Excludes Sikkim, Arunachal Pradesh, Dadra & Nagar Haveli and Lakshadweep as these are not yet covered under the programme.
(ii) Includes all establishments in the public sector irrespective of size of employment and non-agricultural establishments in the private sector employing 10 or more persons.

Source: Economic Survey-2003-04.

goods particularly during 1990s. The contribution of agriculture and allied products in the total exports has been declining continuously. Thus, the brief overview of the performance of the Indian economy throws up a mixture of promises and challenges. The overall growth rate of the economy has picked up well and structural transformation of the economy continues, tertiary sector now accounts for nearly a half of the economy while the share of the secondary sector has witnessed a steady expansion. Trade restructuring is also very much apparent since manufacturing exports now constituted an overwhelming proportion of exports. But one of the most serious and challenging problems is the loss of jobs in the recent years. Thus, even after opening up of the economy in 1991 and joining WTO membership in 1995, India has not been benefited much particularly on employment front.

Table 4
Structure of India's Trade

Year	*Percentage Share in GDP* Exports	Imports	*Percentage Share in Total Exports* Agriculture & Allied Products	Manufactured Goods
1980-81	4.67	8.73	—	—
1985-86	3.92	7.07	25.74	57.65
1990-91	5.73	7.40	13.62	63.33
1991-92	6.74	7.33	12.37	55.17
1992-93	7.17	8.47	14.87	76.97
1993-94	8.12	8.52	18.11	74.90
1994-95	8.16	8.88	16.05	77.49
1995-96	8.95	10.33	19.22	74.69
1996-97	8.68	10.15	20.50	73.54
1997-98	8.54	10.13	18.93	75.83
1998-99	8.03	10.24	18.17	77.64
1999-00	8.21	11.13	15.27	80.93
2000-01	9.63	10.92	13.55	77.90
2001-02	9.16	10.74	13.46	76.14
2002-03	10.33	12.03	12.73	76.34
2003-04	—	—	11.67	75.04

Source: CMIE Report on Foreign Trade & Balance of Payments, Various Issues.

INDIAN ECONOMY UNDER THE WTO REGIME

The WTO was expected to play a crucial role in implementing the new world trade system visualized in the Uruguay Round. It was expected to enshrine the rule of law in international economic and trade relations, thus setting universal rules and discipline over the temptations of unilateralism. This collective profession of faith was expected to mark the end of the Colonial pact and embodied genuine interdependence (Mishra, H.K. 2001). When the WTO was set up, it appeared that every partner of this organisation will be benefited. But in reality it seems that the developed economies are creating new barriers to international trade of developing economies. Under this background, it becomes essential to analyse the expected benefits as well as disadvantages to India being the member of WTO.

(i) Expected Favourable Effects on Indian Economy

The WTO framework offers immense scope for developing countries, who make up most of its membership. On December 31, 2004 the discriminatory protectionism against developing countries' exports of textiles and clothing will come to an end, making a landmark in the multilateral trading system. This will also signal the end of the transition period for product patent protection in some areas of technology such as pharmaceuticals. A stronger intellectual property rights regime may have implications for pharmaceuticals sectors in these countries and their exports, as well as on prices and access to medicines for their people. At the same time, this may give incentives for innovation and patenting. There are several avenues through which India will also gain under WTO regime. Firstly, it was estimated by the GATT Secretariat that the level of merchandise trade in goods will be higher by 745 billion US dollars in the year 2005. The GATT Secretariat further projects that the largest increase will be in the areas of clothing (60 percent), agriculture, forestry and fishery products (20 percent), and processed food and beverages (19 percent). Since our country enjoys potential export competitiveness in these product lines, it is believed that India will obtain large gains in these sectors. It is estimated that if India's share in world exports increases from 0.5 percent to 1 percent then the trade gains for India may range from 3.5 to 7 billion U.S. dollars per year (Economic Survey, 1994-95).

Secondly, due to reduction in domestic subsidies and barriers to trade, there will be improved prospects for agricultural exports as a result of increase in the world prices of agricultural products. India will gain on this count also. In fact, India hopes that the reduction of subsidies in the USA and the European Community will enable it to increase its earnings from agricultural exports. Thus, on the one hand earnings from agricultural exports are likely to increase, on the other hand India has ensured that all major programmes for the development of agriculture will be exempted from the disciplines in the agricultural agreement. Thus, the operation of the public distribution system will not be affected by the provisions of the Agreement, and protection necessary for developing the agricultural sector in the underdeveloped countries might be continued.

Thirdly, it is also believed that the phasing out of the MFA (Multi-Fibre Arrangement) by 2005 will benefit India as the exports of textiles and clothing will increase. In fact, with this the discriminatory protectionism against developing countries' exports of textiles and clothing will come to an end. However, there should be no attempt to replace quotas with other trade protection instruments.

Lastly, the Uruguay Round Agreement which led to the establishment of WTO has strengthened multilateral rules and disciplines. This includes anti-dumping, subsidies and countervailing measures, safeguards and dispute settlement. This ensures greater security and thus create a more favourable environment for the developing countries like India to reap the benefits all round in the new world economic order.

(ii) Expected Unfavourable Effects on Indian Economy

The WTO Agreement carries some disadvantages to the developing countries like India. The most serious disadvantages to India are likely to flow from the Agreements related to TRIPs, TRIMs and GATS.

(a) TRIPS (Trade Related Aspects of Intellectual Property Rights)–

The main argument in favour of protection of intellectual property rights (patents, copy rights, trade marks etc.) is that it encourages innovation by rewarding the inventors with the grant of monopoly rights over the commercial exploitation of their inventions for a specific period (Misra, Puri 2003). In fact, TRIPs under the Uruguay Round has been made more stringent and it is bound to favour the interest of the developed countries. This is due to the reason that the Agreement itself is highly weighted in favour of the patent holders. As the developed countries and their MNCs have vast resources and facilities for research and development, they would be at an advantage to invest and patent processes and products. At the same time, protection of intellectual property rights is, in itself, anti-competition and anti-liberalization and goes against the spirit of opening up the world economy and global integration. The TRIPs Agreement goes against the Patent Act of India, 1970 in almost all important areas. Under Indian Patents Act only process patents can be granted in food, chemicals and medicines, while the TRIPs Agreement provides for granting product patents also in all these areas. The TRIPs Agreement provides 20 years for the general term of patent, but the Indian Patent Act provides for a general term of 14 years, both for product as well as process patents. Indian Patent Act grants process patents only to drugs and medicines.

The extension of intellectual property rights to agriculture has serious consequences for India. It would harm the interests of farmers. It makes no distinction between subsidies to promote food security and self-reliance and those meant to increase exports of farm products. The granting of product patents will also have an adverse affect on the Indian pharmaceuticals industry. The prices of drugs and medicines will rise considerably. It will affect vast sections of the poor on the one hand and many Indian drugs companies may be forced to shut down, on the other. Thus, MNCs belonging to the developed countries are likely to dominate the global economy.

(b) TRIMs (Trade Related Investment Measures)–

The TRIMs Agreement calls for introducing national treatment of foreign investments and removal of quantitative restrictions. It is mainly concerned with provisions for elimination of trade related investment measures which are designed to protect the interests of foreign investors in the developing countries. It is the developed countries that are benefited much more from the Agreement. However, the developing countries have been allowed to deviate from the provisions of TRIMs Agreement on balance of payments ground. But once there is an improvement in the balance of payments, the host country is required to eliminate the identified measures even if there is justification to maintain them on broadest macroeconomic and strategic considerations. The provisions of the TRIMs Agreement will most likely have the effect of undermining any plan or strategy of self-reliant growth for the developing countries. This may also lead to the drain of foreign exchange reserves of the developing countries, adversely affecting their balance of payments position (Dubey, M. 1996). The Agreement has reduced the decision–making powers of national governments. Some developing countries have been facing practical problems in implementing the TRIMs Agreement and, therefore, sought extension beyond the five-year periods.

(c) GATS (General Agreement on Trade in Services)–

The GATS provides a multilateral framework of principles and services which should govern trade in services under considerations of transparency and progressive liberalization. But we know that there is a vast level of difference in the development of services like banking, insurance, telecommunications and shipping between developed and developing countries. Therefore, inclusion of trade in services is bound to benefit the developed countries than developing countries like India. The developed nations insisted for the inclusion of trade in services in the Uruguay Round on the ground that the opening up of trade in services is an important requirement for globalisation and development of world trade. The principal exporters of services are the USA, France, Japan and Netherlands and together they account for about 60 percent share of the world trade in services. It is these countries that will benefit most from the new Agreement on services. Foreign firms will now be free to expand their network in the Indian services sector. They will also be free to remit resources to their parent country in the form of profits, interest, royalties etc. This will lead to foreign exchange burden on India. For Indian firms it will be difficult to compete with the firms supplying services in the developed countries.

CONCLUSION

The Uruguay Round of Agreements which led to the establishment of WTO was one of the significant developments in the area of international trade. Moreover, it had expectations of positive impact attached to it. It has led to the strengthening of the trading system through improved transparency in economic policy making. The Agreement brought agriculture, textiles and service sectors into the mainstream of the multilateral rules. Also, the improved dispute settlement system under WTO is a rule based, thus ensuring that the voice of the developing and the weaker members will not be ignored. But, it is definitely true that there have been certain shortcomings in the Agreements. This, in turn, has led to the loopholes, thereby, providing the scope for non-implementation of the Agreements in their proper spirit. As a result, the expectations attached to it were not actualized. Hence, we have not achieved what we had expected while signing the Agreement. The negotiation has not given us much in tangible terms. The recent performance of the Indian economy particularly in terms of GDP growth rate, employment and exports does not fulfill our expectations of being the member of the WTO. However, trade negotiations are not an end in themselves for developing countries. The government should considerably strengthen its infrastructure for undertaking global trade negotiations. Through negotiations we may pressurize the industrialized countries to reduce their subsidies and provide increased market access. Reduction of subsidies will raise the prices of agricultural products in the world market and this should make our exports more competitive. The liberalisation measures will create market openings which will be available to us. To defend national interests in eventuality of an increasing pace of dumping activities in India by the advanced industrial countries, anti-dumping measures are to be significantly strengthened. Thus, the discussions on TRIPs, services, agriculture, labour standards and environment are likely to dominate WTO's agenda in future and India will have to prepare a national and international strategy to face the challenges. To meet the challenges posed by the developed countries, the developing countries will have to join hands to protect their interests in WTO negotiations in future.

REFERENCES

Aggarwal, Yogi (1994), "Is GATT Really Bad for India?", *The Tribune*, Chandigarh, Vol. 114 (51), Feb. 21.

Alagh, Y.K. (2001), "WTO and India: Getting Facts Right ", *Business Line*, Feb. 9.

Banik, N. (2000), "India and the Post-Seattle Agenda", *The Economic Times*, Jan. 8, p. 6.

Bhandari, Surendra (1999), *World Trade Organisation and Developing Countries*, Deep & Deep Publication Pvt. Ltd., New Delhi.

Bhattacharyya, B. (1995), "World Trade Organisation and India", *Yojana*, Feb. 28. Vol. 39, No. 3, pp. 5-6.

Chadha, G.K. (2001), *WTO and Indian Economy*, Deep & Deep Publication Pvt. Ltd., New Delhi.

Chadha, Rajesh (2000), "Understanding the WTO Regime", *EPW*, March 25.

CMIE Reports, *Centre for Monitoring Indian Economy Pvt. Ltd.*, Mumbai, Various Issues.

Debroy, Bibek (1994), "The Uruguay Round Agreement: An Indian Perspective" in V. Ramachandriah (ed.), *GATT Accord: India's Strategic Response*, Common Wealth Publishers, New Delhi.

Debroy, Bibek (1996), *Beyond the Uruguay Round: The Indian Perspective on GATT*, New Delhi.

Dubey, Muchkund (1996), *An Unequal Treaty: World Trading Order After GATT*, New Age International Ltd., Delhi.

Dutt, R. and Sundharam, KPM (2004), *Indian Economy*, S. Chand and Company, New Delhi.

Gosami, Omker (2000), "Engaging in WTO Trade Policy", *Business Standard*, May 6.

Government of Indian (2004), *Economic Survey – 2003-04*, Ministry of Finance and Company Affairs, Economic Division, New Delhi.

Kumar, A. (2000), "India at the Seattle Meeting", *EPW*, Jan. 15.

Kurien, C.T. (1994), *Global Capitalism and the Indian Economy*, Orient Longman, Hyderabad.

Mishra, H.K. (2001), "Impact of WTO on Indian Economy", in G.K. Chadha (ed.), *WTO and the Indian Economy*, Deep & Deep Publication Pvt. Ltd., New Delhi.

Misra, S.K. and V.K. Puri (2004), *Indian Economy*, Himalaya Publishing House, Delhi.

Puri, Lakshmi (2004), "Reviving Doha – Developing World Can Gain From WTO", *Times of India*, Oct. 29. p. 16.

RBI (2001), *Handbook of Statistics on Indian Economy*, Bombay.

Rao, Harish (1999), "At the WTO, Might is Very Often Right", *Business Standard*, Sept. 20, p. 10.

Sen, A. (1998), "WTO and India's Response", *Yojana*, Sept. Vol. 42, No. 9.

Shukla, S.P. (2002), "From the GATT to the WTO and Beyond", in Deepak Nayyar (ed.), *Governing Globalisation – Issues and Institutions*, Oxford University Press, New Delhi.

Srinivasan, T.N. (1999), "WTO and the Developing Countries", *Journal of Social and Economic Development*, Vol. II, NO. 1, Jan – June.

World Bank (1996), *India: Recent Economic Developments and Prospects*, Washington, D.C.

WTO (1995), "The Results of the Uruguay Round of Multilateral Trade Negotiations: The Legal Texts", *GATT Secretariat/WTO*, Geneva.

17

NEW DIMENSION OF INFORMATION TECHNOLOGY AND MODERNIZATION OF COOPERATIVE BUSINESS ORGANISATION IN THE NEW ECONOMIC ENVIRONMENT

Samwel Kakuko Lopoyetum[*], *P. Selvamani*[**] *and Benjamin K. Muttai*[***]

INTRODUCTION

Information Technology is emerging as the most powerful tool for positive growth of socio economic status of the entire community. This is particularly true in the 21st Century. Modern technology has brought large-number of solutions to the socio-economic problems and many other hurdles facing all the community from different angles. The significance of information technology (IT) is felt on different service sectors such as Education, Health Service, Transportation, cooperative sector and many other business organizations. The Information

* **Senior Post-Doctoral Research Fellow,** (UGC - Min. of HRD), Department of Cooperation, Faculty of Rural Social Sciences, Gandhigram Rural University (Nationally Accredited with Five Stars by NAAC), Gandhigram - 624 302, Dindigul District, Tamilnadu State, India.

** **Research Project Fellow,** Department of Political Science and Development Administration, Faculty of Rural Social Sciences, Gandhigram Rural University (Nationally Accredited with Five Stars by NAAC), Gandhigram - 624 302, Dindigul District, Tamilnadu State, India.

*** **Faculty,** Department of Agricultural Economics and Agri-Business Management, Egerton University, Post Box No. NJORO, Kenya East Africa.

Technology and Communication (ITC) are the subject of great signiricance in the modern times, because the abo\ e mention sectors have grown to become even more complex, public expectation from service sectors are increasing year after year, the new Information Computer Applications and communication system (ITC) in these sectors are also increasing, accessibility of mass media particularly print and electronic (Radio, Television) revolution is also taking place in the most remarkable way which incorporate the internet and multimedia systems. Cooperative education system and training can make use of electronic revolution and use of Information Technology Enable Services (ITES) in the long run and in the 21st Century.

Large number of Cooperative Business Organizations can expect to earn more profits and provide services to the customers and consumers effectively. This can be achieved mainly by applying latest knowledge of Information Technology and Communication in all the functional areas of Cooperative Business Management and Administrations such as

Marketing, Human Resource Management and Development (HRM&D), Financial Management and Resources, Physical Resources, Information Resources, Marketing Management, Office Management and Administration, Export and Import of cooperative products (Foreign trade), Production and Operation Management, Research and Development policy issues, Business forecasting, Leadership Decision-making process, Organizational Behaviour, Planning, Organizing, Staffing, Directing, Communicating, Coordinating, Supervision, Motivation, control etc.,

The ITC sector will help and support business operations of many cooperative business organizations through EC, EB, EW, etc. (E-Commerce, E-business, E-World and E-Banking). In this context Information Technology and Communication would be helpful in bringing-out customers online and becomes powerful technological tool to be adopted by different sectors of the economy in the New Millennium. Cooperative Business organizations in the new era of economic reforms and electronic world (E-World) must make use of the latest information and communication technology. They must also modernize and mechanize their business processing activities. The information and Communication Technology (ITC) is the subject of great significance in the modern times. Agricultural cooperative marketing and processing organizations are undertaking their business activities using the oldest systems, machines and equipments, therefore, there is imperative need to revamp and modernize all these cooperative organizations. The Application of ITC entails the involvement of these cooperative organizations involves recording, creating, storing, retrieving and transmitting information from one area to another organisation to serve the needs and requirements of cooperative sector/ organizations and community at large the new era of electronic revolutions. These organizations are expected to earn surplus and provide adequate services to its members. Therefore, this can only be made possible by the use of Information and Communication Technology (ITC) in the functional areas of business management and administration of cooperative organizations. They can engage themselves in E. Commerce, E-Business, E-World, Web-Marketing, On-line Marketing, Internet, etc., They can bring customers on line and becomes more powerful tool for the growth and development of cooperative business organizations. The use of Information and Communication Technology (ITC) has been demonstrated by Warna – Nagar sugar cooperative mills, National Dairy Development Board (NDDB) and even larger type of cooperative organizations. Infact, now-a-days almost all organizations depends on Information Technology and communication system to enable them to process their business activities in the most effective and efficient manner.

MEANING AND DEFINITION OF INFORMATION TECHNOLOGY (IT)

The term "information technology is used to describe the process involving creating, recording, processing, storing, retrieving, the information and transmitting and again recording of information from the feed back". Also, the

UNESCO consider information technology as "Scientific, technological and engineering disciplines and the management techniques used in information handling and processing, their application, computers and their interaction with men and machines associated with social, economical and cultural matters." Information technology can be defined in simple terms, "as the science of the information storing, accession handling and transferring".

The information and communication technology has assumed greater significant in the 21st Century. The growth and development of service sector in India is extremely enormous. All the service sectors such as Education, Health, Transportation, Business, Tourism, Postal and Telephone service, environment and marketing information system are now days benefiting a great deal from emerging technology and up-gradation of information and communication technology. Subsequently the rural economy is expected to move forward with the help of information and communication technology and bridging the gap between digital divide (Digital) and Non-Digital regions of the country.

COMPONENTS OF INFORMATION TECHNOLOGY (IT)

There are distinct ways of analyzing the components of information technology and can be identified for use in different sectors of the economy. They are;

- Technology and its application for different purposes in sectors such as private, cooperative sector, public, agriculture, tertiary, secondary, industry and service sector.
- Development of equipments machines and tools; and
- Development of software and hardware system etc.,

- **Technology and its Application in Different Sectors of the Indian Economy**

It consists of methods and techniques for collection and transformation of data. Communication links between different geographical places. It is of vital importance for the success of

Information technology based on the feedback and control system. Today, high quality computers are used for communication and different functional areas of organizations. The communication systems and networked environment of different sectors of the economy at present day are making the jobs of connecting different required parts and geographical locations more easily and even become more economical and manageable in handling the Information technology and communication system.

- **Development of Equipments, Machines and Tools**

The development of equipments machines, tools and their peripherals are fast emerging and modernization is taking place at a faster speed. It can take the dimension of

(a) Pattern recognition equipment such as, video cameras and scanners etc.,

(b) Fiber optics and satellite etc.,

- **Development of Software and Hardware System**

The next components in Information Technology are the development and preparation of the software application. There are, relentlessly army of engineers and technologist (technicians) for an effective and efficient use of technological innovations and equipment up-gradations that have been brought in by consistent research and development in the field of information technology and communication system. The hardware system is also being developed and upgraded from time to time.

DEVELOPMENT OF COMPUTER TECHNOLOGY

Computer is the heart of all modern Information technologies. It is an electronic digital device designed to accept input requirement. It can process it and display the output. Computer along with other input devices (keyboard, scanner etc.,) and output devices (printer, plotter etc.,) are referred to as hardware. At present, India's computer density is 0.7 for 1000 population against the world's average of 25 per 1000. The densities are bound to improve in the years to come.

ECONOMIC GROWTH AND COOPERATIVE DEVELOPMENT THROUGH INFORMATION TECHNOLOGY AND COMMUNICATION

Information technology have played significant role in almost all sectors of the economy including agricultural, industry, service, cooperative sector, private, public, tertiary, primary, secondary, business and social sectors. This concept is true for any developed and developing countries such as India and Kenya. Infact, human history has already witnessed the industrial revolution, economic growth and the agricultural revolution which includes Green Revolution and White Revolutions (Milk production system). Whereas, the information technology and communication is emerging as the technological infrastructure for global integration and rapid development of all the sectors of the economic of the country.

In broad terms, information technology dealing all sub-sectors with the generation, transmission and utilisation of information like telecommunication, computers, consumer electronics, media infrastructure etc., The information technology is also as capable of integrating all the development and innovation of different types of programmes/schemes. There has been a revolution of transformation in the economy from old to modern economy based on knowledge-based economy. The development of Information Technology and Communication provides necessary information about the whole structure of the economy in general and necessary information about the market in particular, when the information technology is more efficient and effective it can directly and indirectly help to accelerate the optimum growth of the economy and promote development in all sectors. It is felt, that information and communication technology to day becomes an integral part of the development process of the economy, if only it is geographically and politically (geo-politically) fairly distributed in the country to include the coverage of rural economy.

SIGNIFICANCE OF COMPUTER IN COOPERATIVE BUSINESS ORGANIZATIONS, SERVICE SECTORS AND RURAL DEVELOPMENT ORGANIZATIONS

In order to attain significant rural development and enhanced rural prosperity, eminent scientist Prof. M. Swaminathan advocated for bridging the existing gap between the digital divide among the affluent communities and non-affluent community. Infact, Prof. M. Swaminathan, Chairman, National Commission on Farmers, Founder, M.S. Foundation and Research Center, the architect of India's Green Revolution, was always concerned that all the benefits of science, technology growth and development do not reach the poor!!. He was also greatly concerned about the tremendous differences caused by the new technologies, especially information and communication technologies, which could bridge the gap existing between the rich and the poor. He wanted to use the very same information and communication technologies to bring about greater opportunities for the poor and to usher in an era of job-lead growth. Thus, the ultimate aim is to enhance the growth and development of the rural economy and enhance socio-economic development of rural communication and improve their livelihood management system in the 21st Century.

- **The Speed of Computers and Usefulness for Development**

The computer was initially invented as a high-speed calculator. This has largely led to enormous progress and many scientific projects which were previously impossible to undertake without the use of computers.

Infact, electrical pulses travel at an incredible speed and operations. The units of speed is measured in the microsecond (millionths). The nanosecond (thousand-millionths) and later even the microsecond (million-millionths). It is even interesting to note that, powerful computer is capable of adding together two 18 digit numbers in 300 and 400 nanosecond!!! These benefits and significance can be useful and applied in the development of the service sector, cooperative business organizations and rural development organizations.

- **Storage of Information and Data**

The speed with which computers can process large volume of information has led to the generation of new data and information on a vast scale, in other words, the computer has compounded the information explosion. The IT can store data and information for use in many sectors of the economy including the cooperative business organizations.

- **Accuracy of Computers**

The computers accuracy is consistently becoming higher and higher. Almost, without exception, the errors in computing are due to human rather than to technological weaknesses, i.e., imprecise thinking by the programmer, inaccurate data, or poorly designed systems can contribute to inaccuracy of computers. Accuracy can be useful in taking appropriate decision and relevant data and information in the service sector, cooperative business organizations and rural development organizations.

- **Versatility**

Computers are capable of performing almost any task, provided that the task can be reduced to a series of logical steps and operations.

- **Automation**

A computer is much more than an adding machine or calculator which require human operators to press the necessary keys for the operations to be performed. Once a program is in the computers memory, the individual instructions until the last command which says stop program execution is administered, then it can stop.

- **Diligence**

Being a machine, a computer does not suffer from the human traits of tiredness and lack of concentration etc., If 2 million calculations have to be performed, it will perform the 2 millionth calculation with exactly the same accuracy and speed as the in first instance.

CLASSIFICATION OF COMPUTERS

Large number organizations require the most powerful computers, while individuals may be satisfied with a Personal Computer (PC). The computers are classified according to the size and memory capacity. They are as follows:

Personal Computer

A personal computer or a microcomputer is the smallest general purpose computer system, which can execute programs to process a variety of instructions. It has all the functional elements found in a larger system. These computers usually have a 8, 16 or a 32 bit micro processor. The cheapest variety is one with an 8-bit microprocessor. All 8-bit micros are build around a few popular microprocessors like the z80, 8080 etc., By an 8-bit microprocessor it is understood that it can process 8-bits or 1 byte of data at a time. These microprocessors have a 16-line address bus and hence they can identify a maximum of 2.16 i.e. 64,536 or 64k address locations etc.,

Mini Computers

A minicomputer system is a small general-purpose computer varying in size, from a desktop model to a unit size of a four-drawer filing cabinet. It is quite obvious that, there is tremendous amount of similarity between the more powerful micros and the lower end minis. The same situation exists on the other end where the lower priced mainframes are almost similar to the higher priced minis. Today's typical mini will surpass the PC in storage capacity, speed of arithmetic operations and ability to support a variety of peripherals. Minis are usually with the 16-bit microprocessor but now-a-days they are available only with 32 bit.

Mainframe Computers

A whole series of mainframe models, ranging in size from small to very large, are typically lumped together under a family designation by mainframe manufacturers. Several microprocessors are used in place of the single microprocessor used in micro and minicomputer system. The result is that these systems can process data much faster. They also have the flexibility to operate automatically from 2 to 8 bytes in the same unit of time. The mainframe vendors also have much large libraries of application programmes.

Super Computers

The supercomputers are the most powerful and expensive computers available. Only a few of these computer monsters are made each year because only few people need it. They are designed to perform scientific application and hence the computational speed is very important. To maximize the speed each address location holds 64 bits of information. The time required to execute a single operation may be as slow as nanoseconds.

Software

Software is the means of communicating with the computers. The set of instructions written in a logical sequence are referred as software. They are broadly grouped under two categories-System Software and Application System. System software is the base level software needed to run any application. It has to be present for the application software to function. This software determines which program gets priority in the use of the various resources, such as disk or printer or memory. It translates the application software into a form understandable by the computer.

Application of Software

Application software is a software designed to specifically perform a particular user function or application. This software is for the user to operate the computer to do the processing and give the results needed. In the world of computers, change is permanent than anything else. The change happens like ripples in a tank of water!!. First improvements are incorporated in hardware followed by system software and finally application software.

The computer users are bound to increase as the cost of PC falls at the rate of 40 percent in a year. The percent PC and Taxation of the equipments machines, tools, and peripherals have declined tremendously as recommended by the ministry of finance and Government of India.

Internet Facilities

Internet is a collection of tens of thousands of networks of computers in the globe. It is a vast, worldwide system consisting of people, information, and computers. The Internet is so large and complex as to be well beyond the comprehension of a single human being. Nearly 100 million users have access to Internet and will double within the shortest period. Even perhaps, the best way to understand the organization and importance of the Internet is to compare it to the other great worldwide communication systems like the postal system and the telephone system (communication system). Cooperative business organizations can utilize the emerging and modern Internet facilities in a big way, to compete in the new economic environment.

E-mail

By using E-mail, one can send a message from one computer in the net to any other computer across the Globe. It requires one to run the e-mail programmed, type the message and the receivers address and click a button. The mail popup on the receivers screen a few moments later. If there are no hardware problems, the reply can also be obtained within few minutes-practically for the cost of a local phone call!!! As per several surveys, the number of host computers in Internet crossed the 10-million mark and the annual growth rate is 85 percent per annum.

Newsgroups

These are electronic board with a worldwide fan club, each devoted to some special interest. One can get information, ask questions, canvass opinions, pass on bit of news or get advice form this group-all related to that particular subject. Other users in the group are supposed to read what one has posted and within a few minutes there will be a new posting in response to the earlier query-may be an answer or an explanation. There are newsgroups already for conceivable are of human interest, from agriculture, industry, service to hobbies.

World Wide Web (WWW)

The web is an ambitious client/serve system. This means that you can operate a client (which runs on your computer) to contact a server program (which runs on another computer, some where in the internet). The web offers a simple interface to the vast resources of the Internet. Getting started in easy and just about anyone can start enjoying the web with little preparation.

Moreover, the benefits of Information Technology (IT) have to reach the common man and they should have access to these services even if they are in the remotest part of the country. The convergence of different forms of Information technology services viz., Television, Radio, Telephone, Internet in a single unified environment; is now increasingly possible to have access to Information technology services etc.,

The major expansion in the use of Information technology tools in a recent report by NASSCOM estimate that there are almost 3.25 million Internet users and 0.95 million Internet connections in India as May 2002. It, further predicts that these umbers may go up to 16 million and 6 million respectively by early March 2004. Almost half (49 per cent) of them are in the age group of 18 to 24 years, while 77 percent are male.

LINKING INFORMATION TECHNOLOGY, COMMUNICATION AND COOPERATIVE BUSINESS ORGANIZATIONS

Communication and Information Technology would be the major form of scientific dissemination of information and knowledge in the twenty first century. The use of advance technology such as Internet (www) on communication scenario have offered enormous potential for two-way on-line communication process between distant parties via., the telecommunication technology and computer network spreading all over the entire globe.

The cooperative information and communication technology can provide knowledge on demand to meet local needs using the World Wide Web (WWW), and it does so through a bottom-up process. The process starts with volunteer (cooperative) that help pool the villagers to find out what knowledge they want. Particularly popular among the rural communities are women's health, information, advice on growing local crops and protecting them from diseases, the daily market prices for these crops, local weather forecasts, and clear information about the be wildering array of programs that are provided by the Indian government to aid poor families. Ultimately the cooperative information and communication technology can envisions a global electronic network that connects scientists to people at all levels, locals, regional, state, national, farmers organizations and even the village women can greatly benefit from cooperative information and communication technology. The network will allow them to easily access the scientific and technical knowledge that they need to solve local problems in a technical manner and enhance the quality of their lives, improve productivity, improve profitability, improve economic viability as well as to communicate their own insights and needs back to scientists in the long run.

The current Information Technology and communication revolution has opened huge vistas and opportunities for providing access to readily available information in rural India. Therefore, it is useful for rural development and economic growth in the rural areas. It streamlined the pace of rural economic growth in the new economic environment.

Information Technology can improve village economy and ensure effective utilization of available resources. In today's electrical and electronic revolution, the major dotcoms cooperatives should be used in the grassroot level. The available Internet and E-commerce facilities can make the cooperative members to sell their products in his village itself to the entire country and entire Globe. Moreover, InfoTech can become the backbone of the cooperative marketing activities, functions and operations in the Twenty First Century. Also, the available Information Technologies are widely used to discover new ways and means to sell the products of cooperative business organizations. The E-commerce has provided the basic required infrastructure to effectively communicate and share information among the members of the cooperative business organization. Now-a-days, the farmers have access to the incredibly valuable information provided by the agricultural cooperative business organizations on different aspects such as crop cultivation practices, supply of inputs, sugarcane cultivation practices, pest and disease control etc., Further, they can learn how to market their produce, market their products, understand the process of manufacturing their dairy (Rose milk, milk ice cream etc.,) products and even the processing system of sugarcane to produce ethanol spirit. Moreover, they make use of different types of computerization process/system and maintain up-to-date their financial business transactions and non-financial business transactions. This has been proved in the Sugar-cane factories in Warna-Nagar (Maharashtra State) and Dairy Cooperative Societies in Gujarat including these dairy unions which have adopted "Anand Pattern Dairy System".

NEED FOR INFORMATION TECHNOLOGY AND COMMUNICATION IN COOPERATIVE BUSINESS ORGANIZATIONS

In the era of economic reforms, cooperative business organizations have been engaging themselves in production, processing and distribution activities. The adoption of Information Technology and Communication techniques will promote their distinctive products and enhance their dynamic business activities. In the globalized competitive set up structures the business operations and functions of cooperative business organizations have to undertake their business in the most effective and efficient manner, they must produce high quality products and carryout promotional activities to increase their sales, productivity, profitability, economic performance and create goodwill for their own products in the globalized business market. In this way, cooperative business organizations can survive and become profitable in the New Economic Environment and changing Global Business Scenario.

The Information Technology and Communication have to create effective linkages among producers cooperatives, which would end up in solving many of their business problems. They can enter into new business areas and create new opportunities. The business cooperatives can sell their products to different cooperatives and can pass their products to the consumer cooperatives that have direct touch (or) contact with the consumers. Through, this effective linking, the cooperatives can bring down the market price by selling their products at reasonable price, which should be lower than the open market price. It is possible for the cooperatives to sell their products at a low or responsible price because they make bulk purchases of raw-materials, purchasing the goods directly from the production centers and introducing the cost effective economy and increasing the efficiency in marketing business activities through adoption of Information Technology and Communication in their business operations and functions.

URGENT NEED FOR ADOPTION OF INFORMATION TECHNOLOGY AND COMMUNICATION BY COOPERATIVES BUSINESS ORGANIZATIONS:

The adoption of information technology and communication is to enable cooperatives to make better decisions by providing quality information to their members and consumers. In the modern days of advanced information technology and communication, cooperatives processing and marketing organizations should make use of the latest computers and utilize the available vast variety of database system. The key to building and using effective information system is that, employees need to know how to apply Information and Communication Technology solving cooperative business problems and make suitable and rational decisions. The quality of information system is measured by its ability to provide exact information needed by cooperatives in a proper manner, proper time, proper place, proper coverage etc., The information should be accurate and updated always. This information provide support for managerial decision making process at all levels of business cooperatives, viz., planning, organising, staffing, directing, controlling, coordinating, and management control, decision-making structures.

RELEVANCE OF INFORMATION TECHNOLOGY AND COMMUNICATION IN COOPERATIVE BUSINESS ORGANIZATIONS IN THE NEW ECONOMIC ENVIRONMENT

The Information Technology and Communication system play a significant role in cooperative business organizations such as cooperative processing and marketing organizations, Cooperative Banking, Cooperative Fisheries Organizations, Housing Cooperatives etc., mainly aimed to establish and maintain a direct contact with the potential customers. The cooperative business organizations can establish electronic kiosks (Multimedia machine designed to be user friendly and interactive in the process of delivery of information to the customer) at selected sites often insisted by the potential customers and Web sites on Internet.

Cooperatives can undertake the planning functions of management more effectively and efficiently through using the information technology and communication system. Also, cooperative organizations have to improve its operational performance and services in the era of new centenary and prosper in the 21st Century. Additionally, the relevance of information and communication in cooperative business organizations can be felt in terms of viz.,

- The cooperatives can assess and get adequate information about the views, opinion, taste and preferences of consumers and members from time to time. Their thoughts and behaviour should be measured to solve the problems of the members; therefore, the role of Information Technology and Communication in cooperative marketing is imperative in the new centenary.

- By using the Information Technology and Communication in cooperative business organizations could identify the types of competition that exists in the open market and the ability of private and public sector competitors and other competitors could be identified in the dynamic business world.
- Adopting the Information Technology and Communication system can increase the marketing share of the cooperative products such as dairy products, banking products, tea products, textile products, agro-processed products, fertilizers, fruits and vegetables products.
- Information Technology and Communication can also help the cooperatives such as Consumer Cooperatives, Dairy Cooperatives, Tea Cooperative factories, Sugar Cooperative Mills and Fisheries processing cooperatives etc., through undertaking effective and efficient sales promotional measures in a distinctive manner.
- Advertising is one of the sales promotion techniques which can be effectively used by various cooperative business organizations with the help of Information Technology and Communication, which can be aimed at minimizing the wastages of valuable resources and unnecessary expenditures in their business operations.
- Information Technology and Communication can also provide prompt, adequate, timely and needed information for the administration and management of cooperative marketing and processing business organizations. This information and data bank system could help the cooperative business organizations to take suitable and timely decision by the board of management of the cooperative business organizations.

THE IMPERATIVES OF INFORMATION TECHNOLOGY IN COOPERATIVE BUSINESS AND MARKETING ORGANIZATIONS

The business cooperative societies are important constituent of the Indian Agricultural system. Judging by the rule assigned to them, the expectations they are supposed to fulfill are to serve the members, producers, and the customers. The business cooperative societies play a significant role in rural non-financing and the business in the urban areas has increased phenomenally in the electronic revolution.

In the era of rapidly changing technology and increasing customer expectations, the computerization processes is an imperative need for the cooperative business organizations. Business cooperatives should take appropriate measures for computerization of their entire operations, taking into consideration the volume of business and nature of transactions, number of members, borrowers and other operational activities. This facilitates the business cooperatives to not only improve their operational and administrative efficiency but also in maintaining a competitive edge over their counterparts through a better customer service and customer relationship marketing system. The basic purpose of computerization of business cooperative is to improve customer services, decision-making, increase profitability, sustainability, and productivity. Even now-a-days, some dynamic organizations are adopting the E-CRM etc., Therefore, cooperative business organizations should not lag behind in undertaking computerization process.

While designing the Management Information System and Planning (MISP) for business cooperative societies the modern process and technology is to be used. Moreover, Management Information System and Planning (MISP) gives support to the management to make decisions to design the service strategy to be adopted by the cooperative business organizations. The full MISP for a cooperative processing and marketing societies should cover the following aspects namely customers database, service for business promotions, index monitoring system and upgradation of the human resource. A well-defined business cooperative information system begins and ends with the customers/ members/member-owners, who decide the growth and development of business cooperative societies. The business cooperative information system can disseminate information gathered from the system of developing information to the right personnel at the right time for making right decisions in the cooperative business organizations.

BENEFITS OF INFORMATION TECHNOLOGY TO COOPERATIVE BUSINESS ORGANIZATIONS

A large number of benefits do exist. They are as follows:

- Information Technology can help all the cooperative processing and marketing business organizations to have cost effective and new ways of communication between the customers and suppliers etc. An effective and efficient contact with them is also possible through the Internet and other advanced technology system.
- It provides global choice and reduces the wastages of time, money and energy.
- Manipulation of books can be either prevented or detected promptly because of complete computerization and would eventually enable tallying/balancing of books on daily basis, particularly in the cooperative banking business organizations.
- The reconciliation of business transactions relation to drafts, issued and paid through computerized system would help early detection of fraudulent payments/ irregular business activities in cooperative business organizations.
- The cooperative marketing system can ensure better bargaining power of its members because it provides adequate information through adoption of Information Technology and Communication system.
- Sales through cooperative marketing societies would ensure reduction in the marketing cost through delivering all the necessary, adequate and appropriate Message/Data provide by the Information Technology and Communication Network System located in the cooperative business organizations.
- The Information Technology and Communication linkage system will provide effective information to cooperative marketing societies and processing organizations, which can be used as controlled mechanism, the flow of supplies can also be controlled

and they can also influence the price system, as they are stronger market force in the future.

- Information Technology has more flexibility to add and delete information on produce or products in catalogues, manuals, documents and other records as maintained by the cooperative business organizations.
- The cost of setting the E-commerce website is very low than the retail out let or new office, hence it is not a problem to small and medium size cooperative business organizations.
- Information Technology and Communication provides an alternative to traditional market mechanism to modern market mechanism and also ensure, that cooperative processing and marketing societies can market their produce to their best advantage in the open market economy and new economic environment.

ESSENTIALS OF INFORMATION INPUT IN COOPERATIVE PROCESSING AND MARKETING BUSINESS ORGANIZATIONS

The main aim and goal of business cooperative society for adopting the information input is mainly related to the "need for information and data, services and networks that would enable him to focus on customers". Marketing information is being made as an essential part of business, gets the least attention from the designers of the information systems. The profitability, economic viability and productivity of the marketing cooperative society, their functions depends mainly on the dynamics of market forces and the market information system. Hence, information and communication technology

The information needs of marketing functions in a cooperative marketing society would involve and include 6P's such as product, price, place, promotion, people and procedures information. A marketing information system of cooperative business organizations may encompass the above stated six components marketing mix or 6P's information system as applicable to cooperative business organizations. The information and communication technology is all-pervasive in all the 6P's of cooperative business organizations.

SIGNIFICANCE OF INFORMATION AND COMMUNICATION TECHNOLOGY IN PROMOTION OF EXPORT OF COOPERATIVE PRODUCTS

Through an effective and efficient application of Information Technology and Communication in the cooperative business organizations, they can carry out their export operations is more effectively and efficient manner. They can expect to use ICT to export their agricultural items such as Rice, Jute, Wheat, Mustard seeds and other traditional items. The main motto of adopting the Information Technology and Communication in cooperative business organizations is to make an arrangement for marketing of their members produce in the liberalized economy. They can capture the global market scenario with the help of the Information and Communication Technology (ICT). Even within the information and communication technology SAARC, USA, EU Market, cooperatives can capture nicher market through Information and Communication Technology (ICT).

Even fisheries cooperatives have developed some physical facilities for deep sea fishing and preservation and processing of fish. These physical facilities includes mechanized boats, ice plants, net factory, fish carrier vessels, trucks, etc., The fisherman's products are channalised through adoption of Information Technology and Communication in the fisherman's cooperatives for marketing their products. It leads to ensuring fair price to the fisherman and improves their socio-economic conditions of the fishermen in the new economic environment and globalize world.

ROLE OF GOVERNMENT IN PROMOTION OF INFORMATION TECHNOLOGY AND COMMUNICATION IN COOPERATIVES BUSINESS ORGANIZATIONS

The success of the cooperative business organizations will depend mostly upon their capacity, ability, caliber to adopt and effective use of Information Technology and Communication in their dynamic business activities and operations. This can lead to effectively reducing the price spread between the producer and the consumer without adversely affecting the interests of the consumers. The thrust areas can be emphasized, such as;

- Effective and efficient distribution of essential consumer goods to people at fair price within period of time (stipulated to satisfy the needs and wants of the customers).
- Adequate resources can be raised by way of delivering accurate information and communication to people about the business activity of cooperative organizations.
- An efficient arrangement can be made for processing of produce belonging to the members and non-members with the help of Information and Communication Technology (ICT) system and add-value to the products and commodities in the long run.

STRATEGIES FOR PROMOTING GROWTH AND DEVELOPMENT OF ITC IN COOPERATIVE BUSINESS ORGANIZATIONS

The following are strategies to enhance growth and development of Information and Communication Technology (ICT) in cooperative business organizations in the new economic environment.

Appropriate Planning and Control

While formulating the Information Technology and Communication plans, the cooperative authority of planning and policy planners should give more attention and analysis of implementation of these technology effectively in cooperative organizations and implement in the most efficient manner. Every plan of action on Information and Communication Technology (ICT), should be made to ensure proper and suitable implementation of Information Technology and Communication in the spirit they are made to attain higher growth rate in the long run..

Effective and Efficient Coordination and Communication Process

To ensure effective and efficient coordination among cooperative marketing business societies must work in close tandem and contact with other cooperative business organizations like Credit, Consumer, and Processing Cooperatives etc., This can be established and should pave way for the growth of Information and Communication system horizontally and vertical coordination among various sub-systems of the cooperative business network.

Technical Consultancy and Promotion Services

In the era of electronic and technological revolution, no business can survive without the use of modern technology i.e. Information and Communication Technology (ICT). Therefore, it is the major responsibility of the Government and technical consultancy agencies along concerned with the cooperative business organizations to serve as reliable grass-root cooperative consultancy agency for the cooperative production, cooperative marketing, cooperative service and processing matters in various fields, aspects, operations and functions of these cooperative organizations.

Modernizations, Up-Gradation, Computerization of Processing and Marketing Cooperatives Business Organizations

Every cooperative business society must have complete computerized information system. They can modernize, up-grade and computerize their business operations. So that, it can record all the information about society as well as the members and customers. By doing this, it can easily locate the problem in a few seconds and save their time through solving their problem promptly. Through improved information system it will be more easy for the society to educate its members regarding the changing trends in the market and educate them about the latest trend in the technology and communication system.

Undertaking Effective and Efficient Education Programmes on Computerizations and Modernization

Cooperative Officials, staff, members, farmers should be educated on modernization various ways and procedures of handling agricultural marketing and processing through appropriate modernization process and proper computerization process of cooperative processing, operation, and transaction of marketing societies. They can be educated through knowledge centres, information centres adult education centers, agricultural research centers, and cooperative institutions from time to time.

OTHER DEVELOPMENT AND GROWTH STRATEGIES FOR INFORMATION AND COMMUNICATION TECHNOLOGY IN COOPERATIVE SECTOR

- There is imperative need for setting up of village cooperative knowledge and information kiosks/ shops, that would enable rural families to access a basket of modern information and communication technologies. Motivation and training of educated youth, especially women, in rural areas in operating information and knowledge centers in the rural economy is mandatory and highly essential in the new economic environment.
- There is imperative need for training of the rural youth in the organization and maintenance of the cooperative knowledge system that can generate adequate information technology and communication. Moreover, locally relevant information from generic information and data can be plainly used in the operation of the information and documentation center through cooperative approach.
- The cooperative information and communication center can undertake the maintenance, updating and dissemination of information on entitlements to rural families using an appropriate blend of modern and existing channels of communication. This must be made essential, part and parcel and necessary

components in the cooperative information and documentation center.

- Before installation of the cooperative information and documentation center, it is essential to conduct impact assessment analysis based on the organization of surveys, Participatory Rural Appraisal (PRA), Rapid Rural Appraisal (RRA), Participatory Action Research (PAR), Participatory Learning and Action (PLA), Focus Group Discussion (FGD) and other appropriate methods of data and information gathering for the growth and development of the cooperative information and documentation centers.
- There is imperative need for building of an appropriate model in information dissemination, documentation facilities and exchange units in rural areas that uses advanced information and communication technologies in the rural economy.
- The cooperative information and documentation center can start by elaborately conducting action oriented research on the formation of multi-sectoral partnerships (Private-Public/Government-NGO's) with rural communities to form self supporting and self sufficient, and sustainable model of information and communication technologies for rural areas in the changing economic scenario.
- Development of information and communication technology based applications for rural areas, especially community banking, online health, industry, service, agriculture, education and distance education, to assess their potential to contribute to the sustenance of a rural cooperative information and communication technology programme in the context of changing economic environment and globalization scenario.
- There is imperative need for organizations of cooperative workshops, motivation, training, development and other interactions such as on-site consultations with policy makers to sensitize them to critical issues in the use of cooperative information and

communication technologies to promote human development and cooperative sector located in rural areas.

- There are huge benefits accrued for cooperative information and communication technology such as gaining fully from the exchange of research results with telecenter programmes in different part of the world (cooperatively undertaken) to arrive at a more comprehensive, picture of impact assessment, productivity, profitability, economic viability, and sustainability issues and its possible internationalization of cooperative project implementation and execution in the changing global business scenario and eventually enter into 21st Century with posterity and prosperity.
- Through the setting up of the cooperative information and communication technology Kioks/Centres, it is easy in the development of a set of parameters to make a choice of technical and market access of technology and rural technology for powering the real access devices to the rural communities and rural economy in the Global changing environment.
- There is need for the development of models of cooperative eco-jobs and eco-cooperative entrepreneurship among rural community/rural economy in the 21st Century.
- Through cooperative information and communication technology centre/kiosk, to link cooperative eco-jobs and cooperative entrepreneurship to enhance sustainable development of the rural economy.
- The cooperative eco-entrepreneurship can incorporated all the aspects of the technical, managerial and marketing capacities of the rural women and men to mobilize themselves as cooperative entrepreneurs producing products and services for sustainable development of the rural areas with the help of the cooperative information and communication technology.

- Through cooperative information and communication technology, the concept of cooperative Bio-village and entrepreneurs can be promoted. It is an approach which strengthen the capacity of the rural community to blend sustainable natural management with livelihood security through economically feasible, socially acceptable, economically viable and gender-sensitive interventions under cooperative umbrella.
- By setting up, the cooperative information and communication technology, kiosks/centres it can become people centered approach facilitating the socially and economically disadvantaged groups vis-à-vis class, caste and gender etc.,
- Through the cooperative information and communication technology kiosks/centres the support of Funding Agencies can sourced and used as a leverage to gain access to the commercial bank credits and government resources can be solicited from time to time.
- There is imperative need for evolving a grass-root institutions to take up development initiatives in information and communication kiosks/centres the rural areas.
- Through the cooperative information and communication technology, it will lead to building social capital and linking it with economic capital in the long-run and enhancing the ability of rural community in defining the path of sustainable development in the 21st Century.
- Communication Information Empowerment through cooperative village information and knowledge centers/hub, it would lead to the information empowerment through computer-aided and Intranet connected linking villagers for horizontal transfer of knowledge in the rural economy in the 21st Century.
- The cooperative information and communication technology societies can be treated as local-specific

information empowerment of rural communities leading to less social and economic transaction cost.

- It can be initiated as a hub and communication model and each cooperative information and communication technology center/kiosks can be managed by SHGs or cooperatives in the irrespective villages in the long-run.
- The cooperative information and communication technology can convert and disseminate generic data and information into local specific information documentation to assist in the rural areas decision-making process.
- The cooperative information and communication technology centers/kiosks can communicate information and data every day on various aspects to all interested persons and parties in the rural areas.
- The cooperative information and communication technology used to train villagers in areas like sustainable agriculture, functional literacy and computer literacy proagmmes, to train semi literate villagers and other villagers manage the adult literacy progamme using computers systems, set-up, a web site which provides, all information and data and the website can be managed through cooperative approach/sector.
- The cooperative information and communication technology can lead to expanding and strengthening the network of the grass root institutions. It can fulfill the essence of favouring more towards social and gender equity in the long-run.
- The cooperative information and communication technology can be used for enhancing the village knowledge centers to a region specific virtural academy for rural prosperity and preparing the rural community for the dynamics of the world trade market, world market scenarios, and globalization process linking to export market in the 21st Century.

CONCLUSION

To sum up, in the New Economic Environment, cooperative business organizations are becoming more popular through effective and efficient use and adoption of Information Technology and Communication in undertaking their business functions, transactions, operations, management, administrative functions and dynamic business activities. In the era of economic liberalization and globalization, where there is enormous application of science and technology in almost all the economic field, the processing and marketing organizations, Cooperative Banking, Cooperative Spinning Mills, Agricultural Cooperative Credit, Fisheries Cooperatives, Housing Cooperatives, Industrial Cooperatives, Fertilizers Cooperatives, Consumer Cooperatives, and Weavers Cooperatives etc., must simultaneously take advantage of the E-World. The success and prosperity of cooperative business organizations to a greater extend depends on using an effective and efficient Information Technology and Communication (ITC). This has been demonstrated by large sized and successful cooperative organizations such as Sugar Cooperative Mills in Maharashtra, Dairy Cooperative Organizations in Gujarat and many other states. Also, there is need for use of Information and Communication Technology (ICT) by the New Generation Cooperative Organizations such as SHG'S, etc., Moreover, in the 21st century, the cooperative sector at large must make use of the latest Information Technology and Communication (ITC) in all its sectors and sub-sectors. They can gain competitive advantages and become more productive, economically more viable, more profitable and more sustainable, improve the customer services, promote growth and development of cooperative business organizations in the New Economic Environment and face the New Centenary with Courage, Will power, determination, attain the long-term posterity and prosperity in the cooperative sector in 21st Century.

REFERENCES

Brij pal, (February-2002), "Socio-Economic Transformation Through Cooperative Marketing", Tamilnadu Journal of Cooperation, Vol.2, No.2, Page No.60.

Daman Prakash, (October – December, 2002), "Capacity Building of Agricultural Cooperatives to meet the Market and Human Resources Development Demand: A step-by-step Approach", Cooperatives Perspective, vol.37, No.3, Page No.5-8.

Dodkey M.D., and Hanamashetti J.S. (April - 2002), "Role of Cooperative Marketing in India with special reference to Fruits and Vegetable Marketing Cooperatives", Indian Cooperative Review, vol.36, No.4, Page No.266.

Goel B.B., (1991), "Management of Marketing Cooperatives", Deep & Deep publications, New Delhi, Page No.59.

Goyal R.A., (February-2000), "Relevance of ODI and Information Technology for Cooperatives in the New Millennium", The Cooperator, vol.38, No.8, Page No.382.

ICA, (1987), "Readings in Agricultural Cooperative marketing", Vandana publication, New Delhi, Page No.9-32.

Jayasudha S.M. (June-2003), "Information Technology in Coopratives" Tamilnadu Journal of Cooperation, Vol.3, No.8, Page no.22-36.

Karthikeyan & Karunakaran, (September - 2000), "Marketing Information system for Cooperative Banks", The Cooperator, Vol.38, No.3, Page No.117- 120.

Samwel Kakuko Lopoyetum and Selvamani P., (May 2004), "A Paradigm shift of Cooperative Leadership in the era of Economic Liberalization and Globalization", The Cooperator, Vol.41, No.11, Page No.456-463.

Samwel Kakuko Lopoyetum and Selvamani P., (July-September 2004), "Strategies for Development of Youth through Cooperative Entrepreneurship: 21st Century Perspective", Cooperative Perspective, Vol.39, No.2, Page No.35-48.

18

ECONOMIC REFORMS AND RURAL RECONSTRUCTION: THE ROLE OF PRIs IN INDIA

*B. P. Bulla**

INTRODUCTION

Ours is an age of democracy. Democracy as a form of government, has been becoming a global phenomenon. The fall of the socialist world and domestic and global changes in most of the countries have brought democracy to place and shores where it was undreamt of a few years ago, giving people a taste of freedom. Further, development schemes which arc essentially local in character constitute perhaps as much as one-fifth of the public sector plan outlay. This plan outlay offer much scope for simplification, rationalisation and decentralisation in India. Therefore, decentralization is necessary not only from the centre to the states but also from the state to the local (district/taluka/village) levels.

The central government, over the years, taken the lead in proposing new programmes in the field of agriculture and rural development and in funding them. In doing Sc the scope and content of agricultural programmes which are supposed to be exclusively in the domain of the states, are being increasingly shaped by the centre. The result has been a needless proliferation of programmes often involving duplication and

* Selection Grade Lecturer, P. S. Margol College, Shababad, Gulbanga District, Karnataka.

waste. It also tends to in pose on the states schemes of a uniform pattern, unmindful of the great diversity of conditions in the country. If this process is to be given to PRIs and they should be encouraged to take greater initiative to experiment, innovate and evolve strategies and programmes appropriate to their specific situations.

Globalization, a dominant force in the 20th century's last decade, is shaping a new era of interaction among nations, economies and people. It is increasing the contacts between people across national boundaries- in economy, in technology, in culture and in governance. But it is also fragmenting production processes, labour markets, political entities and societies. As a result, the economic reforms were introduced in India in 1991 and continued in the 21st century as "Second Generation Economic Reforms". Elaborating on the philosophy of the Second Generation Reforms, Finance Minister Yeshwant Sinha stated: "Growth is not just an end in itself. It is the critical vehicle for increasing employment and raising the living standards of our people, especially of the poorest. Sustained, broad-based growth, combined with all our programmes for accelerating rural development, building roads, promoting housing, boosting knowledge-based industries and enhancing the quality of human resources, will impart a strong impetus to employment expansion. There can be no better cure for poverty than this in our country". For implementation, in connections with rural development, the Finance Minister laid down the objectives like (1) Strengthen the foundations of growth of our rural economy, especially agriculture and allied activities and (2) Give the highest priority to human resource development and other social programmes and policies in education, health and other social services, with special emphasis on the poorest and weakest sections of society. Hence, in this paper we concentrate on the evaluation of the rural development and the role of PRIs during the reforms period.

PRI's : A BACKGROUND

It is widely recognized that village communities which were characteristic of agrarian economic have existed in India from the earliest times - The Russian "Mir", German 'Mark' and the Mediaeval 'Manor' of England could be considered as counterparts of such village communities in India which were known here as 'Panchayats'. The important characteristics of these Panchayats were that they have been the pivot of administration, the centre of social life, an important economic force and above all a focus of social solidarity. So much so, Sir Charles Metcalfe, a British Governor of India of the 19th century had called it 'the little republic'.

In India the system of village Panchayats is very old though its form was different from that we have in the modern time based on formal elections. During the British period attempts were made to revive, them again after 1919, when popular ministries were formed under the Government of India Act 1919 and local self-government became a provincial subject. The various provinces passed the village Panchayat Acts in 1919 and after, in their own provinces to revive them. But, the Panchayats formed under these Acts were not democratic bodies and their members were mostly nominated by Government. As a result these Panchayats did not make much headway and these acts remained laws only on paper without any significant effect. It is only after independence that some real progress could be made.

The term "Panchayat Raj" has come into practice recently. Previously the terms were 'village panchayat', 'district board' or 'sub-district board' which were the self-governing bodies at the village or regional level. Rural self-governing bodies play a vital role in rural administration particularly in the field of social service and rural reconstruction. They are the link between the people and the government machinery at the state-level. In fact the powers entrusted to them really make a state democratic.

73RD AMENDMENT ACT (1992)

Economic reforms introduced during 1990's encouraged to bring about deliberate change in Panchayat Raj Institutions for better results with the devolution of power from the centre to the state, states to districts and districts to panchayat units in the true sense. Growth in economy becomes meaningless unless power is exercised by the people at the grass-roots level for the society and political awareness is channelised in the right direction. Accordingly, the 73rd Constitutional Amendment Act, 1992 aims at reducing political and bureaucratic interference in rural development programmes. For this, many states have redefined and redesigned the role of state bureaucracy in order to facilitate effective functioning of Panchayat Raj Institutions. And these states provided power to women, weaker sections and the poor in society there by paving the way for active participation of people in grass root democracy and decision making in process of rural development programmes and implementation.

Further, it was felt that involvement of people was lacking to make use of benefits of reforms and they were not having opportunities to decide the matter which directly affects their life. Therefore, the objective of Amendment act is to improve the participation of the people during the reforms process.

Thus, the PRI's are the basic institutions of democracy where people from village, block and district could participate. Devolution of power and decentralization of function start from this point and also, people at local levels get into the mainstream of development as well as public affairs. The PRI's, especially the 'Gram Sabha' make the concept of 'direct democracy'.

PRIs AND RURAL RECONSTRUCTION: PRESENT POSITION AND A TASK AHEAD

The 73rd Amendment Act 1992 has the noble intention of bringing power to the common people. It provides for decentralized administration through local self-governing Panchayat Raj. Institutions (PRIs) at the district, block and village levels. It provides a platform for direct participation of the people themselves in the Gram Sabha. Thus, the objective is to empower people to have a greater say and role in their own affairs at the grassroots level. In other words PRIs encourage participation of people in the formulation and implementation of various developmental programmes in order to bring a meaningful socio-economic change particularly in rural areas. Thus, the benefits of economic reforms percolate downwards to the people with their active involvement and participation. It creates a system of self-governance which ultimately supersedes the existing bureaucratic system and through which several development works are undertaken.

For the implementation of the Rural Development Programmes through the newly formed Panchayat Raj System during the reforms era will definitely pave the way for alleviation of poverty and development of rural areas in our country. In this part of our paper an attempt is made to look at the present situation of rural development and keeping in view of changing scenario of economy due to economic reforms introduced in 1990's we have discussed about the task ahead for the rapid rural development in the 21st century.

RURAL EDUCATION

Education is universally recognized as a central component of 'human capital'. The role of education as a contributor to economic growth and its impact on population control, life expectancy, infant mortality, improving nutritional status and strengthening civil institutions is well recognized. Moreover, it has been found that education is an important social resource and a means of reducing inequality in society. Therefore, an adequate level of expenditure on education is a basic requirement, to produce the trained manpower that is essential for the rural development in particular and rapid economic growth of the country in general.

Table No.1 provides data for educational expenditure in India. By the year 1981, educational expenditure had risen to a level of 3.0 pe rcent of GDP as against 0.68 per cent and 2.41 per cent in 1951 and 1971 respectively. After this, a gradual increase in educational expenditure was witnessed and it reached a peak level of 4,39 per cent of GDP in 1990. Thereafter, this percentage has declined to 3.62 per cent in 1997. This indicates a lower priority given to education in the post-reform period, despite the fact that the Government has been proclaiming that it intends to increase it to 6 per cent of GDP.

A Task Ahead

It is not enough to start schools and extending other facilities in every village; it is also necessary to provide equal opportunities to all sections of society so as to provide social and economic equality for all. Everybody should be able to get free education. Respect for human beings, respect for work, scientific temper, national consciousness, emotional integration - these are the values that must be inculcated in them.

Table 1
Educational Expenditure In India

Year	*Total Expenditure on Education Expenditure*	*Education Expenditure as % GDP*
1951	64	0.68
1961	260	1.63
1971	1011	2.41
1981	4436	3.00
1990	20491	4.29
1991	22349	4.05
1996	44695	3.89
1997	51683	3.62

Source: 1. Budgetary Resources for Education, Ministry of Human Resource Development, New Delhi, 1991.
2. Economic Survey, 1997-98, Ministry of Finance, Government of India, New Delhi.
3. Selected Educational Statistics, MHRD, New Delhi, 2000.

The rural people should be provided technical education in polytechnic at free of cost. The aged people should be given facility of adult education so that they may get access to the information revolution that is going apace in the world. In short, there must be the realisation by the PRI's that rural development is impossible without educational revolution in the rural sector.

RURAL HEALTH CARE

Health care of the rural population is an important component of rural development. Good health and nutrition increase labour productivity and good health of mothers is crucial to the health of the children they bear. Table 2 shows that the expenditures that have been made in the different plans are very much meager specially in the context of larger problems related to the health and nutrition. After the Fourth Five Year Plan, there is decline in the expenses that were made on the health and it has gone down up to 1.75 per cent of the eighth plan outlay. Likewise, the expenditures on the family welfare has also gone down up to. 1.50 per cent of the total plan outlay in the Eighth Five Year Plan.

Table 2
Pattern of Investment on Health and Family Welfare during different Plan Periods

Period	*Health*		*Family Welfare*	
	Outlay Expenses	*% of Expenses*	*Outlay Expenses*	*% of Expenses*
First Plan (1951-56)	65.20	3.33	0.10	0.01
Second Plan (1956-61)	140.80	3.01	5.00	0.11
Third Plan (1961-66)	225.90	2.63	24.90	0.29
Fourth Plan (1969-74)	335.50	2.13	278.00	1.76
Fifth Plan (1974-79)	760.80	1.93	491.80	1.25
Sixth Plan (1980-85)	2025.20	1.85	1387.00	1.27
Seventh Plan (1985-90)	3688.60	1.69	3120.80	1.43
Eighth Plan (1992-97)	7582.20	1.75	6500.00	1.50

Source: Ninth Five Year Plan (Draft) 1997-2002, Planning Commission, GOI, p.190.

Though, there is an increase in plan outlay for health care schemes in rural areas during the past 50 year, it has not yet reached the level of that in urban areas. Infant and maternal mortality rates are still high. Children die mainly from respiratory infections, malnutrition and diarrhoeal diseases.

TASK AHEAD

Substantial expansion of primary health care is absolutely necessary to protect the health of the rural population. Hospitals in remote areas should be established and adequate finance and qualified staff should be provided. Essential drugs should be supplied to the rural poor who could be identified by the issue of health stamps. Public health and clinical facilities, drug and vaccine quality control have to be improved. Attention should also be paid to research and evaluation of projects of health care and to improve the financial provisions and efficiency of management. PRIs should take care of these activities to protect the health of the rural population.

RURAL INFRASTRUCTURE

Rural infrastructure comprises rural roads and rural housing. Rural road connectivity is an exremely important aspect of rural development. A centrally sponsored scheme has been launched called the Pradhan Mantri Gram Sadak Yojana (PMGSY) which seeks to provide connectivity to all unconnected habitations in rural areas with a population of more than 500 by the end. In order to achieve the objective of the programme, a requirement of Rs.60,000 crore has been estimated. The available source of funds, for the present, is the 50 per cent share of the cess on High Speed Diesel (HSP), amounting to approximately Rs.2500 crore per annum. For the year 2001-02, a sum of Rs.2500 crore has been earmarked for the PMGSY.

According to the 1991 census 3. 1 million household are without shelter and another 10.31 million households reside in unserviceable Kachcha houses. Considering the magnitude of the problem, a National Housing Habitat Policy was announced in 1998 which aims at providing 'Housing for All' and facilitates construction of 13 lakh additional housing units in rural areas annually with an emphasis on extending benefits to the poor and deprived. Government is committed to the goal of ensuring shelter for all by the end of Tenth plan period. The objective of the Indira Gandhi Awas Yojana (lAY) is to provide assistance to the below poverty line households (BPL) belonging to scheduled caste, scheduled tribe and free bonded labour categories. The central assistance under the lAY for 2001-02 is Rs.1618 crore for construction/upgradation of 1.3 rnillion houses.

A TASK AHEAD

Rural road network is an important ingredient of rural development. The farmers in the remote villages have to transport their surplus produce to the towns and other places or they have to go to other villages to promote social relations and communication of information about their agricultural operations; they have also to transport seeds, fertilizers, insecticides and pesticides from the towns to their farms. Good rural transport network is necessary for all these purposes. Therefore, the PRIs should have responsibility of providing rural transport network and should be involved in this exercise. The rural labour force which is actually idle during the off-seasons should be involved in road building on a voluntary basis. A nominal tax on the users of these roads could be levied by the PRIs to meet part of the cost of construction and maintenance.

Further, at present the houses in the rural sector are not planned and designed as to accommodate humans and cattle, sheep, goats and even chicken. In fact they all live together under the same roof. This causes the spread of diseases from the bovine population to humans. The Government should provide, with the help of PRIs, model housing designs making separate provision of accommodation for the bovine population and chicken. The Government should also build model houses which the rural population could copy in building their own houses.

CONCLUSION

The Panchayat Raj Institutions (PRI's) in India are the chief instruments of decentralization at the grassroots level and assume importance owing to the requirement to deal with the relentless demographic pressure and full use of scarce resources for rural development during Reforms period. Also they serve as a vehicle in bestowing upon the people the power that really belongs to them.

REFERENCES

Chakraborthy Krishna and Bhattacharyya Swapan Kumar, "Leadership, Factions and Panchayat Raj", Rawat Publications, Jaipur, 1993.

Dutta Vijaya Rajan, "Gram Sabha-base of Panchayat Raj", Kurukshetra, January 1994.

Economic Survey 2001-2002, Ministry of Finance, Government of India, New Delhi, 2002.

Ghosal Ratan Kumar, "Second Generation Reform and Rural Development", 83rd IEA Conference Volume, University of Jammu, Jammu, 2000.

Gowda Venkatagiri K., "Perestroika and Glasnost for India", Department of Economics, Bangalore University, Bangalore, 1989.

Madan G.R., "India's Developing Villages", Print House (India), Lucknow, 1983.

Mathew George, "Panchayat Raj in Karnataka Today", Institute of Social Sciences and Concept Publishing Company, New Delhi, 1986.

Pai Sudha, "Social Capital, Panchayats and Gross Roots Democracy", Economic and Political Weekly, Vo1.34, No.8, February 24 - March 2, 2001.

Pal Mahi," 11th Finance Commission, Transforming Panchayats", Economic and Political Weekly, Vo1.35, No.50, December 9-15,2000.

Pant. S.K. and Pandey Alok, "Social Sector in Liberalised Era, Challenges Ahead", 83rd IEA Conference Volume, University of Jammu, Jammu, 2000.

Pasayat Chitrasen and Barik Sarmistha, "Strengthening Panchayat Raj Institutions", Kurukshetra, April 1998.

Rajendra T. and Kumarasen B., "Panchayat Raj and Rural Development; 73rd Amendment", Kurukshetra, 1998.

Srivastava K. R., "Reconstructing Panchayat Raj Institution after Constitutional Amendment", Kurukshetra, January 1994.

19

EDUCATION AND EMPOWERMENT OF RURAL WOMEN: A CASE OF HYDERABAD-KARNATAKA REGION IN KARNATAKA

Talwar Sabanna[*] & *Uttam Kamble*[**]

INTRODUCTION

Different developmental programmes designed and targeted to eradicate poverty, inequality, low socio-economic growth, regional imbalance, illiteracy and unemployment to grain rural development have repeatedly failed to bring about change in lives of rural women. Illiteracy of rural women is a major hindrance, which is keeping them away from developmental programmes. Rural women are not informed and educated about the developmental programmes at regular intervals. Women are unaware of the large subsidies available to them under specific schemes.

It is almost universally accepted that women primary role is that of a home maker and it is for the men to provide subsistence to their family. But in recent years, specially after Independence, the traditional status and roles of women in Indian society are gradually changing. Few of the most important causes of such changes are the spread of education among women and the entrance of the educated women in the field of employment. Although, the traditional images of

* Faculty Dept. of Economics, Karnatak University, KRC, PG Centre, Belgaum.
** Research Scholar, Department of Economics, Karnatak University, KRC, PG Centre, Belgaum-591156, Karnatak.

women as helpers to their men-fold, as wives, mothers and home-makers have not changed completely yet, the emergence of women as independent earners and as self-seeking individual entities are being felt increasingly. Their roles and status are undergoing remarkable changes. More specifically, their education and employment outside the home have led to the upliftment of their social status, but at the same time have widened the area of conflicts and tensions, both inside and outside the home. Employed women, as such, are confronting with the problem of striking a balance between home and work.

Occupation has provided a new social prestige to the women, specially their achievement in the performance of occupational roles newly recognised. Several recent studies have shown for that the women employee whatever be the job she holds, is equal in efficiency and performance as the male employee in identical employment situations (Aileen Ross, 1973; Sengupta 1974; Srivastava 1978; Savitri Arputhamurthy, 1990; Srilatha Batliwala, 1998; Mira Seth 2001). Some of the studies even indicate that in certain respects, the women employee is even more efficient. In matters of reliability, promptness and punctuality, she has been found to have an edge over her male counterpart (Ranade and Ramachandran, 1970; Kapur 1974; Kumud Ranjan, 1993 and Anil Bhuuimali, 2004). More specifically, their education and employment outside the home have led to the upliftment of their social status. In order to understand the extend of women education, employment and income of the working women in rural areas of Hyderabad-Karnataka region in Karnataka state this study is undertaken.

OBJECTIVES

The following aspects have been the focus of analysis in the present study:

1. To know the literacy level of rural women in Hyderabad-Karnataka region.
2. To understand the education status and medium of education among rural women in Hyderabad-Karnataka region.

3. To study the type of education, occupation and income level of rural women in Hyderabad-Karnataka region.

DATA SOURCES

Hyderabad-Karnataka region originally consists of the three districts of Bidar, Gulbarga and Raichur (Koppal district formulated from Raichur district in 1997), which belonged to the Hyderabad State and were later added to the Karnataka State (Map). This region is lagging behind in respect of many economic and social indicators such as health, education, transport, communication etc.

The required date on literacy for the period 1981,1991 and 2001 have been collected from the Census reports. Further, the primary data for the present study was collected through an interview schedule. The female respondents who have completed their education above 4th Std were interviewed directly to collect the information. The study covers 600 female respondents from rural areas of Hyderabad-Karnataka region (150 respondents from each district of the region *i.e.*, Gulbarga, Bidar, Raichur and Koppal districts). The data obtained through the interview schedule was tabulated and analysed with the help of simple per centages.

RESULTS AND DISCUSSION

Literacy

Literacy is considered an important determinant of human development. It explains people's capability and thereby their choice. Besides contributing to the ability of the people to read and write, it has significant implications for matters pertaining to life and death like CBR, IMR, TFR, etc (Nanjudappa). Attainments in literacy in Karnataka in general and Hyderabad-Karnataka in particular are still average, notwithstanding significant improvement in the last few decades (Table 1). In absolute terms, the position in rural areas gives cause for concern.

Right upto the 1981 census, rural female literacy in Hyderabad- Karnataka region has increased only up to 9.38

Table 1
Literacy rate of female in Hyderabad-Karnataka region

District/Region State	1981 Male	Female	Gender-difference	1991 Male	Female	Gender-difference	2001 Male	Female	Gender-difference
				Rural					
Bidar	33.95	9.85	24.10	53.85	24.51	29.34	69.95	44.88	25.07
Gulbarga	29.86	8.29	21.57	44.32	16.06	28.26	55.55	29.67	25.88
Raichur jKoppal	32.97	10.00	22.97	44.26	16.48	27.78	56.87	29.38	27.49
H -K region	32.26	9.38	22.88	47.48	19.02	28.46	60.79	34.64	26.15
Karnataka state	41.88	20.04	21.84	60.03	34.76	25.27	70.63	48.50	22.13
				Urban					
Bidar	60.09	35.92	24.17	78.76	55.91	22.85	84.23	67.42	16.81
Gulbarga	57.17	32.63	24.54	79.82	59.93	19.89	80.22	61.70	18.52
RaichurjKoppal	51.92	28.80	23.12	68.53	43.59	24.94	78.19	58.84	19.35
H-K region	56.39	32.45	23.94	75.70	53.14	22.56	80.88	62.65	18.23
Karnataka state	64.69	47.52	17.17	82.04	65.74	16.30	86.85	74.87	11.98

Source: Census of India

per cent, gender– difference works out to be 22.88 per cent. Further, literacy rate for females has increased from 19.02 per cent in 1991 to 34.64 per cent in 2001, through the gender-difference is substantial to the extent of 26.15 per cent in 2001. This is definitely the largest number (per centage) of illiterate rural women existing in any region of the State.

Within the Hyderabad-Karnataka region, census-wise data given in table shows great variations in literacy rates for rural-urban areas. Only 34.64 per cent women living in rural areas, whereas 62.65 per cent in urban areas were literate in 2001 though most of the developmental efforts were directed towards them.

Lower literacy rates in rural areas are primarily due to the more conservative nature of Hyderabad-Karnataka region. The low female literacy rates here bring down the total literacy rate of the region. Lower male literacy in the villages are primarily due to the physical nature of work of agricultural labour and migration of literate men to towns/cities.

EDUCATION LEVEL

There are discriminations and restrictions with regard to the pattern of education and accessibility. In this section we attempted to find major biases against women in access to schooling. We also attempted to explore dimensions like medium of education, educational institutions, girls schools and co-education, dropt-outs and reasons etc.

It is observed from Table 2 that in rural areas of Hyderabad-Karnataka region, 38.00 per cent of women respondents were educated upto primary level, 26.67 per cent women respondents upto secondary level and 9.33 per cent women respondents had PUC education. And 7.33 per cent women respondents studied upto undergraduate, 2.50 per cent women respondents were post-graduates and only 16.17 per cent women respondents completed their 'professional courses'. 38.00 per cent and 26.67 per cent women respondents in rural areas of the total female respondents chosen, the study shows, were completed primary and secondary level education respectively. In many ways, this fact offers a partial explanation that why female workers happened to be located in low-end jobs and activities in the region. This study, further, shows that there are serious constraints to women who have low level education in the way of entering into the labour market in the Hyderabad-Karnataka region.

Table 2
Education level of rural women respondents in all districts of Hyderabad-Karnataka region

Education level	*Bidar*	*Gulbarga*	*Koppal*	*Raichur*	*H-K region*
Primary	46 (30.67)	68 (45.33)	61 (40.67)	53 (35.30)	228 (38.00)
Secondary	48 (32.00)	42 (28.00)	27 (18.00)	43 (28.70)	160 (26.67)
Pre-university	15 (10.00)	13 (8.67)	12 (8.00)	16 (10.70)	56 (9.33)
Graduation	16 (10.67)	09 (6.00)	08 (5.33)	11 (7.30)	44 (7.33)
Post-graduation	10 (6.67)	01 (0.67)	02 (1.33)	02 (1.30)	15 (2.50)
Professional	15 (10.00)	17 (11.33)	40 (26.67)	25 (16.70)	97 (16.17)
Total	150 (100.00)	150 (100.00)	150 (100.00)	150 (100.00)	600 (100.00)

Source: Field study
Note: Figures in brackets indicates per centages

Among districts in Hyderabad-Karnataka region, it is found that female respondents in rural areas who are employed had primary level education constituted 30.67 per cent in Bidar district, 45.33 per cent in Gulbarga district, 40.67 per cent in Koppal district and 35.30 per cent in Raichur district. Among the secondary level educated women respondents in rural areas of these district were 32.00 per cent in Bidar, 28.00 per cent in Gulbarga, 18.00 per cent in' Koppal and 28.70 per cent in Raicnur. Among the pre-university level female respondents in rural areas, 10.00 per cent are in Bidar district, 8.67 per cent in Gulbarga district, 8.00 per cent in Koppal district and 10.7 per cent in Raicnur district. Among those women respondents who have completed Graduation in rural areas, 10.67 per cent are in Bidar district, 6.00 per cent in Gulbarga district, 5.33 per cent in Koppal district and 7.30 per cent in Raichur district. Among those respondents who had Post-graduation degrees in rural areas, 6.67 per cent were in Bidar district, 0.67 per cent in Gulbarga district, 1.33 per cent are in Koppal district and 1.30 per cent are in Raichur district. Further, table reveals that the respondents who had 'Professional' education in rural areas constituted 10.00 per cent in Bidar district 11.33 per cent in Gulbarga district, 26.67 per cent in Koppal district and 16.7 per cent in Raichur district. Thus, it is clear that in all district of rural areas in Hyderabad-Karnataka region, the lower educated working women and 'Professionals' (like TCH and B. Ed. etc.) constituted more. This may be due to the backwardness of the region less importance was given to female education and dominating traditional culture. Low literacy/education level of female workers in Hyderabad-Karnataka region is another manifestation of unequal access to basic, and primary education.

MEDIUM OF EDUCATION

The medium of education is determined by the economic and social benefits that are likely to accrue to the learner. Be it basic education or higher education, the medium of education is determined on the basis of a complex mix of factors. What is significant is that in contexts where specialized education is restricted to a small section of the society, the question of medium is sorted out more easily. Once, education is universalized the problem of medium takes on several unpredictable implications. It is quite clear that in a multilingual country like India education has been delivered through different mediums at different levels for different clientele groups.

The distribution of data about the medium of education of the female respondents in rural areas of Hyderabad-Karnataka region in Table 3 reveals that 90.17 per cent of sample women respondents completed their primary education with Kannada medium (regional language) followed by the 87.63 per cent in secondary level, 73.96 per cent in pre-university level, 68.75 per cent in graduation level, 66.67 per cent in post-graduation level and 53.61 per cent in 'professional courses'.

Table 3
Medium of education of rural women respondents in all districts of Hyderabad-Karnataka region

Education level/Medium	*Bidar*	*Gulbarga*	*Koppal*	*Raichur*	*H-K Region*
1 *Primary:*					
Kannada/Urdu	132 (88.00)	133 (88.67)	137 (91.33)	139 (92.67)	541 (90.17)
English	18 (12.00)	17 (11.33)	13 (8.67)	11 (7.33)	59 (9.83)
Total	150 (100.00)	150 (100.00)	150 (100.00)	150 (100.00)	600 (100.00)
2 *Secondary:*					
Kannada/Urdu	92 (88.46)	70 (85.37)	75 (84.27)	89 (91.75)	326 (87.63)
English	12 (11.54)	12 (14.63)	14 (15.73)	08 (8.25)	46 (12.37)
Total	104 (100.00	82 (100.00)	89 (100.00)	97 (100.00)	372 (100.00)
3 *Pre-university:*					
Kannada	38 (69.09)	30 (76.92)	29 (63.04)	45 (86.54)	142 (73.906)
English	17 (30.91)	09 (23.08)	17 (36.96)	07 (13.46)	50 (26.04)
Total	55 (100.00)	39 (100.00)	46 (100.00)	52 (100.00)	192 (100.00)
4 *Graduation:*					
Kannada	21 (72.41)	11 (68.75)	07 (46.67)	16 (80.00)	55 (68.75)
English	08 (27.59)	05 (31.25)	08 (53.33)	04 (20.00)	25 (31.25)
Total	29 (100.00)	16 (100.00)	15 (100.00)	20 (100.00)	80 (100.00)
5 *Post-graduation:*					
Kannada	07 (70.00)	00 (00.00)	01 (50.00)	02 (100.00)	10 (66.67)
English	03 (30.00)	01 (100.00)	01 (50.00)	00 (00.00)	05 (33.33)
Total	09 (100.00)	02 (100.00)	02 (100.00)	02 (100.00)	15 (100.00)
6 *Professional:*					
Kannada	08 (53.33)	09 (52.94)	22 (55.00)	13 (52.00)	52 (53.61)
English	07 (46.67)	08 (47.06)	18 (45.00)	12 (48.00)	45 (46.39)
Total	15 (100.00)	17 (100.00)	40 (100.00)	25 (100.00)	97 (100.00)

Source: Field study
Note: Figures in brackets denotes percentages

Distribution of data by district about the medium of education reveals that majority of the women respondents in all districts of Hyderabad-Karnataka region (*i.e.*, 88.00 per cent in Bidar distrlct; 88.67 per cent in Gulbarga district; 91.33 per cent in Koppal district; and 92.67 per cent in Raichur district studied their primary education with regional language Kannada/Urdu medium. As there is increase in level of education the per centage of the women respondents studied in regional language Kannada decreases and English medium increases. For instance, the per centage of the women respondents studied with English medium at Graduation level constitutes 27.59 per cent in Bidar district, 31.25 in Gulbarga district, 53.33 per cent in Koppal district and 20.00 per cent and 44.16 in Raichur district. Even in case of the professional and vocational courses, the women respondents studied with English medium accounts 46.67 per cent in Bidar district, 47.06 per cent in Gulbarga district, 45.00 per cent in Koppal district, 48.00 per cent in Raichur district. However, the results shows that the majority of women respondents studied in regional language at primary and secondary level in rural areas of Hyderabad-Karnataka region.

INDEPENDENT/CO-EDUCATION

It is very difficult to assess how female educational opportunity, aside from potential constraints on access, is affected by single-sex as compared with co-educational schooling because of the enormous disparities in the quality of the schools and the social backgrounds of students in them in many educational systems. In principles schooling, within a female environment which affords girls appropriate role models, freedom from the social pressures of competing with males, and enables them to assume leadership positions might provide an incentive to excel-academically, to pursue non-traditional academic subjects and to develop more expansive aspirations for higher education and for professional careers.

Thus, to explore the role of gender-discrimination of female educational history in Hyderabad-Karnataka region, a little further, we asked female respondents to state the type of school/

Table 4

Independent/Co-education schools/colleges in which rural women respondents studied in all districts *of* Hyderabad-Karnataka region

Education level/Type of school/colleges	*Bidar*	*Gulbarga*	*Koppal*	*Raichur*	*H-K Region*
1 *Primary:*					
Independent	35 (23.33)	37 (24.67)	32 (21.33)	42 (28.00)	146 (24.33)
Co-education	115 (76.67)	113 (75.33)	118 (78.67)	*108* (72.00)	454 (75.67)
Total	150 (100.00)	150 (100.00)	150 (100.00)	150 (100.00)	600 (100.00)
2 *Secondary:*					
Independent	35 (33.65)	32 (39.02)	32 (33.71)	43 (44.33)	140 (37.63)
Co-education	69 (66.35)	50 (60.97)	59 (66.29)	54 (55.67)	232 (62.37)
Total	104(100.00)	82 (100.00)	89 (100.00)	97 (100.00)	372 (100.00)
3 *Pre-university:*					
Independent	14 (25.46)	17 (43.59)	09 (19.57)	21 (40.38)	61 (31.77)
Co-education	41 (74.54)	22 (56.41)	37 (80.43)	31 (59.62)	131 (68.23)
Total	55 (100.00)	39 *(100.00)*	46 (100.00)	52 (100.00)	192 (100.00)
4 *Graduation:*					
Independent	04 (13.79)	04 (25.00)	06 (40.00)	04 (20.00)	18 (22.50)
Co-education	25 (86.21)	12 (75.00)	09 (60.00)	16 (80.00)	62 (77.50)
Total	29 (100.00)	16 (100.00)	15 (100.00)	*20(100.00)*	80 (100.00)
5 *Professional:*					
Independent	06 ((40.00)	04 (23.53)	06 (15.00)	*10* (40.00)	26 (26.80)
Co-education	09 (60.00)	13 (76.47)	34 (85.00)	15 (60.00)	71 (73.20)
Total	15 (100.00)	17 (100.00)	40 (400.00)	25 (100.00)	97 (100.00)

Source: Field study

Note: Figures in brackets denotes percentages

college in which they studied. There are 24.33 per cent female respondents studied their primary education in girls independent school and 75.67 per cent studied in co-education schools in rural areas of Hyderabad-Karnataka region. Further, 37.63 per cent female respondents studied secondary education in independent schools and 62.37 per cent in co-education schools, followed by 31.77 per cent and 68.23 per cent in pre-university, 22.50 per cent and 77.50 per cent in graduation, 26.80 per cent and 73.20 per cent In 'professional' education level completed in independent and' co-education schools/colleges, respectively. This shows that in the Hyderabad-Karnataka region, number of independent schools/colleges for rural girls/ women are less.

Cross-tabulation of data on the basis of districts reveals that majority of the rural women respondents who studied their primary level in co-education, *i.e.* 76.67 per cent in Bidar district, 75.33 per cent in Gulbarga district, 78.67 per cent in Koppal and 72.00 per cent in Raichur district. Further, it was found that 60.00 per cent in Bidar district, 76.47 per cent in Gulbarga district, 85.00 per cent in Koppal district, 60.00 per cent in Raichur district studied their 'professional courses' in co-education colleges.

TYPE OF MANAGEMENTS

As is evident from Table 5, at primary level, 79.50 per cent female respondents studied in Government schools and 20.50 per cent in private schools. At secondary education level, 53.76 per cent women respondents have studied in Government schools and 46.24 per cent women respondents in private schools. At pre-university level, 52.60 per cent women respondents have studied in Government colleges and 47.40 per cent women respondents in private colleges. At graduation level, 42.50 per cent women respondents have studied in Government colleges and 57.50 per cent women respondents studied in private colleges. For 'professional' education level, 52.58 per cent women respondents have studied in Government colleges and 47.42 per cent women respondents studied in Private colleges.

Table 5

Type of School/college management in which rural women respondents studied in all districts of Hyderabad-Karnataka region

Education level/Management	*Bidar*	*Gulbarga*	*Koppal*	*Raichur*	*H-K Region*
1 *Primary:*					
Government	133 (88.67)	113 (75.33)	120 (80.00)	111 (74.00)	477 (79.50)
Private	17 (11.33)	37 (24.67)	20 (20.00)	39 (26.00)	123 (20.50)
Total	150 (100.00)	150 (100.00)	150 (100.00)	150 (100.00)	600 (100.00)
2 *Secondary:*					
Government	60 (57.69)	48 (58.54)	34 (38.20)	58 (59.79)	200 (53.76)
Private	44 (43.31)	34 (41.46)	55 (61.80)	40 (40.21)	172 (46.24)
Total	104 (100.00)	82 (100.00)	89 (100.00)	97 (100.00)	372 (100.00)
3 *Pre-university:*					
Government	39 (70.91)	22 (56.41)	12 (26.09)	28 (53.85)	101 (52.60)
Private	16 (29.09)	17 (43.59)	34 (73.91)	24 (46.15)	91 (47.40)
Total	55 (100.00)	39 (100.00)	46 (100.00)	52 (100.00)	199 (100.00)
4 *Graduation:*					
Government	15 (51.72)	06 (37.50)	06 (40.00)	07 (35.00)	34 (42.50)
Private	14 (48.28)	10 (62.50)	09 (60.00)	13 (65.00)	46 (57.50)
Total	29 (100.00)	16 (100.00)	15 (100.00)	20 (100.00)	80 (100.00)
5 *Professional:*					
Government	07 (46.67)	07 (41.18)	22 (55.00)	15 (60.00)	51 (52.58)
Private	08 (53.33)	10 (58.82)	18 (45.00)	10 (40.00)	46 (47.42)
Total	15 (100.00)	17 (100.00)	40 (100.00)	25 (100.00)	97 (100.00)

Source: Field study
Note: Figures in brackets denotes percentages

Table 5, further depicts the district-wise distribution of rural women respondents education level studied in different managements. As is evident from the Table that majority of the women respondents who had their primary level of education from Government schools. For instance, of the total women respondents chosen for the study, 88.67 per cent in Bidar district, 75.33 per cent in Gulbarga district, 80.00 per cent in Koppal district and 74.00 per cent in Raichur district studied in Government schools. Similar trend is found in case of secondary school. However, a significant women respondents (i.e. 48.28 per cent in Bidar district, 62.50 per cent in Gulbarga district, 60.00 per cent in Koppal district and 65.00 per cent in Raichur district), had their graduation level education from private managements.

DROP-OUTS

At the outset, data of the women respondents who dropped their primary education in rural areas of Hyderabad-Karnataka region is presented in Table 6. For the purpose of analysis, drop-out rate was worked out for grades I-IV, V to VII. Of the 600 women respondents chosen for the present study, 228 women

Table 6
Drop-out of rural women education at primary level in Hyderabad-Karnataka Region

Districts	*I-IV*	*V-VII*	*Total*
Bidar	6	40	46
	(13.04)	(86.96)	(100.00)
Gulbarga	29	39	68
	(42.65)	(57.35)	(100.00)
Raichur	15	46	61
	(24.59)	(75.41)	(100.00)
Koppal	14	39	53
	(26.42)	(73.58)	(100.00)
Total	64	164	228
	(28.07)	(71.93)	(100.00)

Source: Field study
Note: Figures in brackets denotes per centages

respondents had primary education (I-VII standard) in rural areas. Of this, 64 (28.07 per cent) dropped their education at lower primary level (between I-IV standard) and 164 (71.93 per cent) dropped their education at higher primary level(between V-VII standard).

The distribution of data according to the district reveals that 6 (13.04 per cent) women respondents in Bidar , 29 (42.65 per cent) women respondents in Gulbarga, 15 (24.59 per cent) in Koppal and 14(26.42 per cent) in Raichur stopped their education at lower primary level (between I-IV standard). Further, it is found that 40(86.96 per cent) women respondents in Bidar district, 39(57.35 per cent) women respondents in Gulbarga district, 46(75.41 per cent) women respondents ill Koppal district and 39 (73.58 per cent) women respondents in Raichur district dropped their education at higher primary (between V-VII standard level). This significant drop-out at higher primary level could be to non-availability of Higher Primary schools in their villages.

REASONS FOR DROP-OUTS

While studying the drop-outs of women respondents In Hyderabad-Karnataka region, it is relevant to study the reasons for drop-outs at the primary education level. The data reveal that the women respondents have given different reasons for their drop-out which are presented in Table 7. Out of 228 women respondents in- rural areas of Hyderabad-Karnataka region, 49 (21.49 per cent) reported the 'need to start earning' followed by 'need for household duties (17.86 per cent); 'got married (14.04 per cent)'; 'school within village was not available (14.04 per cent)'; 'having to take care of younger siblings (13.60 per cent)'; and 'no money to pay fees/purchase books (11.40 per cent)'and 'absence or death of either or both parents (4.39 per cent)'. An analysis of the reasons for the drop-outs of the women in rural areas of Hyderabad-Karnataka region are mainly for 'need to start earning', 'need for household duties', 'got married' and 'having to take care of younger siblings' and' school within village was not available'. The distribution of data according to districts of Hyderabad-Karnataka region also shown the same reasons. It seems that the poor economic condition of their parents and domination of traditional conditions in the region compel them to discontinue their education and engage their

Table 7

Reasons for drop-outs by the rural women respondents from scholl (I-IV std) in Hyderabad-Karnataka Region

Reasons	*Bidar*	*Gulbarga*	*Koppal*	*Raichur*	*H-K Region*
1 Absence or death of either or both parents	03 (6.52)	05 (7.35)	02 (3.77)	00 (0.00)	10 (4.39)
2 Having to take care of younger siblings	06 (13.04)	09 (13.24)	06 (11.32)	10 (16.39)	31 (13.60)
3 Need to start earning	09 (19.57)	14 (20.59)	11 (20.75)	15 (24.59)	49 (21.49)
4 Need for household duties	08 (17.39)	11 (16.18)	13 (24.53)	11 (18.03)	43 (18.86)
5. No money to pay fees/purchase books	05 (10.87)	07 (10.29)	07 (13.22)	07 (11.48)	26 (11.40)
6. Got married	06 (13.04)	10 (14.71)	08 (15.09)	08 (13.11)	32 (14.04)
7. School within village or area was not available	09 (19.57)	10 (14.71)	06 (11.32)	07 (11.48)	32 (14.04)
8. Failed in examination & lost interest	00 (0.00)	02 (2.93)	00 (0.00)	03 (4.92)	05 (2.18)
Total	46 (100.00)	68 (100.00)	53 (100.00)	61 (100.00)	228 (100.00)

Source: Field study
Note: Figures in brackets denotes percentages

girls to various economic activities to supplement the meager family income instead of sending them to schools.

OCCUPATIONAL STATUS:

The exploration into the occupational status of the 600 women respondents in rural areas of Hyderabad-Karnataka reveals that 214 (35.67 per cent) women respondents are self-employed, 176 (29.33 per cent) women respondents belong to agriculture, 111 (18.50 per cent) are Government employees and 99(16.50 per cent) women respondents belong to private sector business sector (Table 8). The district-wise distribution of data reveals the same trend about occupation status of women respondents.

Table 8
Occupation-wise distribution of rural women respondents in all districts of Hyderabad-Karnataka region

Occupation	*Bidar*	*Gulbarga*	*Koppal*	*Raichur*	*H-K region*
Self-employed	77	30	52	55	214
	(51.33)	(20.00)	(34.67)	(36.67)	(35.67)
Agriculture	35	39	51	51	176
	(23.33)	(26.00)	(34.00)	(34.00)	(29.33)
Government	19	33	31	28	111
	(12.67)	(26.00)	(10.67)	(18.67)	(18.50)
Private/business	19	34	16	16	99
	(12.67)	(22.67)	(10.67)	(10.67)	(16.50)
Total	150	150	150	150	600
	(100.00)	(100.00)	(100.00)	(100.00)	(100.00)

Source: Field study
Note: Figures in brackets denotes per centages.

The analysis of data pertaining to the occupational status of the respondents clearly indicates that women's participation in the occupational life is becoming increasingly diversified and they are' achieving top positions in male-dominated occupational fields as well. However, their representation is still very small in Hyderabad- Karnataka region.

MONTHLY INCOME

In the present study, considerable income variation has been found in the income status of rural women respondents in

Hyderabad-Karnataka region (Table 9). For instance, 41.50 per cent of women respondents possess a monthly income upto Rs.1000, 32.67 per cent of women respondents possess a monthly income of Rs.100 1-2000, 11.33 per cent of women respondents possess income ofRs.2001-5000, 13.33 per cent women respondents possess income of Rs.5001-10000, and only 1.17 per cent of women respondents possess income of Rs.1000 and above.

Table 9
Monthly income of rural women respondents in Hyderabad-Karnataka region

Districts	*Upto Rs.1000*	*Rs.1001-2000*	*Rs.2001-5000*	*Rs.5001-10000*	*Rs.10000 and above*	*Total*
Bidar	71	51	16	12	00	150
	(47.33)	(34.00)	(10.67)	(8.00)	(0.00)	(100.00)
Gulbarga	60	55	10	25	00	150
	(40.00)	(36.67)	(6.67)	(16.67)	(0.00)	(100.00)
Koppal	60	38	30	17	05	150
	(40.00)	(25.33)	(20.00)	(11.33)	(3.33)	(100.00)
Raichur	58	52	12	26	02	150
	(38.67)	(34.67)	(8.00)	(17.33)	(1.33)	(100.00)
H-K Region	249	196	68	80	07	600
	(41.50)	(32.67)	(11.33)	(13.33)	(1.17)	(100.00)

Source: Field study
Note: Figures in brackets denotes per centages.

Examining the district-wise monthly income structure of the women respondents, it is found in Bidar that 47.33 per cent have less than Rs.1000 monthly income, 34.00 have Rs.1001-2000, 10.67 per cent have Rs. 2001-5000, and only 8.00 per cent respondents have Rs.5001 to 10000 monthly income. In case of Gulbarga district, 40.00 per cent respondents have less than Rs. 1000 monthly income, 36.67 per cent have income between Rs.I001-2000, 6.67 per cent have Rs.2001-5000, and 16.67 per cent have monthly income between Rs.5001-10000. Further, in Koppal and Raichur districts, 40.00 per cent and 38.67 per cent have income less than Rs.1000, 25.33 per cent and 34.67 per cent have income between Rs.1001-2000, respectively. The income between Rs.2001-5000 constitutes 20.00 per cent and 8.00 per cent, between Rs.5001-10000 constitutes 11.33 per cent and 17.33 per cent in Koppal and Raichur districts, respectively., Only 3.33 per cent respondents in Koppal district and 1.33 per cent in Raichur district have monthly income above Rs.10000. Thus, it is clear that most of the women respondents in rural areas in the present sample have an income less than Rs.1000 and between Rs.1001 to 2000. This shows that these respondents have a lower middle class income status which alone is sufficient to raise these women to a satisfactory position in their family. And if their income is combined with the income of the husbands or of the parents, then these working women are contributing a lot to the economic stability of their family.

MONTHLY INCOME BY EDUCATION

The distribution of income data on the basis of education, it' suggests that there is a unsatisfactory correlation between the education level and income status of the rural women in Hyderabad-Karnataka region. For instance, according to Table 10, the women respondents who had primary education it is found that 57.89 per cent women respondents possess income

Table 10
Monthly income by education of rural women respondents in Hyderabad-Karnataka region (comprising all districts)

Education level	*Upto Rs.1000*	*Rs.1001-2000*	*Rs.2001-5000*	*Rs.5001-10000*	*Rs.10000 and above*	*Total*
Primary	132	78	04	13	01	228
	(57.89)	(34.21)	(34.21)	(5.70)	(0.44)	(100.00)
Secondary	74	64	15	07	0	160
	(46.25)	(40.00)	(9.38)	(4.38)	(0.00)	(100.00)
Pre-university	23	19	08	06	0	56
	(41.07)	(33.93)	(14.29)	(10.71)	(0.00)	(100.00)
Graduation	11	17	06	09	01	44
	(25.00)	(38.64)	(13.64)	(20.45)	(2.27)	(100.00)
Post-graduation	01	05	04	05	0	15
	(6.67)	(33.33)	(26.67)	(33.33)	(0.00)	(100.00)
Professional	08	13	31	40	05	97
	(8.25)	(13.40)	(31.96)	(41.24)	(5.15)	(100.00)
Total	249	196	68	80	7	600
	(41.50)	(32.67)	(11.33)	(13.33)	(1.17)	(100.00)

Source: Field study
Note: Figures in brackets indicates per centages.

less than Rs.1000. 46.26 per cent and 40.00 per cent women respondents who had secondary education posses income upto Rs.1000 respectively. Further, 41.07 per cent and 33.93 per cent women respondents whose education level is PUC have income upto Rs.1000 and Rs. 1001-2000, respectively. 25.00 per cent and 38.64 per cent Graduate women respondents earns Income less than Rs.1000 and 1001-2000, respectively. Only 5 (33.33 per cent) women respondent who had Post-Graduate degree earn income of Rs.5001-10000. Surprisingly, 31.96 per cent and 41.24 per cent women respondents who studied professional/vocational courses possess income of Rs.200 1-5000 and Rs.5001-10000. The study shows that a majority of women in Gulbarga district work in low-earning and low-paying activities and earns low income. Further, it show that there is no correlation between education level and income of the women respondents except professional courses.

CONCLUSION

Since the inception of planning era, making the society more egalitarian, empowering women both in social and economic aspects has remained the stagnant in rural areas of Hyderabad-Karnataka region. For improving literacy and education among women, a number of incentives and programmes were introduced in the region. Besides these socio-economic condition of women still continued to be worst and deprived. Further, the well-established bias against women's schooling, education and employment has been reiterated by the results of the study.

REFERENCES

Anil Bhuimali, 'Education, Employment and Empowering Women', Serials Publications, Delhi, 2004.

Batliwala Srilatha, 'Status of Rural Women in Karnataka', National Institute of Advanced Studies, Bangalore, 1998.

Indira Kumari Y. and Sambasiva Rao B., 'Empowerment of Women and Rural Development', Serials Publications, Delhi, 2005.

Irfan Sabir and Sarfaraj Asgher, 'Rural Women: Work and Health', The Women Press, Delhi, 2005.

Jha Frem Kumar, 'Education for Rural Development', Vista International Publishing House, Delhi, 2005.

Kapur P., 'The Changing Status of the Women in India', Vikas Publishing House, Delhi, 1974.

Kumud Ranjan, 'Women and Modern Occupation in India', Chugh Publication, Allahabad, 1993.

Mira Seth, 'Women and Development: The Indian Experience, Sage Publications, New Delhi, 2001.

Nanjudappa D.M., 'High Power Committee for Redressal of Regional Imbalance (Report)', Government of Karnataka, Bangalore, 2002.

Narayana Reddy V, Vijayakumar S and Nalini, 'Women in Development', Challenges and Achievements', Serials Publications, Delhi, 2005.

Ranade and Ramachandran, , Women and Employment', Tata Institute of Social Sciences Series, No.20, Bombay, 1970.

Savitri Arputhamurthy, 'Women Work and Discrimination', Ashish Publishing House, New Delhi, 1990.

Sengupta P, 'The story of women of Indian', Indian Book Company, New Delhi, 1974.

Srivastava V, 'Employment of Educated Married Women in India', National Publishing House, New Delhi, 1978.

Thota Jyothi Rani, 'Work, Income and Status of Rural Women', Serials Publications, Delhi, 2005.

20

WTO AND SOCIAL CLAUSE IN PERSPECTIVE WITH CHILD LABOUR IN INDIA

Mini Goyal *

INTRODUCTION

In the era of globalisation and liberalisation the world trade has flourished, exports have increased and production has gone up. There was a time when the world market system worked like a well–oiled machine but in the present times it is running at a tremendously increased speed which can be heard clearly by the public (Datta, 1994). In the present times the world market has, no doubt, assumed a great importance. It has become the center of all events as it provides for the worldwide volume of goods, services and capital.

It is true that legislations aimed at affecting improvements in the working conditions of labour have been on since industrial revolutions. Numerous macro legislations in this context were successful in realizing this objective by bringing about a reduction in the number of working hours and ensuring minimum wages. A number of international treaties and declarations were made and acts were enacted to black list the institution of slavery and slave trading.

Since then a general consensus of the people had evolved some core standards of labour to raise the standards of living and to tackle the problems of child and bonded labour, which

* Associate Professor, Department of Economics, Punjab Agricultural University, Ludhiana.

is no less than the problem of slavery and today the developed countries show concern towards its elimination in the third world. For it its advocates want to link the core labour standards with the international trade. They also want to ensure that the benefits of free trade should reach people at large to raise their standards of living. In order to achieve their aim they have moved through World Trade Organisation (WTO) and General Agreement on Tariff and Trade (GATT) to link the core labour standards with trade. It would ensure that the countries violating basic labour rights would be charged with violating their trading commitments, for which sanctions would be imposed. The basic labour rights or core labour standards are known as social in India (Shanker,2001). Bibek (1994), is of the opinion that it is a concept which is not new. Infact, it has evolved over the years in the twentieth century.

ILO, since its inceptions in 1919, has been emphasizing that the failure of any nation to adopt humane conditions of labour is an obstacle in way of other nations which desire to improve the conditions in their own countries . ILO in order to achieve its humanitarian aims has adopted 182 Conventions, 190 recommendations and a few protocols. But the seven conventions which the ILO has declared to be the basic worker rights conventions, concern freedom of association (No. 87), collective bargaining (No. 98), forced labour (Nos. 29 and 105), equal remuneration (No. 100), child labour minimum age (No. 138), and discrimination (No. 111). The minimum core labour standards have been adopted for GATT and WTO, which are based on these seven conventions of ILO.

These conventions have been ratified by a large majority of the ILO member-countries and are considered to be the most fundamental core human rights conventions, which are based on very sound principles. ILO resolved to promote these conventions with renewed vigour. These seven conventions or the core labour standards, qualify to be regarded universally as 'voluntarily agreed labour standards'. But this voluntarism is considered to be both the strength and weakness of ILO. No when the world is moving towards the greater consensus on democracy and market economy, enforcement of minimum or core labour standards internationally, the ILO with its present structure and apparatus based on voluntarism has been found inadequate. In order to incorporate the social clause in the GATT, a serious study about its desirability and its impact on the economy of the world was undertaken. Organisation for Economic Cooperation and Development (OECD), which comprised of 25 developed country-members including the United States, studied the economic aspects and implications of the linkage between the labour standards and the international trade. This study also received the support of Trade Union Advising Committee of the OECD. The conference of the trade ministers in Singapore in 1996 further affirmed the need to consider the labour standards as a part of the WTO discipline. The United States made a strong plea for adoption of the social clause formally as a part of GATT and WTO rules.

The developed countries justify the introduction of social clause in the world trade on the humanitarian grounds to raise the standard of living in the world and to guarantee certain fundamental rights to labour to save them from exploitation. The US President made it clear in his address in Brussels in 1994 when he said, "If we are going to open our borders and trade more and invest more with developing countries, we want to know that their working people will receive a fair share of the benefits of this trade and investment".

The move for incorporation of social clause in trade privileges of GATT is a form of pressure not just on India but also on the entire developing world for the sake of this noble motive. Their logic is based on humanitarian grounds and the cause is just(Swamy, 2000).

It is also claimed to be based on sound economic principles. The prevalence of child and bonded labour may provide a competitive edge to a country that markets its products made with the help of such labour. But this phenomenon will not help to raise the standard of labour in that country because the benefits of the free trade market would be pocketed by the producer and the labour would be left in the quagmire of poverty. This exploitation based on supply of labour would result in depressed labour market ultimately leading to 'the race to the bottom phenomenon'.

The social clause generated massive antipathy. Supachai Panitchapkdi, Thailand's Deputy Prime Minister and Director General designate of the WTO spoke for many governments when he objected to link trade sanctions with labour rights violations. After rejecting the proposal at Marakkesh, the government of India also examined the implications of the social clause very minutely and found it detrimental to the trade and commerce of the entire third world. India stoutly opposed the introduction of social clause in WTO. It also tried that 'all non-aligned countries should stick together as a "block" against social clause endeavours. It wanted that the Non-Aligned Movement (NAM) should serve as a forum to mobilize resistance against it.

In the 5 Conference of the labour ministry of the NAM group, the Indian government put the controversial social clause on its agenda. In the Delhi Declaration the labour ministers argued that the neo–protectionists tie up Uruguay Round of trade with social clauses would endanger the positive results of the Uruguay Round and therefore would be completely unacceptable.

In Singapore the WTO first Ministerial Conference was held on 9-13 December, 1996 the issue of core labour standards there was rejected once again with the active participation of India. The conference claimed that economic growth and development fostered by increased trade and liberalisation automatically contribute to the promotion of these labour standards. Majority of them felt that the whole discussion to link the social clause with the international trade would be protectionist one. And it would not foster the necessary debate on the inter dependency of the liberalisation of the trade and the social development. All the major unions attending the 32nd labour committee session including Center of Indian Trade Unions (CITU), All India Trade Union Congress (AITUC), Indian National Trade Union Congress (INTUC), Hind Mazdoor Sabha (HMS) and Bharatiya Mazdoor Sangh (BMS) supported the stand of the Indian Government on the social clause.

The social clause meant to its critics that whatever is being produced with child labour and forced labour should not form part of the world trade. India, which has this endemic problem as there are about 10.40 million number of child labour in India (NSSO, 2000) should not be allowed to export anything or at least not the products, which have been produced with child labour or forced labour. If the social clause were to be applied to India the country could not export even a blade of grass, a grain of wheat, a leaf of tea, a piece of granite, carpet, bangle, match-box, leather goods, textiles, nothing of this sort because of direct or indirect involvement of the unorganized labour force (Agnivesh, 1999). The economists also suspect the real motive behind it. The real motive behind this move is commercial. The developed countries find their markets flooded with imports from the developing countries and find themselves helpless to check it. These countries under the pressure of their own labour want to take off the competitive edge of the developing countries by linking adherence to the social clause with the international trade. Opposition to the social clause comes primarily on the ground that the developed countries want to restrict the trade of the developing countries in the international market by raising non-tariff barriers in the name of social clause. The motive behind it is commercial.

The Indian government, politicians, trade unionists and social activists all hold uncompromising, attitude of rejection towards social clause. Satyarthi (1999), a trade unionist, is of the view that in the name of social clause, no rich country can impose its own interests against poor countries. It should be introduced through persuasion and not through pressure. The pressure is not justified.

So far as child and bonded labour are concerned, India also share the international concern over it. Child labour is a very acute problem in India. Opposition to the linkage of social clause did not emanate only from its content but also from the procedure adopted to have it enforced .The developed countries have not studied and taken into account the economies of the underdeveloped countries. Because of their backwardness and poverty these countries despite their commitment to combat child labour and bonded labour etc. find themselves at a loss to implement it. The developed countries have miserably failed to fulfill their moral, ethical and economic obligations towards the third world to help them to eradicate those problems to which they express so much concern. After all it is a big problem, which cannot be done away with the stroke of a pen. There should be a time bound programme to phase it out. There should be a provision for incentives in place of sanctions and restrictions, to those countries, industries and children who are affected. There should be a body within WTO to take care of rehabilitating the affected children. Countries like India needs huge funds for it and the developed countries owe a responsibility towards them to float a corporate fund to help the developing countries. But these industrialised countries, which profess to be the well-wishers of the labour have done nothing concrete to solve those problems which are slur on the face of human culture and civilisation. These countries shirk their responsibility knowingly and are to have their own way in every matter, which concerns their trade, commerce, industry and profits. They are playing truant with the problem and are trying to run with the hare and hunt with the hounds. It is a double standard game and by raising the bogey of child labour, these developed countries of the west want to create an atmosphere to bring in their social clause in WTO (Agnivesh, 1999). Moreover child labour is not restricted in export item such as carpets and diamond cutting or polishing but it is more prevalent in unorganized sector. But these developed countries have shown concern with that child labour which is employed in export-oriented activities simply to curtail the share of developing countries in the global trade. That is why the foreign dignitaries fly to Jaipur to see child labour in diamond polishing and cutting industries. It has made the things clear that it was not intended to fight the child labour in this country but to high light child labour in export oriented industry whereas half of the child labour is in agriculture (Agnivesh,1999).

The critics are also vocal about monitoring body of the social clause. They want that it should not be controlled or governed by rich countries or only by the governments. An independent monitoring body under WTO can be constituted inviting top trade unions, Non Government Organizations (NGOs), government representatives and experts from all over the world and from UN agencies.

Due to combined strength of G-15 countries and general out burst against the introduction of social clause in WTO, the US government had to face a retreat and the issue has been deferred. The temporary withdrawal of the social clause should not be seen as a victory of the developing countries. It is quite possible that USA may revive it. Seattle Protest organized on November 30, 1999 is an indication to it. Seattle, the capital of the North Western state of Washington of the US was the scene of the largest protest in the history of the US in which 30000 industrial workers and the industrialists participated against globalisation and demanded protection for the home trade.

Linkage of the social clause with the international trade has divided the world into two groups. One group consists of the developed countries supporting it and the other consists of developing countries opposing it. Both have not viewed it in right perspective. It is clear that during the last fifteen years the adherence to core labour standards has come to stay as an issue on the international agenda. It is based on a worthy idea of eliminating child and bonded labour. Therefore some critics feel that India should not permit the issue of desirable labour standard to become a dividing force in the countries of East and West. It should be given a constructive turn by the concerned countries through dialogue and by working out a consensus for a joint determination on the enforcement, sequence and timing of the compliance of the desirable labour standards. A proper list of labour standards, and a consensus on its enforcement should be finalized through discussion and agreement. The sanctions for non-observance can gradually be made stricter. This approach will be more practical, fruitful and acceptable.

The developed countries should study the economy of the third world and the likely impact of the linkage of the social clause with the global trade on it. More flexibility and liberal attitude towards the poor countries would ultimately facilitate in making the proper atmosphere to link social clause with the international trade. A consensus should be arrived at about social clause in the international trade after mutual discussion.

REFERENCES

Agnivesh, Swamy, (1999), "A Critique of Selective Western Interventions and WTO", in Klaus Voll (ed), *Against Child Labour*, Mosaic Books, New Delhi: 31-38.

Datta, Asit, (1994), *World Trade And World Hunger*, Mundren:21.

Swamy, Subramanian, (2000), *India's Labour Standards and the WTO Framewark*, Konark Publishers Pvt Ltd., New Delhi: 85-86, 102, 170.

Shanker, Gopal, (2001), "American Anti-Globalisation Movement-Reexamining Seattle Protests," *Economic And Political Weekly*, 36(34), August 25.

21

PEOPLE'S PARTICIPATION IN RURAL DEVELOPMENT IN BIHAR: A MICRO ANALYSIS

Sanjay Kr. Jha[*] *& J. P. Sharma*[**]

INTRODUCTION

Active participation and involvement of people in rural development programmes meant for them is an important factor which contributes to the success of these programmes. The catalytic role of popular participation in socio-economic development has gained a special significance in promoting a self-reliant development process in all societies- developed or developing, tribal or non-tribal. The united Nations Economic and Social Council has recommended that the Government should encourage the widest possible active participation of all individuals and non- governmental organisations in development process in setting goals, formulating policies and implementing plans.

People's participation at the time of preparing a programme is very much needed to take dicisions because the programme should be according to the basic needs of local people. The programme should meet the basic needs of the majority of local people as local people are the ultimate beneficiary of any programme.The programme should be for the people, by the

* Lecturer, Deptt. of Economics, T.N.B. College, Bhagalpur, T. M. Bhagalpur University, Bhagalpur (Bihar)

** Lecturer, Deptt. of Commerce, B. N. College, Bhagalpur, T. M. Bhagalpur University Bhagalpur (Bihar) people and of the people. However, it has always been a problem as to how this concept can be practised effectively in such a way that people could be closely associated in the dicision-making process at grass-roots level. It is in this milieu that Mahatma Gandhi has stated, "True democracy could not be worked by some men sitting at the top. It had to be worked from below by the people of every village." (Mahatma Gandhi, Hind Swaraj).

The Balwant Rai Mehta committee (1958) envisaged only a three- tier system of panchayati raj and this committee did not consider the need for a body consisting of residents of the village and to which panchayat could be made accountable. In spite of this the Gram Gavhas (GS) were constituted in a number of states as a forum witch provides opportunities to all the adult villagers to directly participate and suggest what can and needs to be done for their own village and how to accomplish it. Soon after the inauguration of three-tier panchayat raj system based on the recommendations of B.R. Mehta committee; some important recommendations emphasised the need and importance of GS. The conference of Development commissioners as well as the central council of Local Self Government (1959) had recognised possible potentialities of the imtitution of GS and recommended that statutory recognition be given to GS through necessary legislation. The central council of local self Government thus recommended the coustitution of GS as a legal entity and providing for at least two meetings, one for budget and one for review of progress. Thereafter this need was further mooted in a seminar held under the auspices of the National Institute of Community Development in Mussoorie in April, 1962 and later the study team on GS consitituted by Ministry of community Development and co-operation, Gevernment of India, recomended for their establishment. Thus, the institution of GS came into existence in most of the states of Indian union either through statute or otherwise. In most of the states the functions evriseged for the GS includes consideration of annual statement of accounts and audit report of the panchayat, review of progress of work , formulations of plans for the next year and approval of the annual budget previously drawn up by the panchayat.

Infact, the GS in the village level institution developed as an attempt to establish people's participation at the village level for the overall development of the village. Based on the idea that enhancing the powers of Panchayati Raj Institutions (PRIs) world increase the accountability and responsiveness of the government. This institution provides opportunity to electors at the grass-roots level to raise their voice in favour or against the actions of Gram Panchayat (GP). The GP is the elected executive body of the GS, which is considered as the institution of direct democracy by rural communities at the grass-roots level.

With the enactment of the 73rd constitutional (Amendment) Act, 1992,the Panchayat Raj System was revived. This amendment provided a constitutional sanction to the institution of GS, though framework of the concept was left to the wisdom of state governments. Thus, through this amendmend, the GS is not only envisaged to strengthen the participatory process at the local level but also to facilitate elements of transparency, accountability and social control over the activities of village panchayat. Thus, the GS is the unique forum for collective thinking, planning and dicision-making and overseeing different activities in the village. This institution is designed to help in bringing common people to the centre of dicision-making and uplift the status of women and the depressed classes.

The present study on people's participation in rural development programmes in Bhagalpur district of Bihar state was formulated with the following objectives:

(i) To assess the level of people's participation in rural development programme.

(ii) To assess the functioning of the Gram-Sabha.

(iii) To evaluate the role of GS as perceived by the villagers themselves.

(iv) To find out who is responsible for ineffective role of Panchayati Raj in General and Gram-Sabha in particular.

THE EMPIRICAL EVIDENCE

The district of Bhagalpur of Bihar is the universe of the study. Its geographical area is 2,569.5 sq. km. which is 1.47 percent of Bihar.

Population

Place	*Total Persons*	*Males*	*Females*	*Decodal Population Growth (1991-2001) in %*
Bihar	82,878,796	43,153,964	39,724,832	28.43
Bhagalpur	24,30,331	12,94,192	11,36,139	27.2

Literacy rate (Census 2001)

Place	*Total Persons*	*Males*	*Females*
Bihar	47.53	60.32	33.57
Bhagalpur	50.28	60.11	38.83

SOCIO-ECONOMIC PROFILE OF THE SAMPLE RESPONDENTS

The total number of respondent is 100 from five blocks of Bhagalpur district viz. Nathnagar, Sultanganj, Jagdishpur, Naugachia and Bihpur; selecting one village panchayat from each block and 20 respondents were selected from each village panchayat from each block by stratified random sampling plan. The respondents from each village were grouped into four categories *i.e.* Scheduled caste, Scheduled Tribe, Other Backword class and General and five representatives from each category were selected. Thus, total one hundred respondent were included in the study.The responses of the respondents were recorded in the pre- structured schedule by personal interview and data were computed with appropriate statistical methods.

Respondents belonging to different age group; caste/ category; professions were included in the sample which makes it representative as they exist in almost same ratio in the state.

Table 1
Age-wise break-up and gender of the respondents

	Male		Female		Total	
Age Group (Year)	*No.*	*%*	*No.*	*%*	*No.*	*%*
18-35	30	42.85%	18	60.00%	48	48.00%
36-50	32	45.72%	8	26.70%	40	40.00%
More than 50	8	11.43%	4	13.30%	12	12.00%
Total	70	100.00%	30	100.00%	100	100.00%

Table 2
Caste/Category gender break-up of the respondents

	Male		Female		Total	
Caste Category	*No.*	*%*	*No.*	*%*	*No.*	*%*
Scheduled Caste	14	20.00%	6	20.00%	20	20.00%
Scheduled Tribe	15	21.43%	5	16.67%	20	20.00%
Other Backward Classes	16	22.86%	9	30.00%	25	25.00%
General	25	35.71 %	10	33.33 %	35	35.00%
Total	70	100.00%	30	100.00%	100	100.00%

Table 3
Profession of the Respondents

	Male		Female		Total	
Profession	*No.*	*%*	*No.*	*%*	*No.*	*%*
Agricultural	48	68.57%	12	40.00%	60	60.00%
Domestic Work	0	00.00%	16	53.33 %	16	16%
Trade	9	12.86%	0	00.00%	9	9%
Other Work	13	18.57 %	2	6.67%	15	15%
Total	70	100.00%	30	100.00%	100	100%

Table 4
Gram - Sabha : A Basic Fundamental Unit

	Male		Female		Total	
Respondents	*No.*	*%*	*No.*	*%*	*No.*	*%*
Yes	43	61.43%	18	60.00%	61	61.00%
No	27	38.57%	12	40.00%	39	39.00%
Total	70	100.00%	30	100.00%	100	100.00%

Extent of people's participation in rural development programmes under the present study was categorised into three levels *i.e.*

Table 5
Participation in the Gram-Sabha by the Respondents

Whether Participated In Gram-Sabha	*Male* No.	*Male* %	*Female* No.	*Female* %	*Total* No.	*Total* %
Yes	12	17.14%	4	13.33%	16	16.00%
No	58	82.86%	26	86.67%	84	84.00%
Total	70	100.00%	30	100%	100	100.00%

Table 6
Reasons for not participating in the meetings of Gram Sabha by the respondents

Sl. No.	*Reasons (Response)*	*Male* No.	*Male* %	*Female* No.	*Female* %	*Total* No.	*Total* %
1.	Lack of faith in the representatives	18	31.04 %	03	11.54 %	21	25.00%
2.	Lack of awareness among villagers	22	37.93 %	04	15.39 %	26	30.95%
3.	Lack of quorum/dull meetings/mere fornalities	08	13.79%	02	7.69%	10	11.91 %
4.	Purdah Pratha	—	—	12	46.14 %	12	14.29%
5.	Lack of information about programmes	04	6.90%	02	7.69%	06	7.14%
6.	Unawareness about the date of meeting	06	10.34%	03	11.55 %	09	10.71 %
7.	No. of Respondents (Total)	58	100.00%	26	100.00%	84	100.00%

From this table, it is clear that lack of faith in representatives and lack of awareness among villagers and Purdah-pratha among women (46%) are the major reasons keeping people away from GS meetings. Respondents believe that GS meeting is not held due to lack of quarum (13.79%).

(i) The respondents having participation scores below mean minus Standard Deviation (SD.) were grouped under the category of low level participation.

(ii) The respondents obtained scores between mean minus standard deviation to mean plus standard deviation were kept under the category of medium level participation

(iii) The respondents having scores above than mean plus standard deviation were grouped under category of high level participation.

Table 7

Who is responsible for ineffective role of Panchayati Raj in general and Gram Sabha in particular?

Sl. (Response)	*Male*		*Female*		*Total*	
	No.	*%*	*No.*	*%*	*No.*	*%*
1. Politicians	13	18.58 %	04	13.33 %	17	17.00%
2. Bureaucrats	21	30.00%	13	43.33 %	34	34.00 %
3. People's representative of PRIs	25	35.72 %	08	26.67%	33	33.00%
4. Villagers themselves	07	10.00%	03	10.00%	10	10.00%
5. Donot know	04	5.70%	02	6.67%	06	6.00%
6. Total (Respondents)	70	100.00%	30	100.00%	100	100.00%

From Table 7, it is clear that neither the politicians nor the bureancrats and nor their PRI representatives are interested in making GS an effective institution in the development process. There is an on-going tug-of- war among the politicians, bureancrats and local level leadership for larger share of the power cake. If GS becomes vital and functional power centre, position of Mukhiya and Sarpanch in day to day functioning becomes less effective.

Table 8

Level of people's participation in rural development programmes

Participation Level	*No. of respeondents*	*Percentage*	*Mean*	*S.D.*
Low Level Scores < (mean ± S.D.)	19	19.00%		
Medium level Scores (mean ± S.D.) to (mean ± S.D.)	70	70.00%	3.61	2.10
High level Scores> (mean ± S.D.)	11	11.00%		

Table 8 elucidates that participation level of people in rural development programme was medium to low. The reason for medium to low level of people's participation might be lack of awareness among villagers, lack of education and lack of knowledge about different developmental programmes.

SUGGESTIONS

(1) To achieve sustainable rural development, emphasis must be given on three main issues- Public awareness (formal and informal education), rural infrastructure and employment generation. Investment in education, socio-economic infrastructure and employment generating assets should be enhanced. As income generation stands last in the hierarchical order of development goals, any government policy that directly transfers money to poor in rural areas would be like putting the cart before the horse.

(2) In order to motivate elected representatives and staff of GP 'Best GP 'Award' should be introduced at block, district, state and national level. Moreover, Mukhiyas and Sarpanchs should be given honorarium and TA/DA.

(3) To make GP organisation more people oriented, attempts will have to be made to organise training programmes for representatives and staff; review and assess the success of these programmes; and modify the training modules and methods in light of evaluation of the programmes. Government with the help of local NGOs should also educate them through arranging camps, seminars and meetings.

REFERENCES

Ray, G.L. and M. Sagar, 1993, Gram Panchayat Organisation: Effective Management for Rural Development, Naya Prakash Bidhan Sarani, Calcutta.

Singh, B., 1996, Decentralisation, Panchayat Raj and District Planning, Atlanta Publisher, New Delhi.

Palanidurai, G. etal, 1997, Major Issues in New Panchayat Raj System, Kanishka Publishers, New Delhi.

Kumat, R.S., 1997, Panchayat Raj and Poverty Alleviation: Need for New Administrative structure, The Indian Journal of Public Administration, vol. XLIII(2).

Axinn, G.H and N.C. Axinn, 1997, Collaboration in International Rural Development, Sage, New Delhi.

McClelland, D.C., 1961, The Achieving Society, Van Nostrand Reinholt co., New York.

22

PROFILE OF AGED 21ST CENTURY

D. R. Albal & Z. A. Pathan***

INTRODUCTION

Throughout the world 1982 was celebrated as the year of the aged. The increased scientific concern for old age is a recent development and is a result of rapid increase in the population of elderly persons. According to UNESCO estimate, the number of the aged above 60 years of age is likely to go up from 350 million in 1975 to 590 million in 2005. About half of them live in developing countries. India alone has 43 million old people according to 1981 census.

As man grows older, his reduced activities and income and consequent decline in his position in family and society makes his life all the more vulnerable. Modern education, urban influence, mass media and above all the emergence of materialistic and individualist outlook had the tendency to alter traditional kinship and family organization towards nuclear family norms with declining authority of the aged. The joint family system in the past provided the aged needed security, status, love and affection and also mental satisfaction but with its disintegration, the aged are left alone to face the problems of advancing age.

* Reader in Sociology, Karnataka University Kittur Rani Chennamma P.G.Centre, Belgaum

** Research Scholar in Sociology, Karnataka University Kittur Rani Chennama P.G.Centre, Belgaum.

In Indian Society where joint family system still prevails, the aged continues to enjoy respect and power. On almost all-important functions performed in the family, it is a usual practice for sons and daughters to turn to their elders for guidance and support. The obligation of the family to look after the aged and to honor and respect them still continues. However, certain recent developments have given rise to some stresses and strains which have made the position of the aged more problematic.

Technological development which, have brought tremendous changes, in the life style and values have created doubts in the minds of younger generation about the utility of past knowledge and experience in solving present day problems, which greatly reduced their dependence on the aged.

The high cost as well as lack of availability of rental accommodation in cities works as constraints in keeping the aged together with their migrant sons and daughters. The migration of younger generation and the demise of many of their aged members tend to increase the problems of isolation and loneliness for the old staying behind. This is true, for those having no land or productive resource and is dependent on the sale of labor.

The increasing employment of women in offices and factories and their career aspirations lead to the reduced attention towards older members and the increased demand for setting up nuclear family. Gradual breakdown of the joint family following separation or migration of earning members and fragmentation of land holdings.

At times elders have to bear additional economic responsibilities and spend all their savings for educating sons and marrying daughters in addition to meeting family expenses.

Comparatively, aging brings more miseries for women than for men. It is due mainly to the patriarchal character of the society and culturally prescribed norms of seclusion between women and their husbands. The migration, which is male-dominated, also adds to miseries of the women, as they have to shoulder all the domestic and other responsibilities in the absence of working males.

The growing age is hardly of any consequence for the alienation and other problems of the aged; rather poor health, economic dependence and non-working status tend to create among the aged feelings of meaninglessness and powerlessness. The advancing age, when the aged has lost many things including friends, spouse, job, status, power, influence, income, health etc. That cannot be replaced, brings in them intolerance, short temperedness, rigidity of attitude, selfishness and suspicion. This shift in their psychological make-up makes their living and adjustment in society more problematic. They feel hurt when dubbed as conservative, out-of-date or old-fashioned and are neglected in day-to-day life.

Much of the socio-economic problems of the aged have their roots in poor health. Age quite often is found to be associated with respiratory and digestive problems, deficiency diseases, and diseases of reproductive system. While most suffer with functional disorders, some have organic disorders particularly in higher age group. The ailments which are commonly associated with later years include among others falling eye-sight and hearing capacity, slow and faltering steps, declining energy and more acute disabilities such as blindness, forgetfulness etc. However, many such problems go undetected and unattended.

In view of the above an attempt has been made in this paper to analyze:

1. Aging and the Aged
2. Silhouette of aged at global level.
3. A condensed account of aged in India and its neighboring countries.
4. Demographic proportion of aged in India.
5. Problems of the elderly in India.
6. Prevalent policies and programs of the Government & Role of voluntary organizations.

DEFINITION OF THE AGED

The definitions of oldage vary from one country to another and sometimes within a country and of course overtime. It depends on health, sex, labor force participation and socio-economic status. However, in the developed countries all those aged 65 years and above are regarded as aged or elderly, while in the developing countries those aged 60 years and above come under this category.

SILHOUETTE OF AGED AT GLOBAL LEVEL

It is obvious, from the United Nations data of the aged at world level and region/national level (see Table 1) that the world's average percentage of the aged to the total population in 1951 was 5.1 percent. It increased to 5.4 percent by 1970. It stood at 6.2 percent in 1990.

Table 1
Estimates and projections of population aged 65 or over by Major Areas and Region 1950-2025 (Percentage)

Major Area/Region	*1950*	*1970*	*1990*	*2025*
World	5.1	5.4	6.2	9.7
More developed Regions	7.6	9.6	12.1	19.0
Less developed Regions	3.8	3.7	4.5	8.0
Least developed Regions	3.4	3.1	3.0	4.0
Other developing countries	3.9	3.8	4.6	8.7
Africa	3.2	3.1	3.0	4.1
Latin America	3.3	3.9	4.8	8.6
Asia	4.0	4.0	5.0	9.0
Europe	8.7	11.4	13.4	20.1
Oceania	7.5	7.3	9.0	13.9

Source: United Nations 1992- 17

For the same period, population of the aged in the less developed regions and more developed nations gives a different picture. The less developed regions stood with much below the world's average of aged. It was 3.8 percent in 1950. It increased to 4.5 percent in 1990. In the more developed nations the percentage of aged to the total population was higher than the world's average. In 1950, it was 7.6 percent. It increased to 9.6 and 12.1 percent in 1970 and 1990 respectively.

The projections and estimates of aged for 2025 A.D. at world level, less developed and more developed national levels is almost similar to the trend of the yester decades in the respective regions. The world's average of aged population is likely to be 9.7 percent by 2025 A.D. that it is likely to be 8 percent in less developed nations and 19 percent (much above the world average) in more developed nations.

Table 2
Continent-wise, Population (In Millions)

Year	*Asia*	*Africa*	*Europe*	*Latin America*	*North*	*Ocenia*
1	2	3	4	5	6	7
1994	3,392	700	728	470	290	28
19952025	5,017	1,538	731	679	375	39

Source: Ibid.

The continent wise data of the aged (Table 1 & 2) for the corresponding period gives more or less similar picture. Among Africa, Latin America, Asia, Europe and Oceania, Europe has been in lead, with much higher percentage of aged population, followed by Oceania, Asia, Latin America and Africa respectively.

A CONDENSED ACCOUNT OF AGED IN INDIA, AND ITS NEIGHBORING COUNTRIES

Table 3
Age composition of Population of India 1950 to 2000 AD
(In percentage)

Age groupsIn years	*1950*	*1975*	*1990*	*2000*
0 - 14	36.02	39.50	34.48	30.16
15 - 19	10.31	10.23	10.51	09.79
20 - 49	42.04	37.15	40.56	44.19
50 - 59	06.40	6.62	07.14	07.48
60 - 69	03.77	4.13	04.56	05.21
70 +	0.56	2.07	02.75	03.18

Source: P. K. Dhillon, Psycho-social Aspects of Aging of India. Concept publishing house Delhi.

Table 3 shows the age group of Indian population from 1950 to 2000 in terms of percentage, as the population of India is increasing very rapidly but there is very uneven increase in the population on the basis of age group classification, but it can be stated that the growth in the aged population i.e., above 60 years of age is in increase in a gradual manner.

Table 4. deals with comparative picture of aged in India and its neighboring countries of Asia viz., Bangladesh, China and Japan. In 1985, there were 10 percent of aged to the total population in Japan, followed by China with 5.3 percent, India (4.3%) and Bangladesh (3.1%). The aged population (between 65 and 80 years) by 2010 A.D. (see Table-4) would be 5.4 million in Bangladesh, 71.7 million in India. 111.4 million in China, and 24.0 million in Japan. In these countries, elderly population of 80 years above, age group by 2010 A.D. would be highest in China with 17.5 million, followed by India (9.0 million), Japan (4.7 million) and Bangladesh (0.5 million).

Table 4
Probable changes in the Elderly population 1985-2010

	65 years and over		*80 years and over*	
Countries	*1985*	*2010*	*1985*	*2010*
Bangladesh	3.1	5.4	0.3	0.5
India	32.7	71.7	2.9	9.0
China	56.1	111.4	6.1	17.5
Japan	12.1	24.0	2.0	4.7

Source: Ibid.

From the foregoing discussion, it is very much evident that more developed nations have been with higher percentage of the aged to the total population, than in less developed regions. The reasons would be; Increase in life expectancy and steady decline in death rate & fertility rate over the period of time. Because of advancement of medical technology in particular, and the overall development in general.

DEMOGRAPHIC PROPORTION OF AGED IN INDIA:

India's broad population base (548 million in 1971, 683 million in 1981, 830 million in 1991 and 1003 million in 2001 AD) accounts for a sizeable number of people 60+, shows, a definite increasing trend form about 5 percent in 1901 to 6.2 percent in 1991, and it is going to be 10% by 2010 AD.

The demographic dimensions relating to the population 60 years above can briefly be summarizes in quantitative terms as follows.

The number of people, with 60+ age group in 1901 was about 12 million. In 1991, it increased to 42.7 million, registering around 300 percent increase, over 1901. Further it is expected to reach 130.5 million by 2021 A.D. accounting for about 160 percent increase over 1991.

Table 5
India's Total And Aged Population Decennial: Rate Of Growth

Decade	*% Increase Intotal Population*	*% Increase In Population 60 +*
1951 – 1961	21.51	22.40
1961 – 1971	24.80	32.32
1971 – 1981	24.75	31.60
1981 – 1991	22.72	38.00

Source: Census Reports of India.

The rate of increase of the population 60+ is higher than that of general population (Table 5). Among the elderly/aged, males have been with upper hand than their co-eaves in the female segment. Projections for the aged population for 2021 AD also uphold the same feature (Table-6).

Table 6
Projected Population Of Old Persons (60+)

	1971	*1981*	*1991*	*2001*	*2011*	*2021*
Total population	550	682	832	1003	1160	1300
60+ male	14.6	19.9	17.8	36.0	46.8	66.0
60+ female	13.5	17.8	24.9	35.3	47.5	64.5

Source: Census Reports of India, 2001.

The statistical data, about life expectancy in India, is depicted in Table 7. The table reveals that the life expectancy of the Indian population is increasing due to improvement in the medical facilities and health awareness. It can be also observed that the life expectancy of the female is more as compared to the males.

Table 7
Life Expectance Of Males & Females In India (In Years)

Period	*Males*	*Females*	*Total (Average)*
1950 – 55	39.4	38.7	38.6
1960 – 65	46.2	44.7	45.5
1970 – 75	51.2	49.3	50.3
1980 – 85	55.6	55.2	55.4
1990 – 95	60.1	60.7	60.4

Source: Psycho-Social aspects of Aging in India P.K. Dhillon on P.18.

This shows increasing life expectancy has been slowly gaining momentum. Arthur Imhof, a noted German Demographer says. " Certainly it is correct to say that traditional causes of death claimed their victims from all age groups and the life at that time was therefore much riskier business that it is today. But it is also correct to say that the death was more humane than, since most of the infectious and parasitic diseases kill quickly? Today, precisely because we have defeated those diseases; we are living longer, growing older. Simultaneously, however, the dying process in many cases has been lengthened, chronic suffering no longer extends over a period of a few days or weeks but can often last for many months and years so that the death is ultimately viewed as liberation."

Some research studies proved that the marital status of the population 60+, shows a fairly large degree of the population that has widowed status the incidence of which, as may be expected, is much larger among the females than among the males.

PROBLEMS OF AGED IN INDIA

The aged in India, like their Co-eaves elsewhere, experience a range of problems, but the number, nature and type of the problems experienced differ according to their age, sex, marital status, place of residence i.e., rural and urban residence, and economic status.

There are a good number of studies of the aged in India; which have identified some important problems experienced by the aged.

The first and most mundane being that of food, clothing and shelter. These problems do not arise to some extent, for those who are fortunate enough to have some regular source of income like pension or gratuity, etc., But such aged population, according to one study, account for only 11 percent of total aged in India.

India, a country long, known for its joint family system. Providing every facility to the aged on par with other members of the family, the proportion of nuclear families is fast increasing. This means nuclear families fail to provide shelter, food & clothing to the aged, to the extent what they used to avail earlier. Besides, it is common hear, now a days, that old people are often ill treated by their married sons and daughters-in-law.

Many studies have reported that one of the problems of the aged is loss of status in the family and society which, was enjoyed by them before the aging process begins.

Along with the loss of status, more psychological problem, which haunts the aged is loneliness. At this stage people are not only incapable of working and they don't know how to spend their time. It is particularly more acute the aged, when they have lost their spouses.

It is very common to note that aged people are more impaired physically and mentally and less mobile, when compared with the middle aged and young. So 'health care' demands top priority for the aged. This is especially true with our country, where the number of people living in poor health has been increasing particularly because of the modern medical technology and the expansion of primary health programs, which have reduced mortality without sufficiently improving levels of health.

THE POLICIES AND PROGRAMMES OF THE GOVERNMENT

The central & the respective state governments of different states recognized their duties and have been making and amending laws to safeguard the general interest of the elderly. In this directions many provisions have been made to the aged at the Federal and legislative level.

CONSTITUTIONAL AND LEGISLATIVE PROVISIONS:

According to the Article 41 of Indian Constitution: "The state shall, with in the limits of economic capacity and development, make effective provision for securing the right to work, to education and to public assistance in cases of unemployment, old age, sickness, and disablement." This provision is one of the Directive Principles of the state policy: which are considered as fundamental in the governance of the country. According to Article 37: It shall be the duty of the state to apply these principles in making laws.

Section 125 of the Code of Criminal Procedure 1973 requires every person having sufficient means to maintain his father or mother that are unable to maintain themselves. The Hindu adoptions and maintenance Act 1956, Section 20(3), lays down that it is the obligation of a person to maintain his or her aged or infirm parents.

Concern has been expressed from time to time for the care of aged people, particularly those who have no means of support and no near kin to look after them. The problem of care of such people has received attention of several committees and of the Government.

The study group on Income and wages (1978) recognized the needs of old persons not covered by pension or other retirement benefits and suggested that there should be some standardization of the criteria adopted by different states for old age pensions (non-contributory) to the destitute old.

The seventh Finance Commission noted that varying situation in regard to old age pensions (non-contributory) public assistance in different states and observed that it is desirable to have some uniformity in this regard between the states. The sixth Five-year plan of India mentions about the aged, the infirm, and the need for development programs to meet their wants. Of late, aged people are given a new status 'Senior citizens'. They are provided with various facilities such as concessions in Railways and state owned Road transport services etc.

ROLE OF VOLUNTARY ORGANIZATIONS

Voluntary organizations in India have been playing a pioneering role in the care of aged and have shown considerable adaptability and flexibility in meeting the various social service needs of the elderly. In recent years several national level and state level voluntary organizations have been setup for promoting the welfare of the elderly, for urging a greater national priority to their problems and needs, for organizing services. It is identified, recently, that there are around 400 non-governmental organizations working in the field of the welfare of the aged in India. They provide a wide range of services, residential care, day care, geriatric care, medical & psychiatric care, recreation, financial assistance, counseling etc. However, the majority of the agencies and the service, are meant for urbanites. Voluntary agencies have also been active in conducting studies on the problems needs of the elderly and in organizing discussion/seminars/workshops not only on the needs of the elderly but also on the contributions that they can make.

PERSPECTIVES OF THE AGED

From the analysis of the world demographic trends, it is observed that in 21st century the percentage of the aged to the total population is increasing continuously. However, the quantum of the aged to the total population in the more developed nations would work out to be, more than the world's average. This will be less than the world's average for the less developed regions. India being a developing country, its quantum of the aged to the total population in 21st century works to be almost close to the world's average. This trend of increase of the aged is likely to be accentuated with the result of improved expectancy of life at birth as well as at later stage of an individual. In all probability in 21st century, there will a large number of people 60, who have single status-hood.

In view of the increasing acceptance of small family norm and growing urbanization, the aged are likely to be more vulnerable to their care by their offspring. Along with the existing problems the aged will have to experience additional problems such as deprivation of further status, loneliness coupled with psychological tensions and like, due to faster rates of mobility of population from rural to urban centers. As a result the family system in India, long known for its cohesive and filial relations, it vexed on one hand failing to keep the elderly happy and on the other not prepared at the same time allowing them to join the institutional care centers.

Both the center and state government, keeping in view of the problems of the aged, have been making time to time various laws & provisions to combat this social menace. For instance the employees of the organized sectors at the time of retirement are given with terminal benefits, to enable them to lead a peaceful retired life. Also there are different study groups, constituted to look into the problems of the aged, have recommended old age pensions (non-contributory Public assistance). Added to this, there are a good number of schemes to help destitute aged, widows' etc. A few concessions are also there for the aged, like tax rebate for those who come under tax brackets; Senior citizen concessions etc. It is noted by some studies that the schemes are really nice, but they are not reaching the concerned; in the letter and spirit of the scheme. This may be probably, because of the illiteracy among the aged and no proper publicity in the rural areas about such schemes. If these two factors are taken care, the schemes floated for the welfare of the aged will be a success.

There are certain positive factors associated with the problems of the aged. In rural areas they find some sort of employment and make their lives economically better. They don't rate themselves as sick, unless, they are affected severely by certain incurable diseases. But their co-eaves in urban centers face problems ranging from pocket money to health care. In order to overcome these problems, the aged need, Non-Institutional care that takes care of the aged day & night. Such centers should cater the needs of all such aged population, coming from different strata.

Medical care is indispensable for the aged, wherever they are. In this direction, the government hospitals should open separate, outpatient counters and special wards for in-patients of this category. Voluntary organizations which are basically urban based should provide services to the aged in villages also. Psychological problems-loss of status, and loneliness, are considered to be equally serious with the aged. These problems can be solved with in the four walls of the family. It only requires the involvement of aged in all such matters, where they should not feel they are not consulted to.

It is crystal clear that the 21st is going to witness the increasing of the aged at very faster rate and their problems in multitude. Therefore, top priority should be given to arrest the population from growing any further. It is apt to remember the Executive Director of the United Nations Population Fund (UNFPA). Who is optimistic of combating the population of the world at 7.9 billion by the year 2025. Till them it is our onus, to ensure a good living for their peaceful old age. For the act of which we shall remain ever grateful, as their real heirs in the true spirit of Indians.

GROWTH OF AGED POPULATIONS

These United Nations (UN) statistics illustrate the explosive growth of aged populations around the world. By 2050, for example, nearly 30 per cent of the people living in the world's

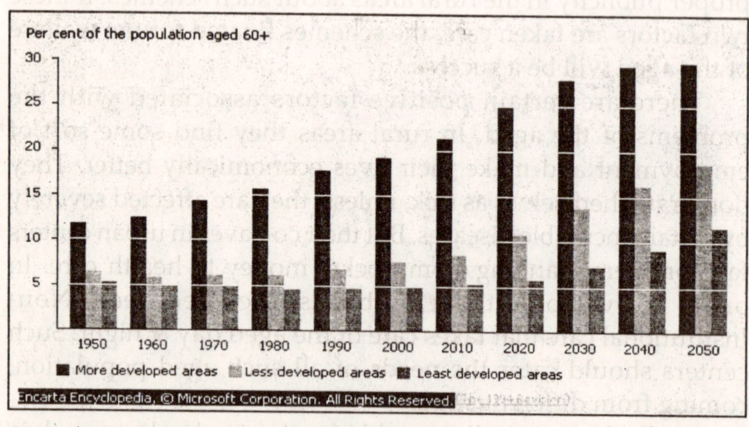

Source: Microsoft Encarta Encyclopedia 2003.

most developed countries—those in North America, Western Europe, and parts of Asia--will be at least 60 years old, up from less than 15 per cent in 1950.

REFERENCES

Davis, K. and Coombs, F. W. 1950, "The Sociology of an aging population", in Goldson, I.(ed), The Social and Biological Challenge of our aging Population, New York: Columbia University Press.

J.N.Pandey, "Constitutional Law of India", law agency, Allahabad, 1984.

M.L.Sharma & T.M. Dak, "Aging in India: Challenge for the Society", Haryana Agricultural University, Hissar, 1987.

Singh, A.K.P.J. Journal of Research 14 (1).1981., Dak T.M. and Sharma, M.L. 1984,

"Status of Males in Old Age", H.A.U.,

Soodan, K.S, "Aging in India, Calcutta", Minerva Associates, 1975.

23

SOCIAL SECURITY FOR THE UNEMPLOYED IN INDIA

*Prakash S. Kamble**

INTRODUCTION

Human resource in general and labour in particular is an important productive resource in absence of which economic development is a mere dream. It is the human resource which plays a vital role in the beginning and development of each and every productive activity, whereby rapid and all round economic development of the economy takes place, whatever may be the state of technology. But in an effort to modernize the economy necessary for the rapid and overall development, the rigorous and to the greatest extent possible attempts are being made either to develop advanced technology or import it. It is a fact that advanced technology is a labour saving and employment declining one. This works as a prominent factor in arising as well as intensifying the problem of unemployment. Imports of goods and services in the globaliasing world have helped in promoting further gravity of unemployment. Hence social security for the unemployed has becoming a burning issue. India has made the process of globalisation dynamic particularly since 1991. This shows an urgent need to study the aspect of social security for the unemployed in India. In this background, the present paper endeavors to examine the issue of social security for the unemployed in India in the globalisation era.

* Leader Dept. of Economics, Shivaji University, Kolhapur, Maharashtra.

CONCEPT OF SOCIAL SECURITY

The term social security at present is only related to the employees employed mainly in industry and tertiary sector. This implies that it has not covered the primary sector in general and agriculture in particular till date in the economies like India. Further unemployed people are totally neglected with a few exceptions in the jurisdiction of social security. But it is the need of hour to think of social security with highest priority in the context of unemployed in the globalising world.

Social security implies protection given by the state of government to the workers to offer minimum standard of living in the crisis like accident, sickness, disablement death etc. It is an attempt to give security to the family members during especially bad conditions of the workers. It is an effective measure on labour welfare maximisation

The meaning of the concept social security can better understand with the help of its major and important definitions. The ILO (International Labour Organisation) defines social security as "the security that society furnishes, through appropriate organizations against certain risks to which its members are exposed. These risks are essentially contingencies against which the individual of small means and meager resources cannot effectively provide by his own ability or foresight alone, or even in private combination with his fellows these risks being sickness, maternity, invalidity, old age and death. It is the characteristic of these contingencies that they imperil the ability of the working man to support himself and his dependents in health and decency." According to Lord Beveridge, "social security is an attack on five giants – wants, disease, ignorance, squalor and idleness." Friedlander defines social security, as, " Programme of protection provided by society against these contingencies of modern life —— sickness, unemployment, old age, dependency, industrial accidents and invalidism – against which the individual cannot be expected to protect himself and his own ability or foresight." In the Encyclopedia of social work, social security has been defined as, "the endeavour of the community, as a whole, to afford itself of the almost extent possible to any individual during periods of physical distress inevitable an illness or injury and from the economic distress consequent on reduction or loss of earnings due to illness, disablement, maternity unemployment, old age, or death of the working member".[1]

SOCIAL SECURITY IN INDIA

Social security is the gift of England to the world. India was under the British rule for a long period. Hence we found the introduction and enforcement of social security measures in the pre-independence period. But it is a fact that the scope and importance of social security has been widened significantly in the post independence period. Thus we find that the evolution of social security in India in the systematized methods of social assistance and social insurance as the result of the influence of the west. The following are the various legislative measures adopted by the Government of India which provide protection to the industrial workers in certain contingencies:[2]

1. Workmen's' Compensation Act, 1923.
2. Employees' State Insurance Act, 1948.
3. Coal Mines Provident Fund and Bonus Scheme, 1948.
4. Dock Workers (Regulation and Employment) Act, 1948.
5. Plantations Labour Act, 1951.
6. Employees Provident Fund Act, 1952.
7. Assam Tea Plantation Provident Fund Act, 1955.
8. Maternity Benefit Act, 1961.
9. Family Pension Scheme, 1964.
10. Seaman's Provident Fund Act, 1966.
11. Employees' Family Pension Scheme, 1971.
12. Survivorship Pension Scheme, 1971.
13. Old –Age Pension Scheme, 1971.
14. Payment of Gratuity Act, 1972.
15. Employees' Deposit – Linked Insurance Scheme, 1976.
16. Employee's Pension Scheme, 1995.[3]

The main statutory provision that has been provided so far in the country in the direction of social security is in respect of:[4]

1. Compensation in case of industrial injury and diseases,
2. Maternity benefits to women workers, and
3. The recent schemes of Health Insurance, Provident Funds, Old age and Family pensions, Gratuity, etc.

The social security measures as provided in various legislations in India are narrow in scope and adequate in the extent of assistance. The coverage of measures is restricted to certain industries and to a specified class of workers, leaving quite many industrial workers outside it. Besides, all the risks are not covered, e.g. there is no unemployment insurance. The types of facilities and the rates and magnitude of benefits are inadequate. The finances for their implementation are small. The agencies for their administration are not sufficient and even appropriate. The process of implementation of these schemes is too much time – taking and it suffers from the evils of red-tapism.

TRENDS IN POST- GLOBALISATION EMPLOYMENT AND UNEMPLOYMENT GROWTH IN INDIA

Estimates based on the data available from the most comprehensive official source, namely, National Sample Survey Organization (NSSO), indicated that these occurred a significant deceleration in the growth of employment over the period following the initiation of major economic reforms towards globalisation in the early 1990s. [5]

Using the Current Daily Status (CDS) criterion, employment grew at 2.5 per cent during 1987-88 to 1993-94, but only at 1.07 per cent during 1993-94 to 1999-2000. Corresponding growth rates of GDP for these periods were 5.8 and 6.7 per cent. A faster growth led to a lower employment growth, particularly during the period 1993-94 to 1999-2000. A decline in employment growth is also observed, when employment elasticity declined, sharply from 0.41 during 1987-88 to 1993-94 to 0.16 during 1993-94 to 1999-2000.

A poor employment performance of the growth during the 1990 can primarily be attributed to a virtual stagnation of employment in agriculture which accounted for 60 per cent of total workers and a significant decline in employment in community, social and personal services, which constituted the third largest employer (among the 9 activity sectors) accounting for 11 per cent of workers, in 1993-94. Manufacturing, the second largest sector after agriculture, accounting for over 11 per cent workers in 1993-94, experienced an employment growth of 2.5 pei cent per annum during 1994-2000. Other sectors, namely construction, trade, transport and finance also registered employment growth of 5 and 6 per cent per annum. Employment growth has been just over one per cent during the 1990s as compared to around 2 per cent in the earlier decade. If period since 1990 is considered, export oriented industries have shown a much better employment growth than others; employment in them grew at 3.36 per cent per annum, as against 2.67 per cent in import- competing and 3.09 in all industries. Expórt- oriented industries are also found to have significantly higher employment elasticity (0.48) than the manufacturing sector as a whole (0.33). Recent data available show employment growth of a rate of over 2 per cent per annum during June 2000 to December 2002.[6]

The failure of the Indian economy to generate adequate employment opportunities has been responsible for taking place the problem of unemployment and its growing gravity. According to NSS (National Sample Survey), there were 3.98 million unemployed in India in 1973-74, which increased to 7.49 million in 1993-94 and as much as 9.15 million in 1999-2000. In the mean time, the incidence of employment (defined as the ratio of unemployed persons to the labour force) increased from 1.64 per cent in 1973-74 to 1.96 percent in 1993-94 to 2.25 percent in 1999-2000. Unemployment rate in Urban areas was 8.99 percent in 1972-73, which rose to 10.34 per cent in 1977-78, but slightly declined to 9.36 per cent in 1987-88. The number of educated unemployed rose from 2.44 lakh in 1951, which rose to 68 lakh in 1992. The current Daily Status Unemployment rate for the Rural male workers was 5.64 per cent in 1993-94 as against 4.58 per cent in1987-88. In March 1994, Usual Status unemployment rate for males and females was 1.4 per cent and 0.9 per cent respectively. Farmers cultivating 75 per cent of land remain involuntary unemployed for 4 to 6 months [7].

NEED FOR SOCIAL SECURITY FOR THE UNEMPLOYED IN INDIA

The trends in the growth of employment and unemployment cited above indicate the need for social security for the unemployed in India. Besides social security for employed especially unsatisfactorily, also social protection should be seriously think of for the unemployed in India as well.

Domination of the unorganized sector with irregular and insecure jobs, low productivity and earnings and no social protection, has been a well-known feature of the Indian employment scene. Employment in the temporary, casual and contract, modes of employment by this sector imply exclusion of even those working for enterprises in this sector not only from the job security but also protection net.[8]

So far as the need for social security for the unemployed in India in post-globalisation is concerned, we find a significant deceleration in the growth of employment is observed, which has been consequently increasing the extent of unemployment indicating the urgent need for its coverage. Employment growth registered only 1 to 2 per cent growth rate in the post-globalisation Indian economy. Agriculture is the main occupation of India on various grounds. But it has shown almost stagnation in employment generation. Besides this, Indian farmers as well as agricultural labours have to remain unemployed for about 4 to 6 months in a year. Disguised unemployment in our country is also an important thing of concern in the context of social security. Manufacturing sector an important sector in the context of employment generation has shown about 8.5 per cent fall in employment generation during 1993-94 to 1999-2000 clearly indicates the need for covering the unemployed in the net of social security. In absolute terms, the number of unemployed has been increased substantially by about 2 million in the post- globalisation era must be considered as a signal of the urgency for enforcing social security measures in our economy. Urbanisation is one of the symptoms of economic development, is very slower in India, but urban unemployment has been rose significantly by about more than one per cent during 1972-73 to 1987-88. Literacy is an ingredient of qualitative population. In India about 35 per cent population is illiterate. But educated unemployment is a thing of serious concern, which stood at 68 lakh people in 1992. The nature of unemployment in India reveals that both the males and females are suffering from the problem of unemployment should be part and parcel of social security. Till date, unemployed are totally neglected component of India's social security along with workers from the agricultural sector. In absence of covering the unemployed in India into the net of social protection, they cannot fulfill even the basic necessities of life necessary of just living as citizens of sub-continent country like India. They must also get the basic facilities like education, health, medical, water etc. for which social protection for them is a must.

VI POLICY IMPLICATIONS FOR SOCIAL SECURITY FOR THE UNEMPLOYED IN INDIA

The above thorough discussions about the various aspects and dimensions of employment and unemployment growth and the need for social security for the unemployed adequately and clearly reveals that, it is the need of hour to introduce and enforce the social security measures for the unemployed in India. The existing all social security measures with their full implementation cannot be a solution for the unemployed social security in our country. But of them, some measures can definitely provide social security facilities to the Indian unemployed. Especially the measures diverted towards insurance, family pension, maternity benefits, old age pension etc. But the social security measures framed based on the following guidelines could be an agenda and a course of action to cover the unemployed into the net of social security system in India.

In absence of an active role assigned to the government, it is rather difficult to get fulfill the goal of social security for the unemployed in India. But at the same time, wherever possible and beneficial private sector of the economy can accompany the government. Like natural calamity fund, the government should create an 'Unemployment Benefit Fund' on the basis of government-private sector participation to provide for employment, basic wants and the necessities like health and medical facilities. Training facilities along with finance should be provided to undertake self-employment activities by the government for the unemployed. Such insurance schemes should be introduced and enforced for the unemployed, without their contribution based on the subscriptions of employed and insurance companies. Attempts should be made to liberalise obstacles and restrictions on the mobility of labours within the country as well as abroad. Union, state and local governments should assign due place to unemployed social security in their annual budgets. Like finance commission, the Unemployment Commission should be appointed after every five years to suggest measures to the government to tackle the problem of unemployment as well as providing social security facilities for the unemployed. The government of India can impose 'Unemployment tax' to mobilize revenue for the unemployed social security measures. It should be made obligatory to government as well as private hospitals to provide free of charge medical facilities in the case of normal sickness and due help of the government for abnormal diseases. On the line of Disinvestments Department, Unemployment Cell should be established at the centre to look at human resource utilization and management, whereby unemployment can be controlled. Family pension benefits should be extended by raising finance from MNCs, IMF, IBRD, and ILO, etc. The World Health organization (WHO) should be given important role in tackling health problems of the unemployed by suggesting measures as well as due assistance. Banks and financial institutions can play a crucial role especially in providing loans & advances whereby employment can be generated for the unemployed through the sources like self-employment and others. The development of export- import oriented industries has potential of generating large employment opportunities on the basis of their post experience. Population control measures and desirable changes in the education system should be brought in the purview of social security measures. Thus, due efforts to generate adequate employment coupled with necessary supply of social security services can be the key of social protection for the unemployed in India.

VII CONCLUSION

The problem of unemployment is a major and important problem before the Indian economy having higher and growing intensity. Hence naturally, it is the need of the hour to protect the unemployed socially. Therefore, introduction and enforcement of the social security for the unemployed is inevitable in the modern India. But the same structure of social protection for the employed cannot be accepted for the unemployed. Only social security measures cannot offer due social protection for the unemployed needed for the labour welfare maximization. Due efforts to promote the level of employment along with the social security measures could offer due social protection for the unemployed in India. Social security policy based on the above suggested policy implications could be a definite solution on this burning problem. This paper is a little bit attempts to look at an important issue of the social security for the unemployed in India in the globalisation era. I could not collect necessary and adequate data needed for the through study and writing of the paper.

REFERENCES

Singh, J.K. (1998), '*Labour Economics*', Deep & Deep Publications Pvt., Ltd., New Delhi, P.115.

Ibid, P.415.

Misra and Puri (2001), '*Indian Economy*', Himalaya Publishing House, Mumbai, P.664.

Dr. Bhagoliwal, T.N. (1976), '*Economics of Labour and Social Welfare*', Sahitya Bhawan, Agra, P.525.

Papola, T.S. (2004), 'Globalisation, Employment and Social Protection: Emerging, Perspectives for the Indian workers', *The Indian Journal of Labour Economics*', Volume 47, Number 3, July – September, 2004, P.543.

Ibid, P.545.

Dr. Kamble, P.S. (2005): 'Business Environment' (Indian Economic Environment), Swaroop Prakashan, Kolhapur (in press).

Papola, T.S, above cited, PP. 545-47.

24

SEASONAL MIGRATORY CHILD LABOUR IN MAHARASHTRA'S SUGAR INDUSTRY

*W. N. Salve**

INTRODUCTION

The sugar industry is claimed to be the second largest in the Indian economy being next only to the cotton textile industry. The claim is based on the extend of labour employed, the amount of capital invested and the value of output. (CSO, 1981).

In this paper, an attempt has been made to study the nature of seasonal migratory child labour in Maharashtra's sugar industry. The specific objectives of the study are:

I. To examine the role of sugar factories in respect of providing educational facilities to children of seasonal migrant workers.
2. To study the position of seasonal migrant workers.
3. To examine the existing labour laws in respect of child and education.
4. To examine the efforts undertaken by the non-governmental organization to eliminate child labour.
5. To know the reasons for nowhere child.
6. To suggest measures for eliminating child labour.

The paper is based on secondary data published in different reports of government agencies. The scope of the present study is limited to seasonal migratory child labour in the sugar factories in the Maharashtra States. This paper based on research study of Kolhapur District.

---

* Lecturer in Economics, Shri Venkatesh College, Ichalkaranji, Maharashtra.

SEASONAL MIGRANTS

The sugar industry plays a very import role in economic development of the Maharashtra State. During the year 2000-2001, there were 190 sugar factories in the Maharashtra State. (daily mahasatta,13 jan, 2001) out of which 132 sugar factories were in operation. Besides, there were 12 lakh sugarcane cutter workers in the state (Lokmat, 22 Feb, 2003), 58 thousand bullock carts and 16 thousand trucks and tractors were engaged in the sugar factories. So far as children of seasonal migrant workers are concerned, it is estimated that more than 2 lakh children are in the age group of 5-14 years. These children are known as nowhere children. The sugar industry is a seasonal character; it depends upon the availability of sugarcane product. The sugarcane is harvested normally from the month of November to the end of April in a crushing season. It is observed that each sugar factory provides employment nearly 5000 to 6000 harvesting labourers for the period of crushing season.

Agricultural is the primary activity in the Maharashtra State. A large tract of the state falls under rain shadow area. However, more than 90 talukas of the state are subject to frequent droughts in each year. As a result, most of the workers belonging to backward castes, landless workers, marginal farmers do not get any job in agriculture after harvesting season. Therefore, they migrate from their villages to sugar factories for Seasonal jobs in a crushing season. Kolhapur district is one of the constituent region of the fertile belt in Maharashtra State. There are 26 sugar factories in the Kolhapur region. Most of the seasonal workers migrate from adjoining districts like Solapur, Satara, Beed, Osmanabad, Ahmadnagar, Bijapur (Karnataka) districts to Kolhapur for seasonal jobs in the sugar factories.

It has been observed that rural seasonal migrate workers are likely to be temporary, poorly educated and from the poorer sections of the community. The mobility is not only characteristics of these workers, life extreme poverty is also, typically most of these workers. It is evident from study (Salve, 1990), that the illiterate workers are forced to migrate from native places to the sugar factories in Kolhapur District. They had no prospects of gainful employment in the drought prone areas. The entire mass of contract basis labour in sugar factories today remains unorganized with the result that their voice is never heard beyond their camps. They have no job security. Their work is unskilled irregular, seasonal and often carried on far from the centers of sugar mills.

CHILD LABOUR

According to 1991 census, the population of child labour in India was 11.28 million, now it estimated to be 25 million. The policy of the government is to ban employment of children below 14 years in factories, mines and hazardous vocations.(Employment News ,Feb 2003). Child labour it consists of__

(a) All economically active children in the age group 9-11;
(b) All economically active children in the age group 12-14 who spend at least 14 hours a week in non-hazardous jobs and;
(c) All economically active children in the age 12-17 in hazardous work.(The Indian Journal of Labour Economics,No.3,2002).

In the case of children of seasonal migrants, there are two types of concepts- (i) Child Labour, (ii) Nowhere children.

Child Labour can be broadly defined to include all children out of school. Nowhere children *i.e.* those who are neither enrolled in schools nor registered as child labour. These children make up approximately 35% of all children in their age group, and the representation of girl is high. They may be engaged in a variety of domestic and other chores that release or supplement adult labour. (Wazir, 2002) As far as children of seasonal migrant workers are concerned, persons below 15 years of age, were treated as children. (Salve, 1990) It was found from study (Salve, 1990) that out of 406 children in the age group of 10-14 years, 227 (55.92%) were going to primary schools but discontinued schools and (44.08%) were not going to schools.

It should be noted that the incidences of dropping out school was about 50% among children of migrant workers due to seasonal migration of labour. However, they migrate. from a comparatively poor environment.(UNESCO,1952). Most of the parents had reported various causes of non-schooling of children such as—

(i) Financial stringency and inability to buy notebooks, books, clothes and other materials.
(ii) Supplementing family income by working them and children needed to do household chores.
(iii) Lack of appreciation of the need for education.

It was found that drop out rate was 74% among boys of migrant workers. However drop out rate is higher in children of seasonal migrants from the first standard up to middle level. This happens because children are required to assist their parents: In the case of girls, almost all girls of seasonal migrant works had discontinued schools due to seasonal migration. Besides, the sugar factories could not provide educational facilities to children of seasonal migrant workers.

Therefore, Khothari Commission 1964-66 pointed out that education of a boy is education of one person, but education to a girl is the education of the entire family. It further states that educational facilities are required for those communities who migrate for several months in a year.

NOWHERE CHILDREN

We want to know the reasons why children are nowhere. It has been observed that the incidence of nowhere children is higher in respect of children of migrant workers in the sugar factories. Nowhere children are children in the age group of 5-14 years who are neither enrolled in schools nor registered as child labour. Because they help their parents and earn a small amount to the family income.

The children as soon as they seven to eight years who become assets to their parents. According to Gayathri' s Study (2002) almost 50% of the female children and 40% of the male children in Karnataka belong to this category *i.e.* nowhere children. As expected, the percentage of nowhere children is lower in urban areas as compared to the rural areas. Children in the age group of 10-14, assist their parents. They sell the leafy head of sugarcane as fodder in the market and thus earn a small amount to the family income.

It is significant to note that all the earning members of family join hands to work in the sugarcane cutting, cleaning, loading process in the sugarcane field. Children in the age group of 10 to 14 years help their parents in the sugarcane cutting and transporting work. Most of the children fall within the age group of 10 to 14 years. As soon as the children cross the age of about 12, where a boy or a girl. The parents look upon them as potential source of income and try as soon as possible to withdraw them from school for earning due to poverty. (Mujumdar 1978). So the poor economic condition of the migrant's people makes it impossible for them to get their children even thought a full elementary course of education. As regards child labour, poverty is the most common factor cited by the parents of children in the carpet industry. Poverty is the main reason non-schooling and drop out of children (Sharma, 2002). Large majority of girls still work within the agricultural sector of rural India. A large sub-set of these deprived children termed as nowhere children (who are neither at school nor at work) consists of over 90 million children in1999. (Gayathri, Chaudhri, 2002). Children of seasonal migrants are deprived from basic education. They never attend formal schools. When the families move from their districts to another districts areas for seasonal work in the sugar factories. The results are retardation of the child and consequent discouragement. (Lowery, 1952). The poorest and depressed sections of the society like agricultural labour, landless labour, marginal farmers and seasonal migrants families have not been able to improve significantly their position in this respect.

Children of poor household belonging to the backward castes, scheduled castes and tribes and minority communities are often highlighted by micro-survey based studies to continue a bulk of child labour. (Lieten, 2002). This study further shows that the bulk of these child workers are in the rural areas. Most of them are engaged in agricultural activities as family hands or as hired agricultural labourers. Generally girls join their mothers at harvest time when contract labour hiring system is adopted in agricultural sector.

Castle, Chaudhari and Nyland (2002) highlight the fact that the highest levels of child labour are associated with a large share agricultural in employment. Most child labour in South Asian countries is found in the agricultural sector. Besides, most of the child labour in India (97.5%) is concentrated in the age group of 10-14 years.

THE EXISTING LEGISLATIONS

Since British period, various legislations have been enacted by the government of India of child labour and education such as the Factories Act, 1881,Mines Act 1901, the report of the Royal Commission on Labour 1931, the Children Act 1933 and 1938, Child Labour Prohibition and Regulation Act 1986, National Policy on Education 1986, National Policy on child labour 2002. Legislation pertaining to compulsory education as well as child labour has existed for over a hundred years. However, the existing legislations were at best superficially implemented at all (Gayatri, 2002).

The declarations of the rights of the child, which were adopted by the general assembly of the UN on 20 Nov.1959. The declaration says that the child is entitled to enjoy special protection for his physical, moral and mental development. He is also entitled to receive education, which should be free and compulsory at least in the elementary stage; he should be protected against all forms of neglect, cruelty and exploitation (NCERT, 1983).

The constitution of India lays down that child labour in factories and other hazardous occupations should be prohibited (Article 24) and that children below the age of 14 years should get free and compulsory primary education (article 45). The article 45 of the constitution of India states that shall endeavor to provide free and compulsory education for all children until they complete the age of 14 years. This article shows that the constitution of India is an extremely powerful instrument against child labour (Mehendale, 2002) the Supreme Court of

India in its judgment 1993 also pointed out "the citizens of the country have a fundamental right to education. Every child of this country has a right to free education until he completes the age 14 years." (Jandhyalaya, 1999).

The Finance Minister Yashwant Sinha (1999) says a major import initiative that Government proposed in the Budget is the Education Guarantee Scheme at National Level, aimed at providing an opportunity to the rural poor, especially those belonging to the Scheduled Castes, Scheduled Tribes and other Backward Classes to secure education for their children.

At present, the project is being implemented in active partnership with the Government in conducting Chalo Abhiyan (School Enrollment Campaign), which seeks to get out of children into primary schools.(Bissell, 2002). According to the Pratichi Education Report of West Bengal, the fundamental right of universal access to elementary education is to be taken more seriously and universalisation of elementary education, expressed as an explicit goal of the 'Sarva Shiksha Abhiyan', the latest government of India Scheme, is to be achieved by 2010 (Jha, 2003).

Many NGOs have taken up the provision of education as an important plunk in their strategy for combating child labour. It is observed that 50 out of 190 Sugar Factories in Maharashtra State have undertaken the project of Sakhar Shala (*i.e.* Balwadi or Seasonal School) for children of seasonal migrant workers. During the year 2002-03, these Sakhar Shala tried to provide facilities of primary education to about 8500 children in the age group of 4-10 years. (Tarun Bharat, 6 Aug, 2003). However, the project of Sakhar Shala (Seasonal School) has not been implemented by all the sugar factories at state level under the Sarva Shiksha Abhiyan as well as Mahatma Phule Education Guarantee Scheme in Maharashtra. It has been observed that poverty is the main cause of child labour. There is evidence that children have been withdrawn from school to work in sugarcane harvesting and transporting work.

Moreover, as long as poverty persists it is difficult to eradicate child labour. (Mehendale, 2002). A country cannot climinate child labour unless there is a more concerted efforts by the state and various partners to end human poverty. (Bissell, 2002). Therefore, the Pratichi Education Report of West Bengal also records several incidences of children not having been enrolled or dropped out or not attending school regularly on account of hunger and other poverty related factors (Jha, 2003). It is observed that nowhere children are increasing in sugar industry due to family poverty.

CONCLUSION

The phenomenon of seasonal migration is important particularly in the Sugar Factories, where labour is actually mobile and drawn from the neighbouring rural areas and drought prone areas to sugar factories. In fact, children of seasonal migrants families are frequently taken out of school in the beginning of winter due to seasonal migration. Children are deprived from elementary education, because they are unable to attend the school, due to seasonal migration and poverty. Family poverty is directly responsible for the persistence of child labour. It is, therefore, worth nothing that even after almost a hundred years there has been very little change in terms of the basic essence of the legislation related to child labour as well as education (Mehendale, 2002).

Poverty is the main reason for child labour. The incidence of nowhere children is higher in sugarcane harvesting and transporting work in the sugar factories. There is a need to protect seasonal migratory child labour from exploitation of contractors and mukadams in the Sugar Factories. Education is essential to our all around development. Therefore mobile labour camp and sugar factory site seasonal schools should be organized in each sugar factory for children of seasonal migrant workers under the Sarva Shiksha Abhiyan and Mahatma Phule Education Guarantee Scheme of the Government. The working hours, and vacation periods, examination, curriculum programme of seasonal schools etc. should harmonize with the environmental of labour camps and crushing season of the sugar factory.

REFERENCES

Bissell Susan L, Gandhi, Elimination of Child Labour-Corporate Options And.

C. Chadha, Shivakumar A. K. (2002), Public Actions, The Indian *Journal of Labour Economics,* Vol. 45.

Castle R. Chaudhuri D. P. and Nyland C (2002), Child Labour in South Asia, Domestic and International Initiatives Including ILO and *WTO The Indian Journal of Labour Economics* No.3.

C So (1982), Annual Survey of Industries, 1981-82, Govt. of India, New Delhi.

Govt. of India (1966) Report of the Education, Ministry of Education. (Kothari Commission), New Delhi.

Gayathri, V. (2002), Situational Analysis of Child Labour Economics, Vol.45, No. 3 (IJLE).

Chaudhuri D.P. (2002), Child Labour and School Education Trends in India, IJLE, VoI. 45, No.3.

Janahyalaya, Tilak B.G.(1999), National Human Development Initiative Education in the Union Budget, Economic and Political Weekly, March, 6-12.

Jha, Jyotsana (2003), Primary Schools in West Bengal, The Delivery of Primary Education, A Study in West Bengal, The Pratichi Education Report, Economic and Political Weekly, No.27.

Liten G.K. (2002), Child Labour and Poverty, The Poverty of Analysis, IJLE Vol. 45, No.3.

Lowery, Nelson (1952), Rural Sociology, New York, American Company, U.S.A.

Majumdar P.S.and Majumdar (1978), Rural Migrants in an Urban Setting, Delhi. Hidustan Publishing Corporation.

Mehendale Archana (2002), Child Rights, Child Labour and Education. A study of Legal Regime IJLE,Vo1.45, No.3.

NCERT (1983), Study of World Problems in Schools, New Delhi.

Salve W.N. (1990), A Socio-Economic Study of Seasonal Migrants in the Co-operative Sugar Factories with Special References to Kolhapur District, Unpublished Ph.D. Thesis, Shivaji University, Kolhapur.

Sinha Yashwant (1999), Finance Minister's Speech on Union Budget 99, The Economics Times, Feb.28, 1999.

Sharma Alakh N. (2002), The Impact of Social Labeling on child Labour in India's Carpet Industry, IJLE, Vol. 45, No.3.

UNESCO (1952), Compulsory Education in India, Paris.

Wazir, Rekha (2002), Eliminating Child Labour, Do NGO Interventions Add Upto strategy. IJLE,Vol. 45, No.3.

PERIODICALS AND NEWSPAPERS

- Employment News, 22-28, Feb, 2003.
- The Indian Journal of Labour Economics, Vol. 45 No.3, (IJLE) 2002.
- Daily Lokmat, 22 Feb, 2003.
- Daily Tarun Bharat, 6 Aug, 2003.

25

SPATIAL PATTERN OF IRRIGATION AND ITS INTENSITY IN BELGAUM DISTRICT- A GEOGRAPHICAL ANALYSIS

*D. K. Kamble * & S. M. Hurakadli ***

INTRODUCTION

Water and land are amongst the most important natural resources and are basic to agriculture, which is the major occupation of the people in Belgaum district. Any appraisal of water resources of agriculture would therefore, would be incomplete without examining the quality, extent and availability of agricultural land to which irrigation can be applied for maximum benefit.

In Belgaum district, the surface water has always received priority in the field of irrigation. This is well evident from a close perusal of past records. The situation has undergone much change since than. In the context of erratic and fluctuating crop yields, development of ground water resources seems to be essential. This is more so, because of facility of surface water irrigation is not available throughout the year, as there is little scope to augment the potential of surface water irrigation the only alternative lies in judicious use of ground water resource which is a more assured source of irrigation.

* Research Scholar, Department of Geography, Karnatak University Kittuer Rani Chennamma P.G.Centre, Belgaum, Karnataka.

** Reader, Department of Geography, Karnatak University Kittuer Rani Chennamma P.G.Centre, Belgaum, Karnataka.

Therefore, an attempt is made in this chapter to investigate the irrigational facilities used for raising various type of crops in Belgaum district. Indian geographers have shown a lot of interest in the study of water sources of the country especially during the last two decades.

CONCEPT OF IRRIGATION

Irrigation is the artificial application of water to supplement rainfall, if and when necessary to satisfy the water needs of crops. The Irrigation is perhaps the most extensive type of environmental modifications made by farmers. Irrigational practices, however primitive, have drastic impact on the land.

Irrigation implies artificial feeding of water to the soil or plants at the time of dry spells, which is very much required for the growth of crops. Right from the early times, man had learnt the art of artificial supply of water to certain crops. This has initiated him to improve upon methods of irrigation by adopting modern technology of continuously. Irrigation occupies the most important position in those bee areas, where the economy is entirely depending on agriculture. Irrigation is the most important requirement in the package practices for intensive and efficient cultivation of the high yielding varieties and also for multiple cropping, irrigation and chemical fertilizers go hand in hand. Without irrigation chemical fertilizer which are costly inputs, cannot be used with advantage to the farmers. Better results from the high yielding varieties depend largely on controlled application of water.

Therefore, an attempt is made in this chapter to investigate the growth of irrigation, spatial pattern of different sources of irrigation and regional imbalances in the utilization of water which will be useful for analysing the agricultural development in the region.

STUDY AREA

The study area is located in the north western part of the Karnataka state and falls within the northern maidan region. The Belgaum district (named after its Head Quarters-Belgaum) extends between 15°23', and 16°58' north latitude and 75°5' and

75°8' east longitude. The district is bounded in the north by Sangali and Kolhapur districts, and on the west by parts of Kolhapur and Ratnagiri of Maharastra state and Goa, on the east by Bijapur district, South by Dharwad and Uttar Kannada districts. It measures about the 168 kilometers north to south and 80 to 138 kilometers east to west.

The geographical area of the district according to the central statistical organisation of the government of India is 13,44,382 square hectares or 13,415 square kms which is 6.99 per cent of the total geographical area of the state and consists

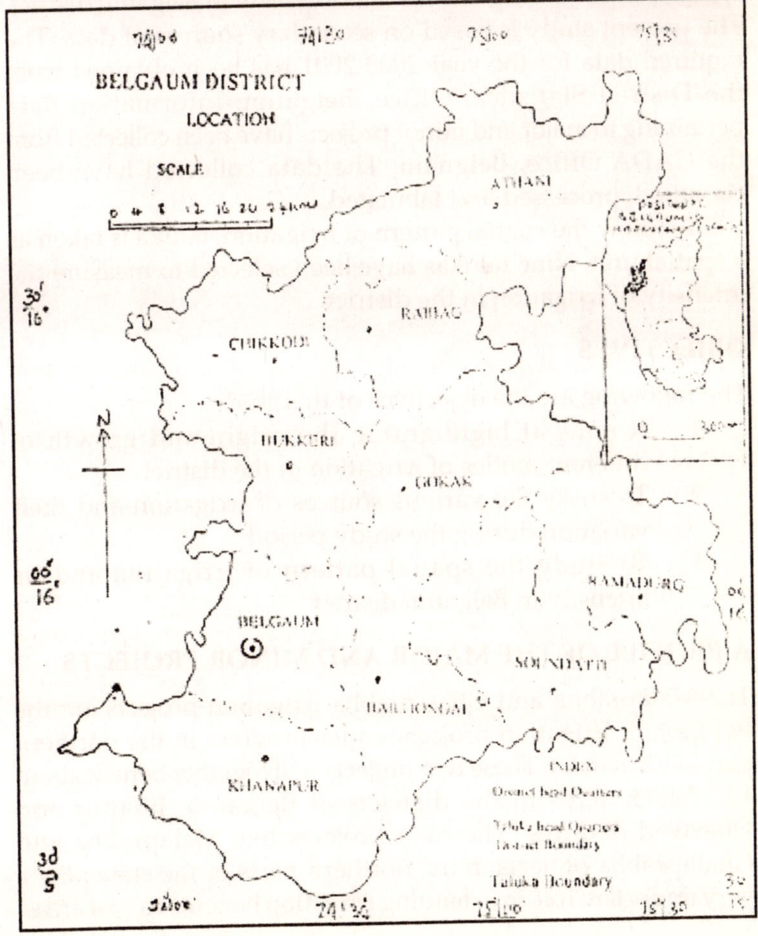

of ten talukas. As per the 2001 census Belgaum districts population is about 4,267,264 persons and it ranks second in top among the districts and in terms of area the districts occupies 5th place among the districts of Karnataka state. The general slope of the district is from the north west to the south east, its average height above the mean sea level varies from 450 to 500 meters.

METHODOLOGY

In the present study an attempt has been made to study the spatial pattern of irrigation and its intensity in Belgaum district. The present study is based on secondary sources of data. The required data for the year 2000-2001 has been obtained from the District Statistical Office, Belgaum. Information data pertaining to major and minor projects have been collected from the CADA Office, Belguam. The data collected have been classified, processed and tabulated.

To know the spatial pattern of irrigation, taluka is taken as a spatial unit. Nine talukas have been selected to measure the intensity of irrigation in the district.

OBJECTIVES

The following are the objectives of this study:-

1. It aims at highlighting the origin and growth of different modes of irrigation in the district.
2. To study the various sources of irrigation and their variation during the study period.
3. To study the spatial pattern of irrigation and its intensity in Belgaum district.

A PROFILE OF THE MAJOR AND MINOR PROJECTS

The Malaprabha and Ghataprabha irrigation projects are the twin major irrigation projects under progress in the northern part of Karnataka. These two projects will together benefit about 13.17 lack acres in the districts of Belgaum, Bijapur and Dharwad districts. The twin projects like Malaprabha and Ghataprabha projects in the northern parts of the state play a very important role in extending irrigation benefits to vast areas.

These areas have been traditionally known for their scarcity and draught conditions. The average rainfall which varies from 28 to 32 cms per annum is meager and is not only erratic but also is undistributed. The soil in this area are very fertile and have exhibited bumper crops whenever proper distribution of rainfall occurs which is of course very rare.

MALAPRABHA PROJECT

Malaprabha Reservoir Project consists of a storage reservoir constructed across river Malaprabha at Peacock gorge near Manoli in Soundatti taluka of Belgaum district, with canal system on both banks to provide irrigation over an area of 2.13 lakh hectares in Dharwad, Belgaum and Bijapur Districts. Masonry dam 507 feet long and 147 feed high above river bed is constructed to form a storage reservoir for an impounding capacity of 37.7 TMC of water. The work of the project was started during 1963 and completed in 1974, the cost of the project was about 274.57 crores.

Due to construction of this dam, 43 villages affecting about 41,000 persons and about 1,33,55 hectares of land has come under submersion. In addition, some portion of 3 interconnecting roads viz-Soundatti, Bailhongal, Kittur, Saundatti-Manoli, have also been affected.

The Malaprabha left bank canal pierces through the left abutment hills by means of a 7 furlong tunnel and further runs for a length of 168 kms. Enroute, the left bank canal is negotiated through three more tunnels, twin tunnel near Katkol in 30 kms and at Mudakavi in 66kms. A left point in its 9 kms reach is provided and termed as Yergatti lift irrigation scheme. The irrigable area under left bank canal is 53,150 hectares.

The Malaprabha right bank canal takes off from the head regulator constructed in the right bank foreshore of the reservoir, cuts through the Yellamma range of hills through a 5 kms long tunnel and further runs for 138 kms. The irrigable command under right bank main canal is 81,100 hectares and under Nargnd branch canal is 47,570 hectares. The total irrigable command is 1.28 lakh hectares. A right bank canal which takes off from the existing Kolchi weir lower down the Malaprabha dam site had an irrigable area of 1275 hectares only. Now it is extended to run for a length of 64 kms, with an irrigable command of 8100 hectares.

Apart from this, for the foreshore of the reservoir on both banks, 8 (eight) lift irrigation schemes introduced to irrigate an area of 23,360 hectares, mainly to provide amenities to the expropriated riots have also been constructed. The total utilization under Malaprabha project is 46 TMC.

In Belgaum district, there are three talukas had an irrigational facilities viz-Soundatti taluka had an area about 1,10,973 hectares, Bailhongal 9,363 hectares and Ramdurg taluka 32,880 hectares.

GHATRPRABHA PROJECT

Efforts were made to utilize the water of Ghataprabha river as early to 1852. A scheme for construction of a masonry weir across Ghataprabha about 21/2 miles above Gokak falls was sanctioned during 1877 and the Dhupdal weir and Gokak canal on left bank was completed by 1897.

In order to utilize fully the water of the river, the comprehensive scheme was taken up and the Ghataprabha valley development scheme was approved in 1949 by the former government of Bombay vide resolution No-9194-36 dated 5th April 1949. The entire scheme as conceived now consists of the following components to provide irrigation over an area of 3,88,200 hectares in Bijapur and 4,67,371 hectares in Belgaum district.

In the I stage, a storage dam at Hidkal with a storage capacity of 5.16 TMC feet, and in IInd stage, the left bank canal taking off from Dhupdal weir for a length of 116 kms, to command an irrigable area of 1.62 lakh hectares, ultimately when lining is completed, and in the IIIrd stage, Ghataprabha left bank canal for a length of 220 kms and Chikkodi branch canal of 86 kms length and to provide foreshore lift irrigation from the Chikkodi branch canal. The storage reservoir has been formed by construction of 175 feet high and 14700 feet long composite dam comprising of earth dam, rockfill dam, masonry spillway and non-spillway section. In addition two dykes of 17010 feet and 1700 feet length have been plugged with earth dam. The total impounding capacity is about 51.16 TMC. As a result of this, 18 villages with 4 hamlets and total of 3728 families have rehabilitated in 22 centers, and the cultivated area of 7383 hectares of land has come under submersion due to formation of this reservoir.

Ghataprabha left bank canal taking off from Dhupdal weir runs for a length of 116 kms. This canal with distribution system will be lined to command 1.62 lakh hectares. Out of total irrigated area from this canal four talukas have benefited in Belgaum district, Viz-Gokak (342634 hectares), Athani (4748 hectares), Chikkodi (8337 hectares) and Raibag (33995 hectares). The right bank canal takes off from the right bank of Hidkal dam and runs for a length of 202 kms. The total irrigable area in this right bank canal was about 1,55,567 hectares benefited by six talukas in Belgaum district Viz-Gokak (4076, hectares), Hukkeri (10413 hectares), Ramdurg (2686 hectares), Soundatti (1739 hectares), Chikkodi (14,730 hectares) and Raibag (8665 hectares).

PROPOSED PROJECTS

There are three major projects proposed, they are as follows:

Firstly, the Dudha ganga project is proposed. It is an inter state multi-purpose project between Karnataka and Maharashtra which will irrigate 19,440 hectares in Chikkodi taluka. The Hippargi Barrage is also another proposed scheme at Hippargi village in Jamkhandi taluka of Bijapur district, which will irrigate part of Athani and Chikkodi talukas of Belgaum district. The Harinala is another minor project, which is proposed to construct across the Harinala river which is a tributary of Malaprabha river. It will supply the water to Tigadi village of Bailhongal taluka of Belgaum district.

GROWTH OF IRRIGATION

Irrigation is undoubtedly and age-old art as old as civilization itself. The rapid of irrigation is the effect of increasing need for crop production by growing population through the world.

The importance of irrigation in the Indian agriculture cannot be over estimated in view of the peculiar nature of the rainfall in the country. Irrigation, therefore, has been the principal pre-occupation with India since time immemorial. In India the country's early development of irrigation took place in the Gangetic and Indus valley. However the first "anicut" was built on the river Cauvery during the second century.

It is in this context that an analysis of the development of irrigation in Belgaum district is made against its requirements in the part and the till the day. As a result, irrigation facilities are being well developed in the Belgaum district over last three decades. According to 1968-69 the total net irrigated area in the district was less, that is 65,498 hectares, before the commencement of the water discharge through Malaprabha and Ghataprabha projects. By 1978-79 it has been increased to 1,35,196 hectares and during 1988-89 the total irrigated area in the district was 2,13,273 hectares. During the decade of 1998-99, the district had 3,11,305 hectares of land under irrigation in the district and it has increased to 4,44,688 hectared during 2000-01.

Table 1
Decadel variation of Area under Different Sources of Irrigation in Belgaum District

S. No.	*Sources*	*1968-69*	*1978-79*	*1988-89*	*1998-99*	*2000-01*
1	Canals	24183	47562	83401	89790	111693
		(36.92)	(35.18)	(39.01)	(28.85)	(25.11)
2	Wells	32290	56080	65038	121345	236913
		(49.29)	(41.48)c	(30.49)	(38.98)	(53.27)
3	Tanks	6317	9705	5788	5436	4548
		(9.64)	(7.18)	(2.71)	(1.75)	(1.02)
4	Other Sources	2708	21844	59046	94734	91534
		(4.13)	(16.16)	(27.68)	(30.43)	(20.58)
	All Sources	65498	135196	213273	311305	444688
		(100%)	(100%)	(100%)	(100%)	(100%)

Note: Figures in Brackets indicate percentage of total irrigated area.

SPATIAL PATTERN OF IRRIGATION

Irrigation plays a vital role in the agricultural regeneration of a district. As such, great importance has been laid on accelerating the extension of water in the dry season within the shortest possible time. The rabi cultivation depending on irrigation suffers because of low moisture retention capacity of the soil. The major sources of irrigation are the wells and canals (Malaprabha and Ghataprabha projects), which supplies water through left and right bank canals, and also small irrigation schemes extend irrigation facilities within the region. The

Belgaum District
Decadal Variation of Different Sources of Irrigation

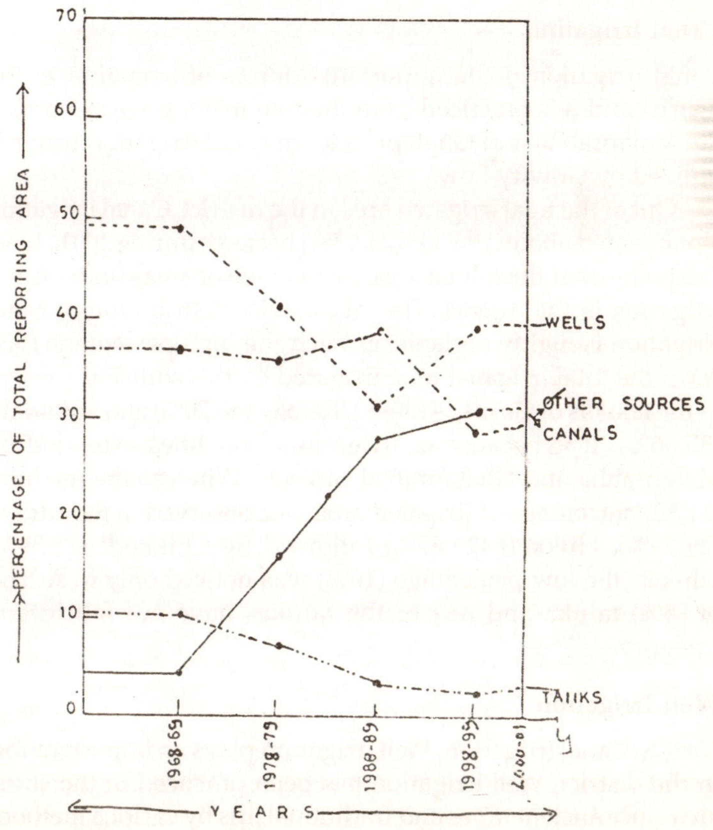

sources of irrigation are greatly affected by the geological, physical ana climotalogical conditions. According to the availability of surface of ground water, type of relief, soils and moisture requirements of crops, the sources of irrigation have been categorized.

The important irrigation sources available in the study area fall into four traditional types, namely canals, wells, tube wells, bore wells, tanks and other sources of irrigation. The different modes of irrigation were characterized by the change in their ranking order. Consequently the canal, and well irrigation system is the most dominant and it irrigates larger area than any other system. Next come to other sources of irrigation, and tank irrigation.

Canal Irrigation

Canal irrigation is the important sources of irrigation in the district and it is practiced from the two major projects namely the Malaprabha and Ghataprabha. In canal irrigation water is utilized by Gravity flow.

Out of the total irrigated area in the district, Canal irrigation alone shared about 2,96,306 (24.13%) hectares during 2001. Table 2 explains that the taluka wise percentage of areas under canal irrigation in the district. The taluka wise distribution of canal irrigation is highly variable, as such the high percentage (>31 %) of the total irrigated area irrigated by this source is present in the talukas of Gokak (41.43%), Raibag (40.20%) and Soundatti (35.66%). It is because of irrigational facilities extended by Malaprabha and Ghataprabha projects. Whereas the medium (11.30) percentage of irrigated area was observed in Ramdurga (29.29%), Hukkeri (25.67%) followed by Chikkodi (13.59%) talukas. the low percentage (10%) was noticed only in Athani (4.25%) taluka and rest of the talukas have not fall in any category.

Well Irrigation

Next to Canal irrigation, Well irrigation plays an important role in the district. Well irrigation has been practiced in the study area since ancient times and traditional lifts by various methods

Table 2
Utilisation of Different Sources of Irrigation in Belgaum District (2000-2001)

Sl.	Talukas	Canals	Tanks	Wells	Bore Wells	Tube Wells	Other Sources	Wet
1	Athani	9341	3079	83645	23078	76354..	24097	219594
		(4.25)	(1.40)	(38.09)	(10.50)	(34.77)	(10.97)	(100%)
2	Bailhongal	NA	172	7953	61630	3236	NA	77191
			(0.22)	(10.30)	(79.84)	(4.190		(100%)
3	Belgaum	NA	373	24236	5994	1602	70	31825
			(1. 1 7)	(76.15)	(18.83)	(5.03)	(0.21)	(100%)
4	Chikkodi	18555	NA	36981	13995	2460 (2.01)	51423	121784
		(13.59)		(30.36)	(11.96)		(42.22)	(100%)
5	Gokak	106781	NA	44576	29133	9443	67803	257736
		(41.43)		(17.24)	(11.30)	(3.66)	(26.30)	(100%)
6	Hukkeri	15290	1652	16263	2884	12534	10987	59550
		(25.67)	(2.77)	(27.30)	(4.84)	(21.04)	(18.45)	(100%)
7	Khanapur	NA	10260	6057	17421	3403	13418	50165
			(20.45)	(12.07)	(34.74)	(6.78)	(26.74)	(100%)
8	Rai bag	71539	NA	73627	7139	NA	44629	77934
		(40.20)		(41.37)	(4.46)		(25.08)	(100%)
9	Ramdurg	26588	NA	16425	16434	4896	27596	90774
		(29.29)		(18.09)	(18.10)	(5.39)	(27.97)	(100%)
10	Soundatti	50272	419	25646	28568	29106	NA	140971
		(35.66)	(0.29)	(18.19)	(20.26)	(20.64)		(100%)
	Total in District	296306	15905	336009	206246	143034	164923	1227524
		(24.13)	(1.29)	(27.37)	(16.80)	(11.65)	(13.43)	(1 00%)

Note: Figures in bracket indicate percentage of irrigation area to the net irrigation area.

like Charsa and Rent, Kapli, Moht it means leather container based on human and animal energy were used for the purpose and are still in practice. Nowadays mohts are replaced by oil engines and electrical motors.

In the present study well irrigation was dominated allover the district. Out *of* the total irrigated area well irrigation accounts for an area about 3,36,009 (27.37%) hectares in the district during 2001.

Table 2 explains that the taluka wise distribution *of* well irrigation in Belgaum district. In general, where canal irrigation is less, well irrigation is more and vice-versa, and it is true it occupies first place among the sources *of* irrigation in the district. However, its spatial distribution at taluka level has varied from one taluka to another. The high percentage (>30%) *of* irrigated area was observed inthe talukas of Belgaum (75.15%), Raibag (41.37%), Athani (38.09%) and Chikodi (30.36%). Whereas the medium percentage (15-30) of irrigated area was confined to four talukas *of* the district, viz-Hukkeri (27.30%), Soundatti (18.19%), Ramdurg (18.09%) and Gokak (17.29%) talukas. The low percentage (15%) *of* irrigated area was observed in two talukas namely Khanapur (12.07%) and Bailhongal (10.30%) talukas. This variation was mainly due to variation in the amount of rainfall in these talukas.

Tube Well Irrigation

The fluctuation of rainfall and erratic monsoon the district experiences severe problem of water for irrigation. When the open wells are dried up the farmers are not able to practice agriculture in the district. The tube wells represent a modern scientific and efficient method of exploiting ground water and has greatly contributed to success of new agricultural technology. There are 52, 623 bore wells in the district which irrigated about 1,43,034 (11.65%) hectares during 2001.

The spatial distribution of tube well irrigation at taluka level varied from one taluka to another. As such the high percentage (>10%) of tube well irrigated area was observed in Athani (34.77%), Hukkeri (21.04%) and Soundatti (20.64%) talukas.

Whereas the medium percentage (5-10%) was irrigated area was confined to three talukas of the district viz - Khanapur (6.78%), Ramdurg (5.39%) and Belgaum (5.03%). The low percentage (5%) of tube well irrigated area concentrated in three talukas of the district namely in the talukas of Bailhongal (4.19%), Gokak (3.66%) and Chikkodi (2.01%) and Raibag taluka was not fall in anyone of the category, it is because of non-availability of data.

Belgaum District
Intensity of Irrigation- 2000-2001

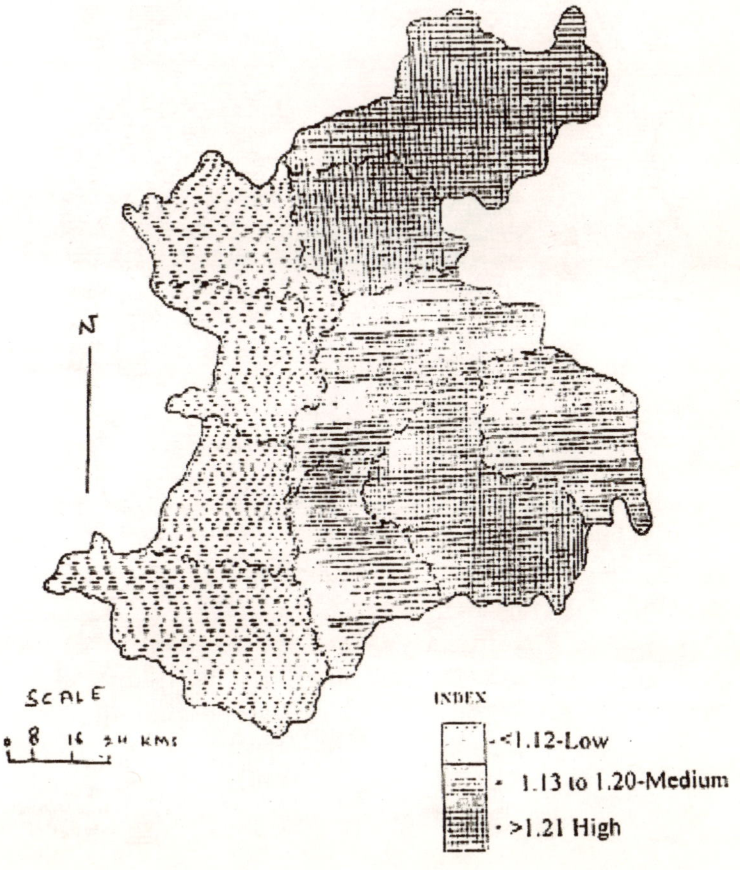

Bore Well Irrigation

Bore well irrigation represents a modern scientific and efficient method of exploiting ground water through modern technology. There are as many as 60920 bore wells in the district, which irrigates about 2,06,246 (16.80%) hectares during 2001.

Table 2 explains that the spatial distribution of bore well irrigation in the district.

Belgaum District
Taluka wise area Under Different Sources of Irrigation 2000-2001

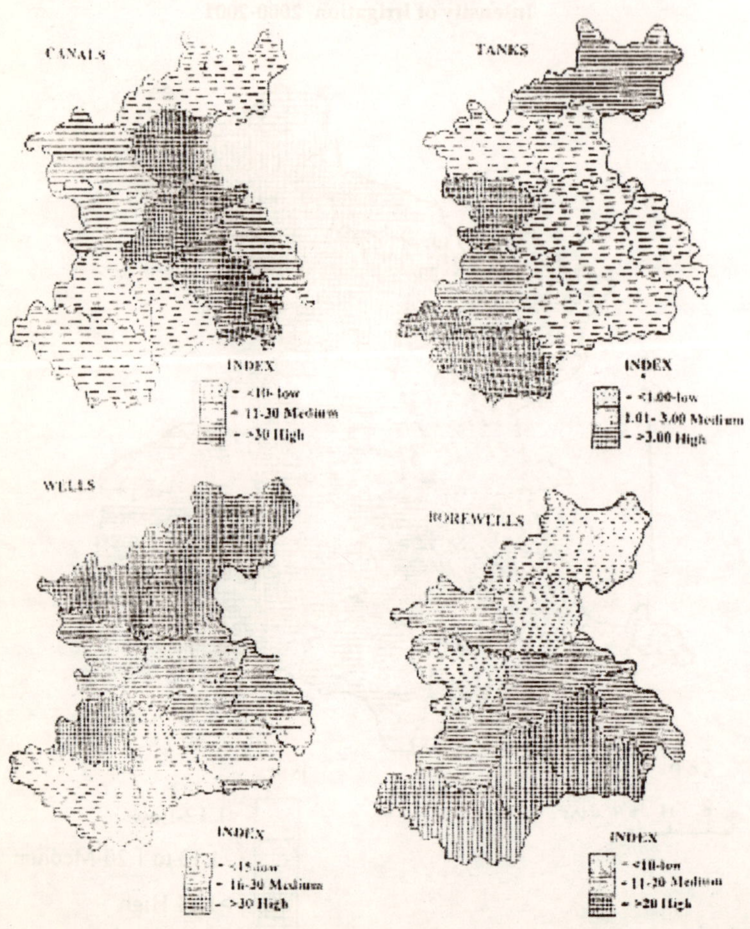

As such the high percentage (>20%) was observed in three talukas namely Bailhongal (79.84%), Khanapur (34.72%) and Soundatti (20.26%) talukas. Whereas the medium percentage (10-26%) of this category of irrigation was confined to large area in the district mainly in the talukas of Belgaum (18.83%), Ramdurga (18.10%), Chikkodi (11.46%), Gokak (11.30%) and Athani (10.50%) talukas. The low percentage (<10%) was confined to only two talukas of the district viz - Hukkeri (4.84%) and Raibag (4.46%) talukas. It is because of dominance of otheT irrigational facilities in the district during 2001.

Other Sources of Irrigation

In addition to irrigation by Canals, Wells and Tanks other sources of irrigation is also in practice. This source of irrigation includes lift irrigation by streams and rivers. A lift is an installation of pump, of a height close to the river banks, that taps water from rivers, streams and allows it to reach the field through small channels constructed for this purpose. There are as many as 1,27,162 electrical pumpsets and 3654 diesel pump sets in the district, are being intensively used for irrigation purpose. It is because of erratic rainfall condition.

The area and irrigation by this source was about 1,64,923 (13.43%) hectares during 2001. The other sources of irrigation

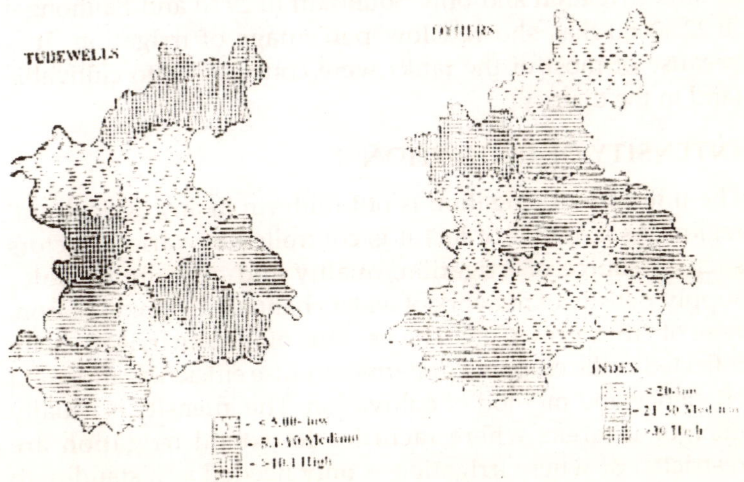

is important almost in the entire district. Among all the talukas of the district there are two talukas fall under the category of high percentage (>31 %), of this category of irrigation, viz-Chikkodi (42.22%) and Ramdurga (37.97%). Whereas the medium percentage (20.30%) of other sources of irrigation was confined to Khanapur (26.74%), Gokak (26.30%) and Raibag (25.08%) talukas. The low percentage (< 20%) was seen in the talukas of Hukkeri (18.45%), Athani (10.97%) and Belgaum (0.21%). This type of irrigation is only practiced where the well and canal irrigation is absent.

Tank Irrigation

There are as many as 886 tanks in the district and most of them are seasonal in their nature. Out of the total number 409 tanks are being intensively utilized for the irrigation purpose. These tanks are feed by rivers and rainfall and many of them have be constructed by bunds across the streams and most of the tanks are found in Khanapur and Athani talukas.

The area under tank irrigation for the year 2001 was about 15,905 (1.29%) hectares, out of the total irrigated area of the district. The high (>3%) percentage of tanks are concentrated in Khanapur taluka, followed by Hukkeri (2.27%), Athani (1.40%) and Belgaum (1.17%) talukas, have medium percentage of tank irrigation and only Soundatti (0.29%) and Bailhongal (0.22%) talukas showed low percentage of irrigation. It is because of most of the tanks were converted into cultivable land in the district.

INTENSITY OF IRRIGATION

The intensity of irrigation is not uniform in any agricultural region. As a matter of fact it is controlled by various factors such as source of irrigation, quality and quantity of water supply, density of network of water channels, cropping season, type of crops grown etc. The benefits of intense irrigation are reflected in the cropping patterns, landuse efficiency, area yield efficiency and method of cultivation. The intensity is usually meager in areas where facilities to extend irrigation are restricted or where irrigation is only needed as a standby to overcome the moisture facility in otherwise heavy rain areas. In an agricultural region, other things being equal, the intensity of irrigation will increase with decrease of rainfall and vice-versa.

Generally the intensity of irrigation is expressed in two ways viz- (1) The percentage of gross irrigated area to net irrigated area, (2) The percentage of net-irrigated area to new sown area.

Belgaum district is not irrigated fully. The researchers have calculated the intensity of irrigation by applying the second method as mentioned above.

The term "intensity of irrigation" here refers to percentage of net area irrigated to net-sown area. The intensity has been calculated to evaluate the existing use of irrigation facilities in cultivated area. This can be expressed as under.

$$\text{Intensity of irrigation} = \frac{\text{Net irrigated area}}{\text{Net sown area}} \times 100$$

1. Gross Irrigated Area x 100
   Net irrigated area
   Suits for very intensively irrigated area
2. New Irrigated Area
   Net sown area

Suits well for the area where irrigation area is low and medium.

Table 3

Taluka wise Intensity of Irrigation in Belgaum District (2000-2001)

Sl.No.	*Talukas*	*Net Irrigated Area*	*Net Sown Area*	*Intensity of Irrigation*
1	Athani	219594	125383	1.75
2	Bailhongal	77191	65824	1.17
3	Belgaum	31825	28232	1.12
4	Chikkodi	121784	115076	1.05
5	Gokak	257736	213414	1.20
6	Hukkeri	59550	53396	1.11
7	Khanapur	50165	50757	0.98
8	Raibag	277934	152893	1.81
9	Ramdurg	90774	76073	1.19
10	Saundatti	140971	82925	1.69

SPATIAL PATTERN OF INTENSITY OF IRRIGATION

In Belgaum district, the intensity of irrigation is not uniform. In fact, it is controlled by various factors as mentioned. Earlier.

Belgaum District
Utilisation of Irrigation in Belgaum District 2000-2001

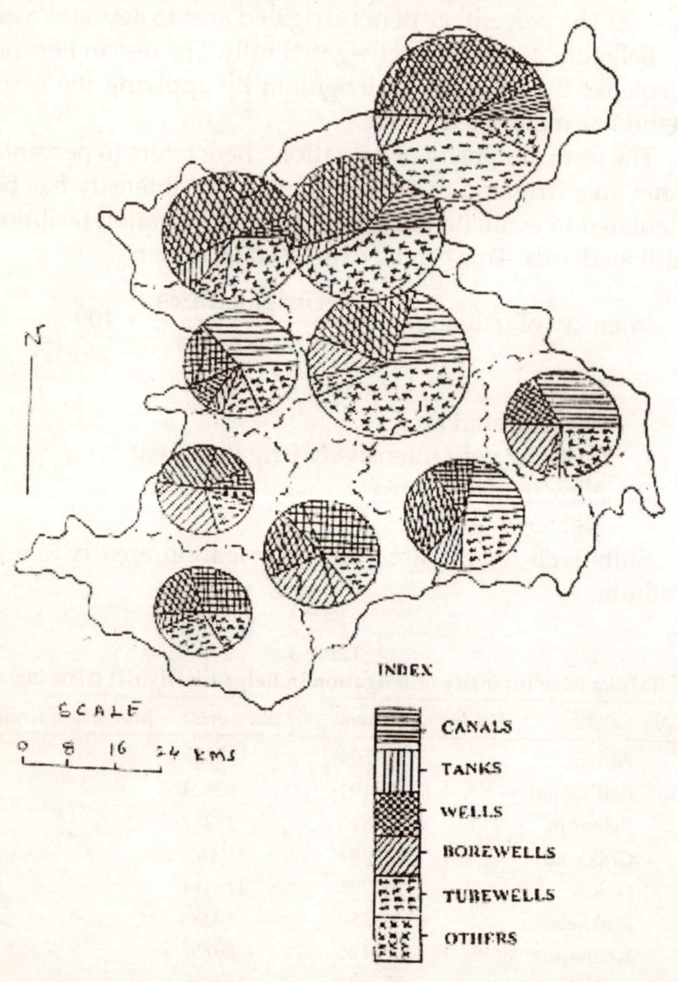

Table 3 depicts that the taluka wise regional distribution of intensity of irrigation in Belgaum district. It reveals that relatively high intensity was observed in three talukas of the district namely in the talukas of Soundatti, Athani and Raibag talukas. It is because, these talukas got perennial water supply through Malaprabha and Ghataprabha and Krishna river lift irrigation, and also contributed by well irrigation during the study period of 2001.

The medium intensity of irrigation was observed in six talukas of the district, namely in the talukas of Chikkodi, Hukkeri, Belgaum, Bailhongal, Ramdurg and Gokak talukas. It is mainly due to lift and bore well irrigation and also perennial water supply through Malaprabha and Ghataprabha projects.

In the district the low intensity of irrigation is found in non-irrigated areas, where tank, well irrigation and other sources of irrigation is practiced. During 2001, only one taluka i.e. Khanapur showed low intensity of irrigation. It is mainly because of undulating topography, canal irrigation cannot reach beyond certain level, hence canal irrigation is absent and this low intensity of irrigation depend on only rainfall, as a result of this the intensity of irrigation is comparatively low in this taluka during 2001.

REFERENCES

Majid Hussain (1996), Systematic agricultural geography. *Rawat Publication, Jaipur,* pp.213-270.

Mohammad N. (1978), Agricultural landuse in India. *Intra Inda Publications,* New Delhi.

Morgan W.B. and Morton R.J.C. (1992), Agricultural geography, *Methuen and Company Ltd.,* London.

Pawar C.T. (1989), Impact of Irrigation Himalaya a regional perspective, *Publishing Published House, Bombay,* Ph.D. Thesis.

Ram Mohan Rao & Samhadri (1989), Development dynamics in command areas of major irrigation project. *Inter, India Publications,* D-17, Raja Garden Extension, New Delhi.

Reddy K. V. & Reddy K.S. (1976), Agricultural efficiency In Andra Pradesh, *The Deccan Geographers,* Vol. 16, No.2, pp.157-162.

Shinde S.D., (1988) ed. Readings irrigated farming, In *Vishwanil Publication,* Pune.

Shafi M. (1960), Measurement of agriculutral productivity in Uttar Pradesh. *Economic Geography,* Vo1.36, pp.295-305.

26

MULTIVARIATE STATISTICAL ANALYSIS OF DETERMINANTS OF DENTAL CARIES, PLAQUE DEPOSIT AND PERIODONTAL DISEASE

S. B. Javali & Parameshwar V. Pandit***

INTRODUCTION

Oral health is an integral part and very much important for the achieving & maintenance of general health. Dental caries and periodontal disease are two major oral diseases, which impair the quality of life of people, adverse effects on the vital organs of the body and affects the lives of a large proportion of the inhabitants of this world. Changes in our knowledge of etiology of dental caries and periodontal disease and the recognition of the potential importance of susceptibility factors as they affect initiation and progression of these major diseases, led to intense study of specific determinants of these oral diseases. The prevention of dental caries and periodontal disease depends mainly on the manner in which individuals conduct their lives (Blinkhon A. S. 1978). The presence of dental plaque on the teeth and oral tissues is recognized as being a requirement for the initiation of dental caries (Fehr et al. 1970) and periodontal disease (Koch G., & Linde J., 1965, Loe H et al 1965, Suomi J. D. et al. 1971). Thus frequent removal of plaque or the prevention

* Lecturer in Bio-statistics, Department of Public Health Dentistry, SDM College of Dental Sciences and Hospital, Sattur, Dharwad-580 009

** Senior Grade Lecturer, Department of Statistics, Karnataka Arts College, Dharwad-580 003 of its formation may be considered effective for the prevention of dental caries and periodontal disease. The better understanding of the determinants which influence pattern of behavior would greatly aid health educators in their efforts to establish sensible socio-economic-demographic, eating habits, oral hygiene habits, and other deleterious habits. A countable number of studies have been conducted to ascertain the socio-economic-demographic and other factors related to dental caries (Javali et al. 2001, 2003, 2004, Javali S. B., and P. V. Pandit, 2004), periodontal disease (Vander Velden U., 1984) and plaque deposit on the teeth (Cohen L. et al. 1983). In order to gain further information about the determinants associated with good dental health status especially dental caries and periodontal disease, the decision was made to study this problem multivariately.

Therefore, the primary purpose and aim of this study was to determine the influence of the socio-economic-demographic and other factors related to oral health status on development of dental caries, accumulation of plaque deposit and occurrence of periodontal disease.

The specific objectives of the this study are as follows:

1. To find the most important determinants affecting development of dental caries, accumulation of plaque deposit and occurrence of periodontal disease separately
2. To select the key discriminating determinants between subjects with positively and negatively health oriented towards development of dental caries, accumulation of plaque deposit and occurrence of periodontal disease separately.

METHODS AND MATERIALS

A total of 500 subjects were selected by using simple random sampling procedure, who are attending the Out Patient Department (OPD) with oral health problem of SDM College of Dental Sciences and Hospital, Dharwad, Karnataka, India. The selected subjects were called for free dental examination. The dental examination of dental caries, plaque deposit and periodontal disease was carried out by using plane mouth mirror, dental explorer, disposable gloves and sterilized instruments under artificial light for each subject. The findings of the dental caries examination were recorded by using diagnostic criteria recommended by World Health Organization (WHO 1997). The dental caries was recorded by DMFT and DMFS indices, the Silness and Loe Plaque index was used for assessment of visible plaque and periodontal disease status (dichotomous) was recorded by Community Periodontal Index (CPI). All these indices are taken as dependent/response variables. The data on selected explanatory variables were collected by structured questionnaire and interview method. The explanatory variables are as follows:

Socio-economic-demographic characteristics:

Socio-economic-demographic characteristics were assessed in terms of Sex (male=1, Female=2), Age (in years) as continuous, place of residence (Urban=1, Rural=2) Religion of the subject (Hindu=1, Muslim=2, Sikh=3,Christian=4), Caste of the subject (SC/ST=1, OBC=2, GM=3, others=4), Education of the subjects were assessed on scales ranging from 1 to 7 (i.e. Illiterate=1, Primary=2, Secondary=3, PUC=4, Graduate=5, PG=6, professionals or others=7),. Two dummy variables constructed yielding the categories 1=lower education including no education/Primary/Secondary/PUC and 2=higher education including Graduate/PG/professionals/others, Occupation (Farmer=1, Agriculture labour =2, Unskilled worker=3,Skilled worker=4, Business=5, White-collar worker=6, Professional and Others=7), Income of a family (as a continuous), Desire family size (as a continuous).

Food Habits

Food Habits were assessed in terms of Staple (main) food (Wheat=1, Rice=2,Maize=3, Jowar=4, Bajra=5 and others=6), Main source of drinking water (Pipe tap=1, Tube well=2, Hand pump=3, Pond=4, River=5, others=6), Type of food (Vegetarian=1, Non-Vegetarian=2, Mixed=3)

Eating Habits

Eating Habits were assessed in terms of Frequency of sweet consumption (per day) (Once=1, Twice=2 and more than twice=3), Duration of sweet consumption (During meals=1, In between meals=2, during & in between meals=3),

Oral Hygiene Practices

Oral hygiene practices are measured in terms of materials used to clean the teeth (Finger=1, Brush=2, Datun=3, others=4), Frequency of brushing (Once=1, Twice=2, after every meal=3, don't clean every day=4), Timings of cleaning teeth/brushing (Morning only=1, Night only=2, Morning and Night=3, after meals=4), Methods of brushing (Horizontal=1, Vertical=2, Circular=3), Type of materials used to clean the teeth (Tooth paste=1, Tooth powder=2, others=3), Types of toothpaste / powder use to clean teeth (Colgate=1, Colgate-gel=2, Close-up=3, Pepsodent =4, Vicco=5, Babool=6,Forhans=7, others=8), Duration of change of toothbrush (1-3 months=1,4-6 months=2, 6 months +=3), Rinsing habit (Never=1, Some times=2, Always=3).

Deleterious Habits

Deleterious habits were assessed through Smoking habit (Yes=1, No=2), Chewing habit (Yes=1, No=2) and Alcohol habit (Yes=1, No=2).

Further more, for analytical purpose the present study subjects were divided into two groups according to increasing subject's clinical values (Javali et al. 2004). This was done by DMFT, DMFS and PLAQUE index scores, but not by CPI index scores, because of the occurrence of periodontal disease was taken as qualitative character. The two groups of the subjects were classified on the basis of mean±SD. A total subjects were separately classified into two groups according to increasing individual indices values (DMFT, DMFS, PLAQUE). According to classification, the subjects of the first group with index values were less than or equal to mean-SD values were combined in the positively health oriented group and the subjects of the second group with index values were more than the mean+SD values were combined in the negatively health oriented group.

The mean and SD values were determined for DMFT, DMFS and PLAQUE index values separately for positively and negatively health oriented subjects. The Karl Pearson's correlation coefficient technique has been utilized to determine the associations between selected determinants with DMFT, DMFS and PLAQUE indices values.

The step-wise multiple regression analysis of selected 23 independent determinants were used in order to determine best predictors of dental caries experience (DMFT, DMFS) and accumulation of plaque deposit on the tooth surfaces (PLAQUE index) separately. The following procedure has been used in step-wise multiple regression analysis. First the variable having greatest power of influence is selected. Then the effect of this variable is eliminated from the information content of all the other variables. The variable, which then has the highest power of influence after the above elimination procedure is ranked as the second etc. Thus, the variables are listed in decreasing order those have the probability of the additional information gained from entering further variables was less than 0.05. Lastly, the variables having the weaker influence power may drop from the final analysis. Therefore, there may be some variables out side the final list, which in fact have greater individual influence power. The multiple logistic regression analysis is also used to determine the best predictors having independent effects on the probability of occurrence of periodontal disease by CPI scores.

The step-wise multiple discriminant function analysis of selected 23 determinants were used in order to obtain scores of positively health oriented and negatively health oriented group subjects. The same procedural steps of step-wise multiple regression analysis are used in step-wise multiple discriminant function analysis. In order to weigh significance of each chosen variable in discrimination, its partial lambda values and standardized coefficients of each variable was computed. The discriminant power of the whole set of variables and as a whole was measured with eigen values, canonical correlation and Wilk's Lambda criteria.

Lastly, the chi-square test has been used to assess the association between independent variables and development of dental caries experience, plaque accumulation and occurrence or severity of periodontal disease. A statistical analysis was performed by using SPSS 11.0 (2001).

Results

The mean DMFT, DMFS and PLAQUE index values for the total study subjects studied was 4.3463±2.0191, 13.4323±6.8510 and 0.7092±0.1693 respectively. The mean and standard deviation values of DMFT, DMFS and PLAQUE indices according to positively health oriented and negatively health oriented subject groups are presented in the table 1.

Table 1
Mean Clinical Records of Selected Subjects Divided into two Groups Classified by DMFT, DMFS and PLAQUE index

Group	*DMFT (Mean±SD)*	*Classifier DMFS (Mean±SD)*	*Plaque (Mean±SD)*
First (Positively)	3.2037±1.9612	9.3704±4.8241	0.6497±0.1666
Second (Negatively)	5.6952±2.1448	26.2282±8.8924	0.7790±0.1595
	DMFS (Mean±SD)	DMFT (Mean±SD)	Plaque (Mean±SD)
First (Positively)	10.3559±9.6548	3.3220±3.2111	0.7126±0.1920
Second (Negatively)	14.4883±11.6579	5.4927±2.04447	0.7043±0.1493
	Plaque (Mean±SD)	DMFS (Mean±SD)	DMFT (Mean±SD)
First (Positively)	0.7045±0.1786	11.2558±6.3035	3.2326±2.7065
Second (Negatively)	0.7127±0.1750	15.4300±7.2180	5.4300±3.5510

A frequent sweet consumption was seen more commonly among negatively health oriented subjects than the positively health oriented subjects by DMFT (chi-square=20.4845, <0.05,S), DMFS (chi-square=18.1767, <0.05, S) and PLAQUE index (chi-square=30.8862, <0.05, S) (Table 2).

Table 2: Frequency distribution of frequency of sweet consumption as reported by positively (+) and negatively (-) health oriented subjects as measured by DMFT, DMFS, and Plaque indices

Frequency of sweet consumption	*DMFT* +	*DMFS* -	*Plaque* +	-	+	-
Once	53	111	71	105	57	154
Twice	113	59	142	64	112	64
Thrice	55	35	46	29	31	39
More than thrice	44	30	35	8	15	28
	χ^2=20.4845, <0.05,		χ^2=18.1767, <0.05,		χ^2=30.8862, <0.05, S	

A significantly higher number of positively health oriented subjects brushing their teeth frequently than the negatively health oriented subjects in accordance to PLAQUE index (chi-square=28.1009, <0.05, <0.05). But non-significant difference was estimated between positively health-oriented and negatively health oriented subjects in DMFT (chi-square=1.995, >0.05, NS) and DMFS (Chi-square=2.1334, >0.05, NS) at normal level of significance (Table 3).

Table 3: Frequency distribution of frequency of brushing as reported by positively (+) and negatively (-) health-oriented subjects as measured by DMFT, DMFS, and Plaque indices

Frequency of brushing	*DMFT*		*DMFS*		*Plaque*	
	+	-	+	-	+	-
Once	118	112	125	89	108	68
Twice	71	64	86	52	57	124
After every meal	32	34	49	28	35	37
Don't clean every day	44	25	34	37	15	56
	χ^2=1.9995, NS >0.05,		χ^2=2.13342, >0.05, NS		χ^2=28.1009, <0.05, S	

Significantly more number of positively health oriented subjects were seen among who are brushing their teeth by using vertical method than the horizontal and circular methods. However, a statistical significant difference was observed between positively and negatively health oriented subjects by DMFT (chi-square=33.0319, <0.05, S), DMFS (chi-square=12.4606, <0.05, S) and PLAQUE index (chi-square=15.3201, <0.05, S. (Table 4).

Table 4: Frequency distribution of method of brushing as reported by positively (+) and negatively (-) health-oriented subjects as measured by DMFT, DMFS, and Plaque indices

Method of brushing	DMFT		DMFS		Plaque	
	+	-	+	-	+	-
Horizontal	41	117	83	107	64	192
Vertical	167	80	147	62	125	152
Circular	57	38	64	47	26	40
	χ^2=33.0919, <0.05, S		χ^2=12.4606, <0.05, S		χ^2=15.3201, <0.05, S	

Table 5: Frequency distribution of rinsing habit as reported by positively (+) and negatively (-) health oriented subjects as measured by DMFT, DMFS, and Plaque indices

Rinsing habit	DMFT		DMFS		Plaque	
	+	-	+	-	+	-
Never	91	124	58	114	43	106
Sometimes	143	79	142	64	112	117
Always	31	32	94	28	60	62
	χ^2=10.3678, <0.05,		χ^2=29.5317, S <0.05,		χ^2=9.9559, <0.05, S	

Similarly, a rinsing habit with water after every meal was seen commonly among those classified as positively health oriented than the negatively health oriented subjects. A statistical significant difference was observed between positively and negatively oriented subjects in DMFT (chi-square=10.3678, <0.05), DMFS (chi-square=29.5317) and PLAQUE index values (chi-square=9.9559, <0.05, S) (Table 5).

A non-significant difference was observed between positively and negatively health oriented male and female subjects by DMFT (chi-square=2.6979, >0.05, NS), DMFS (chi-square=0.0001, >0.05, NS) and PLAQUE (chi-square=1.7892, >0.05, NS) at normal level of significance. Significant higher number of negatively health-oriented subjects was seen more in urban subjects than the rural subjects by DMFT index (chi-square=16.0438, <0.05, S). But non-significant difference was observed between them according to DMFS (chi-square=0.1300, >0.05, NS) and PLAQUE index (chi-square=1.7000, >0.05, NS) values.

Similarly, a non-significant higher number of positively health-oriented subjects were seen among different religion of the study subjects by DMFT (chi-square=0.6307, >0.05, NS), DMFS (chi-square=2.5079, >0.05, NS) and PLAQUE index values (chi-square=0.8569, >0.05, NS).

In generally, non-significant differences were estimated between positively health oriented and negatively health oriented subjects by three indices (DMFT, DMFS and PLAQUE) with respect to occupation of the subjects, different food habits, and types of toothbrushes, different materials used for clean the teeth at 5% level of significance.

STEP-WISE MULTIPLE REGRESSION:

The results of the regression analysis carried out with respect to development of dental caries experience (DMFT and DMFS), accumulation of plaque deposit on the tooth surfaces (PLAQUE index) and occurrence of periodontal disease (CP index) are being presented separately in this section.

DENTAL CARIES EXPERIENCE (DMFT INDEX)

Out of 23 independent determinants/variables, only eleven variables included in the model and they emerged as statistically significant at respectively 5% and 1% level of significance. The results of step-wise regression estimates of selected eleven independent determinants with respect to dental caries experience (DMFT) are given in Table 6.

The results of the Table 6, indicate that the existence of a strong positive relationship between the duration of change of toothbrush and development of dental caries experience by DMFT index values. The regression coefficient of duration of change of toothbrush was positive and statistically significant at 1% level of significance. The value of the coefficient that has decreased considerably in regression analysis implied that decrease the duration of change of toothbrush by within 1 to 3 months may reduce the dental caries experience or DMFT values.

As results indicated by table 6, the variable method of brushing emerged as statistically significant with a regression estimate denoting powerful yet expected negative influence on dental caries experience. It appears that regular brushing of teeth with vertical method may reduce the dental caries experience.

Table 6
Step-wise regression estimates with dental caries experience (DMFT index) of the subjects as dependent variable

No.	*Independent variable*	*Regression estimates*	*SE of regression estimates*	*t-value*
Constant		8.3730	2.2419	3.7348*
1	Duration of change of tooth brush	-2.2293	0.5745	-3.8807*
2	Method of brushing	-1.5339	0.5286	-2.9015*
3	Area of residence	-1.1592	0.6565	-2.9015**
4	Method of cleaning a teeth	0.7135	0.3082	2.3149**
5	Frequency of brushing	-0.6108	0.2963	-20.0616**
6	Sex	1.3032	0.6478	2.0115**
7	Chewing habit	-1.2883	0.6567	-1.9612**
8	Occupation	-0.3060	0.1560	-1.9612**
9	Education	-0.286	0.1467	-1.9604**
10	Frequency of sweet consumption	0.6699	0.3420	1.9591**
11	Desire amily size	0.3718	0.1905	1.9520**

R=0.8985, R^2=0.8074, Adjusted R^2=0.7808, F=30.3850*, SE of estimate=2.5989

Note: * Indicates significant at 1% level of significance,
** Indicates Significant at 5% level of significance

The variables income of family, sex of the subject, frequency of sweet consumption and desire family size are emerged as statistically significant and positive with development of dental caries experience by teeth wise. In another words, these variables are supporting to increase the development of dental caries experience. But, the areas of residence, frequency of brushing, occupation, education of the subject and chewing habit have significant negative impact on dental caries experience. It means that, these variables are decreasing the development of dental caries in the study population concern.

DENTAL CARIES EXPERIENCE (DMFS INDEX)

Out of selected 23 independent determinants, only thirteen variables included and emerged as statistically significant with dental caries experience (DMFS) at 5% and 1% level of significance in the step-wise regression analysis. As results are indicated in Table 7, the variables like different materials used for clean the teeth, timings for cleaning the teeth, the main source of drinking water, desire family size, frequency of sweet consumption and tobacco habits have positive impact on dental caries experience by DMFS index values. It means that, larger family members in family have a frequent sweet consumption & tobacco habit and cleaning their teeth irregularly by other than toothpastes and tooth powder (finger etc.) in tube well water or hand pump water have higher rate of development of dental caries by DMFS values. In another words, all these variables or determinants are increasing the development of dental caries.

Table 7
Step-wise regression estimates with dental caries experience (DMFS index) of the subjects as dependent variable.

No.	*Independent variable*	*Regression estimates*	*SE of regression estimates*	*t-value*
Constant		32.6391	9.4189	3.4653*
1	Materials of cleaning a teeth	4.1434	0.9679	4.2808*
2	Method of brushing	-8.1969	0.0788	-3.9431*
3	Duration of change of tooth brush	-8.8725	2.2891	-3.8759*
4	Occupation	-2.2533	0.6464	-3.4862*
5	Duration of sweet consumption	-4.6651	1.3490	-3.4581*
6	Cleaning time for teeth	4.7730	1.4758	3.2341*
7	Drinking water	2.9892	1.0183	2.8354*
8	Food habits	-5.2477	1.8995	-2.7627*
9	Desire family size	1.9416	0.7776	2.4969**
10	Frequency of sweet consumption	3.5995	1.4769	2.4372**
11	Area of residence	-6.1227	2.6821	-2.2828**
12	Rinsing habit	0.0007	0.0003	2.1307**
13	Tobacco habit	2.5882	1.2999	1.9900**

R=0.9035, R^2=0.8163, Adjusted R^2=0.7885, F=29.3960*, SE of estimate=10.6777

Note: * Indicates significant at 1% level of significance,
** Indicates Significant at 5% level of significance

Similarly, various brushing methods, duration of change of tooth brush, occupation of a subject, duration of sweet consumption, types of food habit, area of residence and rinsing habit with water after every meal have significant negative impact on dental caries experience. It means that these mentioned determinants are decreasing the development of dental caries experience by DMFS index values.

ACCUMULATION OF PLAQUE DEPOSIT (PLAQUE INDEX)

Out of selected 23 independent determinants, only twelve variables included and emerged as statistically significant with accumulation of plaque deposit of the tooth surface (PLAQUE Index) at 5% and 1% level of significance in the step-wise regression analysis.

Table 8
Step-wise regression estimates with accumulation of plaque deposit (PLAQUE index) of the subjects as dependent variable.

No.	Independent variable	Regression estimates	SE of regression estimates	t-value
Constant		1.6347	0.4587	3.5638*
1	Smoking habit	0.9116	0.1859	4.9037*
2	Chewing habit	0.3008	0.1859	4.6206*
3	Education	-0.9320	0.2584	-3.6068*
4	Frequency of sweet consumption	0.3111	0.0900	3.4563*
5	Materials used to clean the teeth	0.7411	0.2510	2.9526**
6	Method of brushing	-0.6506	0.2238	-2.9071**
7	Age	0.3589	0.1258	2.8530
8	Duration of sweet consumption	0.5996	0.2214	2.7082**
9	Desire family size	0.6420	0.2658	2.4530**
10	Sex	0.8316	0.3568	2.3307**
11	Frequency of brushing	-0.4567	0.2009	-2.2733**
12	Main (Staple) food	-0.4313	0.2147	-2.0088**

R=0.8321, R^2=0.6923, Adjusted R^2=0.6619, F=19.6310*, SE of estimate=11.8312

Note: * Indicates significant at 1% level of significance,
** Indicates Significant at 5% level of significance

As, results indicated in above table 8, smoking habit, chewing habit, frequency of sweet consumption, materials used to clean the teeth, age of the subject, duration of sweet consumption, desire family size and sex of the subject have significant positive impact on accumulation of plaque deposit of the surfaces of the tooth. In another words, all these variables increasing to support the accumulation of plaque deposit on tooth surfaces.

But, education of the subject, various methods of brushing, frequency of brushing and main (staple) food have significantly negative impact on accumulation of plaque deposit on the tooth surfaces. It means that, these determinants are support to decrease the accumulation of plaque deposit on tooth surfaces.

OCCURRENCE OF PERIODONTAL DISEASE (CP INDEX)

In order to determine the relative strengths of the associations identified in Table 9, a logistic regression analysis was conducted with a dichotomous dependent variable consisting of a zero score representing the subjects without periodontal disease and a one score representing subjects with periodontal disease by CP index.

Out of selected 23 independent determinants, only thirteen variables emerged as statistically significant with occurrence of periodontal disease (CP Index) at 5% and 1% level of significance are presented. The frequencies of sweet consumption, duration of sweet consumption, duration of change of toothbrush, staple food, materials used to clean the teeth and ages are the best determinants, which are significantly and positively associated with occurrence of periodontal disease. In another words, these variables are increasing the chance of occurrence of periodontal disease.

But educations, caste, food habits, method of brushing and occupation of the subject have negative and significant association with occurrence of periodontal disease. It means that, all these determinants are decreasing the chance of occurrence of periodontal disease in the study.

Table 9
Multiple Logistic Regression Estimates with Periodontal Disease (CP index) of the Subjects as Dependent Variable

Independent variable	*Regression estimyates*	*SE of regression estimates*	*t-value*
Constant	4.6338	3.1414	1.4751
Frequency of sweet consumption	-0.5707	0.1213	-4.7033*
Education	-0.2777	0.0592	-4.6917*
Caste	-0.3866	0.1219	-3.1715*
Duration of sweet consumption	0.2292	0.0831	2.7590*
Food habit	-0.3910	0.1420	-2.7527*
Frequency of brushing	0.2583	0.1033	2.4991**
Sex	-0.3901	0.1608	-2.4267**
Duration of tooth brush	-0.2808	0.1163	-2.4138**
Staple or main food	0.3020	0.1326	2.2782**
Materials to clean the teeth	-0.1943	0.0875	-2.2201**
Method of brushing	-0.3993	0.1878	-2.1260**
Occupation	-0.4153	0.1974	-2.1037**
Age	-0.2682	0.1359	-1.9742**

Note: * Indicates significant at 1% level of significance,
** Indicates Significant at 5% level of significance

DISCRIMINANT FUNCTION ANALYSIS:

The 23 independent determinants were taken for possible relationships with dental caries experience (DMFT, DMFS), accumulation of plaque deposit on tooth surfaces (PLAQUE index) and results are presented in the proceeding section.

DENTAL CARIES EXPERIENCE (DMFT)

Out of 23 determinants, 17 determinants were significantly related to the dependent variable i.e. development of dental caries experience by DMFT index with magnitudes ranging from low scores/positively and high scores/negatively health oriented groups.

The step-wise discriminant function analysis was used to determine if a linear combination of the 17 determinants significantly correlated determinants could be used to predict the development of dental caries experience. Of 17 related determinants, only 11 determinants found to be best discrimination power on development of dental caries experience (Table 10).

Table 10

Step wise Multiple Discrimination Analysis Atatistically significant Factors of Positively Health Oriented (+) and Negatively Health Oriented (-) Subjects by DMFT index Scores

Independent variables	*Mean±SD* +	-	*Partial Lambda*	*Standard coefficients*	*Wilk's Lambda value*	*F-value*
Duration of sweet consumption	2.1463±3.33	6.1864±3.00	0.8341	0.5616	0.7562	17.3001*
Frequency of sweet consumption	3.1425±2.35	5.2874±4.32	0.8405	0.5415	0.7542	16.5038*
Desire family size	3.1546±4.98	6.654±2.96	0.8719	0.6365	0.7451	12.7801*
Income of a family	2.8965±3.1	5.3980±3.10	0.8900	0.4718	0.7401	10.7520*
Frequency of brushing	3.1865±2.33	4.2587±5.02	0.9286	-0.3838	0.7301	6.6896*
Area of residence	2.9872±3.98	5.6873±3.11	0.9363	0.3112	0.7282	5.9200*
Cleaning materials of teeth	2.6514±4.21	4.8014±4.00	0.9511	-0.3396	0.7247	4.4777**
Change of tooth brush	3.0124±2.68	5.0236±2.99	0.9552	-0.2803	0.7237	4.0758**
Method of brushing	2.8857±2.32	4.6325±3.24	0.9603	-0.2621	0.7225	3.5970**
Sex	3.2564±2.77	4.2587±2.35	0.9704	0-0.2085	0.7202	3.2488**
Type of tooth paste	3.1657±3.33	5.0111±2.68	0.9770	0.2129	0.7187	2.6493**

Note: * Indicates significant at 1% level of significance,
** Indicates Significant at 5% level of significance

The discriminant function analysis resulted in an overall classification rate of 96.00%, in which 98.14% of the correctly placed in the group of positively health oriented and 93.47% of the subjects placed in the negatively health oriented.

The mean discriminant score for positively health-oriented subjects (-0.2933) was significantly different from negatively health-oriented subjects (0.4220) (Wilk's Lambda=0.7110, chi-square=128.3716 with 11 df). The analysis resulted in an eigen value of 3.3020 and canonical correlation of 0.8773. The most distinguishing characteristics of positively health orients (DMFT), when compared with negatively health oriented subjects can be determined by examining the standardized discriminant function coefficients.

Table 10: Step wise multiple discrimination analysis statistically significant factors of positively health oriented (+) and negatively health oriented (-) subjects by DMFT index scores

As the indicated results in the above table, duration of sweet consumption, desire family size, income of a family, frequency of brushing, method of brushing and type of toothpastes are most important discriminant determinants of positively health oriented group subjects and were less likely to be frequency of sweet consumption, materials used to clean the teeth, duration of change of tooth brush and sex of the subjects. The details about mean (±SD), partial Lambda, standardized coefficients and Wilk's Lambda values are presented for further information (Table 10).

DENTAL CARIES EXPERIENCE (DMFT)

Twenty-three independent determinants were examined for possible relationship with dental caries experience by DMFS index. Of these 18 determinants were found to significantly related to the dependent variable i.e. dental caries experience.

The results of the step-wise discriminant function analysis showed only ten determinants were found to be best discriminating determinants of dental caries experience by DMFS index. The discrimination function analysis resulted in an overall correct classification rate of 72.00%. Positively health

Table 11

Step wise Multiple Discrimination Analysis Statistically Significant Factors of Positively Health Oriented (+) and Negatively Health Oriented (-) Subjects by DMFS Index Scores

Independent variables	*Mean±SD* +		*Partial Lambda*	*Standard coefficients*	*Wilk's Lambda value*	*F-value*
Caste	8.255±5.41	24.368±7.38	0.9524	-0.5650	0.7790	4.4484*
Education	9.699±6.254	25.687±8.87	0.9532	0.6293	0.7782	4.3662*
Staple food	7.955±5.987	23.654±7.96	0.9589	0.5677	0.7730	3.8149*
Rinsing habit	8.897±7.133	22.398±9.10	0.9716	-0.5223	0.7616	2.6053**
Age	8.136±5.324	23.258±5.32	0.9772	0.4060	0.7567	2.3758**
Brushing methods	9.001±5.970	23.987±6.01	0.9848	-0.3605	0.7501	2.3718
Materials used to clean the teeth	7.895±5.291	24.111±8.00	0.9848	-0.4096	0.7457	2.2707**
Type of drinking water	8.0124±4.62	23.023±7.12	0.9851	0.3363	0.7498	2.0134**
Frequency of sweet consumption	7.205±5.021	24.350±8.004	0.9887	0.2859	0.7468	1.9987**
Frequency of brushing	8.574±6.156	23.241±7.25	0.9895	-0.3263	0.7460	1.9762**

Note: * Indicates significant at 1% level of significance,
** Indicates Significant at 5% level of significance

oriented subjects were correctly classified about 85.24% of the time where as negatively health oriented subjects were correctly classified 51.28% of time. The mean discriminant score for positively health-oriented subjects (0.3991) was significantly different from negatively health-oriented subjects (0.6243) (Wilk's Lambda=0.7490, chi-square=29.4880 with 10df) in this index also. The analysis resulted in an eigen value of 0.3542. According to scores of DMFS index, the most distinguishing characteristics of positively health-oriented subjects when compared to with negatively health oriented subjects can be determined by examining the standardized discriminant function analysis (Table 11).

The best discriminating determinants of positively health-oriented subjects by DMFS score values were education, staple/ main food, rinsing habit of mouth with water, source of drinking water and frequency of brushing and were less likely to be caste ·age of the subject and methods of brushing.

ACCUMULATION OF PLAQUE DEPOSIT (PLAQUE INDEX)

Twenty-three independent determinants were examined for possible relationship with accumulation of plaque deposit on the tooth surfaces by PLAQUE index. Of these 14 determinants were found to significantly related to the dependent variable i.e. accumulation of plaque deposit on the tooth surfaces.

The results of the step-wise discriminant function analysis showed only eight determinants were found to be significant determinants are discriminates the accumulation of plaque deposit on the tooth surfaces by PLAQUE index.

69.00% of an overall correct classification rate was found by the discrimination function analysis results. About 61.00% of subjects correctly classified in the group of positively health oriented subjects. The corresponding percentage for the negatively health oriented subjects was 75.43%. This indicates that, the determinants chosen by discrimination function analysis possess a significant amount of discrimination information.

Table 12

Step wise multiple discrimination analysis statistically significant factors of positively health oriented (+) and negatively health oriented (-) subjects by plaque index scores

Independent variables	*Mean±SD* +	-	*Partial Lambda*	*Standard coefficients*	*Wilk's Lambda value*	*F-value*
Frequency of brushing	0.6591±0.15	0.7894±0.18	0.8532	0.7944	0.7958	12.8036*
Frequency of sweet consumption	0.6345±0.13	0.7986±0.17	0.8675	-0.6702	0.7864	11.6952*
Duration of sweet consumption	0.6493±0.15	0.8014±0.21	0.8761	-0.4631	0.7701	9.1631*
Education	0.6681±0.19	0.8054±0.24	0.9212	0.5411	0.7625	6.2635*
Duration of change of tooth brush	0.6212±0.11	0.8235±0.16	0.9332	0.4865	0.7515	4.3684*
Method of brushing	0.6887±0.11	0.7564±0.19	0.9529	0.4546	0.7460	3.6874**
Sex	0.6561±0.18	0.7891±0.18	0.9777	0.3654	0.7317	3.0241**
Staple food	0.6517±0.10	0.7654±0.12	0.9797	0.5301	0.7081	2.9987**

Note: * Indicates significant at 1% level of significance,
** Indicates Significant at 5% level of significance

The mean discriminant score for positively health-oriented subjects (-0.5368) was significantly different from negatively health-oriented subjects (0.4050) (Wilk's Lambda=0.7184, chi-square=23.0352 with 8df) in this index also. The analysis resulted in an eigen value of 0.3219.

According to scores of PLAQUE index, the most distinguishing characteristics of positively health-oriented subjects when compared to with negatively health oriented subjects can be determined by examining the standardized discriminant function analysis (Table 12).

As indicated results in the table 12, The most important discrimination determinants of the positively health oriented groups were frequency of brushing, duration of sweet consumption and education of the subject, duration of change of tooth brush and were less likely to be frequency of sweet consumption, method of brushing, sex of the subject and main or staple food by PLAQUE score values.

DISCUSSIONS

A study was conducted to determine the determinants associated with different dental health status i.e. dental caries experience, accumulation of plaque deposit on the tooth surfaces and periodontal status. The classification of the subjects into two groups (positively and negatively health oriented) by DMFT, DMFS and PLAQUE index values seemed to be a perfect and good method to differentiate subjects into groups of good and bad dental health status. However, it is interesting to note that in the groups that have no correlation between indices was found. This finding confirms the conception that there is neither directly synergistic nor directly antagonistic correlation among dental caries experience (DMFT and DMFS index values), plaque deposit scores and CP index scores in the same subjects (Heikki M.H. et al. (1984), Ainamo J et al. (1971), Javali et al. (2004)).

Explaining the dental health status, which at a certain time is an end result of varying dental health behavior raises many difficulties, which are inherent in the available methods. The majority of the variability in the clinical indices remains unaccounted for. This inability of the predictor variables to make an important contribution towards explaining the variations in the oral health status indicators was of the same direction was found in the studies done by (Heikki M.H. et al. (1984), Cohen et al. (1971) and Javali and P. V. Pandit (2004), Javali S. B., Prasad K. V. V. and Tippeswamy V. (2004)).

The present study findings showed that, the frequent sweet consumption was seen more in negatively health oriented subject group and frequent tooth brushing with vertical method and rinsing habit were commonly seen in the group of positively health oriented by DMFT, DMFS and PLAQUE indices. The same findings were estimated by Javali S. B., Prasad K. V. V. and Tippeswamy V. (2004). Regular tooth brushing is accepted as a key determinant in the prevention of development of dental caries experience and in controlling the accumulation of plaque deposit on the tooth surfaces and occurrence of periodontal disease. This result is very much coincides with studies done by Chestnut et al. (1998), O'mullane et al. (1997) and Javali S. B., Prasad K. V. V. and Jithendra A., (2004).

The occurrence of dental caries experience is depends on intake quantity and frequency of sweet consumption. Hence, the dental caries experience and accumulation of plaque deposit have strong association with sweet consumption. Eija KK et al. (1982), Guttaffson et al. (1954) and Javali, Prasad K. V. V. and Jithendra A., (2004) found same result between the dental caries experience and accumulation of plaque deposit.

In variety of brushing methods, some methods have been described very much in dental literature. Proponents of one method or another have traditionally been vehement in the decrease of their methods efficiencies. The relationship between method of brushing with development of dental caries experience, accumulation of plaque deposit and occurrence of periodontal disease was found to be negative and statistically significant in the present study. Vertical method and circular method of brushing found to be common in positively health oriented subjects group in DFMT, DMFS and PLAQUE index scores. Sangness et al. (1992), Rajala M. (1980) have explained similar findings.

The age is one of most important determinant of accumulation of plaque deposit on the tooth surfaces, because the stronger relationship was found between them. But surprisingly, no significant relationship between age and development of dental caries, it could be. In the recent further studies Brain et al. (1993) and Javali et al. (2001), Javali S. B. and Pandit P. V. (2004) and Javali, Prasad K. V. V. and Jithendra (2004) found that age has significant positive relationship with development of dental caries.

The development of dental caries was seen significantly more in urban subjects compared to rural subjects as the easy availability of sticky foods in urban areas. Javali S. B. and Pandit P. V. (2004) and Elani P et al. (1996) derived that no relationship between area of residence and dental caries experience. But in the present study, accumulation of plaque deposit and occurrence of the periodontal disease have no relationship with area of residence.

In generally, family of income is important determinant of individual in relation to development of dental caries, accumulation of plaque deposit and occurrence of periodontal disease. Milan A. (1987) has estimated similar findings between income of family with dental caries and plaque deposit in Finland.

Discriminant function analysis can be taken to a one of the best important and useful descriptive method, when many predictor variables are studied simultaneously. According to discriminant function analysis, duration of sweet consumption and frequency of sweet consumption are the most important determinants related to lower DMFT score values followed by family size, income of a family, frequency of brushing. The same findings are highlighted by Javali et al. (2004). Caste, education of the subject are the best determinants of related DMFS score valued compared to staple food, rinsing habit with water after every meal, age of the subject, method of brushing. Frequency of brushing, frequency of sweet consumption is the best discriminant determinants in relation to accumulation of plaque deposit on the tooth surfaces.

CONCLUSIONS

The results of the study confirms that duration of change of tooth brush, methods of brushing, frequency of brushing, frequency of sweet consumption, desired family size, area of residence are important determinants in relation to dental caries experience. Age, sex, education of the subject, frequency of brushing, methods of brushing, smoking habit, and chewing habits are best predictors of plaque deposit on the tooth surfaces. Also frequency of sweet consumption, duration of sweet consumption, frequency of brushing, methods of brushing are the best predictors of occurrence of periodontal disease.

Frequent tooth brushing with vertical method was more common among those classified as positively health oriented group and frequency of sweet consumption and duration of sweet consumption was most commonly seen among the group of negatively health oriented subjects by DMFT, DMFS and PLAQUE index values. Duration of sweet consumption was the one of the important determinant related to higher DMFT, frequency of sweet consumption related to lower DMFT.

Caste and education of the subjects are the best determinants related to lower DMFS values and only age is the best related to higher DMFS values. Education of the subject, frequency of brushing and methods of brushing are highly and negatively influence and age, sex and sweet consumption have highly positive influence on accumulation of plaque deposit. Frequency of sweet consumption best determinant in related to high rate of occurrence of periodontal disease and education of the subject in only one determinant related to low rate of occurrence of periodontal disease.

REFERENCES

Ainamo J. (1971), The Seeming Effect of Tobacco Consumption –the Occurrence of Periodontal Disease and Sental Caries. Suom. Hammslaeaek Tiom, 67: 87-94.

Blinkhon A. S. (1978), Inference of Special Norms on Tooth Brushing Behaviors of Preschool Children. Community Dent Oral Epidemiol, 6: 222-226.

Brain A. B., Stephen A. E. & Donald W. L. (1992), Dentistry, Dental Practice and the Community, 4th Edition, W. B. Saunders Company, *Harcourt Brace Jovanovich, Inc. London.*

Chestnut I. G. & *et al.* (1998), The Influence of Tooth Brushing Frequency and Post Brushing Rinsing on Caries Experience in caries clinical trail. *Comm. Dent Oral Epidemiol,* 26: 406-411.

Cohen L., Snyder T., Labelle A. (1983), Determinants of Oral Health in University Students. *Clin Prev Dent,* 5: 17-21.

Eija K. K. & Leena R. (1982), Relationship between Oral Hygiene and Sugar Consumption to risk of Caries in Children. *Community Dent. Oral Epidemiol.* 10: 224-233.

Eleni Petridou, T. Athanassouli, H. Panagopoulos & Revinthi K. (1996), Socio Demographic Factors in Relation to Dental Health among Greek Adolescents, *Comm. Dent Oral Epidemiol,* 24, 307-311.

Fehr F. R., Vonder, Loe H., and Theilade E. (1970), Experimental caries in man. Caries Res. 4:131-142.

Gustafsson B. E., Quensel C. E. & *et al.* (1954), The Vipeholm dental caries study. The Effect of Different Levels of Carbohydrate Intake on caries Activity in 436 Individuals Observed for five years. *Acta Odont Scand,* 11: 232-364.

Heikki Murtomaa H., Lauri T., and Inkeri R. (1984), Differentiating Positively and Negatively Health Oriented Finnish University Students by Discriminant analyses. *Comm Dent Oral Epidemiol,* 12: 243-248.

Javali S. B, Tippeswamy V, and Prasad K. V. V. (2001), Determinants of Dental Caries Experience. *J. Ind. Dental Research,* XII (4): 230-233.

Javali S. B, Tippeswamy V, and Prasad K. V. V. (2001), Relative Importance of risk Factors in Dental caries Experience (Accepted for publication in the journal of *The Indian Association* for the Study of Population "Demography India").

Javali S. B. and Pnadit P. V. (2004), Statistical Analysis of Data from some Determinants of Dental Caries Experience. *Journal of Pierre Fauchard Academy* (JPFA), 18 (3): 59-66.

Javali S. B., Prasad K. V. V. and Tippeswamy V. (2004), Segregation of Positively and Negatively Health Oriented Subjects by Discriminant Analyses. *Karnataka State Dental Journal,* 23 (3), 74-78.

Koch G. and Lindhe J. (1965), The effect of Supervised Oral Hygiene on the Gingival of Children: the effect of Tooth Brushing, *Odontol Revy*, 29:28-45.

Loe H. Theilade E. and Jensen S. B. (1965), Experimental gingivitis in man. *J. Periodontol*, 36:177-187.

Milan A. (1987), Role of Social Class in Caries Occurrence in Primary Teeth. *Int J Epidemiol;* 16: 252-256.

O'Mullane D.M. and *et al.* (1997), A three year Clinical Trail of a Combination of Trimetaphosphate and Sodium Fluoride in silica Toothpastes, *J Dent Res* 76:1776-1781.

Prasad K. V. V, & Javali S. B. (2001), Socio-demographic and other factors in relation to dental caries experience among adolescents of Karnataka state, India. *J. Ind. Dent. Assoc.*, 72: 349-351.

Rajala M., Honkala E. *et al.* (1980), Tooth Brushing in relation to other Health Habits in Finaland, *Comm. Dent Oral Epidemiol.* 8:391-395.

Sangness G., Zachrisson B., Gjermo P. (1972), Effectiveness of vertical and Horizontal Brushing Techniques in Plaque Removal. *J Dent Child*, 39: 94-97.

Statistical Package for the Social Sciences (2001), SPSS users guide, *Chicago:* SPSS Inc.

Suomi A., *et al.* (1971), The effect of Controlled Oral Hygiene Procedures on the progression of Periodontal Disease in adults: results after third and final year. *J Periodontol*, 42: 152-160.

World Health Organization, (1997), Oral Health Surveys, Basic Methods. WHO Geneva.

Dr. Kamble, P.S. (2005), 'Business Environment' (Indian Economic Environment), Swaroop Prakashan, Kolhapur (in press).

Papola, T.S, above cited, PP. 545-47.

27

DYNAMICS OF URBAN POPULATION GROWTH –A CASE STUDY OF HUBLI – DHARWAD TWIN CITIES

Mahadevi Kotyal[*] *& S. I. Biradar*[**]

INTRODUCTION

Population growth in an area is an index of its economic development, Social awakening, cultural background historical events and political ideology. Moreover most of the other population characteristics are intimately related with the growth patterns experienced by the region and derive their meanings and significance from it. An understanding of growth of population in any area is, thus fundamental to the understanding of inherent correlations not only between various demographic phenomena, but also non-demographic phenomena.

The term growth of population is used in its broadest connotation to cover change in population numbers inhabiting a territory during a specific period of time, irrespective of the fact whether the change is negative or positive (Chandna & Sidhu-1980). This change/growth can be measured both in terms of absolute numbers and percentage. The term urban generally means relating to cities and towns. The definition of urban settlement is however, a difficult one. Most of the countries define their urban settlements on the basis of

* Lecturer, Department of Geography, JSS College, Dharwad, Karnataka.

** Reader, Department of Geography, Karnatak University, Dharwad-3, Karnataka.

minimum qualifying size of population. The size may very from country to country and from plane regions to mountainous regions. The criteria of functions, administrative status, lay out and amenities are also combined with the criterion of minimum size of population.

As population grows in a place the space content of that place changes and resultantly the morphological dimensions of the place are also changed. The growth of populations in urban centers has registered an alarming rate during the recent decades. Such tremendous growth of population in urban places has brought about many environmental problems.

STUDY REGION

Hubli-Dharwad twin cities urban region has been presently selected as study area. The study region lies in northern part of Karnataka State and has been recognized as the second largest urban agglomeration in the state.

The twin urban centers, Dharwad lie between 15° 23' & 15° 30' north latitude and 74° 58' & 75° 5' east longitude and Hubli lie between 15° 20' & 15° 30' north latitude and 75° 5' and 75° 11' east longitude with a total area of 202.28 sq. kms. The total area of Dharwad city is 149.82 sq. kms and Hubli covers 54.86 sq. kms.

Dharwad is situated at an altitude of 2500' (762.19 meters) above mean sea level and Hubli about 2200' (670.75 meters). The higher altitude is the reason for Dharwad having pleasant and healthy climatic conditions. The temperature of Dharwad ranges from 67.9° F to 86° F. The Dharwad represents semi malnad area. The average annual rainfall at Dharwad is 32.5" (812 mm) and at Hubli 26" (or 666 mm).

The variation of humidity in Dharwad is 96 to 61% while in Hubli it is 79 to 30%. The twin cities urban system has elongated shape (See figure – 1) and connected with Pune and Bangalore by national highway – 4 and broad guage railway line of south western railway zone. The Hubli urban center is facilitated by aerodrome. The total population of these two urban centers is 7,86,018 (2001 census) with density of 3891 (2001 census) persons per sq. kms. The entire urban system consists of 67 wards.

OBJECTIVES

In this paper researchers have made an attempt to trace out dynamics of urban population growth in Hubli – Dharwad twin cities. The main objectives of this paper are,

1. To analyse the trend of population growth in Hubli – Dharwad twin cities.
2. To examine the magnitude and temporal changes in major demographic aspects such as literacy, male – female ratio, religious break up etc.
3. To analyse the occupational structure of Hubli – Dharwad twin cities.
4. To study the spatio temporal variation in the areal expansion of the twin cities.

Figure 1

METHODOLOGY

The dynamics of population growth like trend of population, literacy, population according to religion, mobility etc, has been assessed on the basis of secondary data collected from different offices namely Hubli – Dharwad Municipal Corporation, District Statistical Office, JSS's Economic Research Institute Dharwad, etc.

The trend of population growth of twin cities is expressed by a simple graph which depict the growth of population clearly (see graph – 1). For this, variable selected for the study are population and time. The data was collected from various government, semi government offices and private agencies.

ANALYSIS OF TEXT

The Hubli-Dharwad urban system has the total population of 7,86,018 (2001 census) which is distributed among 67 wards. The population of Hubli-Dharwad twin cities in the year 1901 was only 81,143 (see table-1). Till 1921 i.e., for 20 years the population increase was slow. But next decade i.e., 1921-31 the increase in population was double than that of the decade 1911-21. After 1941, every decade the population increase was very high i.e. about 50,000 to 1,00,000.

Table 1
Decennial growth of population of Hubli-Dharwad 1901-2001

Year	*Total Population*	*Increase in Population*	*% Growth*
1901	81,143	-	-
1911	91,031	9,888	12.18
1921	1,00,992	9,961	10.94
1931	1,24,398	23,406	18.81
1941	1,43,504	19,106	13.31
1951	1,96,180	52,676	26.85
1961	2,48,489	52,309	21.05
1971	3,79,166	1,30,677	34.46
1981	5,27,108	1,47,942	28.06
1991	6,48,298	1,21,190	18.69
2001	7,86,018	1,37,720	17.52

Source: District Census Hand Books.

The percentage growth in population was high after 1951. It is clearly observable in the graph which is showing decennial growth of population of Hubli – Dharwad twin cities. Increase in the growth of population results, increase in the density of population. The density of Hubli-Dharwad was only 2,761 persons per sq. kms in 1981 and it increases to 3395 persons/ sq. kms in 1991, and it further increased to 3891 in 2001.

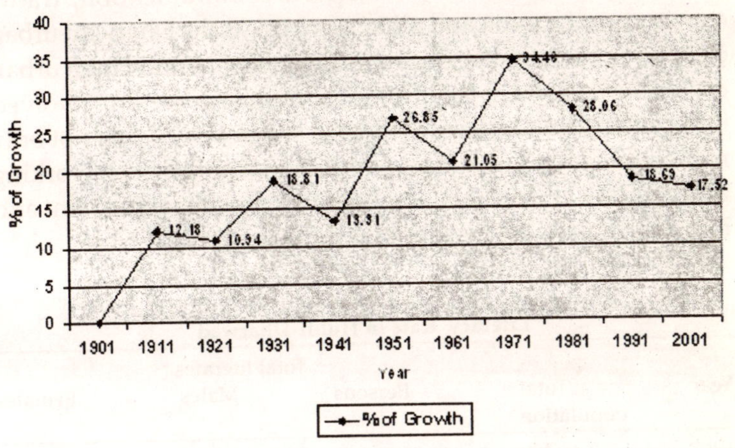

The literacy rate of twin cities in 1961 (table-2) was only 50.34 percent (65.4% males and 34.58% females). During the recent decades this literacy has been increased due to better educational facilities. There is a tremendous increase (66.38% in 2001) in the rate of literacy among the females because of the awareness among the public. It was only 34.58% in 1961, which increased to 66.38% in 2001. The total literacy rate also increases from 50.34% in 1961 to 72.13% in 2001 i.e. during the recent four decades. The male female ratio of twin cities is 949 females per 1000 males (2001 census).

The number of births during 2002 in these cities is 11,311 (5810 males and 5,501 females) and number of deaths during same year is 5,034 (3,202 males & 1,832 females), showing a wide gap between the birth and death rates. This ultimately results in high population growth in the twin cities.

OCCUPATIONAL STRUCTURE

As the Hubli-Dharwad twin urban centers considered as city / town in 1951 most of the people were engaged in secondary and tertiary activities (see table –3). In 1961 people engaged in primary activities were 9.7%, secondary 34.17% but in tertiary more than half of the working population was engaged. This occupational structure is continued till today. According to 1991 census also most of the population (55.42%) has been engaged in tertiary activities like transport, communication, trade, commerce, education and other services. As the Dharwad urban center is known for its educational institutions and Hubli urban center for its market facilities most of the people are involved in secondary and tertiary activities. It is observed that not only male population but female population has also been working in secondary and tertiary activities to a considerable extent and is also gradually increasing in recent decades.

Table 2
Literacy Rate in Hubli-Dharwad

Year	Total population	Total literates		
		Persons	Males	Females
1961	2,48,489	1,25,100 (50.34%)	81,830 (65.41%)	43,270(34.58%)
1971	3,79,166	2,07,212 (54.64%)	1,30,087 (62.7%)	77,125(37.22%)
1981	5,27,108	3,05,692 (57.99%)	1,84,650 (60.40%)	1,21,042(39.59%)
1991	6,48,298	4,11,065 (63.40%)	2,37,517 (57.78%)	1,73,548(42.21%)
2001	7,86,018	5,66,981 (72.13%)	3,12,902 (77.59%)	2,54,079(66.38%)

Source: Dharwad District Statistical Report.

The Hubli-Dharwad urban centers attract the people of different places belonging to different regions. These two urban centers, particularly Dharwad attracts the people from different

Table 3
Occupational Structure

Year	Total Workers			Primary Activities			Secondary Activities			Tertiary Activities		
	Persons	*Males*	*Females*	*Persons*	*Males*	*Females*	*Persons*	*Males*	*Females*	*Persons*	*Males*	*Females*
1961	73,001	63017	9984	7154	5164	1990	24947	21823	3124	40900	36030	4870
	(29.3%)			(9.7%)			(34.17%)			(56.02%)		
1971	105804	92212	13592	16597	12312	4285	27677	24250	3427	61530	55650	5880
	(27.9%)			(15.6%)			(26.15%)			(58.15%)		
1981	146941	126356	20585	20463	14624	5839	6207	4351	1856	120271	107381	12890
	(27.8%)			(13.9%)			(4.2%)			(81.8%)		
1991	181723	155971	25752	23247	17396	5851	57747	51875	5872	100729	86700	14029
	(28.0%)			(12.79%)			(31.77%)			(55.42%)		
2001				NA	NA	NA	NA	NA	NA	NA	NA	NA

Source: District Census Hand.Books to the concerned years.

neighbouring and far places as it possesses various advanced educational facilities. When we observe the population of these twin cities religion wise two third (70.56% in 1971) of the people belongs to hindu religion (see table 4). These urban centers includes people belonging to religions, like hindu, muslim, christian, jain, buddhist, sikhs etc. However the people belonging Christian, jain Buddhist, Sikhs are very less in number.

Before 1961 these two centers had separate Municipal Corporation with total area of 88.59 sq kms. In 1964 the single municipal corporation was established for these two urban centers. Both the centers are expanding in their outward direction. In 1970-71 the area of these cities was 182. 30 sq kms and it become 190. 94 sq kms in 1981. As per 2001 census including Narendra (a village) the total area of Hubli-Dharwad twin urban centers is 202.8 sq kms. Due to the areal expansion the number of words have also been increased. At present these twin city centers have 67 wards in total.

Occupational Structure

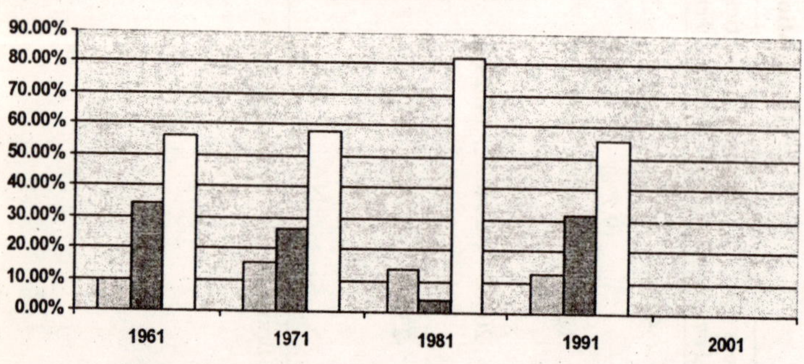

POPULATION PROJECTION

The essential growth trend of future population is termed as population projection. Population forecasting is one of the most complicated ones as it is based on a number of assumptions, regarding the future trend in fertility, mortality and migration (Agarwal 1977). To estimate the population for year 2011 and

Table 4
Religion wise distribution of population

Year	*Total Population Persons*	*Hindus*	*Muslims*	*Christians*	*Jains*	*Buddhist*	*Sikhs*	*Other*
1961	248489 (130718) (117721)	NA	NA	NA	NA	NA	NA	NA
1971	379166 (201286) (177880)	P 267489 70.5% M)142685) F (124804)	P 89623 23.6% M (46872) F (45751)	P 16634 4.3% M (8600) F (8034)	–	P 831 0.2% M (315) F (516)	P 462 0.1% M (340) F (122)	P 25 .006% M (13) F (12)
1981	527108 (275703) (251405)	NA	NA	NA	NA	NA	NA	NA
1991	648298 (3365586) (311712)	P4507129 69.5% M (234958) F (215761)	P 163404 25.2% M (84087) F (79317)	P 23249 3.5% M (11620) F (11629)	P 9024 1.3% M (4841) F (4183)	P 98 0.015% M (53) F (45)	P 738 0.1% M (421) F (317)	P 381 0.05% M (214) F (167)
2001	786018 (403270) (382748)	NA	NA	NA	NA	NA	NA	NA

2021 the Registrar General's method has been applied. For this method the following simple formula is used.

Religion Wise Distribution of Population 1991

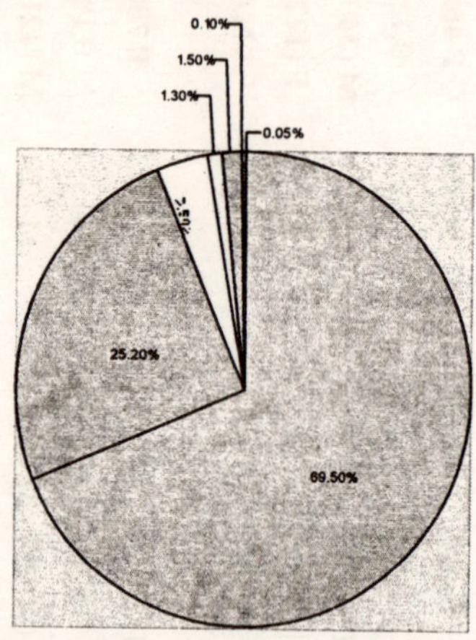

☐ Hindu ☐ Muslim ☐ Christian ☐ Jains ☐ Buddhist ☐ Sikhs ☐ Others

$$Pt = P1 \frac{P_1(P_1 - P_D)}{P_O} \times \frac{1}{100}$$

Pt - Projected Population
P1 - Population of the later Period
P0 - population of the earlier period
t - Time interval
Population of 2001 - 7,86,018
Population of 1991 - 6,48,298
Net increase - 1,37,720

$$\% \text{ of increase } - \frac{1,37,720 \times 100}{6,48,298}$$

$$= 21.2\%$$

If 21.2% increase over the population of 2001 is considered, then the projected population for 2011 will be (786018 + 159674)

927692 persons. Similarly the projected population for 2021 will be (927692+273439) 1201131. This indicates changes in status and size class of Hubli-Dharwad urban centers in forthcoming

Religion wise Distribution of Population 1971

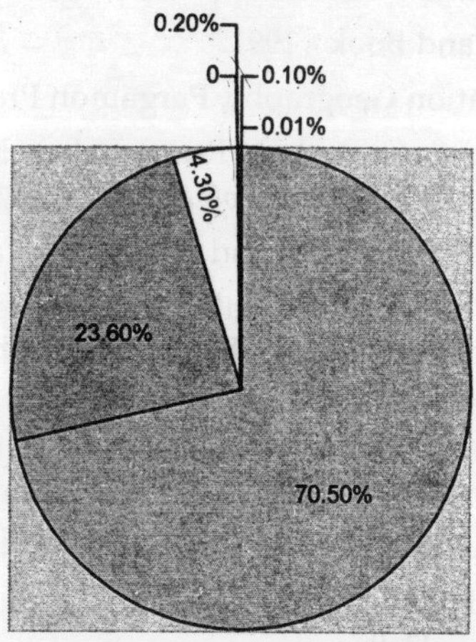

Hindu Muslim Christian Jains Buddhist Sikhs Others

years.

FINDINGS & SUGGESTIONS

It is noticed that there is a direct relationship between the growth of population and the areal expansion of the urban centers and with the religion and occupational structure.

The twin cities selected for the study are growing at a faster rate and are the second largest urban agglomerations in Karnataka State. It is observed that the growth of population in these cities is very fast, which is resulting in several problems and is dangerous in view of the public health conditions, and other environmental problems.

The twin city system requires a more rational comprehensive developmental plan to overcome the unforeseen problems.

REFERENCES

Bose A (ed) Patterns of Urban Growth 1951-61 Allied Calcutta, 1967.

District Census Hand Book - 1961.

District Census Hand Book - 1971.

District Census Hand Book - 1981.

District Census Hand Book - 1991.

Clarke J.I., Population Geography, Pergamon Press, Oxford, 1996.

Dayal P. Population Growth & Rural Urban Migration in India. *National Geographical Journal of India* 5, 6, 1959.

District Statistical Office, Dharwad, Statistical Handbook, 2002-03.

Gosal G.S. & Chandna R.C, Population Geography in Moonis Raza (ed), A Survey of Research in Geography, 1969-72, Allied Publishers Pvt. Ltd. Bombay 1979.

Hubli - Dharwad Municipal Corporation, Population Statistics. Mazid Hussain, Human Geography Rawat Publications, New Delhi.

JSS's Economic Research Center, Population Statistics.

Chandna R.C. and Manjit Sidhu 1980, Population Geography Kalyani Publisher, New Delhi.

Gazetteer of Dharwad District, 1995.

28

THE PRESENT POSITION OF RURAL WORKERS IN LABOUR MARKET AND RURAL NON-FARM SECTOR IN INDIA

*W. N. Salve**

INTRODUCTION

Agricultural forms the backbone of Indian economy. It employs 65 per cent of workforce and provides livelihood for nearly three forth of our population. Though the share of agriculture in the GDP is declining, it still remains a significant contributor. The Indian economy is primary producing because agriculture contributes 32 % of national income while 70% of the labour force is engaged in agricultural. Indian economy is passing through the process of transition from an agricultural economy to an industrial economy. After independence, the non-agricultural sectors of the economy have grown faster than the agriculture sector.

This paper attempts to study the present position of rural workers in labours market and rural non-farm sector in India. The study has used relevant data from different sources.

WORK PARTICIPATION RATE

The ratio of working population to population is referred to as the participation rate. The workforce/labour force, therefore, be defined as that proportion of population which belongs to

* Shri Venkatesh College, Ichalkaranji, Kolhapur District, Maharashtra.

the age group of 15-59. A worker is defined as any person who participates in some economic activity or the other. According to the census of 1991, workers are classified into two categories: Main Workers and Marginal Workers. Main workers are those who had worked for the major part of the year i.e. 6 months (183 days) or more, while Marginal Workers are those who had worked for major part of the year i.e. less than 6 months, (Dutt & Sundharm, 1995).

Table 1 shows that out of 306 million total working population in the country in 1991, 278.9 million were main workers and 27.1 million were marginal workers. It may be noted that marginal workers increased from 5.7 million in 1971 to 27.1 million in 1991. According to the census of 2001, the total workers and non-workers are 39.26% and 60.74% respectively. Out of total workers, 7.80% are main workers and 22.20% are marginal workers. Besides, male marginal workers are 12.69 % of the total workers and 42.81 % are female marginal workers. The proportion of female marginal workers is higher than the male marginal workers both in rural and urban areas.

Table 1
Classification of Working Population

	1991	1981	1971
Total workers of which	306.0	242.0	180.7
Rural	241.7	195.1	149.1
Urban	64.3	46.9	31.6
Male	218.6	179.3	144.4
Female	87.4	62.7	36.3
Main	278.9	220.7	175.0
Marginal	27.1	21.3	5.7

Source: Statistical Outline of India, 2001-02.

Table 2 shows the work participation rate during 1981 to 2001. The total work participation rate has shown an increasing trend from 1981 onwards. WPR was 36.7 % in 1981. it improved to 37.7% in 1991. it increased to 39.26 % in 2001.

In the case of males, there has been a slight decline in work participation rate from 52.6 % in 1981 to 51.6 % in 1991. it has almost remained constant around 51.93 % in 2001. Besides, the work participation rate for females has been shown an increasing trend both in the rural and urban areas. The total females work participation rate improved from 19.7% in 1981 to 22.3% in 1991, and further increased to 25.68 % in 2001.

Table 2
Work Participation Rate In India 1981-2001

Total Rural Urban	*Persons Males Female*	*Total workers as % of total population Years*		
		1981	*1991*	**2001*
Total	Persons	36.7	37.5	39.26
	Males	52.6	51.6	51.93
	Female	19.7	22.3	25.68
Rural	Persons	38.8	40.1	41.97
	Males	53.8	52.6	52.36
	Female	23.1	26.8	30.98
Urban	Persons	30.0	30.2	32.23
	Males	49.1	48.9	50.85
	Female	8.3	9.2	11.55

Source: 1> Statistical Outline of India, 2001-2002.
2> * The Indian Journal of Labour Economics No.1 ,2002.

During 1981 to 2001, rural female work participation rate increased from 19.7% in 1981 to 30.98 % in 2001. Urban female work participation rate improved from 8.3 % to 11.55 % during the same period. Besides, urban total female participation rate increased from 30.2% in 1991 to 32.23% in 2001. However, the female participation ratio is lower than the male participation owing to unfavourable socio-economics conditions for female labour force. Women are mostly engaged in agricultural and household activities in rural areas. In the informal and unorganized sector women tend to be concentrated in the least remunerative and less skilled activities. As regards gender displsparity, Human Development Report 1995, stated that women's economic contributions are generally undervalued or are not valued at all. (Gill, 2001).

SECTORAL SHARE OF GDP

It has been observed that the share of the primary sector in GDP has gone from t 56% in 1950-51 to 31% in 1990-91 and further declined to 29% in 1999-2000. The share of secondary sector in GDP has increased from % in 1950 -51 to 29% in 1990-91 and to still lower figure at 24% in 1999-2000.

The share of tertiary sector in GDP has increased from 29 % in 1950-51 to 40% in 1990-91 and further increased to 47% in 1999-2000. it may be noted that the share of service sector in GDP has been increasing than primary and secondary sectors during the periods 1951-2001.

SECTORAL SHIFF IN EMPLOYMENT

Table 3 gives distribution of working population by industrial categories. Table 3 shows that the employment in the primary sector reduced from 71.7% to 66.8% during the period 1901 to 1991.

The share of cultivation reduced from 50.6% in 1901 to 38.4 in 1991 and further declined to 31.71% in 2001. Besides, the share of agricultural labourer has gone up from 16.9%in 1901 to 1907% in1951 and further increased to 26.4% in 1991 and 26.69 in 2001 (Census of 2001).

Table 3

Distribucion of Working Population By Industrial Categories (%)

	1901	*1951*	*1991*
I. Primary Sector (1+2+3)	71.7	72.1	66.8
1. Cultivators	50.6	50.0	38.4
2. Agricultural Labourers	16.9	19.7	26.4
3. Livestock: Forestry Fishing, Plantation, Etc	4.2	2.4	1.9
II. Secondary Sector (4+5+6)	12.6	10.6	12.7
4. Mining & Quarrying	0.1	0.6	0.6
5. Manufacturing: I. Household Industry II. Other Than Household Industry.	11.7	9.0	10.2
6. Construction	0.8	1.0	1.9
III. Tertiary Sector(7+8+9)	15.7	17.3	20.5
7. Trade &Commerce	6.1	5.3	7.5
8. Transport, Storage & Communication	1.1	1.5	2.8
9. Other Services	8.5	10.5	10.2
Total	100.0	100.0	100.0

Source: K.k.deweet, Verma,Sharma,Indian Economic,2000.

The role of secondary sector has remained steady *i.e.* 12.6% in 1901, and 12.7% in 1991. The employment in tertiary sector increased from 15.7 % in 1901 to 17.3% in 1991. It may be noted that the service sector has been growing steadily in the Indian economy. The service sector is divided into two parts: 1>organized and 2>unorganized . The organized sector workers are employed on the basis of qualification only, the qualified persons can be absorbed in the organized sector. In case of unorganized sector the situation is more subtle (Desai, 2000).

As shown by table 2 the tertiary sector has grown steadily at a faster pace than the primary and secondary sectors. The category of service producing economic activities includes wholesale and retail trade, hotels and restaurants, transport, business service, sanitary service, other services. The share of the service sector employment in the total workforce has increased from 17.3 % in 1951 to 20.5% in 1991.

NEW ECONOMIC POLICY

The government adopted new economic policy in 1991. There are three components of new economic policy *i.e.* Liberalization, Privatization, Globalization. Liberalization of the economy in the 1990s and encouragement of private investment in industry and infrastructure have induced sustained high growth in service sectors. As a consequence, the share of service sector in GDP increased from a level of 28% in the early 1950's to 41 % in 1990-91 and further around 49% in 2000-2001 (The Economic Times, 24 Feb, 2001). Although the share of non-agricultural activities in employment has been increased-overtime, rural India continues to remain primarily an agrarian economy, with a high proportion of its working population still engaged in agricultural activities.

According to the Censuses of 1981, 1991, the proportion of workers in manufacturing activities decreased from 11.3% in 1981 to 10.2 % in1991 both for males and females. Besides, the proportion of workers in household industry has decreased from 3.55 in1981 to 2.4% in 1991.

According to the Censuses of 2001, household industry workers are 4.7%. Moreover, rural household industry female workers are 5.44%, which improved from 2.1 % in 1991 to 5.44% in 2001. As regards urban household industry, female workers increased from 2.1 % in 1991 to 12.93% in 2001. The proportion of household industry female workers has shown an increasing trend both in the rural and urban areas.

The class of semi-landless and marginal farmers has been growing at a progressively fasters rate both in absolute and relative terms. As a result, the proportion of casual labourers has risen appreciably.

JOBLESS GROWTH

Table 3 shows distribution of labour force, India is witnessing, what is called jobless growth. According to K.Sundharam, since independence, agriculture actually witnessed a reduction in jobs. In 1993-94, agriculture employed 239 million people. In 1999-2000, the figures came down by three million to 236 million. Other sectors did record growth but only marginally, over the past 10 years, jobs in the manufacturing sector increased by a merge 3.7 million to touch 4.4 million. (Business Today, June 26, 2001). According to Dewett, verma, Sharma (2000), even after more than four decades of planned economic development in India, the secondary and tertiary sectors put together account or only 33% of: the country's working population in 1991. This shows that there is a very uneven distribution of India's labour force among the various occupations. It shows an unbalanced and, therefore, the unstable economy. The main cause of this unstable and unbalanced state of our economy is the lack of mobility of labour, from agriculture to secondary and tertiary sectors. Besides, populations is increasing at such a tremendous rate that there is an increase in this undo dependence on agriculture, because the development of industries has been relatively slow. The proportion of the non-farm sectors contribution to total rural employment rural employment is around 20 %.

According to the census of India 2001, about 31.71 % of the total working population worked as cultivators. While as high a proportion as 26.69 % were engaged in agriculture as labourers having no land in a fewer hands with smalls and marginal farmers being disposed of their land, thereby swelling the ranks of landless agricultural labours (Dewett-2000): About 65% of the rural families have either no land or land below one hectare. The pressure of population on land has resulted in low wages for agricultural labours. Fragmented landholding and static yields, agricultural cannot provide for them any more. Disguised unemployment in rural areas is the result of heavy pressure of population on land and the absence of alternative employment opportunities in the villages. These people suffer from low level of literacy and income, indebetness, low asset-holding etc. compared to other sections of the rural population. Most of the scheduled caste household and scheduled tribe households in the rural sector are in debt. Despite the introduction of rural banking and credit societies, the small and marginal farmers still go to the moneylenders and become victims of usurious capital.

According to the Dewett, Verma, Sharma (2000), near stagnation of non-agricultural sector and non-availability of alternative employment opportunities in industrial and tertiary sectors are responsible for the worsening condition of agricultural labour. The non-farm sector in rural areas has failed to increase employment opportunities. At present, about 20 % of the rural workers are employed in non-farm sector in rural areas.

POLICY OF RURAL INDUSTRIES AND EMPLOYMENT

After Independence, the industrial policy resolution 1948, had set the tone the policy of development for rural industries. Khadi and number of rural industries received government support. Since 1951, rural industries have been developed under five year plans. The industrial policy resolution 1956 further reaffirmed the state support and protection for small and village industries. To overcome the problem of rural industries, six all India Boards for Handloom, Handicrafts, Coir, Sericulture, small scale industries and khadi and village industries were established. The village small industries sector (VSI) includes such as small-scale industries (SSI) Coir industry, Khadi and village industry (KVI), Handlooms, handicrafts, Powerlooms,

Wool industry, Sericulture and Food Processing industries. The VSI sector provides employment opportunities to the rural workers. The Food Processing Industry continues about 18% of the total output of the industrial sector and provides employment about 1.5 million persons.

Industrial Estates and Rural Industrialization programs introduced during the third five year plan and continued during the succeeding plans. The integrated Rural Development Program (IRDP) was launched in 1978-79 for target group, which includes small and marginal farmers, agricultural labours, tenants, share croppers, rural artisans, scheduled caste and scheduled tribe population in the rural sector.

Industries, services and business (ISB) components was built into the IRDP programs in Feb. 1979 with the object of maximizing employment opportunities to the rural poor in the secondary and tertiary sectors in view of the limited absorption of the farm sector. Government has provided grants and subsidies to selected persons under ISB components as per the IRDP. Besides, the scheme of training at Rural Youth for self-employment TRYSEM) was launched on August 15, 1979 with the object of training the rural youth (age group 18-35) possessing necessary skills and technology to enable them to I take to vocations of self-employment in the primary, secondary the tertiary sectors. However, with the extension of the IRDP to all blocks, with effect from April 1981, the TRYSEM became a component scheme of the IRDP.

The committee of training for fuller employment had earlier identified eight trades, viz., rural electrification, automechanic, tractor and farm mechanic, bakery, tailoing and embroidery, leather goods making, carpentry and furniture making, blacksmithy, and sheet metal and welding.

The total number of youth trained under the TRYSEM scheme in India during period 1979-80 to 1982-83 was 4.18 lakhs, while the total number of these who were self-employment during the corresponding period was 1.85 lakhs account for about for about 45 % of the former (NIRD, 1984).

Small Sector Industrial Policy: The government announced its policy towards the small sectors on 6th August

1991. The small-scale industrial sector, which plays a private role in the Indian economy in terms of employment. Industrial activity in the eight plan has been based on the new industrial policy of 1991, which aimed at industrial development through greater competitiveness, increased efficiency, strengthening of indigenous capabilities, deli censing, deregulation and larger flow of foreign investment, while initially the rate of industrial growth was low, in1993-94 it showed a sharp rise from 2.3 % to 6%. This rose further to 8.6 % in 1994-95 and 12.2 % in 1995-96. this increase in industrial growth is attributable to the various revival measures taken by the government.(The Ninth Five Year Plan 1997-2002).

As regards small-scale industries, it has been observed that the number of small-scale units have grown from 1.4 lakhs in 1950-51 to 32.251akhs in 1999-2000. During the same period, 50 years, employment has grown from 1.7 million to 17.7 million and output out put has increased from Rs.2603 crores to Rs.578299 crores. (Statistical Outline of India,2001-2002). According to the Ninth Five Year Plan (1997-2002), animal husbandry and dairying will receive greater attention for development during the Ninth Plan as this sector plays an important role in generating employment opportunities and supplementing incomes of small and marginal farmers, and jobless labours, especially in the rained drought prone areas.

Over the last decades, there has been a considerable decline in the incidence of rural poverty. However, a large number of persons continue to live below the poverty line. Hence there is a need for continued direct state intervention for poverty alleviation. While the programs for self-employment would continue in the Ninth Five Year Plan. They would also be integrated with various sectoral programs as well as the area development programs within the Umbrella of the Panchayat Raj Institutions (Ninth Five Year Plan Draft). However, the plans did not emphasize sufficiently the development of small scale and cottage industries but concentrated on large-scale producer goods with very limited employment generation effects.

POVERTY ALLEVIATION

It is difficult to assert how many people are under the poverty line. Planning commission estimates that in 1993-94 about 36% of the population was under the poverty line, and 37.3% of the population was under the poverty line in rural areas, while it was 32.4% in urban areas (SOl, 2001-2002). Though some non-government figures place it around it around 40%, it may be said that in India between 35 to 40 % population is under the poverty line. According to Thorat s.k.(Bheempatrika,2002) about 30 % people live below the poverty line in India of these, 60% belong to scheduled caste and scheduled tribe people and 65 % of the people are casual workers. This is the position of India after five decades of independence; alleviation of poverty remains a major challenge before the nation (Rao,1999)

Agriculture offers only a seasonal occupation. As a result, the employment opportunities are not sufficient to absorb the rural labour force. At present, nearly 27% of the population is below poverty line (1999-2000). They suffer from cronic unemployment. The marginal and landless households continue to remain unemployed, under employment due to lack of self-employment opportunities. Majority of which are scheduled castes scheduled tribes and weaker sections of the society.

Nearly half of the rural poor are small and marginal farmers according to the estimates of the planning commission. Agriculture labour households continue 26% of the total labour force, and of these, 60 % live below the poverty line. Hence, the incidence of poverty is higher in states where agricultural labours constitute a higher proportion of the rural workers. Andhra Pradesh, Uttar Pradesh, Bihar, Maharashtra, Madhya Pradesh and Tamil Nadu States in India account for 70% of the agricultural labour. Besides, the literacy rates are lower in six states of India such as Andhra Pradesh, Uttar Pradesh, Bihar, Maharashtra, Madhya Pradesh, Rajastan, and Orissa. The total literacy rates are lower than all India total literacy rate of 52 % according to 1991 census.

UNORGANISED LABOUR

Agricultural labours, landless labours constitute the largest segment workers in the unorganised sector. Besides, the badli workers (casual), domestic servants, hotels and restaurant workers, rickshaw pullers, building and construction workers, Brick kiln workers, Handloom/Power loom workers, Bidi and Cigar workers, Carpenters, Cobblers, Fisherman, Head load workers (Mathadi workers, and coolies doing loading and unloading work) Railway workers, Primary Milk producers, Auto-rickshaws drivers, sweepers and scavengers, Salt workers, Tendu Leaf collectors, Toddy Tappers, Anganwadi workers, private motor transport workers, sericulture workers, other categories of home based workers and casual, contract and unprotected labour, etc. fall in categories of unorganized labour (NLLA, 1994). Most of the workers migrate from rural areas to urban area in order to find out jobs. They do not have employment security, work security. The Eight Five Year Plan acknowledges that poverty still remains a problem of considerable magnitude. Though there is evidence that the incidence of poverty is on the decline, the percentage of the population below the poverty line is estimated to be about 27%, which in absolute numbers comes to about 230 million. The total number of persons requiring employment would be 58 million during 1992-97 and 94 million 'during the period 1997-2002. (Subrahmanya, 1995).

REFERENCES

Datt Ruddar, Sundhram, K.P.M. (1995), Indian Economy, S.chand & Comp. Ltd. New Delhi.

Deweet, K.K. Verma, J.D. Sharma, M.L. (2000), Indian Economy, S.chand & Comp. Ltd. New Delhi.

Desai H.N. (2000), Paper on Role of Service Sector in Present Time, 42nd Annual Labour Conference, Jabalpur, Dec. 9-11, 2000.

Gill Kanwaljit Kaur (2001), "Diversification of Agriculture & Women Employment in Punjab". The Indian Journal of Labour Economics, Vol. 44, 2001.

Govt. of India (1997), Approach Paper to Ninth Five-year Plan 1997-2002 Planning Commission, New Delhi.

NIRD (1984), (NLLA) Course of Financing the Rural Poor, Hydrabad National Labour Law Association The Indian Labour Code, 1994 (Draft), New Delhi.

Rao, S.R.K. (1999), India & Internal Debt Trap, Forum of Free Enterprises, Mumbai.

Subrahmanya, R.KA. (1995), Evolution & Status of Social Security System in India, Friedrich Ebert Sifting, New Delhi.

Thorat, S.K. (2002), 'Poverty In India', Bheem Patrika, Vol.18, September 2002.

JOURANAL AND OTHERS

- Business Today, June 6, 2001.
- The Indian Journal of Labour Economics Vo1.45, 2002.
- Statistical Outline of India 1996-97, 2001-02.
- Bright Mini Year Book 2002.
- The Economics Times, 24 Feb. 2001.

The twin city system requires a more rational developmental plan to overcome the unforeseen problems comprehem.